The Poseidon Project

The Poseidon Project

The Struggle to Govern the World's Oceans

DAVID BOSCO

OXFORD
UNIVERSITY PRESS

OXFORD
UNIVERSITY PRESS

Oxford University Press is a department of the University of Oxford. It furthers
the University's objective of excellence in research, scholarship, and education
by publishing worldwide. Oxford is a registered trade mark of Oxford University
Press in the UK and certain other countries.

Published in the United States of America by Oxford University Press
198 Madison Avenue, New York, NY 10016, United States of America.

Library of Congress Cataloging-in-Publication Data
Names: Bosco, David L., author.
Title: The Poseidon project : the struggle to govern the world's oceans /
David Bosco.
Description: New York, NY : Oxford University Press, [2022] |
Includes bibliographical references and index. |
Identifiers: LCCN 2021030644 (print) | LCCN 2021030645 (ebook) |
ISBN 9780190265649 (hardback) | ISBN 9780190265663 (epub) |
ISBN 9780197582916
Subjects: LCSH: Law of the sea—History.
Classification: LCC KZA1145 .B678 2022 (print) |
LCC KZA1145 (ebook) | DDC 341.4/5—dc23
LC record available at https://lccn.loc.gov/2021030644
LC ebook record available at https://lccn.loc.gov/2021030645

DOI: 10.1093/oso/9780190265649.001.0001

1 3 5 7 9 8 6 4 2

Printed by LSC Communications, United States of America

For James, Lael, and Josephine

Contents

Acknowledgments

This project began while I was at American University and was written from my new home at Indiana University's Hamilton Lugar School of Global and International Studies. The deans at these institutions, Jim Goldgeier at American and Lee Feinstein at Indiana, have been enormously supportive. Padraic Kenney and Purnima Bose were unfailingly helpful as department chairs. Dave McBride at Oxford University Press embraced the idea of the book from the beginning and guided me expertly through its various stages.

A fellowship through the College Arts and Humanities Institute at Indiana University provided an invaluable semester to complete writing, and the Institute for Advanced Studies supported a conference to review the manuscript. I am grateful to Barbara Breitung for her work in arranging that conference (and for countless other forms of assistance). I benefited enormously from comments by David Balton, Nick Cullather, Taylor Fravel, Tamar Gutner, Kate Hunt, Stephanie Kane, Adam Liff, Stephen Macekura, Jessica O'Reilly, Lincoln Paine, Alexander Proelss, Scott Shackelford, and Justyna Zayac. Douglas Guilfoyle, Jim Goldgeier, and Emma Chanlett-Avery were kind enough to comment on late versions of the draft. Colin Koh shared his expertise on freedom of navigation operations. Mark Strauss, my friend and former colleague at *Foreign Policy* magazine, provided several rounds of superb edits.

A wonderful group of students at both American University and Indiana University pitched in at various stages of the project, including Jong Eun Lee, Sunny Aldrich, Henry Farrell, and Rachel Myers. Alejandro Barrett Lopez and Megan Chapman went above and beyond the call of duty in their work on the project.

I am grateful to the 21st Century Japan Politics and Society Initiative for financial support that allowed me to make a trip to Japan and have enlightening discussions with a range of officials there. In Tokyo, my friend Tomoaki Ishigaki generously helped me find the right interlocutors. Kristina McReynolds expertly facilitated the logistics of the trip.

During the pandemic year, this project became an extended family affair. Relatives who took up the gauntlet include my father, Joseph Bosco (who served in the US Navy), and my father-in-law, Jim Wallace. My sister Carla, a history buff, offered salient thoughts. My brother Stephen (also a former naval officer) helped with several chapters. My sister Alessandra provided superb comments and editing throughout. My wife, Shana Wallace, buoyed my spirits when the project seemed overwhelming and gently but firmly urged important structural changes. Our children, Josephine, Lael, and James, expressed only intermittent interest in the project but had pronounced views on the cover design.

Introduction

On December 11, 2019, several Japanese Coast Guard vessels patrolled the waters near the Senkaku Islands in an otherwise desolate stretch of ocean. The vessels and their crews were far from home (Figure 0.1). Hundreds of miles of often turbulent waters separate Japan's main islands from the Senkakus, a clutch of eight rocky outcroppings about 120 miles northeast of Taiwan. Sea conditions around the islands that day were manageable if not hospitable.

The patrol was a familiar one for the crews. Japan's Coast Guard devotes a significant percentage of its budget to monitoring these waters.[1] To aid in the effort, Japan has built a network of defense installations, including a coast guard base housing hundreds of personnel on the nearby island of Ishigaki. Japanese aircraft fly regular patrols in the area, and the government created an elite ground force that can be deployed quickly if the Senkakus are threatened.

The strenuous effort is centered on islands that have no residents and scant resources of their own. The largest island in the chain has an area of just two square miles, and the smallest feature barely breaks the water line. Japan first staked its claim to the Senkakus in 1895 on the premise that the islands were unclaimed and therefore free for the taking. A 1900 survey by several Japanese scientists found an array of birds (including albatross), wild cats, and swarms of mosquitoes and bottleneck flies. With permission from the government, an intrepid Japanese businessman harvested and exported bird feathers and snails. At its peak, the business employed dozens of people. The isolation and harsh conditions ultimately prevailed, and by the late 1930s the Senkakus were once again uninhabited.

What the islands lack in onshore human activity, they have more than compensated for in offshore drama. When imperial Japan surrendered at the end of World War II, the Senkakus came under the control of the United States. In the 1950s, US forces used several of the islands as bombing ranges. As Washington finally prepared to hand back control to Japan in the late 1960s,

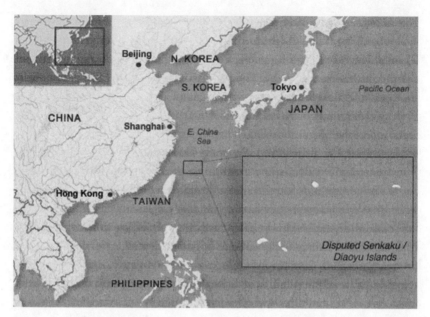

Figure 0.1 The Senkaku Islands; courtesy of Michael Lipin/Voice of America

China objected. Its government insisted that the islands, which it calls the Diaoyu, have always been Chinese. Beijing's interest in the islands coincided with a report suggesting that the waters near the islands might hold plentiful oil and gas reserves. In the decades since, groups of nationalist protesters from China, Taiwan (which also claims the islands), and Japan itself have voyaged to and occasionally clambered onto the rocky islands. In 1978, a Japanese group apparently introduced goats, which multiplied, turned feral, and ravaged one island's vegetation.

Once an occasional irritant to relations between Beijing and Tokyo, the Senkakus have become a nearly constant source of tension. A collision between Chinese fishing boats and a Japanese Coast Guard vessel in 2010 raised the temperature of the dispute. Controversy ratcheted up further in 2012 when the Japanese government, prodded by the nationalist mayor of Tokyo, purchased three of the islands from their private Japanese owner. While that move did not alter Japan's international legal position, it made several islands government property and was seen in China as a provocation. In several Chinese cities, protesters gathered outside Japanese consulates and businesses. In 2016, an armed Chinese navy vessel appeared for the first time in the waters around the Senkakus.

This fraught history—and the threat of an even more serious confrontation—hangs over every Japanese patrol. An incident at sea could easily escalate, and it might well draw in the United States. Successive American leaders have made clear that they see US treaty obligations to Japan as encompassing the Senkakus. The United States has the means to intervene quickly; US aircraft and a sizable force of US Marines stands ready on Okinawa, a few hundred miles from the contested islands. In the summer of 2020, a group of security experts conducted a wargame that began with a Chinese move to take control of the Senkakus. In the simulation, clashes between Chinese and Japanese naval forces escalated into a conflict that involved Chinese ballistic missile strikes on a US aircraft carrier and US submarine attacks on Chinese ships.[2]

These risks notwithstanding, China appears determined to keep the dispute simmering, and it has used an expanding coast guard and a large fishing fleet to do so. Since mid-2012, Chinese government vessels have been an almost constant presence in the waters near the islands. Chinese fishermen have also shown keen interest in the area. In the summer of 2016, as many as 300 fishing boats congregated near the islands, straining Japan's ability to monitor their movements. Usually, Chinese ships loiter beyond the boundary line that separates international waters from the 12-mile-wide territorial sea that encircles the islands. Once or twice a month, however, Chinese vessels make sure to cross the line.

At approximately 10:30 A.M. on December 11, 2019, four Chinese Coast Guard vessels did just that. The Japanese crews immediately radioed their objections as they maneuvered to intercept the interlopers. Japan has developed an elaborate protocol for intervening while minimizing the chances of an armed confrontation. Crews follow a script in their radio communications. Electronic billboards affixed to the vessels flash firm but polite warnings in Chinese. Loudspeakers convey the same message. Powerful water hoses stand ready in case more vigorous methods become necessary to ward off the intruders.

While well practiced and almost ritualistic, these encounters are perilous. The Coast Guard immediately transmitted news of the December incursion to Tokyo, and the mobile phones of officials in the prime minister's office buzzed with the news. As has been their custom, the Chinese vessels departed the territorial sea after a decent interval. About an hour after the initial alert, an all-clear signal followed. For the Japanese Coast Guard, the lonely vigil around the deserted islands resumed.

The disputes in Asian waters, where the Senkakus are only one of multiple points of friction, have attracted worldwide concern. Small islands, rocks, and reefs that might otherwise be of little significance threaten to instigate major-power conflict. At stake in these areas is less the contested land than the influence it permits over the waters around them. Asia's maritime outcroppings raise old questions in human affairs: who controls the oceans and what are the rules for their use?

***

In ancient Greece, those questions often received an otherworldly answer. Poseidon, the brother of Zeus, had the power to still or roil the waves. He could even raise new land from the deep. The island of Delos, birthplace of Apollo, was said to be the product of the sea lord's exertions. Often depicted sitting astride seahorses and brandishing a trident, Poseidon was venerated throughout ancient Greece. Around 440 BCE, one of the largest temples to the god was constructed on Cape Sounion, a promontory in southern Greece overlooking the Aegean Sea. Archaeologists believe it featured more than 30 marble columns and an enormous bronze likeness of the god. Sailors likely frequented the temple, particularly before long voyages.[3]

Yet Poseidon was a capricious and inconstant guardian of the oceans. He often left his ocean realm untended as he pursued amorous conquests on land or consorted with fellow gods on Mount Olympus. Even when his attention was focused on the waters, Poseidon was hardly a neutral arbiter. He picked favorites and carried bitter grudges. Homer depicts Poseidon as an unusually vengeful deity. "All of the gods pitied Odysseus except for Poseidon," he wrote in the opening of *The Odyssey*. Employing storms, Poseidon delayed the beleaguered mariner's return home for months to punish him for several perceived insults. (In fairness, one complaint was serious: that Odysseus had blinded the god's one-eyed son, Polyphemus.) When particularly agitated, Poseidon might unleash earthquakes by striking his trident on the ground. For ancient peoples who relied on but could scarcely fathom the ways of the ocean, Poseidon's temperament was appropriate. Like the sea, he was unpredictable, almost always in motion, and dangerous.

The modern world has accumulated vast knowledge of the oceans and their patterns. Mercurial deities have been unseated, and management of the oceans is now a thoroughly human affair. Yet mortal dominance has not produced calm on the waters. Disputes about ocean control extend well beyond the South and East China Sea. Greece and Turkey feud bitterly about maritime rights in the Mediterranean and the Aegean. Russia and Ukraine have clashed over rights in the Black Sea. Arctic countries disagree about who can control passage through northern waters. Reports have surfaced of Russian submarines lingering near undersea communications cables, and security experts have warned that these vital conduits are vulnerable to sabotage.[4] In the crowded Straits of Malacca and off the coasts of Africa, the age-old phenomenon of piracy remains a threat, as modern marauders in Zodiac boats waylay tankers, siphon off their liquid cargo, and then disappear into the night. For those working the oceans, abusive captains are often more menacing than pirates. Working conditions on some fishing boats approximate forced bondage. Stowaways unlucky enough to be discovered on certain merchant vessels have disappeared without a trace.

Evidence of maritime discord is even more overwhelming when it comes to the natural environment. International observers worry that certain fish stocks are in steady, and perhaps terminal, decline. Scientists have documented the increasing acidification of the oceans, a phenomenon that bleaches coral reefs and threatens entire ecosystems. In the Arctic, melting sea ice jeopardizes animal habitats and may be accelerating global warming by increasing the amount of heat the ocean absorbs from the sun. Thousands of feet beneath the surface, mining companies are testing devices for harvesting minerals from the ocean floor, stirring concern about damage to fragile and poorly understood ecosystems.

Drawing on many of these threads, popular accounts have often described the oceans as chaotic, anarchic, and beyond the reach of the law. "Few places on the planet are as lawless as the high seas," one particularly intrepid correspondent has argued.[5] Another journalist described the ocean "not merely as a wilderness that has always existed or as a reminder of the world as it was before, but also quite possibly as a harbinger of a larger chaos to come."[6] That sentiment has been echoed by diplomats, environmentalists, and human rights activists. According to a former British foreign minister, "The high seas are in a state of anarchy."[7] A US congressional committee heard testimony that the oceans are a "lawless Wild West, far from any enforcement authority."[8]

These descriptions capture important and sometimes horrifying realities, and the perception of ocean lawlessness is potent enough that it has seeped into popular culture. In an episode of *The Simpsons*, Homer took to the ocean in a quest to buy alcohol on a Sunday. As he passed out of US waters onto the high seas, he witnessed a small armada of vessels hosting otherwise illegal activity—interspecies marriage, an Old West shootout, a bull fight, and unauthorized rebroadcasting of sports events. "We made it, son," he exults to Bart, "international waters—the land that law forgot."[9]

Yet the story of maritime lawlessness tends to obscure both the past and future of ocean governance. In fact, there has been a system for the oceans in place for several centuries: "freedom of the seas." For nearly 400 years, that doctrine helped answer questions about how the oceans could be traveled, exploited, and managed. More than a historical accident or the mere absence of governance, the doctrine represented a conscious choice with a coherent philosophical grounding. Implementing and maintaining it required sustained diplomatic, legal, and military effort by powerful countries and commercial actors. "Freedom of the seas was not given to mankind," a veteran US diplomat has pointed out. "It was won—won through scholarly and legal debate and in naval engagement."[10]

A central contention of this book is that key elements of that doctrine have been lost and that others are fading. Recognizing that process and the emergence of new forms of governance is critical to understanding contemporary maritime challenges. Just as it obscures aspects of the past, the story of ocean lawlessness has trouble describing the transformation that is under way. In fact, the world's oceans are subject to more rules and regulations than ever before. National governments have created many of these, but others are international in nature. These layers of national and international regulation are enforced unevenly and leave ample room for disorder, but there are also new and meaningful limitations on what ocean users can do. It is not possible to chart trends in ocean governance without understanding the past.

The Free Sea

The idea that the seas should be owned by nobody and free for all to use was advanced most famously in the early 17th century. The young jurist Hugo Grotius and the Dutch corporation that he represented had particular political and economic reasons for making that argument. But his case for *Mare Liberum*—a "free sea"—was potent enough that it transcended the specifics of the dispute he was addressing. Grotius leaned heavily on what he saw as the distinctive nature of the oceans in making his case for freedom. The seas were fluid and could not be occupied in the way that land could. Their resources were, at least to Grotius's eye, abundant and likely inexhaustible, and so there was no need to divvy them up and apportion ownership. Finally, the oceans were natural highways connecting different lands, almost purpose-built for facilitating commerce across long distances.[11]

Grotius's polemic inspired plenty of opposition, but the principle of free use of the oceans that he championed has powerfully influenced international lawyers, politicians, and the general public ever since. Freedom of the seas has resonated particularly in the United States, the leading maritime power since at least the Second World War. More than 300 years after Grotius wrote, President Woodrow Wilson described freedom of the seas as "sacred." On the eve of the US entry into the Second World War, Franklin Roosevelt was even more expansive:

> All freedom—meaning freedom to live, and not freedom to conquer and subjugate other peoples—depends on freedom of the seas. All of American history—North, Central, and South American history—has been inevitably tied up with those words, "freedom of the seas."[12]

Since then, US leaders across the political spectrum have routinely emphasized the importance of ocean freedom.

Before advancing too far, some clarity about what this ubiquitous phrase means is important. It has been used as a slogan for centuries, and for a variety of agendas. For much of its history, the United States embraced the concept to preserve its ability to remain neutral in European conflicts and, as a result, trade lucratively with all sides. As European powers struggled repeatedly for primacy in the 19th and early 20th centuries, French and then German leaders used the idea of ocean freedom as a way of assailing Britain's maritime supremacy. For their part, landlocked countries have seen freedom of the seas as a guarantee of their right to access the ocean and its resources and to fly their flag on oceangoing vessels.

The phrase has been used to sell products and services as well as policies. In 2006, the cruise company Royal Caribbean christened its newest vessel *The Freedom of the Seas*. Equipped with a theater, ice rink, and multiple pools and spas, the 1,100-foot vessel transports thousands of passengers on pleasure cruises around the globe. A company spokesperson described the ship as "really all about freedom of choice. Freedom to explore. Freedom to relax. Freedom to make one's own vacation plans reflective of one's own tastes and interests."[13]

Scholarly definitions of the concept have sometimes been little more precise than those offered by corporate publicists. One book-length exposition on freedom of the seas began by acknowledging that the term "has always meant many things to many men" and ended almost tautologically by defining it as the "measure of liberty in the use of the sea accorded by international law."[14] I elaborate below what I view as the core components of the traditional doctrine of freedom of the seas. To some degree, these elements have all been reflected in international legal instruments over the years, but they cohere into a doctrine that is broader than (and in some ways distinct from) the current state of international maritime law.

The starting point for freedom of the seas is an insistence that the oceans are and must remain different and separate from the land. Specifically, it requires *that the open ocean should not be claimed as territory by states.* Grotius and most other thinkers have distinguished between waters close to the coast, which can legitimately fall under state control, and the open ocean, which cannot. Generations of negotiators have wrestled with precisely where the dividing line should be between state-controlled and international waters. But the principle of restricting state control and maintaining a substantial open ocean has rarely been contested. Its logic is powerful: if too much of the ocean becomes state territory, or something akin to it, then the seas are not really free anymore. Coastal countries might choose to let them be free, but that freedom can be revoked at any time, just as it can be on land.

From this basic assumption, several additional principles follow. The first of these is that *vessels (and now aircraft) from all states should have unimpeded access to the world's oceans.* "The use of the sea and air is common to all," Queen Elizabeth told a vexed Spanish envoy who was protesting the late 16th-century voyages of Sir Francis Drake. The navigational freedom she defended includes merchant ships and military vessels alike (although the distinction between the two has not always been clear, as Drake's voyage demonstrated). During conflict, it has long been understood that belligerents may impose some restrictions on shipping, but they should avoid interfering with most neutral shipping.

Maintaining ample freedom of navigation, even during conflict, respects the ocean's value as a highway between societies and an open channel for commerce. That value has grown exponentially since Grotius's time. Every day, fleets of enormous container ships carry everything from new automobiles to recycled cardboard across the world's oceans. In all, more than 80 percent of the world's trade is carried at sea. The transported goods total about 10 billion tons annually with an estimated worth of more than \$4 trillion.[15] This flow has become so routine that it attracts notice only when it is interrupted. The March 2021 grounding of the *Ever Given* in the Suez Canal, for example, reminded the public of how dependent modern economies are on a steady stream of seaborne goods.

The seas are much more than just a conduit. They are a source of sustenance and wealth. *Freedom to fish and to otherwise exploit the open ocean's resources is another element of traditional freedom of the seas,* one that Grotius emphasized. Fish and other sea creatures caught on the open ocean belong to those who catch them, and ever more efficient and powerful oceangoing fishing fleets derive profit from the principle of free access. In 2018, more than 90 million tons of fish were harvested by an industry that uses more than 4 million vessels and employs about 39 million people.[16]

Meanwhile, the last half-century has made clear that there are many valuable resources in the sea other than fish. Oil- and gas-drilling operations have moved steadily seaward. Researchers and entrepreneurs have learned more about the mineral resources that lie on the deep seabed and have devised new means to harvest them. Scientists have recently managed to extract genetic material from marine life and then develop it for commercial applications. Knowledge of the resources that the oceans host has thus expanded over time, but the doctrine of freedom of the seas provides that all people have a right to exploit them.

To this point, the foundations of ocean freedom have been negative in character. Countries can maintain that freedom mostly by *inaction*: not claiming ocean space as national territory, not interfering with navigation, not preventing others from fishing, and not impeding drilling, mining, and other open ocean activities. Absent meddling from jealous sovereigns, the theory holds, peaceful maritime commerce and activities will flourish.

There is another aspect of freedom of the seas that requires involvement rather than restraint from rulers on land. Since maritime commerce began several thousand years ago, shipping routes have been intermittently plagued by violence. An ocean on which vessels may be attacked at any time is not free in any meaningful sense, and suppressing disorder has usually required powerful players to take action. At times, the merchants who benefit most from ocean commerce have fended for themselves, but for most of history they have required assistance from rulers. History's roster of pirate-hunters is long and features Rome's Caesar and Pompey, a frustrated 9th-century

Korean merchant, Ottoman bureaucrats in Istanbul, and the commanders of modern NATO warships off the Somali coast.

The negative and positive dimensions of freedom of the seas exist in some tension with each other. The powerful navies and coastal security forces that can most effectively suppress maritime violence also have the means to disrupt shipping when they choose and assert national control in other ways. Missions to maintain order on the oceans can easily slide into naked assertions of maritime power and influence. One of the fundamental challenges facing an ocean regime that prizes freedom of access is keeping the forces that maintain order from asserting dominion.

In no historical period have all these elements of freedom of the seas been present continuously and consistently. Still, the period between the British victory in the Napoleonic Wars and the outbreak of the First World War represents the high point of the freedom of the seas. As described in Chapter 2, British leaders abandoned their claims to own substantial ocean space and consistently resisted the claims of other states to expand control of the ocean. Britain also used its maritime power to suppress piracy and other threats to shipping. That coercive power, joined with a number of other factors, produced a substantial decline in private maritime violence in many parts of the world. However tenuous open access to the ocean was during this period, it best conformed to the Grotian vision of the "freedom of the seas."

The Advancing Sovereigns

That era has ended. The doctrine of freedom of the seas has been attacked directly and indirectly for decades, and it is buckling under the strain. The most powerful force arrayed against it has been the desire of sovereign governments to control more of the ocean. The legal history of the oceans, writes one scholar, "has been dominated by a central and persistent theme: the competition between the exercise of governmental authority over the sea and the idea of freedom of the seas."[17] For much of history, the vastness and unpredictability of the oceans limited the reach of those governmental authorities. As the capacity of rulers grew, the doctrine of freedom of the seas emerged as a conceptual bulwark against states claiming the oceans as their own.

Since 1945, however, the balance has tilted sharply toward sovereign control. The percentage of the oceans that is under some form of national jurisdiction has increased dramatically. Moves after the Second World War toward greater national control prompted several rounds of multilateral diplomacy designed in large part to restrain that trend. That process culminated in 1982 with the creation of the United Nations Convention on the Law of the Sea (the focus of Chapter 5). Often dubbed a "constitution for the oceans," the Convention remains to this day the clearest answer the international community has provided to the questions of who controls the ocean and how it should be used. In key respects, the Convention acquiesced to unilateral state bids for greater control of the oceans—for example, by creating a large economic zone in which coastal countries had exclusive rights. But it did so as part of a broader effort to stabilize maritime law by ending national appropriation, limiting the ability of countries to stake additional ocean claims, and ensuring that "freedom of the seas" remained meaningful.

The Convention notwithstanding, the pressure for countries to expand into the oceans has continued in myriad ways. In 2007, a small Russian deep-sea submersible planted a titanium Russian flag on the bottom of the Arctic Ocean. While that act was unusually theatrical, it accurately represented what is happening in areas of the seabed around the globe. Dozens of countries are seeking exclusive rights on what is called the "extended continental shelf," which can reach hundreds of miles from the coastline. Experts at the United Nations are dutifully reviewing those submissions, many of which will be finalized in the years to come.

Other forms of appropriation have been more subtle. For example, the Convention left unclear whether the maritime economic zone should be considered part of the open ocean or whether it was more akin to territorial waters. In practice, many coastal states, including major powers such as Brazil, China, and India have tried to tip the balance toward territoriality by enacting regulations forbidding military and research vessels from operating within that zone, at least without explicit permission. A few countries with large bays or networks of offshore islands have drawn their ocean boundaries such that large areas of open ocean are converted into internal waters. In the 1980s, for example, Canada issued new maritime "baselines" that placed most of the famous Northwest Passage under its control. China's sweeping maritime claims in the South China Sea (described in Chapters 7 and 8) may pose an even more fundamental threat to the Convention structure. Beijing claims special rights to all waters encompassed by a "nine-dash line" that in some places extends more than 1,000 miles from the Chinese coast.

Unilateral assertions of national control over the oceans could continue. Maritime history provides abundant evidence that unilateralism, particularly by powerful countries, has shaped modern rules. It is far from certain that over the long term, the Convention will be able to control this dynamic. The world's leading maritime power, the United States, has repeatedly refused to join the Convention, and its stance is a reminder of the persistent gap between sovereign authority and international ocean rules. China has joined the Convention but appears willing to challenge some of its fundamental provisions through unilateral assertions. Thus, as this book charts the erosion of freedom of the seas, it will also document the testing of the world's still fragile ocean constitution.

While the decades-long process of national appropriation of formerly open waters has unfolded, other pillars of freedom of the seas have crumbled. The world wars of the 20th century shattered the existing rules protecting maritime commerce during wartime (a process outlined in Chapter 3). Belligerent states—including the United States—declared vast and unprecedented ocean zones in an effort to advance their war aims; some neutral countries tried a similar approach to shelter themselves from the voracious conflict. The absence of sustained major-power conflict since those wars means that those kinds of maritime restrictions have largely been forgotten, but there is no reason to believe they would not reemerge quickly in the context of renewed conflict between maritime powers.

The traditional freedoms to fish and exploit the ocean's resources have also come under significant pressure. As countries have cemented new ocean rights, they have often excluded foreigners from fishing in these waters—and even beyond. National governments watching foreign fishing fleets operate in nearby waters have been tempted to extend restrictions even further than current ocean rules permit.[18] China's periodic harassment of foreign fishing vessels has received most attention, but countries with stronger multilateral credentials, including Canada, have pushed the legal envelope to protect their domestic fishing industries from competition.

It is unclear where this process of national expansion into the oceans will end. With the lonely exception of Antarctica, just about every square mile of dry land has now been parceled out to some sovereign state or another. There are still disputes—occasionally bloody—about exactly where these lines should fall, but few argue that land should not belong to some state or another. Grotius notwithstanding, it is not obvious that the oceans should be different.[19] Technological change has made the idea of controlling or occupying ocean space much less fanciful than in the past. Modern, well-functioning states have resources for maritime control that earlier generations could scarcely imagine. From drones to orbiting satellites and underwater sensors, many of today's governments know a great deal about who is using their waters and have mechanisms for preventing activity they do not countenance.

Internationalizing the Ocean

If national pressure to own and regulate the oceans is the most powerful force eroding freedom of the seas, increasing international control is another. The idea of internationalizing the oceans received its most famous endorsement in November 1967. In an unusual speech, the ambassador from newly independent Malta, Arvid Pardo, declared the Grotian conception of ocean freedom outdated and called for the oceans to be treated in the future as the "common heritage of mankind," with robust international supervision and control. In Pardo's mind, this concept would not eliminate ocean freedoms but preserve them for a world very different from the one Grotius inhabited.[20]

Pardo's expansive vision has not yet been realized, but international supervision of the oceans has advanced in fits and starts. The International Maritime Organization, a specialized United Nations agency that crafts rules for ocean commerce, has expanded its responsibilities. A UN commission populated by technical experts is issuing opinions that help decide how far into the ocean countries can claim undersea rights. More than a dozen regional fisheries organizations generate rules for high-seas fishing. There are more international courts and tribunals than ever before, including one specifically devoted to maritime issues. Through these bodies, international judges issue influential rulings about the oceans and their use.

The area where international control of the ocean has moved closest to reality is the deep seabed. What galvanized Pardo's UN speech was the possibility that lucrative seabed mining would spur a scramble by states to claim undersea territory. In one of its most controversial sections, the UN Convention addressed that concern by creating an International Seabed Authority (ISA). US objections to that international body and its powers remain the most significant obstacle to the United States joining the Convention. The ISA is a remarkable creation; it has the power to assign rights to an area of approximately 150 million square miles. At least in theory, international officials working in a modest headquarters in Jamaica exercise authority over more territory than any sovereign on land. The internationalization of the oceans may advance even further. A major negotiation is under way at the United Nations that could significantly restrict high-seas activities, including fishing, and bolster and expand the international architecture for managing the oceans.[21]

****

Over the centuries, the oceans have become comprehensible, accessible, and exploited in ways that earlier generations could scarcely contemplate. Gone is the conceit that the sea is somehow beyond human influence or control. Sovereigns and seafarers with advanced technologies have tamed the ocean and made it serve their economic, military, and recreational ends. As the ability to use the ocean has grown, so too has the desire to control it and the capacity to despoil it. The notion that "freedom of the seas" itself could provide order for the oceans has been tested and found wanting. As that doctrine succumbs, the work of building a stable new foundation for governing the oceans is only beginning.

This book traces the evolution of ocean governance through a narrative history of diplomatic, military, commercial, and scientific developments. It identifies the historical circumstances and political choices that made and unmade freedom of the seas as the centerpiece of ocean governance. The more contemporary chapters sketch the complicated mix of expanded national and international control that is emerging to replace freedom of the seas. Whenever possible, conceptual shifts are illustrated through events at sea, diplomatic communications, and individual accounts. Large political and economic forces have shaped the story of contemporary ocean governance but so too have shipwrecks, pirate attacks, environmental protests, naval clashes, and scientific breakthroughs. The leading maritime powers, Britain in the 18th and 19th centuries and the United States after the mid-20th century, feature in this account, as they must. China becomes prominent in the later chapters. Smaller countries, from Iceland to Malta to the Philippines, have written themselves into the narrative. Individuals, including anti-slavery activists, writers, and modern eco-vigilantes, are part of the story as well.

Understanding the tangled historical roots of ocean governance is particularly important at this moment. Competition for ocean resources is pushing governments and companies into deeper waters. The pace of environmental change is forcing even reluctant governments to construct new mechanisms to protect the oceans. Meanwhile, ocean rules have emerged as a leading irritant between the world's superpower and its main challenger. If open conflict does break out in Asia, it is likely that "freedom of the seas" will be a battle cry. The history of humanity's attempt to create rules for the oceans is alive and relevant.

1

The Oceans Become Global

(to the 1700s)

In 1183, a government clerk from Andalusia, Ibn Jubayr, left his native Cádiz to begin the Hajj. From Spain, he crossed the Strait of Gibraltar, the thread of water through which the Atlantic Ocean mingles with the Mediterranean Sea. Once in North Africa, Ibn Jubayr boarded a Genoese ship that was transporting fellow Muslims as well as some Christians. He marveled at the ease with which the vessel traveled from North Africa to within sight of Sardinia, close to the Italian coast. But there a "mighty storm" rose up, leaving them "unable to distinguish the east from the west."[1] A week later, he endured even more ferocious weather before finally landing in Alexandria, Egypt (Figure 1.1). Once the vessel had docked, the passengers' often terrifying isolation ended, and sovereign authority abruptly appeared. A customs official interviewed the travelers, carefully inspected their cargo, and ensured that they paid the requisite taxes.

Even back on land, Ibn Jubayr felt reverberations from events at sea. He encountered a group of captured Syrian Christians who, he was informed, had been harassing Muslim pilgrims at sea until "valorous Moorish sailors" apprehended them. In the Red Sea port of Aydhab, on the border between present-day Egypt and Sudan, he saw men harvesting pearls from the sea. He spotted merchant ships from as far as India and Yemen and complained that unscrupulous shipowners often loaded passengers into boats "like chickens crammed into a coop." As he crossed the Red Sea toward Jidda—a stretch of water notoriously difficult to navigate—he praised the skill of the ship's crew. "They would enter the narrow channels and manage their way through them as a cavalier manages a horse that is light on the bridle and tractable."[2]

After completing the Hajj, the pilgrim journeyed through present-day Iraq and Syria, where Crusaders periodically battled resurgent Muslim forces. In the port city of Acre, he located another Christian vessel to carry him back west. Progressing across the Mediterranean, the vessel suffered more storms,

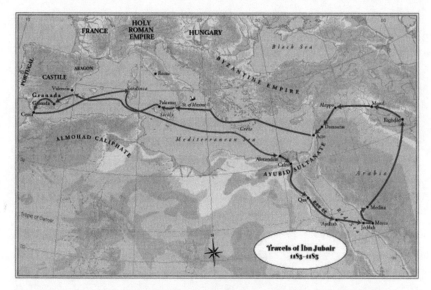

Figure 1.1 Ibn Jubayr's Mediterranean journey; courtesy of The Ibn Jubayr Project, University of Virginia.

and the passengers wondered whether they had been driven off course. Despairing, Ibn Jubayr turned to religious verse:

> The sea is bitter of taste, intractable:
> No need of it have I.
> Is it not water and we earth?
> Why then do we endure it?

The exhausted traveler endured at least one more tempest before completing the last leg of his voyage and landing back in Spain.

Ibn Jubayr's account offers an unusual glimpse into the premodern maritime world. For all his doubts about the wisdom of sea travel, he witnessed vibrant interactions between the land and the sea. But the power of sovereign rulers did not extend far into the water. There is no sign that the vessels he traveled on had to seek permission to journey through the Mediterranean from one land to another. So far as we are told, the vessels encountered sovereign authority only when they entered port. Nature imposed many more restrictions than rulers. Even when not buffeted by storms, mariners had a limited ability to control their own course. What's more, the sea that Ibn

Jubayr traveled was just a fragment of the global oceans. The vast waters of the Atlantic and Pacific were little known to his contemporaries. The nature of the world's oceans was a matter of lively debate at the time of the voyage, and one popular theory posited that land was surrounded by an "ocean river."[3]

Even in these conditions of limited control and incomplete knowledge, the contours of future debates about managing the oceans were emerging. This chapter provides a sketch of early efforts to set rules for the oceans. It considers some of the dynamics at work before the extent of the world's oceans were known and then describes the unexpected rise of freedom of the seas as the dominant doctrine.

The Narrow Seas

The notion of states or kingdoms owning swathes of the ocean was not nearly as prominent in early history as it has become in modern times. Seventeenth-century publicists debating ownership of the seas worked hard to demonstrate the classical roots of their preferred maritime policies, and they plumbed ancient and medieval records for support. But the evidence of ancient claims to ocean spaces is confused at best. Polynesian navigators were among the very few ancient mariners able to traverse large areas of ocean with confidence, but they made no effort to exercise political or legal control of the waters through which they journeyed. For their part, the Phoenicians built some of the earliest large merchant vessels and strung together a trade network in the Mediterranean that reached its greatest extent around 700 BCE. But even their maritime achievements fell well short of establishing sovereignty over the sea.

Part of the explanation is that the marine environment limited the coercive power of sovereigns. Armed vessels could stay at sea only for short periods and often relied on tactics and weapons derived from land combat. As the historian Lincoln Paine has noted, "Until the end of the age of sail in the 19th century, most naval engagements were decided in boarding actions in which ships served as little more than floating battlefields."[4] Over the centuries, tactics and technologies developed that were more specifically suited to maritime warfare, including boarding ramps, ramming spars, pots of fire hung from the prows of ships, and on-board archers. But for most of recorded history, naval vessels had a limited ability to control the seas.

If command of the sea was elusive, one of the principal modern motivations for drawing and enforcing lines in the sea—protecting local fisheries—was also reduced. The determination to exclude outsiders from fishing grounds became acute later, as fishing techniques improved and as the range and capacity of fishing vessels increased. For most of history, harvesting marine resources was a local affair, and in many places it focused first on rivers rather than the sea. As early as 3000 BCE, people used seines to trap fish in rivers, a technique that eventually depleted freshwater stocks and pushed fishermen into coastal waters. Archaeologists in Britain, for example, have found evidence that consumption shifted from freshwater to ocean fish around 1050 CE.[5] Innovations eventually cleared the way for fishing even farther afield. Chinese fishermen constructed sealed compartments on board that could flood with water and keep captured fish alive at sea, permitting longer voyages. Vikings developed the technique of drying fish on board. Around the 15th century, the use of trawl nets began in earnest. Before the 16th century, however, there was scant precedent for efficient long-range fishing that has become so prominent in the modern world.

Even with limited means and motive to control large areas of the oceans, numerous sovereigns boasted about their maritime exploits. Ancient accounts suggest that the Persian king Darius cut a channel from the Nile to the Red Sea—a forerunner of the modern Suez Canal. Not to be outdone, his son Xerxes constructed a "bridge of boats" so that his army could cross the Dardanelles. In the wake of victory over the Persians around 480 BCE, the Greeks apparently attempted to enforce limits on where Persian ships could sail. Historians debate whether that conflict ended with a formal treaty, but those who believe it did contend that the agreement included strict limitations on how close Persians could come to the Aegean Sea.[6] It is beyond dispute that Athens, having vanquished the Persians, then built its empire on the basis of naval power—a strategy that a Spartan general bitterly described as "fornication with the sea."[7] For certain periods, the Athenians were able to exclude enemy vessels from parts of nearby seas. Plato described the Greeks as "frogs around a pond," and the most capable of these periodically attempted to control the pond.[8]

Rome eventually established a stronger claim to "owning" ocean space. By about 60 CE, Roman territory completely encircled the Mediterranean, effectively rendering it a Roman lake. In the Imperial period, Rome established standing naval units that policed the coasts, helped put down uprisings on land, transported dignitaries, and escorted merchant vessels.[9] Certain observers have cited Rome's domination of the Mediterranean—known as "mare nostrum" to proud Romans—as a vital precedent for the right of states to control and administer large ocean spaces. Whether the Romans actually saw the Mediterranean as their own territory has been a point of vigorous debate, and there is ample material for historians litigating the question. The poet Ovid, who wrote during the reign of Emperor Augustus, seemed to offer support for Rome's ownership of the waters:

By definite limitation land was given to other nations,
The space of the allotment of Rome is the same as the entire world.

The Roman, now as victor possesses the whole world,
How the sea, the earth, and the stars run together.[10]

Yet the Digest of Justinian, a 6th-century attempt to compile Roman law, contains an oft-quoted passage casting doubt on Rome's ownership of the sea: "By the natural law, then, the following things are common to all men: the air, flowing water, the sea, and consequently, the shores of the sea."[11]

Whatever the formal character of Rome's maritime dominance, it began to crumble in the 3rd and 4th centuries. To restore order and protect merchants, new players eventually dominated portions of the ocean. Around 1000, Venice became the most powerful naval presence in portions of the Adriatic, in the process routing pirates based on the Dalmatian coast. Profits from the lucrative spice trade, which Venetian merchants helped extend, provided resources for a robust merchant fleet and navy. Venetian leaders even "wed" the sea in an annual ceremony recognizing the society's deep relationship with the waters around it. "We wed thee, Adriatic, as a sign of our true and perpetual dominion," the doge declared, before tossing into the waters a golden ring.[12] Few states rivaled Venetian pomp, but others, including Genoa and Pisa, sometimes claimed exclusive rights to the waters around them. Yet these assertions were ephemeral, tenuous, and rarely formalized.

In the Indian Ocean and in Asia, there is less evidence that sovereigns sought to exercise sustained control of maritime space. A few rulers in the Indian Ocean required passing ships to pay taxes, and officials in the kingdom of Sri Vijaya (based on the island of Sumatra) apparently hung a chain across one strait to prevent unwanted ships from passing.[13] Such tactics seem to have been exceptional. The scholar Hassan Khalilieh has argued that Islamic rulers generally respected freedom of navigation in the Mediterranean and the Indian Oceans.[14]

Ahmad Ibn Majid, the 15th-century Arab navigator and cartographer who became an accomplished mariner while in his teens, insisted that the seas could not be owned. "Know, o seeker, that every man knows his own coast best; the Chinese, China; the people of Sofala, Sofala; the Indians, India; but the sea is not peculiar to anyone of these peoples."[15] The Sultan of Makassar (in modern-day Indonesia) deemed it "unheard of that anyone should be forbidden to sail the seas."[16] Contemporary scholar R. P. Anand concurs: "Persians and Arabs, Indians and Ceylonese, Chinese and peoples of Southeast Asian states all used the seas for trade and enjoyed its bounties in perfect peace."[17]

At least one powerful player in Asia consciously chose not to pursue dominance of the oceans. In 1405, as Europe's historic maritime expansion was beginning, China's emperor dispatched a series of great fleets, including several under the command of Zheng He, who had risen to prominence in the early Ming dynasty. The fleets traveled as far as the Persian Gulf, India, and the coast of Africa. While the voyages promoted maritime trade and attempted to build goodwill, they also projected military strength. Chinese forces confronted and routed several pirate bands they encountered. They landed troops and captured or executed a handful of local rulers who refused to pay fealty. The Ming "were engaged in that early form of maritime colonialism by which a dominant maritime power took control (either through force or the threat thereof) of the main port-polities along the major East-West maritime trade network, as well as the seas between, thereby gaining economic and political benefits."[18] China's bid for maritime control was brief, however. Even as these fleets were completing their voyages, Chinese rulers decided against further forays at sea, a decision that altered significantly the course of history.

The claims of later partisans notwithstanding, the premodern world left no simple answer to whether sovereigns could legitimately claim even those areas of the ocean that were known. The vastness of the waters made those questions almost impertinent. "No absolute 'command of the sea' was possible, for neither side in war could deny the use of the sea to an enemy," one scholar of English maritime policy has written. "The sea was always a debatable space, available to whoever possessed a sea-coast and cared to use it."[19] Even when certain ancient and medieval societies did exercise local maritime dominion, they did not create a clear legal precedent for the modern world. The concept of a formal body of law or even multilateral treaties governing different societies scarcely existed. "Rulers knew that dominance at sea was desirable and possible; those who could obtain it did so," a naval historian has written. "But that question, as a question of law and right, had not yet emerged, because the concept of interstate law itself had not emerged."[20] Yet the hunger of rulers for maritime control was already evident, and without any clear prohibition on claiming the oceans, there was nothing inevitable about the doctrine of freedom of the seas.

Early Rules of the Road

While sovereign claims to ocean dominion in the ancient and medieval world were vague and incomplete, other mechanisms for regulating maritime activities were clearer and more elaborate. The most detailed rules centered on trade and exchange by sea. Sustained maritime trade began as early as 3000 BCE and came to involve several distinct networks, the most developed of which were in the Mediterranean Sea and Indian Ocean. These early trade routes were limited. Most mariners preferred to navigate in sight of the coast, and only occasionally did seafarers break out of their regional waters into the vastness of the open Atlantic or Pacific. Even this constrained trade put merchants from different societies in direct contact. And as maritime commerce became a regular feature of life, a succession of maritime codes and rulebooks emerged to smooth the edges of transactions among merchants and to govern conduct aboard ship.

Between the 6th and 3rd centuries BCE, the Aegean island of Rhodes was a focal point for both seaborne trade and rules governing that trade. The "Rhodian Sea Law" stands as the most influential early maritime code for the Mediterranean world. While many details of those early rules have been lost, their influence is apparent in frequent references by others. As Rome began to engage in maritime commerce, its legal authorities frequently referenced Rhodian law as they settled maritime commerce disputes.

Other societies also found it necessary to create special rules and institutions for maritime activities. The Arthashastra, a treatise compiled in India between 300 and 200 BCE, included detailed provisions on maritime commerce, as did the Hindu legal text Manusmriti. As Muslim influence in the Mediterranean grew, Islamic scholars formulated their own maritime codes. A *Treatise Concerning the Leasing of Ships*, for example, drew on Rhodian and Byzantine rules but added novel features on the financing of maritime commerce.[21] In Asia, the port of Melaka, near the Strait of Malacca, was the source of a 13th-century maritime code that helped structure commerce throughout the region. In northern Europe, the Rolls of Oléron, a

12th-century maritime code, was widely used. Legal experts in Barcelona later produced the *Consolato de Mar*, a compilation of existing maritime law that incorporated elements of Rhodian law, Islamic law, and other sources.

A central goal of all these codes was sharing the substantial risks of commerce at sea. An exigency that demanded particular attention was the jettisoning of cargo to save a vessel. How should those losses be apportioned? One answer, which emerged as early as the 8th-century BCE, was the law of "general average." It provided that all parties sending goods on a given ship agree in advance to share any losses proportionally, and versions of the law of general average appear repeatedly in different maritime codes.

Maritime codes also delved into the details of shipboard life and established authority for those beyond the reach of powers on land. The Rhodian Sea Law, for example, stipulated the compensation scale for masters, boatswains, sailors, and cooks. It also prohibited the frying of fish or the splitting of wood on board without the permission of the captain. Drunken disorder by sailors was a perennial concern, and the Rolls of Oléron provided a measure of protection for shipowners:

> If any of the mariners hired by the master of any vessel, go out of the ship without his leave, and get themselves drunk, and thereby there happens contempt to their master, debates, or fighting and quarreling among themselves, whereby some happen to be wounded: in this case the master shall not be obliged to get them cured, or in any thing to provide for them, but may turn them and their accomplices out of the ship.[22]

The intricacies of these codes are of interest mostly to specialists in admiralty law, the rules and doctrines that govern private commercial relationships at sea. Two points are important for this account. First, these codes reinforced the notion that the sea was different from the land and required its own set of rules. As the stormwracked Ibn Jubayr had asked, "Is it not water, and we earth?" A statement attributed to the Roman emperor Antoninus anticipated this distinction: "I am indeed lord of the world, but the law is lord of the sea." The Code of Melaka continued that theme:

> Let these Laws be followed towards all Countries, in as much as the Laws of the Sea which relate to the Sea only, and the Laws of the Land, which relate to the Land only, are defined, because those of the Sea cannot interfere with those established on shore.[23]

Second, these codes implicitly acknowledged the limited reach of rulers on land. They were codes for and by merchants and mariners. When they are mentioned at all, rulers appear largely as outsiders who are admonished to treat mariners fairly. Only occasionally is there a suggestion that mariners owe an obligation to sovereigns on land; the Rolls of Oléron provide, for example, that mariners who fish off the seashore should provide a percentage of their haul to the "lord." But sovereigns were not driving the regulation of maritime affairs, as they would at later stages. It does not appear that there was even a necessary connection between a sovereign and a vessel. Most vessels had home ports, of course, and a merchant in distress might seek the assistance of his sovereign. Yet there was no real equivalent to the "flagging" and registration process that has become so central to modern maritime governance.

Pirates and Kings

Storms, running aground, and collisions were the risks that precipitated the law of general average and other risk-sharing maritime rules. Robbery at sea was yet another preoccupation. As soon as maritime commerce became significant, the practice of plundering ships and taking hostages began. Ancient Egyptian sources record battles by the Pharaoh Rameses against the "sea peoples," tribes of unknown origin that relied on small, quick boats to raid Egyptian cities and towns. Looting and the capture and trading of slaves was common on the waterways around ancient Greece. Inscriptions found on the island of Rhodes memorialized a member of the Rhodian navy who died "fighting against the pirates."[24]

Centuries later, prominent Romans were seized at sea and even from roads along the Italian coast. A young Julius Caesar himself fell into pirate hands, likely while voyaging to Rhodes for a course of study.[25] According to Plutarch's account, Caesar was displeased by the modest ransom sought by the pirates and insisted that they demand a more fitting sum. The future emperor languished with the pirates for several months, apparently building a rapport with his captors. (Once freed, however, Caesar expeditiously assembled a small fleet and captured and crucified the pirates who had held him.)[26]

Caesar's experience has understandably received lavish attention, but private violence has been a nearly constant feature of life at sea. The island of

Socotra, off the coast of Yemen, was cited by Muslim travelers as a haven for pirates. In the 1180s, a Crusader transported several dismantled vessels to the Red Sea, reassembled them, and then commenced raids against Muslim ports and travelers.[27] Multiple sources suggest that India's Malabar coast was a locus for piratical activity by the 12th century. Japanese raiders pillaged the Korean coast in the 13th century. One group, the Matsura band, seems to have raided Korean territory nearly a dozen times in the space of a few decades.[28]

Certain ancient writers questioned whether piracy should even be seen as dishonorable or illegitimate. Homer's poems evince some ambiguity on the subject. As the historian Philip de Souza has pointed out, "Homer does not actually use a word for 'piracy', and the activities of those who are la-belled 'pirates' are virtually indistinguishable from the deeds of his heroes and warriors, who seem to share the same predatory motives and achieve similar results."[29] Occasional uncertainty about the moral and social status of violent men at sea persisted through the centuries. In the *City of God*, the early Christian theologian St. Augustine sympathetically recounted an ex-change between a captured pirate and the emperor Alexander:

> The Emperor angrily demanded of him, "How dare you molest the seas?" To which the pirate replied, "How dare you molest the whole world? Because I do it with a small boat, I am called a pirate and a thief. You, with a great navy, molest the world and are called an emperor."[30]

However intriguing, these passages should not obscure the broader reality that "pirate" has mostly been employed as an epithet since ancient times. In 44 BCE, Cicero classified pirates as actors not worthy of the protection offered by traditional moral convention:

> If for example, you do not hand over to pirates the amount agreed upon as the price for your life, this is not perjury, not even if you have sworn an oath and do not do so, for pirates are not included in the category of lawful ene-mies, but they are the *enemies of all mankind*.[31]

The power of Cicero's formulation made the accusation of piracy—or aiding pirates—a favored rhetorical weapon of rulers (not unlike the term "ter-rorism" today). Charges of piracy have been leveled against a range of actors with very different motives and characteristics. Pirates sometimes operated as independent bands, but they often were part of land-based societies that functioned almost as political units of their own. In these cases, accusations of piracy were often little more than a way of delegitimizing an enemy society.

Even when seaborne marauders could make no plausible claim to sovereignty, their relationships with established societies were often complex. Purveyors of violence at sea have often been useful to rulers. What later became known as privateering—raiding with permission from a sovereign ruler—has long historical roots. For much of history, "men accused of robbery and murder at sea went free if they enlisted to rob and murder in the king's name."[32] Rulers often traded accusations with rivals about consorting with pirates. An Egyptian pharaoh accused the ruler of Cyprus of working with pirates; the king responded that his ships too were being assaulted. The Persians accused the Athenians of being in league with pirates. A few centuries later, the Romans alleged that Mithridates, a nemesis of Rome in the 1st century BCE, was aligned with pirates then ravaging the Greek coast. Japanese rulers in the 12th century hastened to ensure suspicious Korean counterparts that they were not supporting the work of Japanese pirate bands—and they executed dozens of suspected bandits to prove it.[33]

It is clear enough that sovereigns at times employed pirates and raiders to further their own aims. Yet unsanctioned violence at sea has been a recurring problem throughout the ages. Even today, suppressing piracy is a daunting challenge. It requires not mere agreement on norms and rules, but the ability and willingness of public authorities—or merchants themselves—to deploy resources to ensure security. Early maritime societies certainly had an incentive to do so; promoting law and order at sea was often an economic imperative. Acting to suppress piracy was recognized from ancient times as the kind of feat great rulers achieved. The Greek historian Thucydides, writing around 400 BCE, credited (the likely mythical) King Minos of Crete with having "cleared the sea of piracy as far as he was able."[34] Whether Minos himself existed, there is evidence that the Minoan navy did suppress piracy in the eastern Mediterranean for several centuries.

Athens, which had established an empire based on sea power, made occasionally energetic efforts to stamp out piracy. Rhodes, so prominent in the development of maritime codes, can claim to have opposed piracy even more consistently. Its naval forces regularly endeavored to keep the Aegean safe for commerce. Like the Greek city states before it, Rome was heavily dependent on grain imports, and predation at sea therefore aroused intense public anxiety. In 67 BCE, the Roman commander Gnaeus Pompey enhanced his already considerable fame by clearing the Mediterranean of pirates in a matter of months. With more than 200 ships at his disposal, Pompey divided the entire sea into 13 naval districts and systematically isolated and defeated pirate bands. The campaign was enormously popular, and grain prices in Rome apparently plummeted soon after Pompey took command. Modern historians have been circumspect in their evaluations of Pompey's success, but it stands at the very least as a public relations coup. In the centuries that followed, the Roman imperial navy had counter-piracy as one of its missions, and Roman domination produced a boom in Mediterranean commerce.

As with Pompey's famous campaign, counter-piracy has mostly been a unilateral affair that typically fell to the dominant naval power or to a local ruler particularly affected by piracy. There are few examples of sustained coordination between societies to suppress crime at sea, but provisions on piracy appeared occasionally in some treaties and diplomatic agreements. For example, Athenian and Rhodian treaties with other states in the region sometimes included provisions demanding an end to all cooperation with pirates. Rome apparently worked with Rhodes on anti-piracy initiatives.

When sovereigns working alone or in concert proved unable to stem violence at sea, prominent individuals occasionally took matters into their own hands. Chang Bogo, a Korean merchant, grew so frustrated at piracy, slave trading, and abduction in the Yellow Sea that in the early 9th century he apparently petitioned the king for permission to develop a fleet of his own. Based on Wando Island, off the southern tip of the Korean Peninsula, Chang tamped down banditry and emerged as the principal maritime authority in the area. He is credited with preventing the abduction of Koreans by slave merchants, and his vessels were sought out as the most secure way to ship cargo in the area.[35] Thousands of miles away, in northern Europe, merchants settled on a similar approach. The Hanseatic League, a confederation of northern German traders that coalesced in the 1100s, had as one of its primary objectives safeguarding its members' shipping. Eventually, the League required all of its ships to carry certain types of armaments and sometimes arranged convoys of vessels to dissuade pirates.[36]

The fact that merchants themselves periodically took the initiative against piracy underlines an important reality: few sovereigns have had the naval resources regularly to combat violence at sea. Only a handful of premodern societies—including the Roman Empire, Athens, and Venice—possessed the means and the inclination to build standing navies tasked with maintaining law and order at sea. Throughout history, even major powers have often decided that investing in permanent navies was not worth the considerable cost and opted to raise fleets only when exigencies demanded.

Sovereigns have been inconstant and often negligent custodians of order at sea, but both ancient and medieval experiences make clear that suppressing disorder at sea was usually viewed as a common good. Cicero's description of pirates as the "common enemy of mankind" reflected a gathering consensus. Centuries later, it stands as a fair description of modern international law on the subject.

Christian Condominium

Knowledge of the full extent of the oceans emerged in the late 15th and early 16th centuries as Europeans began crossing first the Atlantic and then the Pacific Oceans. The critical breakthroughs occurred within the space of a few remarkable years. On his way to what he hoped was the Indies, Christopher Columbus collided with the Americas in 1492. The oceans around this newly discovered land were vacant of competing navies or maritime commerce of any scale. The indigenous peoples that Columbus encountered mostly used canoes, and Columbus could justifiably feel that he was (as he would soon be titled) the "Admiral of the Ocean Seas."[37]

Once confirmed, Columbus's finds occasioned considerable tumult in Europe and, in particular, between the competing Spanish and Portuguese monarchies. On his return voyage, Columbus docked briefly in Portugal, where the explorer Bartholomeu Dias questioned him suspiciously about his travels. The Portuguese realized that Spain, having sponsored Columbus's voyage, now stood ready to reap its rewards.

Columbus's breakthrough occurred just as Portugal was opening the sea route from western Europe to the Indies. Dias himself had reached the Cape of Good Hope in 1488. A decade later, three Portuguese ships under the command of Vasco da Gama rounded the Cape, sailed up the eastern coast of Africa, and emerged into the Indian Ocean. Unlike Columbus, they found a body of water well traveled by merchants, many of them Arab and Indian. Following the monsoon winds, ships routinely traversed the Indian Ocean, with several Indian ports serving as entrepôts.

As da Gama's modest flotilla engaged with local rulers in the area, the Portuguese captain quickly resorted to demonstrations of force to ensure access to trade and supplies. The ability of Portuguese vessels to project power from a distance appears to have been their decisive advantage. The historian Sanjay Subrahmanyam writes:

> What was fundamentally new about the Portuguese in the Indian Ocean was thus not the fact that they used force on water: it was the degree of expertise with which they did so, the fact that they did so over such large maritime spaces, separated moreover by such a distance from anything that could be thought of as their home territory, and the relatively systematic effort they brought to bear in this sphere.[38]

Portuguese naval dominance in the Indian Ocean was not a given. The massive Chinese fleets commanded by Zheng He had stalked those waters less than a century before. "It can only be imagined what might have occurred had the first Europeans to visit the Indian Ocean encountered the treasure fleet, whose smallest support junks would have towered over the puny Portuguese caravels," William Bernstein has written. "[But] when Vasco da Gama breached the Indian Ocean, the playing field had just been vacated by the one force capable of repelling him."[39] It was long believed that one of da Gama's navigators during his voyage was Ahmad Ibn Majid, the Arab navigator who had insisted that the oceans could not be claimed by anyone.[40] Their collaboration would have been deeply ironic. Da Gama and the Portuguese who would follow him into the Indian Ocean were developing a quite different conception of the oceans.

With superior armaments and a conviction of their right to dominate the region, the Portuguese soon claimed dominion over broad areas of the Indian Ocean. Commercial and religious motives overlapped, and an extraordinary vision of ocean dominance became part of the emerging national narrative. In his epic poem completed around 1570, Luis Vas de Camoes placed his countrymen's achievements in a rarefied company:

> Boast no more about the subtle Greek
> Or the long odyssey of Trojan Aeneas;
> Enough of the oriental conquests
> Of great Alexander and of Trajan;
> I sing of the famous Portuguese
> To whom both Mars and Neptune bowed.[41]

Controlling trade allowed Portugal to ensure its own supply routes and gather taxes and duties from other merchants seeking access. Domination of the Indian Ocean also could cut into the lucrative Arab trading routes down the Red Sea and Persian Gulf, thereby weakening the Islamic world; control of the Indian Ocean could simultaneously make Portugal rich and strike a blow for Christianity. After a decisive battle in February 1509, when a Portuguese fleet routed a combined Gujarati and Egyptian force, no naval power in the region challenged Lisbon's dominance. The Portuguese did not delay in capitalizing; within a few years, they had established a system of *cartazes*, or passes, that vessels had to possess to engage in commerce. "Portuguese captains, to justify capture of ships, put forth the argument that their ruler was the 'Lord of the Sea.' "[42] Portuguese warships prowled the Indian Ocean to enforce compliance.

The competing Spanish and Portuguese discoveries in the West and East, and the prospect of access to vast new territory and resources, prompted the most important supranational figure of the time to mediate. By the time of Columbus's voyage, a series of papal proclamations had already attempted to smooth relations between the expansionist Christian kingdoms, and Pope Alexander VI tried his hand again in 1493. Drawing on his mediation work, the two kingdoms a year later agreed to what still stands as the most audacious attempt to divide the oceans between sovereign powers. The Treaty of Tordesillas, signed in 1494, acknowledged that "certain controversy exists between the said lords, their constituents, as to what lands, of all those discovered in the ocean sea up to the present day . . . pertain to each one of the said parts respectively." To resolve that "controversy," the treaty divided the oceans into two spheres based on a north-south line 70 leagues to the west of the Cape Verde islands. Spain was given control of areas to the west of that line; Portugal had preeminence to the east. Leaving nothing to chance, the treaty called for a joint maritime mission to meet at the Cape Verde islands and establish the line to both parties' satisfaction.[43]

Tordesillas did not make these enormous ocean realms sovereign territory, exactly.[44] The concern of the treaty was clearly land that had been or might be discovered in these parts of the oceans, and not the oceans themselves. But it did give the kingdoms the right to exclude others from their vast maritime zones. It required each kingdom not to dispatch ships through the other's ocean realm unless necessary to reach their own possessions. Any vessel passing through had to proceed directly, without carrying out any exploration, an arrangement foreshadowing the modern doctrine of "innocent passage" through territorial waters.

Growing knowledge of the oceans soon outpaced the treaty arrangement. Less than three decades after the Treaty of Tordesillas was signed, the remaining crew from an expedition led by Ferdinand Magellan straggled back to the Spanish port of Seville. Magellan, who was Portuguese, had successfully enlisted the support of the Spanish Crown for his voyage, which began in the summer of 1519. For the next two years, his ships traveled from Spain to South America, through the strait that now bears his name, and then across the vastness of the Pacific before finally landing in Guam and then picking their way back to Europe. The survivors—and there were not many—were gaunt and ridden with scurvy, but they had accomplished the first ever around-the-world voyage. Magellan himself did not complete the circuit. He was killed in the Philippines, where he had intervened unwisely in a local conflict.

The ghastly toll of the voyage could not diminish its accomplishments: proving definitively that the world's great oceans were linked and providing, for the first time, a reasonably accurate picture of their extent. Two decades later, the German cartographer Sebastian Munster produced one of the first known maps to label the Pacific Ocean.[45] Its merits in terms of expanding knowledge aside, Magellan's mission posed an immediate complication to the Tordesillas settlement that had been reached between Spain and Portugal. If Magellan could sail from Europe westward around the world, the dividing line established by that treaty was useless, because each kingdom could claim that *everything* was to the east or west of the Tordesillas line. (The Portuguese court realized this and made several attempts to intercept Magellan's voyage.) In the wake of Magellan's success, the Spice Islands—now known as the Moluccan—became the focal point of the dispute. The result was a 1529 treaty that established a new north-south line in Asia. Portugal would control the Indian Ocean and a slice of the Pacific. Spain would have control of the Philippines and the vast bulk of the Pacific to their east.

The Christian kingdoms had at least temporarily repaired their joint condominium of the world's oceans, but momentum in maritime affairs was already shifting to other players, and they were not inclined to honor the Tordesillas arrangement. By the end of the 16th century, the ocean privileges of Spain and Portugal produced what still stands as the seminal controversy on governance of the oceans.

"Battle of the Books"

One individual keen to challenge Spanish pretensions to ocean control was Sir Francis Drake. In 1578, he famously circumnavigated the globe with tacit approval from Queen Elizabeth to raid Spanish shipping in the Pacific. Denounced as a pirate by the Spanish, Drake captured several Spanish treasure galleons and returned to England a hero. Elizabeth swore Drake and his crew to secrecy about her role in the voyage, but she did at least rise in defense of free navigation when the Spanish complained. "The use of the sea and air is common to all," the queen apparently responded. "Neither can any title to the ocean belong to any people or private man, forasmuch as neither nature nor regard of the public use permitteth any possession thereof."[46] A decade after Drake's voyage, the failure of the Spanish Armada struck a blow against Spanish naval supremacy.

For all the drama of England's confrontation with the Spanish, it was Dutch resistance to Portugal's dominion in the Indian Ocean that brought the matter of ocean control to a head. The Dutch had multiple reasons to challenge the Iberian claims. The Spanish and Portuguese kingdoms merged in 1580, just a year before the northern Dutch provinces achieved de facto independence from Spain. But the Dutch struggle continued, and a blow against the Portuguese in the Indies would also strike directly at the oppressors. More broadly, the Dutch realized that maritime commerce would be essential to developing their economy. With neither vast territory nor rich farmland, the Dutch path to riches went through the sea. So in the 1590s, the Dutch began a bid to break into what had become Portugal's lucrative monopoly on the spice trade. In 1602, after several earlier experiments, the Dutch formed the United East India Company (known by its Dutch initials as the VOC).

Lisbon did not share its prize easily. Early Dutch attempts to establish trading routes met with violent opposition from Portuguese and local rulers in league with them. In 1601, 17 Dutch sailors were lured into port, captured, and ultimately hanged at a Portuguese-run prison in Macao. Two years later, the Dutch struck back. With the assistance of a sympathetic local ruler, the Sultan of Johore, a Dutch admiral ambushed the Portuguese vessel *Santa Catarina*, which was groaning with fruits of the trade. The Portuguese crew finally yielded, and the *Santa Catarina* was sailed to Amsterdam. Its contents were auctioned off for the extraordinary sum of 3 million Dutch guilders. In a disorganized but energetic decision, a Dutch court ruled that the seizure was entirely legal.

The VOC seemed to understand that a more thorough and careful defense was necessary to win support internationally, and its board of directors contracted a legal prodigy named Hugo Grotius, just 20 years old at the time, to provide it. Grotius's product, a pamphlet titled *Mare Liberum*, appeared in 1609. It vigorously defended the right of Dutch merchants to trade in the Indian Ocean and justified the seizure of the *Santa Catarina*. (Grotius's name was not attached, and the author described himself as an "artist skulking behind his easel, to find out the judgement of others.") Written in Latin, the pamphlet circulated widely among European scholars. Grotius was fortunate in the timing of his publication. By chance, other events in 1609 sharpened the debate about how much of the ocean any ruler could claim.

Across the North Sea from the Netherlands, England's King James I announced new restrictions on the right of foreign vessels—primarily Dutch—to fish in the waters off his coast. James had a variety of motives, including concern about the depletion of fishing stocks and the decrepitude of England's fishing industry. English fishermen could only watch with envy as modern, well-equipped Flemish *busses* hauled in their catch, sometimes just a few miles off the coast. Dutch fishermen had mastered the technology of salting and barreling herring on board, allowing them to stay at sea for long periods rather than rush home to offload their catch. The prospect of revenue from taxing foreign vessels likely piqued the English king's interest, and in 1609 he issued a proclamation preventing fishing by unlicensed foreigners.

The move sparked immediate Dutch protests, and *Mare Liberum*'s arguments now stood ready to combat English pretensions to ocean control just as they had the Portuguese. The English had plenty of problems other than Grotius's pen, however, and the government struggled to put the new policy into practice. Dutch *busses* continued to fish the waters, and the grand visions of a reinvigorated English fishing fleet did not materialize. But the controversy did at least stir several scholars to defend the English king's actions. Together, the Dutch push into the Indian Ocean and the English insistence on protecting what they saw as their historical fishing grounds produced the "Battle of the Books." Aspects of that debate have little resonance today—including sparring over the bearing of scripture and the relative weight of various Roman authorities—but its main contours remain salient.

At the heart of Grotius's argument that the Dutch were justified in seizing the *Santa Catarina* was an insistence that the seas cannot be owned in the way that land can. Once that premise is accepted, Portugal's attacks on the Dutch interlopers becomes unjustified aggression and the Dutch response a legitimate countermeasure. Grotius defended his central assertion in several ways. He argued that the ocean's nature, and the shifting direction of the winds, make clear nature's design of the oceans as a pathway between societies:

> For even that ocean wherewith God hath compassed the Earth is navigable on every side round about, and the settled or extraordinary blasts of wind, not always blowing from the same quarter, and sometimes from every quarter, do they not sufficiently signify that nature hath granted a passage from all nations unto all?[47]

It was evident to Grotius that the mere presence of vessels in these ocean pathways did not create ownership. A ship passing through waters, he argued, leaves no right to possession behind it. "Nature doth not permit it but commandeth it should be common." Nor does suppressing piracy or ensuring safety at sea more generally create ownership. Those assertions of order "happened not by any proper right but of the common right which also other free nations have in the sea."[48]

Grotius also leaned on what he described as the inexhaustibility of the ocean's resources, a quality that made it different from land. There is a logic to parceling up the land so that its resources can be more rationally managed and to ensure that those who have labored to produce crops reap the benefit. What sense does that make in the vast ocean with its limitless resources?[49] "For by using, the sea itself is not at all impaired, and it needs no cultivation to bear fruit."[50]

The most elaborate response to Grotius came from the English lawyer John Selden, who published *Mare Clausum* (The Closed Sea) in 1635. He directly contradicted Grotius's central claim, first by resort to religious authority. The Bible made clear, he argued, that God gave man dominion over the land and the sea equally. Ancient Jewish law, said Selden, was also clear that "the Sea was every jot as capable of private Dominion, as the land." In ancient history, Selden found what he saw as ample precedent for ownership of the sea—including by the Phoenicians, Greeks, Romans, and Venetians.

If the lessons of history were clear to Selden, he also saw nothing in the nature of the ocean that made it immune from ownership. The fluidity of the sea, he argued, should not preclude ownership. After all, nobody disputes that sovereigns can rule rivers and lakes. If Grotius could admit (as he did) that bays and inlets were subject to ownership, why not the open ocean? Selden acknowledged that controlling the entire ocean would be very diffi- cult, but he did not see any principled reason why it could not come under the sway of a powerful enough ruler. Intently focused on England's claims, Selden devoted much of his work to proving the particular claim of the English to their own nearby seas. He combed through records for historical evidence of English control and found plenty, including frequent references to English kings as "Lords of the Sea."[51]

There were other entrants into the battle of the books. In 1615, Scottish lawyer William Welwod directly challenged several of Grotius's arguments, including his assertion that the resources of the sea were inexhaustible. Welwod's principal concern was to protect Scottish fishing grounds that, in his view, had been depleted by Dutch interlopers. A Portuguese friar, Serafim de Freitas, penned his own defense of the right of sovereigns to control the ocean. Like Welwod and Selden, Freitas disputed Grotius's insistence that the seas were by nature open to all.

But Grotius emerged as the most influential by far. His renown derived not just from the clarity and force of his prose, but also from his reliance on nat- ural law rather than scripture. While firmly grounded in Christian thought, Grotius drew on the nature of the ocean to craft arguments that could be persuasive across the fierce religious divides of the time. As one admirer has written, he "cut himself free from theological argument and was able to em- brace the whole of mankind in his purview."[52] He published his masterpiece, *De Jure Belli ac Pacis* (On the Law of War and Peace), in 1625. The Dutch prodigy was far from alone in expounding a more secular version of inter- national law, but his work met the needs of the time. As Europe struggled to extract itself from decades of religious wars, Grotius and others provided a framework and language for a new system of international relations between sovereign and juridically equal states.

The Dutch scholar's prominence and the evocative titles that he and Selden chose sometimes made their disagreement appear even more stark than it was. Grotius distinguished the open sea from other bodies of water more sus- ceptible to control, including bays, rivers, and that part of the ocean "that can be seen from the shore."[53] For his part, Selden acknowledged that sovereigns could likely never govern the vastness of entire oceans. But the conceptual differences between the two tended to overwhelm that practical overlap.

The Gathering Fleets

As Grotius, Selden, and others traded learned salvoes, the ability of Europe's rulers to wage real battles at sea was improving markedly. The 1648 Peace of Westphalia formalized the end of Europe's long-running religious wars and allowed rulers to funnel resources into other projects. The centralization and bureaucratization of once fissiparous European kingdoms was a major trend in the years after Westphalia, which scholars of international relations have often used to mark the beginning of the modern international system.

At sea, that trend resulted in larger and newly professionalized national navies that could sail faster, deploy farther afield, and shoot with greater accuracy and effect. The Dutch in the 1650s sought to build on the stunning success of their merchant shipping and authorized a 100-ship navy (although their efforts to build a cohesive force suffered from excessive decentralization). Under the energetic guidance of Jean-Baptiste Colbert, France poured money into training its naval officers and furnishing them with a world-class fleet. In the space of five years, from 1666 to 1670, the French produced more than 80 warships. Vigorous French efforts to become a naval power included the publication of a new maritime code.

Yet it was in England that the professionalization of the navy had the most dramatic and lasting impact. In 1637, during the reign of Charles I, the Royal Navy took possession of the enormous and provocatively named *Sovereign of the Seas*. With three decks and more than 100 cannon, the ship was the largest and most extravagant an English fleet had ever featured. The ship's name and iconography were a direct endorsement of Selden's view of the oceans. Her transom featured carvings of Neptune and evoked early English rulers associated with maritime power. The ship "was used to support Charles's political ideology that attacked Grotius's *Mare Liberum* and encouraged maritime empire," the historian Benjamin Redding writes. "The *Sovereign of the Seas* declared that Charles owned the sea."[54]

The vessel was among the most dramatic examples of what became known as "ships of the line," which one naval historian has described as "the most expensive, technologically advanced, and visually impressive weapon of its day [that represented] the measure of national naval power, like the dreadnought of World War I or the aircraft carrier of World War II."[55] These vessels were much larger than earlier warships, carried scores of cannon, and were designed to concentrate overwhelming firepower on opposing vessels.

Fifty years after *Sovereign of the Seas* first sailed, the English navy had grown to more than 170 vessels. "From being an assembly of vessels provided for by the monarch and certain nobles and merchants, it became a national force, paid for by regular votes of Parliament," writes the historian Paul Kennedy. "From being an occasional and motley body, it became a standing and homogeneous fleet."[56] A controversial tax raised revenue for building the fleet, and for the first time, the Royal Navy undertook regular patrols around the British Isles.

In stages, that newly cohesive fleet helped Britain develop maritime supremacy. The defeat and dispersal of the Armada in 1588 had diminished the Spanish as a naval competitor. Beginning in 1652, the English and the Dutch commenced a series of naval wars for commercial dominance. The first of these wars began when a Dutch admiral refused to offer the demanded "salute" to an English warship in the Channel in recognition of English maritime dominion. The ensuing struggles ended inconclusively, but the Dutch proved unable to stem England's naval rise.

In the 1660s, the French made their own concerted bid to rival the British at sea. British and French naval forces clashed over the course of a decade in the War of Spanish Succession, but the French, like the Dutch, struggled to overcome key British advantages. By the early 18th century, one of those assets was control of Gibraltar, the rocky peninsula jutting south from Spain toward the narrow strait between Europe and North Africa. British forces helped oust the Spanish in 1704 and then formalized their conquest through the Treaty of Utrecht. Britain now controlled a spit of land that would give it enormous influence over entry to and exit from the Mediterranean.

Around this time, Britain began stationing vessels away from their home bases year-round, a key step toward fielding a global navy. The Seven Years' War, from 1757 to 1763, saw several European fleets deploy well outside of European waters, and the historian Martin Robson has argued that the sprawling conflict served as a hinge moment for Britain in particular:

In 1754–6 Britain was a country that was still very much European in outlook. By 1763 that had changed, Britain was an imperial power trying to balance European colonial concerns. The war was, therefore, for Britain about the great contest for maritime empire and it relied on the Royal Navy.[57]

Key battles still lay ahead, but the British were on course for prolonged maritime domination. As it stood on the cusp of hegemony, the British navy carried with it a conception of the ocean that owed as much to Selden's idea of proprietary waters as to Grotius's insistence that the seas were open to all.

2

Britannia's Rules

(1750–1914)

Writing in 1704, the year English forces scrambled onto Gibraltar, the Dutch scholar Cornelius Bynkershoek tried to cut through what he saw as the "empty twaddle" confusing the issue of sovereignty over the sea. Revisiting some of the ground covered by Grotius—but differing with his illustrious countryman in certain respects—Bynkershoek argued that states can occupy and therefore own the sea, but only in very distinct circumstances:

> We do not concede ownership of a maritime belt any farther out than it can be ruled from the land, and yet we do concede it that far; for there can be no reason for saying that the sea which is under some one man's command and control is any less his than a ditch in his territory.

How far out can the sea be ruled from land? For Bynkershoek, the answer was simple: "Control of the land [over the sea] extends as far as cannon will carry; for that is as far as we seem to have both command and possession."[1] That formulation was the most influential statement of what became known as the "cannon-shot rule." Within the reach of a cannon, a distance often estimated to be three miles, a coastal state could legitimately claim to occupy and control the sea. The cannon-shot rule had a defensive rationale as well as an acquisitive one. Coastal states did not want foreign warships battling close to their villages and towns, as musket and cannon shot from naval battles sometimes fell on innocent coastal observers. An established three-mile territorial sea offered at least some protection to those on shore.

In 1758, the Swiss jurist Emer de Vattel published a landmark tome that "dominated the philosophy of international law from the middle of the 18th century to the end of the First World War."[2] Vattel confidently rejected the validity of national claims to the open ocean. Following Bynkershoek, he limited national control to the "space of the sea within cannon-shot of the coast."[3] Vattel's work circulated widely on the continent. It also crossed the

Atlantic and found its way into the libraries of several American founders. In thanking a French acquaintance for sending it, Benjamin Franklin noted that the volume "came to us in good season, when the circumstances of a rising State make it necessary frequently to consult the law of nations."[4] In an era in which the law of nations was more the product of scholarly opinion than multilateral agreement, the "free sea" seemed to have prevailed.

Yet vessels in the 18th century often found Grotius's influence elusive. Britain still required ships passing through the English Channel to dip their flags in a sign of obeisance. This "channel salute" was mostly an annoyance, but it signaled that the leading maritime power remained tempted by the idea of a closed sea. More important, the freedom of vessels to navigate the high seas was interrupted by occasional forced boarding, inspection, impressment, and even armed assault and scuttling. The 18th century featured shifting but nearly constant hostilities among at least some of the European major powers; Britain and France were at war almost half of the time between 1700 and 1815. As the European powers struggled for primacy, merchant vessels on the high seas became frequent prizes.

The British, with their growing naval superiority, most actively harassed shipping that might benefit adversaries, and London's strategic needs dictated its view of the international legal environment. While other countries insisted that ships flying the flags of neutral states should be immune from search and seizure—"free ships make free goods" was the slogan—the British often claimed the right to seize any good (even carried in neutral vessels) destined for adversaries. The American War of Independence provided particular impetus for Britain to flex its maritime muscle. Royal Navy ships and privateers routinely intercepted vessels carrying supplies to the rebellious colonies.

That policy reverberated through the continent and infuriated Russia, in particular, which had ambitions of becoming a maritime power. British seizures at sea spurred the creation in 1780 of a "League of Armed Neutrality," which undertook to protect (by force of arms if necessary) the freedom of neutral merchant vessels to trade. Led by Russia, the league eventually included Sweden, Denmark, Prussia, Austria, and Portugal. The initiative's efficacy is not easy to measure, but it vexed the British by compelling them repeatedly to justify their seizures.

War between Britain and revolutionary and then Napoleonic France, which began in 1793 and continued with only brief interruptions until 1815, provoked more interference with shipping. The first major naval engagement of that conflict, in June 1794, foreshadowed warfare by economic blockade. Desperate for grain after a crop shortage, the French arranged a massive convoy laden with supplies to sail from the eastern United States. A British squadron stalked the convoy and then engaged. From time immemorial, naval battles had taken place close to shore and were typically named for some coastal feature. But the Battle of the Glorious First of June occurred so far out to sea that it was not associated with any particular landmark.[5] Not decisive on its own, the battle demonstrated the increased range of navies and the possibility of naval blockades over much larger areas. Beginning in 1793, the British imposed a blockade on the port of Brest. Later, the British seized Dutch and French vessels unlucky enough to be in its ports and imposed new restrictions on colonial trade. Britain's aggressiveness at sea spurred the creation of a second armed neutrality league in 1800, although its impact was limited.

The French navy had little more success than neutral states in coping with British maritime power. Near parity with the British in 1700, the French then fell behind. By 1800, the French navy boasted just over 200 vessels while the Royal Navy numbered more than 500.[6] Zealous revolutionaries purged the French navy's aristocratic officer corps, and the hemorrhaging of trained personnel accentuated Britain's numerical advantage. The defeat of the combined French and Spanish fleet off Cape Trafalgar in 1805 cleared the way for an even more stifling British blockade imposed the next year. Napoleon responded with a counter blockade, dubbed the Continental System. French ships attempted to prevent all British maritime trade with the continent, but Britain's dominance of the seas rendered the French strategy mostly ineffective and likely counterproductive.[7]

French propaganda during the long conflict was rife with complaints about Britain's tyranny over the seas. Preparing his troops for battle against the Austrians, Napoleon described them as allies of England without whom the French "would have avenged six centuries of injury and restored the freedom of the seas."[8] A tract written by one of the general's favored intellectuals described metastasizing British maritime influence:

> English vessels cover every sea: she sends soldiers, arms, gold, agents to the four quarters of the world; there is no colony so remote that her distant expeditions do not threaten it; there is no empire, however much a stranger to European intercourse, to which she does not labour to procure access and to secure exclusive establishments there . . . and as she extends the

realm of nautical geography, she enlarges at the same time that of English maritime domination.[9]

Britain's insistence that it could stop and search neutral vessels to check for contraband contributed to the outbreak of war in 1812 between Britain and the United States. John Adams, still active in his post-presidency, warned a correspondent in 1808 that "the Trident of Neptune is the Scepter of the World and that unlimited Despotism on the Ocean for which Britain avowedly and openly contends would be a more dangerous Domination over the civilized World than any that Napoleon ever can accomplish."[10]

The resentment of "perfidious Albion" and its maritime dominance complicated British efforts to organize and nourish opposition to Napoleon. But the privation and dislocation imposed by Britain's blockade also generated dissatisfaction within Napoleon's realm and emboldened those on the continent willing to challenge him. As those forces gathered and finally defeated Napoleon in 1815, the British took from the experience the decisiveness of their naval supremacy and the utility of economic warfare waged by sea. It was a lesson that would remain salient for decades to come.

Surrendering the Salute

With Napoleon vanquished, it was safe for the British elite to recommence the "Grand Tours" of the continent that had become customary in the late 17th century. Usually accompanied by tutors, young noblemen would cross the Channel, spend time in Paris (perhaps acquiring some French), and then typically proceed to Italy. Rome, of course, had to be seen, but another Italian destination exerted a particular pull—Venice. The city state that had once held sway in the Adriatic and swathes of the broader Mediterranean was a diminished power by the time the Grand Tour tradition commenced. Its history was compelling, though, and British visitors flocked in particular to the annual ceremony in which the doge—embarked upon his stylized barge, the *Bucentaur*—would cast a ring into the waves and wed the sea. The ceremony "set parallels vibrating" and reminded British visitors of the "gap between past hegemony and present debility."[11] A naval historian has written, "This long defunct Italian republic had assumed a critical place in the intellectual and cultural world of imperial Britain. . . . [I]t was an ideal case study of the rise and fall of maritime empires."[12]

Its territory eroded and its navy in decay, Venice traded on its past glories and burnished its reputation as a playground for the European elite. A somewhat dissolute Lord Byron arrived in 1816 and penned portions of *Childe Harold's Pilgrimage* while residing in the city. A loosely autobiographical sketch of a young man's search for meaning through travel, *Childe Harold* launched Byron's fame. He is sensitive in it to Venice's historical resonance for Britain, and he laments the decay he sees around him.

> Thy lot
> It is shameful to the nations, —most of all,
> Albion! to thee: the ocean queen should not
> Abandon Ocean's Children; in the fall
> Of Venice think of thine, despite thy watery wall.

What could Britain do to avoid Venice's fate? For those hawkishly inclined, the lesson was to maintain naval supremacy at all costs. Venice, some argued, had lost its maritime focus and let itself be drawn into too many disputes on land. Others attributed Venice's fall to the corruption of its internal institutions. Byron himself had few policy prescriptions, but he did offer a vision of the ocean and its relationship to sovereign power likely influenced by Venice's decline. The open water featured in *Childe Harold* as a liberating force ultimately beyond the grasp of even mighty rulers.

> Roll on, thou deep and dark blue ocean, roll!
> Ten thousand fleets sweep over thee in vain;
> Man marks the earth with ruin,
> His control stops with the shore . . .[13]

Harried by romantic and financial entanglements, Byron had personal reasons for hoping that sovereign control would stop at the water's edge. Still, it is noteworthy that a British aristocrat in the years after Napoleon's defeat would so passionately advance the idea that the sea should be beyond the control of land. After 1815, the Royal Navy adopted a global posture that saw more and more of its vessels stationed far from Britain, including in the Mediterranean, the East Indies, and off the coast of Africa. A string of naval bases—including Gibraltar, Malta, Bermuda, and Halifax—made the Royal Navy the decisive player in multiple theaters. In the decades after Napoleon's defeat, "British sea power exercised a wider influence than has ever been seen in the history of maritime empires."[14]

Britain's unparalleled naval resources coupled with the recent precedent of a successful maritime blockade might have led the "mistress of the seas" to more forcefully and effectively assert sovereignty over the nearby maritime domains that she had long claimed. Even more ambitious, London might have attempted to fashion an instrument like the Treaty of Tordesillas for a world dominated by Britain. Yet the maritime hegemon chose a different path, and Byron's encomium to ocean freedom meshed in certain respects with policy in London.

At its most basic, Tordesillas had been a mechanism for allowing two expansive powers to simultaneously extend their realms without clashing. Britain in the 18th and 19th centuries demonstrated repeatedly that legal and political control of the ocean was not necessary for the acquisition of new territory. Captain James Cook reached New Zealand in 1768 and Australia a year later. Undeterred by the presence of indigenous groups, he expeditiously claimed the new lands for the Crown. Britain established itself in West Africa, starting in Sierra Leone, in the early 19th century. In the 1820s, building on the work of the Stamford Raffles, London cemented control of Singapore. Those new possessions made the British Empire a globe-straddling enterprise.

If excluding others from the ocean was not necessary for Britain's empire building, the country's finances also pulled it in the direction of maritime freedom. Pressure was growing for Britain to do away with long-standing nationalist restrictions on shipping and trade with colonies. Henry Martyn, an early and prominent advocate of free trade, marveled at the way the sea brought the world's riches to Britain's shores:

> Why are we surrounded by the Sea? Surely that our Wants at home might be supply'd by our navigation into other Countries, the least and easiest Labour. By this we taste the spices of Arabia, yet we never feel the scorching Sun which brings them forth; we shine in silks which our Hands have never wrought; we drink of Vineyards which we never planted; the Treasures of those Mines are ours, in which we have never digg'd; we only plough the Deep and reap the Harvest of every Country in the World.[15]

Since the 1650s, through a series of measures collectively known as the Navigation Acts, Britain had required that this plowing and reaping occur via British vessels, with mostly British crews. (To retain its status as a British ship, a vessel normally needed three quarters of the crew to be British.)[16] As other countries, including the new United States, developed efficient merchant fleets, that requirement came under pressure, not least from British merchants eager to trim shipping costs. In 1849, Britain finally repealed the Navigation Acts; the world's leading maritime power was becoming a full-throated advocate of open trade.

More important for this account, Britain's post-Napoleonic maritime dominance coincided with abandonment of expansive claims to the seas around the British Isles. British rulers ceased enforcing exclusive rights to large fishing grounds. "The extensive claims which were formerly made to the dominion of the English or British seas were practically abandoned in the eighteenth century."[17] The shift in policy was gradual and marked by inconsistencies, but ultimately profound. In 1805, the year of Nelson's victory off Cape Trafalgar, Britain ended entirely its insistence on the "channel salute."

> This told the world in unequivocal terms that no stretch of salt water—not even that peculiarly personal one which divides Shakespeare Cliff from Gris-Nez—was our sea. Like every other stretch it was "free sea." Again, both then and since, whenever the knotty question of territorial waters arose, Britain has invariably stood for narrowing them to the minimum.[18]

In part, the change reflected a recognition that the expense and trouble required to enforce these claims was exorbitant. The once fearsome Dutch fishing industry had stumbled, easing one of the major domestic incentives to exclude others from local waters. More fundamentally, British officials seem to have recognized that a world with *less* coastal state control of the ocean worked to the benefit of the largest naval power. No other country could match Britain's naval reach, and a system of open seas in effect gave the British the freest hand.

Britain's emerging conception of itself as a benevolent but firm custodian of ocean freedom may have reached its artistic zenith around mid-century. In 1846, Prince Albert commissioned a painting by the noted Scottish artist William Dyce. The result was *Neptune Resigning to Britannia the Empire of the Sea* (Figure 2.1). The god of the sea sits astride several stallions and is captured in the act of transferring his crown to a female figure of Britannia, who already possesses the sea god's trident. Britannia holds it gingerly, almost as if wondering whether and how she should wield it.

Figure 2.1 Neptune Resigning to Britannia the Empire of the Sea.

Those on the receiving end of British naval power saw no such hesitation; London's turn against expansive ocean claims must have appeared hollow to the merchant ships still periodically falling victim to Royal Navy vessels. What did it matter that Britain opposed expansive territorial seas if that policy created larger high seas on which Britain could effectuate its ample interpretation of belligerent rights? However opportunistic, abandoning the Selden closed-sea doctrine in favor of a (mostly) Grotian view was consequential. The world's dominant naval power now stood as a firm opponent of coastal state pretensions to control more than the customary three miles. And the British turn against appropriation of the oceans by coastal states was accompanied by several important innovations in managing the use of the oceans.

Corralling the Privateers

Britain began a concerted effort in the wake of the Napoleonic Wars to manufacture greater security on the oceans by tamping down private violence. Those efforts took on new formality and contributed to early multilateral governance of the oceans. As with its volte-face on the territorial seas, there was rich historical irony in Britain's new distaste for private violence at sea. For centuries, English monarchs had tolerated and sometimes encouraged private raiding in their struggles against the Spanish and French in particular. As early as 1243, English kings had issued *marques* and distinct letters of reprisal allowing private vessels to plunder foreign shipping. Marauding at sea—particularly if it could be privately encouraged and publicly disavowed—was quite convenient, as Sir Francis Drake's voyages attested. But reliance on private actors to inflict harm on adversaries also fed processes that could spin beyond the sovereign's control. The political scientist Janice Thomson describes the dynamic:

> The tediously repetitive process went like this: The State would authorize privateering, which was legalized piracy, during wartime. When the war concluded, thousands of seamen were left with no more appealing alternative than piracy. The state would make some desultory efforts to suppress the pirates, who would simply move somewhere else. With the outbreak of the next war, the state would offer blanket pardons to pirates who would agree to serve as privateers, and the process would start all over again.[19]

That pernicious cycle endured through the Napoleonic Wars, when both Britain and France reached for whatever tools they could find in their epic struggle. But Britain's naval dominance and its increasing reliance on ocean trade was gradually making private violence less appealing. As early as 1670, the English entered into a treaty with Spain that called for an end to privateering. Compliance with its terms was spotty, but the atmosphere in London was turning more foul for once celebrated privateers.

William Kidd had the misfortune of serving as a signal of growing official disapproval. For years, he operated in the Atlantic with the blessing of the British authorities, who had authorized him to hunt French vessels. He seized dozens, often appropriating the cargo and then scuttling victimized vessels. In the late 1600s, Kidd moved his operations east, and in the Red Sea he captured the *Queddah Merchant*, a French-flagged vessel owned by a powerful Indian trader. Outraged Indian merchants demanded that the East India Company rein in privateers and compensate those affected. Realizing that its vital interests were at stake, the company lobbied in London for a more serious anti-piracy effort and for Kidd's apprehension. Several British vessels were dispatched, and the notorious captain eventually stood trial in London and was hanged. For three years, his body hung over the River Thames as a warning to other would-be adventurers.[20]

The effort to restrain non-state violence extended across regions. In the Americas, London exerted pressure on colonial authorities to cease their intermittent support for pirates operating from the eastern seaboard. In parts of the Caribbean, maritime violence had grown to alarming proportions, as out-of-work privateers parlayed their skills. The Bahamas hosted a particularly dangerous collection of pirates in the early 18th century who resisted all efforts to instill sovereign control and even fashioned a "pirate republic." That effrontery pushed British officials to respond. Ironically, they selected for the job Woodes Rogers, who had earned fame as a globe-circling privateer tormenting the Spanish. Stealing a trick from Rome's Pompey, Rogers offered some of the pirates plots of land if they would cease their marauding. Others were hunted down. The famed Blackbeard—an Englishman likely named Edward Teach—met his end at the hands of a British lieutenant off the coast of North Carolina.

In the Mediterranean as well, the British and other Western powers pushed to secure sea lanes. The 17th and early 18th centuries featured regular seizures of shipping in the region. Not infrequently, passengers and crew were abducted and held for ransom. Operating from Malta, Christian pirates seized Ottoman ships and ransomed captives. For European ships, the danger emanated mostly from the Barbary states, nominally under the control of the Ottoman Empire but often functionally independent. While there were strong religious overtones to Mediterranean marauding, a vibrant market for men capable of maritime violence often transcended confessional divides. European privateers sometimes took employment with the Barbary states and even assumed senior positions in their ranks.

For the major European powers, the solution to the vulnerability of their shipping often proved to be overwhelming military force. On several occasions, European powers bombarded Barbary ports and extracted bilateral agreements in which Algiers, Morocco, and Tunis agreed to cease their attacks. (In 1831 France went a step further and simply occupied Algiers, finally putting an end to its maritime attacks.) Seeking new sources of revenue and keen to avoid punishment by powerful European players, the Barbary states increasingly focused on ships of weaker European powers. After gaining its independence, the United States was added to the list of convenient marks. The eventual American response included the creation of a small fleet capable of operating a world away. Its several victories—of which the most famous was Stephen Decatur's daring raid in Tripoli—began the legacy of what would in time become the world's most powerful naval force.

The decades-long struggle against pirate enterprises produced several notable developments. Efforts to tamp down Mediterranean piracy forced a new reckoning with questions of sovereignty and the nature of piracy. Were the Barbary states sovereign entities? If so, wouldn't attacks by their vessels be acts of warfare rather than piracy? That question arose in other theaters as well. One treaty among several European states and Arab powers attempted to clarify the distinction between warfare and marauding:

If any individual of the people of the Arabs contracting shall attack any that pass by land or sea of any nation whatsoever, in the way of plunder and piracy and not of acknowledged war he shall be accounted an enemy of all mankind and shall be held to have forfeited both life and goods.[21]

The treaty went on to distinguish between "an acknowledged war" that was "ordered by government against government" and all other types of violence at sea.[22] That formulation left the status of privateers murky, but Cicero's notion of pirates as the common enemy of all governments had endured through the ages and taken modern legal form.

The turn against private maritime violence in Europe eventually manifested itself in multilateral form—and it came to explicitly encompass privateering. The context for that codification was the Crimean War between Britain and France, on one side, and Russia. The conflict ran from 1853 to 1856, and a joint naval blockade of Russian ports emerged as a key British and French strategy. Harmonizing their naval actions required agreement about which ships could be seized, and that in turn forced the British to reconsider their (very unpopular) insistence that their warships could seize even neutral vessels trading with the enemy.

Britain was willing to make that concession, and it realized that in so doing it might be able to extract something of value from other powers: a ban on privateering, which was increasingly seen as a threat to Britain's naval dominance. As the war clouds gathered, the *Economist* called for the British government to both relent on its view of belligerent rights and to work together with France and the United States to outlaw privateering. "Henceforth, privateering shall rank with piracy," the editors suggested. "That would be a great step forward in the regulation and humanizing of war."[23] The prime minister, Lord Palmerston, put the case to the queen in terms of the country's long-term interests:

> It seems to the Cabinet that as Great Britain is the power which has the most extensive commerce by sea all over the world, which Privateers might attack, and has on the other Hand the largest Royal Navy which can do that which Privateers would perform, Great Britain would find it for her Interest to join in an agreement to abolish Privateering.[24]

The Declaration of Paris was duly signed in 1856. Seven European powers signed the instrument, which was remarkably spare by modern standards of multilateral drafting. It lamented the "deplorable disputes" that had plagued maritime law, and particularly the rules during conflict. It provided simply that "privateering is, and remains, abolished." The declaration also protected neutral shipping (except for contraband) and tightened the rules on when a belligerent could declare an enemy port to be under blockade. Britain therefore gave up something (its expansive interpretation of belligerent rights) to secure the broad ban on privateering that it now favored. One scholar has described the Declaration of Paris as not merely a decisive policy shift but also a new approach to international governance. The declaration "marked a revolution in how international law is made. . . . [T]he seven [signatory] powers took the unusual step of inviting every nation on the planet to join their legal project and accede to the treaty, highlighting a path towards universally recognised global norms that we still follow today."[25]

Despite entreaties from European powers, the United States shunned the declaration. Secretary of State William Marcy described US reluctance as a byproduct of its suspicion of standing military forces. If privateering was outlawed, he reasoned, the United States would have no choice but to greatly expand its regular naval forces. "A large force ever ready to be devoted to the purposes of war is a temptation to rush into it," he wrote.

> The policy of the United States has ever been, and never more than now, adverse to such establishments, and they can never be brought to acquiesce in any change in International Law which may render it necessary for them to maintain a powerful navy or large standing army in time of peace.[26]

US abstention notwithstanding, there is substantial evidence that maritime predation declined significantly during the 1800s as military, diplomatic, and legal pressures made the oceans less receptive to purveyors of violence. Indications of success came from the merchants who relied most directly on free transit through the ocean. More and more commercial ships chose to sail unarmed, and insurance rates on oceanic voyages dropped steadily.[27] Oceangoing ships could deliver a newly diverse array of cargoes with much greater regularity.

Loosening Chains at Sea

Sometime in 1769, the *Neptune*, under the command of one Ebenezer Price, set sail from London bound for West Africa. After the transit, the ship's mostly British crew guided the vessel down the African coast, eventually securing from local brokers a complement of 350 human beings. Once the vessel headed into the Atlantic, these persons were kept mostly below decks in cramped and stifling quarters. Ten of the enslaved did not survive the infamous "middle passage," and their bodies were likely thrown overboard with little ceremony. After 88 days at sea, the vessel reached Charleston, South Carolina, where it offloaded the survivors.

By the brutal standards of the time, the *Neptune*'s voyage was unremarkable. Indeed, the science of transporting humans via vessel evolved substantially during the 18th century, and captains and senior officers had a financial incentive to keep their human cargo alive. The 18th century "is when the commercial acumen that had been perfected in the carriage of cargo was adapted to that of people."[28] Some of that acumen was devoted to moving willing passengers, but the greater part went to honing the ability to transport the enslaved. British merchants and vessels expanded a trade from western Africa to the Americas that the Portuguese had begun in the 15th century. In all, it is estimated that British vessels transported nearly 3 million Africans to the Americas.[29]

Spreading awareness of the slave trade's horrors began to have an effect on public opinion. The case of the *Zong*, in particular, helped galvanize opposition. During a voyage from West Africa to Jamaica in 1781, the *Zong*'s crew ordered more than 120 slaves—some of them ill—hurled overboard, in an apparent bid to conserve scarce drinking water. Months later, the *Zong*'s Liverpool owners brought a case against the voyage's insurance providers, demanding payment for the jettisoned slaves. The shipowners successfully argued that the long-standing maritime rule of "general average"—used when a crew jettisoned cargo to save a ship in distress—should apply. In legal terms the case was not remarkable. Insurers had long provided coverage for slave voyages and had elaborated rules for when slave deaths would be covered by standard policies. Shipowners could usually secure compensation for slaves killed to put down an insurrection on board, for example, but not in cases when a slave "destroys himself through despair."[30] In this case, the judges decided that the crew had reason to jettison some slaves and awarded them compensation.

A persistent English lawyer, Granville Sharp, followed the lawsuit closely and circulated transcripts of the court proceedings. He failed to persuade the government to bring murder charges against the crew, but he at least succeeded in making the *Zong*'s atrocities part of the abolitionist brief. When abolitionist leader Thomas Clarkson published his influential anti-slavery tract in 1786, the details of the *Zong* case reached an even wider audience. In part because of the publicity generated by the case, a group of activists in England coalesced and began to convince the broader public of the need for reform. In 1788, Parliament for the first time regulated the slave trade, capping the number of humans that could be transported on a given vessel. (Abolitionists split over the legislation, with some fearing that it would legitimize a fundamentally inhumane trade.)

Much more dramatic legislation followed. In 1807, Parliament prohibited British subjects not only from directly engaging in the slave trade but also from helping crew, navigate, procure, or outfit a ship involved in the slave trade. The British might have left the matter at that, content that there were now domestic consequences for the involvement of its nationals. But as the naval hegemon, it had the power to export its swelling moral outrage. "During the first half of the nineteenth century British governments translated a moral crusade against the slave trade from the domestic to the international sphere."[31]

The legal basis for that effort changed over time. In the first years after the act, the British relied on an expansive—and to foreign eyes, very strained—view of its rights as a belligerent in the war against Napoleon. British courts declared that its wartime rights included boarding and searching vessels from multiple states, including neutral countries, to ensure that they were not carrying slaves. In part, British courts relied on the fact that several countries whose vessels engaged in the practice had enacted domestic prohibitions on the slave trade. All the Royal Navy was doing, British admiralty courts sometimes insisted, was helping these states to enforce their own laws.

These arguments were thin, and British judges began to question the basis for the boardings and seizures. In an 1817 case, Lord Stowell rose in defense of ocean freedoms as he saw them:

> All nations being equal, all have an equal right to the uninterrupted use of the unappropriated parts of the ocean for their navigation. In places where no local authority exists, where the subjects of all states meet upon a footing of entire equality and independence, no one state, or any of its subjects, has a right to assume or exercise authority over the subjects of another. . . . I can find no authority that gives the right of interruption to the navigation of states in amity upon the high seas.[32]

A combination of this pushback from Britain's own courts and complaints from other governments forced a change in the legal justification. At the Congress of Vienna, which convened from 1814 to 1815, British Foreign Secretary Lord Castlereagh strove for a multilateral mechanism to combat the slave trade, but he was able to secure only precatory language declaring the slave trade "repugnant to the principles of humanity and universal morality."[33] Unable to achieve meaningful enforcement provisions, Britain replaced reliance on belligerent rights with a strategy centered on a series of bilateral and a few plurilateral agreements with other maritime countries. In these agreements, sometimes extracted only after considerable diplomatic pressure, foreign governments accepted that British vessels had the right to board their vessels to check for slaving activity. To save face, the treaties often made the right to board mutual, although in practice it was almost always British vessels doing the boarding.

Britain entered such agreements with a host of smaller maritime states including Denmark, Portugal, and several Italian sovereigns. In 1841, Austria, France, Prussia, and Russia inked the so-called Quintuple Agreement with the British for the suppression of the slave trade. Several innovative "mixed commissions"—comprised of judges from Britain and its treaty partners— were formed to help adjudicate seizures of ships on the basis of involvement in the slave trade.

The Americans, watching from a distance, thought the entire exercise reeked of hegemony. When the French ultimately failed to ratify the Quintuple Agreement, a Detroit newspaper celebrated the "overthrow of this deep-laid scheme to retain the 'dominion of the seas.'" The editors saw behind Britain's lofty rhetoric an obvious bid for maritime control:

The object of the treaty was ostensibly the suppression of the slave trade on the coast of Africa—the real object at least on the part of England was . . . to constitute her navy the "police" of the ocean, to yield up to her "protection" the commerce of the world. It was a virtual acknowledgement of "supremacy on the Ocean" to England.[34]

A few years later, the same newspaper lauded the US envoy who had opposed the treaty (and may have helped encourage France's defection) as a "hero of the freedom of the seas."[35] Only during the Civil War did Washington finally abandon its opposition and fall in line, signing a treaty with the British allowing boarding of each other's vessels upon suspicion of slave-trading activity.[36]

Together, the network of treaties between the leading naval power and other countries "brought into being an international maritime police force, the Royal Navy, armed with its right to search, and international courts for the suppression."[37] Still, the practice of the anti-slavery patrols at sea was inconsistent. Some British naval commanders exercised the authority with relish, and a dedicated naval squadron focused on confronting slave traders off Africa's west coast. At other times, the anti-slavery vessels languished. Lord Palmerston, the longtime foreign minister and then prime minister, complained that "the Board of Admiralty have never cared a farthing about the suppression of the slave trade, and have considered the Slave Trade Suppression Service as a sort of penal duty and have sent to it all the old tubs that were fit in their opinion for nothing else."[38]

Even when it was pursued energetically, the British campaign certainly did not end the slave trade; in fact, the number of slaves transported from West Africa to the Americas likely increased temporarily after Britain began its policing. The British patrols do seem to have forced up insurance rates on slave-trading voyages, increasing the overall cost of the enterprise and per-haps restraining growth in the trade. In the end, the American Civil War and Cuba's belated decision to close its ports to slaving vessels were more decisive in finally breaking the Atlantic trade.

Whatever its effectiveness, Britain's anti-slavery campaign stirred intense debate about the rules at sea. Skeptics pointed out repeatedly that the British policy was a challenge to the conception of freedom of the seas that had existed to that point. For a government that still saw itself as defending ocean freedoms, that charge resonated. One way of defending traditional freedom of the seas while attacking the slave trade was to insist that slaving was little more than piracy, which was already acknowledged as universally illegal and a cause for boarding and capture on the high seas. The notion that piracy and slave trading were the same thing (forms of robbery at sea) had a certain logic: The two activities had been tightly linked for centuries, and the passengers and crew of ships waylaid at sea were sometimes sold into slavery.

In a few narrow contexts, the unitary theory of piracy and slave trading did gain traction. In 1820, somewhat surprisingly, the United States Congress declared slave trading a form of piracy.[39] Britain signed a treaty with Brazil that did the same.[40] But the conflation of the two concepts never really took hold, and the right to board vessels suspected of slave trading should be seen as an emerging additional exception to the traditional freedom of the seas.

Britain's period of maritime dominance in the 18th and 19th centuries therefore produced several critical developments in ocean governance and shaped the modern conception of freedom of the seas. Most fundamental, it helped tilt the balance of international practice against state ocean claims. A naval hegemon that might have made expansive claims to the oceans instead opted for the bare minimum. While not universally accepted, the concept of a three-mile territorial sea, which Britain endorsed, commanded significant international support. Belatedly and inconsistently, Britain also tamped down private violence on the oceans and advocated rules that delegitimized marauding as a tool of state policy. The ease with which privateers became pirates convinced London and other governments that rooting out privateering was essential to ending piracy. The shift against privateering altered international norms, but it did so in a way that was consistent with a long-standing international aversion to private violence and the desire for the oceans to be a usable space for all.

Britain's anti-slavery campaign—and its push for the right to board vessels suspected of carrying slaves—marked a sharper break with the past. It established what would eventually become a welcome and universally acknowledged exception to ocean freedom, but it also demonstrated the power of naval hegemons to alter ocean rules in ways that were more unilateral than consultative. What's more, the British remained tempted by a vision of belligerent rights that many other states found antithetical to freedom of the seas.

From Coffeehouses to Conferences

The gradual reduction in maritime violence and the period of major-power peace that prevailed after 1815 helped accelerate a boom in maritime commerce. Between the 1770s and the 1790s shipping passing through British ports increased from 900,000 tons to more than 1.7 million. In the decade after the Napoleonic Wars ended, the total increased by another million tons.[41] The nature of seaborne commerce had changed significantly since the 17th century. Commodities including sugar, coffee, tea, and textiles surpassed spices as the most common cargo.

More crowded shipping lanes produced new pressures, not least from commercial interests, to ensure the reliability of the vessels transporting valuable goods. As in ancient and medieval times, some of the most consequential early efforts to improve safety at sea derived not from national governments but from the commercial interests themselves. In the 1680s, one of the more consequential private actors was an enterprising Welshman named Edward Lloyd. He founded one of London's early coffeehouses, which were popping up to sate the country's growing thirst for the beverage. Lloyd's establishment became a social club for those in the shipping business, and for maritime insurance underwriters in particular. In addition to libation, the members shared morsels of information regarding oceangoing vessels and their seaworthiness. In time, the informal club evolved into an organization that published a regular Register of Shipping and employed dozens of surveyors and inspectors to evaluate the condition of vessels.[42]

By the 1830s, these maritime inspectors were compelled to turn their attention from sails and wooden hulls to new methods of propulsion and new forms of construction. In 1837, the *Sirius* became the first steam-powered vessel to cross the Atlantic. The shift to steam and steel did not stem the losses at sea, however, and concern about safety at sea became more acute as ships carried more paying passengers. The danger of shipwreck, once the preoccupation of sailors and their families, was now more widely shared. In September 1854, the paddle steamer *Arctic* was sailing in fog off the coast of Newfoundland when it collided with a French ship, the *Vesta*. Four hours later, the *Arctic* sank, leaving 350 people dead. That disaster helped spur some of the earliest international shipping regulations. In 1863, Britain and France agreed on "Articles for the Prevention of Collisions at Sea." Several dozen countries subsequently adopted them. These articles established early "rules of the road"—elaborating which vessels should give way when in proximity to another.

At the national level, even more ambitious attempts at regulation began. In Britain, Samuel Plimsoll emerged as the leading figure in a campaign to make life at sea safer and more tolerable. A self-made man elected to Parliament,

Plimsoll enraged shipping interests by demanding government regulation of the maritime industry. In speeches and pamphlets, he marshaled evidence that none of those tasked with ensuring the safety of vessels—insurance companies, underwriters, shipowners—were adequately performing the function. Plimsoll pointed, in particular, to the practice of overloading ships. Excess cargo rendered vessels unstable and prone to foundering in heavy weather. He labeled these vessels "coffin ships," a moniker that stuck with the public and stung shipowners and insurers. By 1873, the British government appointed a royal commission to examine maritime safety. Soon thereafter, Parliament required that ships have visible markings on their sides to make clear when they were overloaded. To this day, they are known as "Plimsoll lines."[43]

Navigational safety and conditions on board ships both received attention at what stands as the first major international conference on maritime safety. In October 1889, delegates from 21 countries met in Washington. "For the first time in the history of the world," one of the US delegates said, "a conference of all the maritime powers has assembled to formulate a code."[44] Those recognized as maritime powers were still mostly Western, but the gathering included China, Japan, and Siam (although the last was represented by a British official). Chile, Guatemala, and Mexico sent envoys as well. For almost two months, the delegates worked through an array of safety issues, including traffic-separation schemes and regulations for saving lives at sea. At times, the debates delved into questions as precise as how long a ship's fog-horn blast should be. Papers presented to the delegates included calls for universalization of maritime regulations. "In the navigation of the ocean, the highway at sea of all nations, a universal law system should be obeyed."[45]

Yet there were limits to the diplomats' appetite for creating international machinery to advance that universal law. For example, the delegates considered but could not agree on the creation of an international maritime commission. "However desirable such a result would be," the conference proceedings reported, "a majority of the committee do not believe it to be possible to carry it into effect and are of the opinion that it cannot be regarded as one of practical feasibility at the present time."[46] Left unsaid was that Great Britain itself had led the opposition to a permanent maritime commission. The dominant maritime power proved deeply suspicious of any encroachments by international authorities; that dynamic would recur a century later when the next maritime power faced the prospect of international control of ocean resources.

Maps, Passages, and Canals

Britain may have balked at a permanent international infrastructure, but it was contributing significantly to an edifice of public knowledge regarding the oceans. In 1806, a ship carrying an employee of the East India Company wrecked in the South China Sea. In the aftermath of the disaster, the passenger, James Horsburgh, dedicated himself to producing clear and accurate maps. He seems to have been the first modern mapmaker to identify several features in the South China Sea, including the Spratly Islands (which he called Storm Island). Updated editions of his work appeared for decades.[47]

At the same time, dozens of Royal Navy ships were developing new awareness of ocean features and currents. Britain created the Royal Hydrographic Office in 1795, and it soon surpassed its European counterparts in producing reliable charts. "From a humble beginning, one hydrographer . . . one assistant, and a draftsman, the British Admiralty eventually became one of the chief sources of supply for the maritime world, furnishing charts and hydrographic information to all nations."[48]

For centuries, maritime maps had been closely held; safe paths through the ocean and around coastal waters were a valuable strategic asset. In 1821, in keeping with its more open maritime policy, the Royal Navy changed tack and made its maps available for purchase.[49] The sale of the maps may have been the product of bookkeeping as much as beneficence; the Hydrographic Office helped fund itself through the sales proceeds. Still, the willingness of the government to see its charts circulate freely reflected a new attitude. The corpus of maritime knowledge that became available via the British ranged from charts of the Red Sea, notorious for its reefs and difficult currents, to detailed renderings of the Turkish coastline. US naval officers were even known to complain that they needed British maps to safely navigate the US coastline.

The most consequential of British mapmakers was the irascible and eccentric Sir Francis Beaufort, named chief of the Hydrographic Office in 1826. Already well known for developing a scale for the force of winds, Beaufort's passion was the production of meticulous charts and the spread of the knowledge they contained. Not content with his official duties, the admiral often rose early to work on maps for a private organization called the Society for the Diffusion of Useful Knowledge, which offered maps and other informational brochures to the general public at low prices.[50]

As understanding of ocean space was growing, new channels for ocean commerce were being carved out, by negotiation, exploration, and construction. Since its conquest of Constantinople in the 15th century, the Ottoman Empire had exercised near dominion over the Black Sea. As Russian power increased, however, the weakened Ottomans gradually yielded control. At first, access was limited to Russian vessels (although some European merchants apparently used the Russian flag as a way of circumventing Ottoman restrictions). By the 1820s, European merchant ships had been granted permission as well. "From the late eighteenth century, the [Black Sea] was slowly reintegrated into a pan-European—and for some goods, genuinely global—commercial network that had not been seen since the demise of the Italian trading colonies in the fifteenth century."[51] But the Ottoman Empire drew a line at allowing military vessels to pass through the Dardanelles. That distinction still resonates today: many countries willing to concede freedom of commercial navigation near their shores hesitate to accord military vessels the same privileges.

Even as the Black Sea was opening to international shipping, several British vessels set out in 1850 to explore whether transits were possible in the Arctic. An expedition led by British captain Robert McClure endured for more than four years in the region before completing for the first time the long-sought Northwest Passage. Dispatched in part to discover the fate of an earlier expedition, McClure eventually left his vessel icebound, but he and his crew concluded the passage by sledge and returned to England on another navy ship. The ordeal was hardly an advertisement for the route, but it at least signaled the possibility of an Arctic link between the Atlantic and the Pacific.

As McClure and his crew were ending their Arctic trek, a French diplomat-turned-developer, Ferdinand de Lesseps, cobbled together the funding and permission he needed to connect the Mediterranean and the Red Sea. With mostly French money and with permission from the ruler of Egypt and Sudan, de Lesseps broke ground on what would become the Suez Canal. When the canal opened in 1869, it cut more than 4,000 miles from the journey between Europe and the Far East and reduced use of the route around the Cape of Good Hope that the Portuguese had pioneered in the 15th century. The Suez Canal Convention of 1888 provided that the waterway "shall be always free and open, in time of war as in time of peace, to every vessel of commerce, without distinction of flag" and that it would not be subject to blockade.[52] The bulk of the traffic was soon British, and London in 1875 took an ownership stake in the waterway.

Other maritime openings were less peaceful. The Royal Navy forced open Chinese commerce in the 1840s, in the wake of the Opium Wars. Britain's naval superiority delivered several decisive victories, and the Chinese emperor agreed in the Treaty of Nanking to cede Hong Kong and to open Chinese ports to British merchants. In 1853, a United States Navy squadron under the command of Commodore Matthew Perry sailed into Japan's Edo Bay and trained its guns toward land. Perry's threats eventually produced the intended result; the following year, Japan's rulers signed a treaty allowing US ships access to two Japanese ports. Perry's success in accessing Japanese markets led to quick succession of agreements between Japan and other Western powers.

Throughout the 19th century, Western naval power was used repeatedly to pry open, dominate, and extract from non-Western societies. The coincidence of that pattern with the dominance of the Grotian view of the ocean inevitably raises the question of the connection between the two. Was freedom of the seas simply the handmaiden of colonialism and domination? In later years, as formerly colonized countries secured seats at international negotiations, several diplomats insisted on a connection. In one sense, the relationship is clear: with freedom of the seas as the dominant doctrine, well-equipped Western navies were free to roam the world's oceans and exert their will. Yet it is not clear that an alternative ocean regime would have been any less friendly to colonialism. As we have seen, the Tordesillas system of closed seas was used just as effectively to subjugate and dominate. Had the British opted for a closed seas regime in their period of dominance, it is hard to imagine it being designed in a way that would constrain their imperial ambitions. Western military dominance and an unwillingness to recognize sovereign rights of most non-Western societies were the decisive factors—not the specific ocean rules advanced by the British.

The British experience in southeast Asia, in particular, suggests a more subtle connection between colonialism and freedom of the seas. As in other parts of the world, the British in the 19th century saw suppressing piracy and tamping down the slave trade as core missions for the Royal Navy. In the waters between what is now Singapore and Borneo, both maladies had become common. In the course of anti-piracy campaigns—which can plausibly be viewed as defending freedom of the seas—the British found it convenient to raid and briefly occupy coastal land used by sea marauders. In some cases, British agents were appointed to ensure that local rulers did not again permit piracy. One of the most active British officials in the region, Stamford Raffles, saw involvement in local politics as essential to effective anti-piracy:

Nothing can tend so effectually to the suppression of Piracy, to the encouragement and extension of lawful commerce, and to the civilization of the Inhabitants of the Eastern Islands, as affording a steady support to the established Native Sovereigns, and assisting them in the maintenance of their just rights and authority over their several Chiefs.[53]

In making these pleas, Raffles realized that many of his superiors had little desire to administer additional foreign territory and he insisted that safeguarding freedom of navigation was the sole aim. In one missive, he assured a correspondent that "the object is solely and exclusively confined to the abolition of Piracy, without any views whatever to aggrandizement or Territory."[54] Yet the perceived need to eradicate piracy ended up directly and indirectly fueling several extensions of British control—including through the efforts of Raffles and, later, James Brooke (who became known as the "White Rajah" of Sarawak). After one punitive raid in Borneo, Brooke explained what he saw as the rationale for British involvement. "Our invasion of their country, and destruction of their forts and town," Brooke informed the local chiefs, "was not for the purposes of pillage or gain to ourselves, but as a punishment for their repeated and aggravated acts of piracy."[55] A century later, newly decolonized countries would remember the ways in which a professed desire to secure ocean freedom had led to domination on land.

What Lies Beneath

As commerce across the oceans intensified and expanded, knowledge of what lay beneath the ocean accumulated. Accounts from whalers and fishermen working in deeper waters and more systematic soundings by navy crews generated a hazy image of the deep. In 1855, Lieutenant Matthew Fontaine Maury, a US naval officer, published *The Physical Geography of the Sea*, one of the first comprehensive works of oceanography.[56] Maury had an avid reader in Jules Verne, the French author who published *20,000 Leagues Under the Sea* in 1870. Verne's enigmatic Captain Nemo several times cited "the learned Maury" as he expounded on undersea wonders to the captive but curious Professor Aronnax.

Efforts by Maury and others to plumb the depths began to reveal the complexity of the seafloor. It had long been assumed that the seafloor was relatively smooth. The measurements that Maury had collected from several US Navy ships provided stunning evidence to the contrary. As Maury wrote:

> Could the waters of the Atlantic be drawn off, so as to expose to view this great sea-gash, which separates continents, and extends from the Arctic to the Antarctic, it would present a scene the most rugged, grand, and imposing. The very ribs of the solid earth, with the foundations of the sea, would be brought to light, and we should have presented to us at one view the empty cradle of the ocean.[57]

Over the next several years, that cradle became more visible. In 1857, a US survey vessel operating off the coast of California discovered the first submarine canyon. The feature, now known as Monterey Canyon, provided additional support for Maury's conception of the ocean floor as irregular.

The effort to understand the contours of the ocean floor had immediate practical implications. Since the invention of the telegraph in the 1830s, the idea of linking the continents telegraphically had been tantalizing. In 1850, the first attempt was made. Ships laid a cable between Dover, England, and Calais in France, but it was poorly insulated and failed almost immediately. A redesigned cable laid the next year proved more effective. Several efforts to bridge the broader Atlantic also foundered at first, and furious investors even alleged that the entire scheme was a fraud. It was not until 1866 that the *Great Eastern* finally put those accusations to rest when it successfully laid a submarine cable from Ireland to Newfoundland.[58]

The mariners and engineers who laid those cables wrestled with an array of logistical and political complications. But one question that did not appear to vex them was whether they had the right to lay cables across the depths. Given the expense of the undertaking, and from today's vantage point, it is remarkable that the question of who controlled the thousands of miles of seabed on which the cables lay scarcely emerged. The unquestioned assumption that the ocean floor was free for all to use testified to the power of the Grotian vision of ocean freedom.

Within the space of two decades, it was realized that some kind of international instrument was necessary to safeguard the cables that had been so laboriously placed. The result was the 1884 Convention for the Protection of Submarine Cables, which required those on the high seas to avoid cables and cable-laying vessels. Yet even the drafters of that treaty did not feel it necessary to state the obvious: that states had the right to lay cables across the seabed under the high seas. "It was evident that freedom of use was conceded by all," two legal scholars have written, "and that the real concern was to adopt measures for protecting cables from other, sometimes physically incompatible, uses of the ocean."[59]

If the seabed's utility was becoming apparent, there also emerged the first glimmers of potential riches there. Between 1873 and 1876, the Royal Navy ship HMS *Challenger*, a steam-assisted sailing vessel, embarked on what seems to have been the world's first dedicated marine research mission. Its voyage "marks the transition from Victorian to modern science: from the world of the gentleman naturalist to that of Big Science, with its requisite institutional, collaborative and multidisciplinary framework and national funding support."[60] Specifically outfitted and crewed with dozens of scientists and technicians, *Challenger* traveled almost 70,000 miles and collected hundreds of specimens. Her crew eventually produced several careful volumes describing the results of their dredging. They detailed the red clay, various classes of "ooze," shark's teeth, and other substances found on the floor. Among the most intriguing finds were the hard nodules her trawls brought up repeatedly:

> In some regions of the ocean the *Challenger* discovered ferro-manganic concretions in great abundance, the minute grains giving a dark chocolate color to the deposit, while the dredges and trawls yielded immense numbers of more or less circular nodules or botryoidal masses of these oxides of large dimensions.[61]

On several dredging attempts, the ship's log records hundreds of these nodules being brought to the surface. For the moment, *Challenger*'s discoveries were curiosities rather than incentives to begin harvesting. The expedition was all but unique, and no state had the wherewithal to mount a similar operation with the aim of advancing knowledge of the undersea world for a number of years.

The *Challenger*'s crew sought to generate knowledge of the undersea world from atop the waves, but others, with different motives, were approaching from the shore. Oil drilling had been a terrestrial exercise for most of its short history, which began in earnest in the 1850s. By 1894, a man named Henry Williams was drilling wells on a California beach. Designed to tap the lucrative Summerland oilfield, the wells were productive. Williams realized that the oilfield likely extended into the Pacific. Two years later, he and his crew constructed a pier and began drilling into the ground beneath the shallow water.[62] When that well also proved productive, more than a dozen companies joined the action. This early drilling all occurred close to shore, but Williams and his collaborators had initiated a technique that would eventually move much farther into the ocean. An industry magazine speculated that "possibly in some future age, when all known petroleum fields shall have been drained of their richness, oil men may seek refuge in King Neptune's realm."[63]

Interpreting "The Book of Nature"

The shift from sail to steam that was convulsing the maritime world had profound implications for the fishing industry as well. In the 1870s, several of the first steam-powered trawlers embarked from British ports. On a small scale, trawling—when a collecting device is dragged over the sea floor—had been attempted for hundreds of years. More powerful and maneuverable vessels turned the technique into a major industry practice.

Certain fishing communities in coastal England and elsewhere became convinced that the trawlers were depleting fish stocks. As these concerns mounted, however, authoritative voices reassured the public about the health of fisheries. A British commission of inquiry concluded that stocks were plentiful. The *Toronto Leader* in 1872 told its readers that "the quantity of fish taken out of the sea by the hands of men is so small, in proportion to the whole or to the number destroyed by their natural enemies, that the abstraction could make little or no impression on the immense shoals of the ocean."[64] Perhaps most influential, the leading British scientist Thomas Henry Huxley in 1883 described the notion of overfishing as essentially nonsensical:

> Any tendency to over-fishing will meet with its natural check in the diminution of supply. . . . I believe, then, that the cod fishery, the herring fishery, the pilchard fishery, the mackerel fishery, and probably all the great sea fisheries, are inexhaustible; that is to say, that nothing we do seriously affects the number of the fish. And any attempt to regulate these fisheries seems consequently, from the nature of the case, to be useless.[65]

At sea, however, a conviction that marine resources were in fact exhaustible sometimes produced friction. Canadian and American fishermen clashed in the 1870s over access to North Atlantic herring fisheries. In 1893, a decade after Huxley's reassuring exposition, Denmark announced an exclusive fishing zone around Iceland (then under its sovereignty) in a bid to protect its lucrative cod-fishing operations from efficient new British steam trawlers. That declaration met immediate opposition from the British, and Danish patrols seized several fishing boats that challenged the restrictions.

As Britain and Denmark feuded, a panel of eminent officials convened in Paris to arbitrate a different dispute between Britain and the United States over the hunting of fur seals in the Bering Sea. Soon after acquiring Alaska from Russia in 1867, the US government had sought to profitably and sustainably manage the large herds of fur seals centered on the Pribilof Islands, a few hundred miles from the Alaskan mainland. Washington imposed strict rules on the harvesting of seals and stationed personnel on the islands to enforce them.

In the 1880s, however, the Americans noticed that British vessels had begun harvesting seals during their annual trek from the islands to the California mainland and back, a route that took them out of US territorial waters and onto the high seas. The dispute crested in 1886 when US patrols seized and imprisoned the crews of several British ships. Britain objected on the grounds that their nationals had been seized outside the three-mile territorial sea. Conceding that point, the United States insisted that it still had the right to protect seal populations in the waters around Alaskan territory.

Apparently realizing that their formal legal ground was thin, the US lawyers making their case to international arbitrators leaned heavily on arguments about nature and natural justice. The seals were more like domesticated animals than wildlife, they insisted, and allowing their destruction was against all international morals. In a formulation that might make later generations of US lawyers squirm, the lead US counsel contended that freedom of the seas was only conditional—it really meant freedom for *innocent* purposes. Bludgeoning to death hundreds of seals, he continued, did not fit the bill. At one point, a US lawyer insisted that government policy comported with the "Great Book of Nature." That claim seemed to have finally exasperated one of the arbitrators. "What are your authorities? My Lord. The Book of Nature—what page and what edition?"[66]

To the extent prevailing international law drew on the Book of Nature at all, it was a Grotian-inspired edition predicated on boundless oceanic resources. The arbitrators in the fur seal case delivered a decisive victory for Britain by insisting that the three-mile limit was sacrosanct and that the

United States had no right to enforce restrictions on the high seas. The same logic ultimately prevailed in the Icelandic fishing dispute: in 1901, a chastened Denmark signed an agreement restoring the traditional three-mile fishing limit and making clear that British vessels were free to fish beyond that line.[67]

Battleships on Parade

The US willingness to arbitrate the fur seal dispute and Britain's ability to stifle Denmark's claims to expanded fishing grounds owed a great deal to British naval wherewithal. The small squadron sent to remind the Danes of the futility of confrontation belonged to a British navy that Parliament had insisted must be the equal of any two rivals combined. In 1897, the navy marked Queen Victoria's Diamond Jubilee by parading 165 warships in lines that stretched for five miles. The fleet of battleships and armored cruisers that observers witnessed that day reflected a technological transformation that had been under way for decades. Many of the ships were driven by powerful steam turbine engines and carried heavier and more accurate guns than ever before.

With these new capabilities came new military strategists, who emphasized the decisive influence of naval power. Most famously, Captain Alfred Thayer Mahan, a US naval officer, published *The Influence of Sea Power upon History* in 1890. Its more than 500 dense pages insisted that powers became great and maintained their greatness through naval power. Expounding on the decisive influence of the British navy in defeating Napoleon, Mahan wrote, "Those far distant, storm-beaten ships, upon which the Grand Army never looked, stood between it and the dominion of the world." Mahan saw maritime control as fundamentally a question of force rather than law:

> The possession of that overbearing power on the sea which drives the enemy's flag from it, or allows it to appear only as a fugitive; and which, by controlling the great common, closes the highways by which commerce moves to and from the enemy's shores. This overbearing power can only be exercised by great navies.[68]

Mahan's paean to naval power did not go so far as to suggest that states should seek to own ocean space; he still envisioned the oceans as a "great common." But he was prescient in viewing it as a common that increasingly powerful navies could close as they saw fit during war. The spectacular success of Mahan's work helped push navies to the forefront of national strategy. Germany's Kaiser Wilhelm owned multiple copies of the book and ordered it distributed widely among his commanders. For Germany, the construction of a navy to rival the Royal Navy became a national priority. In retrospect, it is evident that the naval competition between Germany and Britain was pushing Europe toward a cataclysm that would shatter the international system, with major consequences for the British-led maritime order.

But in the years before the First World War, it was possible to imagine that the freedom of the seas was stable. The periodic claims of states to control more of the ocean, such as Denmark's fishing zone, were generally stifled by a combination of diplomatic, economic, and military pressure. The scholar Joseph Nye concisely summarized the state of play at the end of the 19th century:

States claiming jurisdiction beyond 3 miles from the coast (Scandinavia, Iberia, Mexico, Uruguay) accounted for little of the world's coastline and less than 10 percent of world shipping. In 1902, after the American victory over Spain, Mexico reluctantly went from a 9- to a 3-mile limit. In 1905 British protests led Uruguay to release a ship seized for fishing in its contested waters, and in 1909 British diplomatic pressure led Portugal to accept a 3-mile limit fishing jurisdiction. In 1915, Germany enforced a 3-mile limit against Sweden.[69]

What's more, there was evidence that this basic regime of ocean freedom was being managed moderately and intelligently on multiple fronts. Piracy and privateering were much reduced. An International Council for the Exploration of the Sea was born in 1902, to study the "rational use of fisheries." Headquartered in Copenhagen, the council identified herring and cod migration and the threat of overfishing in the North Sea as its priorities.[70]

Five years later, another international conference addressed the specter of mines at sea, which were used extensively in the Russo-Japanese War of 1905. The assembled diplomats lamented the impossibility of banning the devices altogether. Still, "inspired by the principle of the freedom of sea routes, the common highway of all nations," they placed strict limits on the kinds of mines that countries could deploy.[71] Even more important, the British ceded additional ground on the cherished right to interfere with neutral shipping during conflict. In 1909, the British government signed the London Declaration, which reaffirmed the view that neutral vessels should be mostly immune from seizure and narrowed the right of belligerents to impose economic blockades by sea.

In terms of safety at sea, there was international progress as well. The 1912 *Titanic* disaster galvanized relatively prompt international action. In January 1914, sixteen countries signed an agreement on safety at sea that committed them to ensure that their vessels were adequately stocked with life vessels. Thirteen countries even agreed to fund the operations of an International Ice Patrol in the North Atlantic, under the leadership of the United States. Other participating states agreed to help defray the costs of the US patrols.[72]

If an observer could hope that the seas were becoming better organized, they were also very much open for business. In 1914, more than 43 million gross tons of cargo were shipped around the world. That total included one of the world's newer bulk commodities—oil. After experimenting with shipping oil in barrels, shipping companies developed specialized "tanker" vessels capable of holding thousands of gallons in their holds. Many of the merchant ships, laden with commodities both old and new, enjoyed shorter transit times than in the past. The same month that the convention on safety at sea was signed, an old French crane vessel became the first to transit the newly completed Panama Canal, which slashed travel time between the Pacific and Atlantic. The canal, one historian has written, was "an expression of that old and noble desire to bridge the divide, to bring people together."[73]

By the early 20th century, the oceans were being employed to bridge divides in remarkable ways. Ships traversed the seas with unprecedented speed; undersea cables linked several of the continents; newly efficient vessels brought in unprecedented hauls of fish and other marine life; and coastal countries still claimed only a fringe of ocean as their own. There were discordant notes, but the Grotian ideal of the oceans as an unoccupied avenue of free commerce and exchange, open to all, appeared to be in full bloom.

3

The Unraveling

(1914–1945)

On the afternoon of May 7, 1915, a German submarine, the U-20, fired one torpedo at a ship sailing near the coast of Ireland. The captain, an officer named Walter Schwieger, was targeting the *Lusitania*, one of the world's largest passenger liners. The British-flagged Cunard Line ship had begun its transatlantic voyage a week earlier in New York and was just a few hours from Liverpool, its planned destination. Unlike many torpedoes used early in the war, the one that Schwieger loosed that day both found its target and detonated. Charlotte Pye, who was on board the *Lusitania* with her two-year-old daughter Marjorie, recounted the aftermath:

> We were sitting at luncheon when the torpedo struck us. A few minutes earlier I had been talking with a woman who sat opposite me, and I told her I intended upon staying on deck all night as we were in the danger zone and I feared something might happen . . . and then the crash came. Everybody stood up, and my friend shouted *'She's going down!'* I picked up Marjorie and ran on deck.

The scene there was chaotic, as the ship listed sharply to starboard. In the confusion, someone managed to strap a life belt around Pye and her daughter. They were loaded into a lifeboat, but it foundered within minutes and the mother and daughter were thrown into the cold water of the North Atlantic. Pye felt herself being pulled under. "The suction underneath the water dragged [Marjorie] out of my arms and she was gone forever. I shall never forget the agony of it: while I was under the water I felt my end had come."[1]

Through his periscope, Schwieger watched the liner in its death throes. The haphazard lowering of the lifeboats (many of which overturned) suggested to the captain that there was widespread panic on board. After a few moments, Schwieger ordered his vessel down to a depth of 20 meters and away from the area. Not long after, he sighted another vessel in the vicinity and maneuvered the U-boat to line up a shot.[2]

Likely thanks to the life belt, Charlotte Pye surfaced, alive but unconscious. Rescuers aboard the *Flying Fish*, one of several vessels that raced to the scene, plucked her from the sea. The child's body was recovered several days later. Of the more than 1,900 passengers and crew on the *Lusitania*, only 767 survived. "Never before had a single act of war caused so many noncombatant deaths," one military historian has concluded.[3]

News of the sinking reverberated around the world. Newspapers filled their pages with survivor accounts and images of the mass burial of victims. President Woodrow Wilson, determined to avoid being drawn into the European war, received the news coolly and made no public statements for several days. In the weeks that followed, however, he wrote several stiff complaints to the German government objecting to its violation of the "sacred freedom of the seas."[4] For the rest of the war, the *Lusitania* served as an Allied rallying cry, and Pye and several other survivors became active in the wartime recruiting effort. Schwieger, the German submarine captain, did not survive the war. Having claimed more than 40 Allied ships, he died when his own U-boat went down in September 1917.

Questions about the *Lusitania* sinking have echoed through the decades. Before she sailed, the German government took out advertisements in New York newspapers warning passengers that the waters near Britain were "a war zone" and that any British or Allied vessel could be targeted. Given this, should she ever have sailed with passengers? (The ship's owners were confident that the vessel was fast enough to outrun submarines.) A host of other questions persist. Did the captain respond adequately to warnings about U-boats nearby? (He altered course shortly before the attack, but this maneuver inadvertently brought him closer to the U-20.) Was the *Lusitania* armed and therefore a combatant? (There is no evidence that she was.) Did Schwieger fire a second torpedo? (No, but a secondary explosion on board led many to believe that he had.) Was the *Lusitania* carrying weaponry for the British? (Yes, thousands of rounds of rifle ammunition.) Why did the British leave her unescorted and vulnerable? (Historians still debate this point.)

Enveloped in tragedy and controversy, the *Lusitania*'s demise marked a consequential moment for freedom of the seas. For most of the 18th and 19th centuries, maritime nations had sparred over what restrictions belligerents could impose on shipping. Elaborate rules had evolved on what kinds of blockades were permissible and when belligerents could search or seize neutral vessels. The 1909 London Declaration—endorsed by all major European powers—attempted to codify those norms. It specified that blockades must be limited, defined a limited category of contraband, and set rules for when neutral vessels could be detained. In exceptional circumstances, it allowed for the destruction of captured merchant ships, but it required that "all persons on board must be placed in safety."[5] Less than six years elapsed between the solemn signing of the Declaration and the attack on the *Lusitania*.

How did the edifice of norms protecting freedom of navigation crumble so spectacularly? With some justification, the German government argued that the British had started the unraveling. In late 1914, Britain declared the entire North Sea a "military area" and warned that any ship entering without permission would face the "most grave danger."[6] Britain's navy managed to blockade this vast area (at least its surface traffic) by controlling the English Channel and the expanse of ocean from Great Britain to Norway. London had ready answers to complaints from Germany and affected neutral countries that its "military area" far exceeded permissible blockades. The British accused the Germans of using neutral ships to scatter mines across the North Sea, a violation that they said justified the British closure. A second available response was legalistic: while the British had endorsed the 1909 London Declaration, its government never ratified the document.

Those responses rang hollow. Even if true, the accusations of German mine laying did not seem to justify such an enormous closure of the seas. Nor was the London Declaration's nonbinding status persuasive. The agreement was designed to clarify *existing* customary law, which neutral states viewed as already binding on Britain. In September 1914, the US secretary of state protested at length the British unwillingness to respect neutral rights. In the weeks that followed, the United States objected again as the British detained and diverted US ships headed to European ports. The *Washington Post* labeled British policy a "declaration of war on American commerce."[7] For Germany, the British blockade was just the kind of maritime strangulation it had long feared. Like the French before them, Germans often depicted the Royal Navy as the real enemy of ocean freedom and insisted on the need to counterbalance British sea power. Freidrich Ratzel, an influential German strategist, wrote before the war that "the only guarantee of freedom of the seas against exclusion by a dominant power was a system of oceanic equilibrium."[8] German propaganda from the period depicted Britain as strangling ocean freedom with tentacles that reached to distant bases and possessions (see Figure 3.1).

In the face of Britain's maritime chokehold, Berlin saw unrestricted submarine warfare as a legitimate method for restoring that equilibrium. In the months before the *Lusitania* sinking, German diplomats warned their US counterparts that a response to the British blockade was coming and expressed frustration that neutral states had not more forcefully and effectively protested British policy. Certain scholars of the period have concurred that the US failure to robustly confront the initial British blockade led inevitably to the unwinding of maritime rules. "The established system of international maritime law broke down in 1914 not because of its own flaws," John Coogan has argued, "but because [Wilson] refused to uphold it."[9]

In the wake of the *Lusitania* sinking, anger from the United States and other neutral countries did persuade Germany to retreat from unrestricted submarine warfare. That reversal was controversial at home, however, where many had welcomed the attack on the British liner. A leading German newspaper

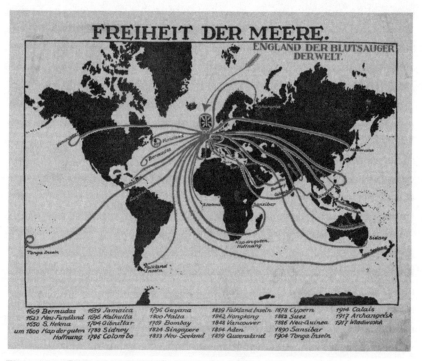

Figure 3.1 German propaganda poster during World War I; image courtesy Cornell University – PJ Mode Collection of Persuasive Cartography.

heralded the sinking as "the end of the epoch of English supremacy of the seas," and a German artist designed a medal commemorating the event.[10] As Britain's maritime blockade wore on and economic privation in Germany worsened, the clamor to restart unrestricted submarine warfare increased. In February 1917, the gloves came off and the undersea offensive against shipping resumed.

Taken together, the British and German restrictions on free navigation demonstrated the limits of law and norms in regulating force and protecting traditional ocean freedoms. Treaties, declarations, and custom struggled to compete with the strategic imperatives of powerful countries engaged in what they increasingly viewed as a fight for survival. One naval historian concluded, "The realities of the law as it affects the use of force at sea are strikingly simple: power decides."[11] In the context of what strategists have described as "total war," broad restrictions on maritime commerce—whether through a naval embargo or unrestricted submarine warfare—had a powerful logic. All manner of goods that might be immune from seizure in more limited conflicts, including food, clothing, and basic commodities, could now be seen as vital to the war effort. Tactics once rejected as inhumane suddenly appeared proportionate. Whether even influential neutral countries could have held back the brutal tide is unclear.

Woodrow Wilson himself certainly acknowledged no responsibility. He placed defending freedom of the seas at the heart of his rationale for declaring war on Germany. When he addressed Congress on April 2, 1917, the president described German barbarism in sinking vessels on sight. "International law had its origin in the attempt to set up some law which would be respected and observed upon the seas, where no nation had right of dominion and where lay the free highways of the world." Germany's submarine campaign, Wilson declared, "is a warfare against mankind."[12]

Yet the US entry into the war showed just how hard it was to reverse the cycle of maritime restrictions. Once in the conflict, Washington advocated one of history's more remarkable attempts to block access to the "free highways" of the ocean. The idea was to lay thousands of mines—a "barrage"— to prevent German U-boats' movement from the North Sea into the broader Atlantic. The British had made limited use of mines and nets for this purpose already, but the new initiative dwarfed those efforts. The operation began in 1918, and the commander of the US squadron described the goal as creating "a barrier of high explosives across the North Sea—10,000 tons of TNT, 150 shiploads of it, spread over an area 230 miles long by 25 miles wide and reaching from near the surface to 240 feet below."[13] The wall of mines had some success in restricting U-boat activities, but those results came at the cost of creating yet another impediment to free navigation during the war's final years—and in its aftermath. Despite a sustained effort to clear the mines once fighting ended, they continued to claim victims for months.[14]

Freedom of navigation lost vital ground during World War I. The disruption that the major combatants created for ocean commerce far exceeded that of previous conflicts. As important, the war set in motion broader geopolitical and diplomatic dynamics that would dramatically change the 19th-century dispensation regarding use of the oceans. Critical to that shift was the decline of Great Britain as the dominant naval and maritime power.

Passing the Trident

As Europe emerged exhausted and stunned from the Great War, public opinion clamored for major changes to the model of international relations that had allowed such a destructive conflict. The moment seemed to demand new forms of international governance and control. Jan Smuts, the South African leader who played a central role in postwar diplomacy, predicted that "the greatest opportunity in history would be met by the greatest step forward in the government of man."[15] Fully caught up in that spirit, a leading German academic proposed full international control of the oceans, complete with an "international sea police" that would "be used for the general police purpose of repressing any violation committed by any one nation upon the seas."[16] Another suggested radical changes to the rights of military vessels that would "forbid the high seas to the man-of-war of any nation whatsoever, to relegate them to territorial waters, and to permit only such small cruisers as are necessary to prevent privateering."[17]

That still jealous and suspicious governments actually moved in the direction of international governance owed a great deal to the US president, who marshaled diplomatic and public support for what would become the League of Nations. In that quest, safeguarding freedom of the seas remained central. The second of Wilson's proposed "Fourteen Points" to guide the postwar peace process was "absolute freedom of navigation upon the seas, outside territorial waters, alike in peace and in war." The only exception Wilson envisioned was "international action for the enforcement of international covenants," an acknowledgment that the future League might need the power of maritime blockade to defeat an aggressor state.[18]

Protective of the Royal Navy's ability to blockade continental adversaries—as it had Germany—the British became nervous about explicit references to "freedom of the seas," which they now viewed as being a direct attack on their wartime rights. The influential British lawyer and strategist Julian Stafford Corbett wrote:

> It comes then to this—that if Freedom of the Seas is pushed to its logical conclusion of forbidding altogether the capture and destruction of private property at sea, it will in practice go far to rob fleets of all power of exerting pressure on an enemy, while armies would be left in full enjoyment of that power. The balance of Naval and Military power, which has meant so much for the liberties of the world, would be upset, and the voice of the Naval Powers would sink to a whisper beside that of the Military Powers.[19]

At the very least, the British wanted assurances that the United States would not challenge its increasingly fragile naval dominance; British officials realized full well that Washington could become the world's leading naval power if it chose that path. At the Paris peace negotiations in early 1919, US and British naval officers exchanged harsh words about future American shipbuilding plans, and their disagreement came close to derailing the conference. In the end, Wilson and British Prime Minister Lloyd George restrained the feuding admirals and brokered a compromise. The final Covenant of the League, signed in the summer of 1919, was less explicit on ocean freedom than Wilson would have liked; instead of ensuring freedom of the seas it more obliquely encouraged League members to "make provision to secure and maintain freedom of communications and of transit and equitable treatment for the commerce of all Members of the League."[20]

After playing a decisive role in shaping the League, the United States famously abjured membership when the treaty fell a handful of votes short in the Senate. But Washington did participate in several novel diplomatic exercises designed to prevent a new naval arms race. The poisonous Anglo-German naval competition was fresh in the minds of diplomats seeking to construct a durable peace. Beginning in the early 1920s, Britain, France, Japan, Italy, and the United States gathered for conferences in Washington, Geneva, and then London, where their representatives bargained and bickered over an acceptable ratio of naval forces. The 1922 Washington conference recognized the new prominence of the United States by giving it parity with the British in major warships. "For the first time in centuries, the Royal Navy had declared itself content with mere parity rather than naval mastery," Paul Kennedy writes. "And it had agreed to have its strength bound by international treaty rather than based upon a consideration of its own defence needs."[21] Japan, acknowledged as a rising power, secured the right to build its naval capacity to 60 percent of American and British levels.

As the negotiations moved from Washington to Geneva and from battleships to other naval forces, the relations between the reigning maritime power and the heir apparent again soured. Washington and London failed to agree on more detailed naval restrictions, and the 1927 Geneva conference broke up acrimoniously. British statesmen insisted that there was a critical difference between their situation and that of the Americans: for Britain, control of the sea lanes was a matter of survival. Winston Churchill fumed, "There can be no parity between a power whose navy is its life and a power whose navy is only for prestige."[22] The British insisted that a significant number of navy cruisers was necessary for "policing" purposes, suggesting that their navy served an international constabulary function. Far from convincing the Americans, these British claims to a global maritime role often activated deep distrust of British sea power:

> American history had begun with a revolution against supposed British tyranny, and Americans were taught that the War of 1812 had been a struggle to protect American seamen from impressment by the Royal Navy. . . . In the 1920s an increasing number of Americans were led to believe that U.S. entry into World War I had been engineered by the Allies, led by the crafty British.[23]

In this fraught atmosphere, the long-standing dispute over what maritime restrictions were permissible during war remained the most sensitive. While the United States had ultimately linked arms with Britain in the war, it had not forgotten the economic impact of Britain's blockade of Germany. US legal specialists desirous of preserving freedom of navigation during conflict viewed with alarm the precedent created by the world war. "Today the law governing the use of the sea in time of war is in a state of unprecedented confusion and chaos," an American scholar wrote in 1930. "If a war occurred today a belligerent could with Allied precedent justify almost any conceivable practice."[24] As in the past, Britain supported a broad right to seize neutral shipping if necessary in some future conflict while the United States viewed that policy as an unacceptable infringement of maritime freedom. According to British Foreign Secretary Austen Chamberlain, "Blockade is therefore the root of our difference with the US over naval limitation & is the one question which might lead to war between us. Unless they are belligerents, the US will never again submit to such a blockade as we enforced in the Great War."[25]

The British feared that the United States might seek international support for its view of maritime law and the rules on freedom of navigation. That concern was well founded. Influential US Senator William Borah, chair of the Senate Foreign Relations Committee, advocated an international conference on maritime law. Legal uncertainty, he argued, made "the seas subject to no definite rules save that of force and commerce [and] to no ultimate protection save that of battle fleets."[26] President Herbert Hoover also put the British on the back foot by casting traditional US concerns about free shipping in humanitarian terms, proposing that vessels carrying foodstuffs be treated like hospital ships and be protected from attack. "The time has come," the president said, "when we should remove starvation of women and children from the weapons of warfare."[27] To deflect mounting US pressure, Britain signaled a willingness to review belligerent rights and hurriedly convened several committees to examine its policy and consider changes.

Negotiations over relative numbers of battleships and cruisers consumed diplomats, but the most transformative issue was submarines. Soon after World War I ended, London pushed for a complete prohibition on the vessels that had nearly strangled its commerce. That view had some support in other capitals. Suspicion of submarine warfare ran deep in some militaries, including among traditional naval officers who had spent their careers above the waves. But France and several other powers realized that submarines offered a relatively low-cost means of acquiring sea power and they balked at a ban. The leading naval powers could at least agree that there should be no return to unrestricted submarine warfare that menaced all merchant shipping. As late as 1936, almost all major naval powers declared that submarines must follow what was referred to as "cruiser rules"—that they must stop and search merchant vessels before detaining or sinking them.[28]

In retrospect, the interwar naval negotiations appear tragically irrelevant. As the diplomats parried in ornate conference rooms, political earthquakes were rendering their efforts largely meaningless. Three years after the 1930 London agreement, Adolf Hitler rose to power in Germany, and Japan began its campaigns of conquest in East Asia. Arms control agreements were soon a thing of the past. By the mid-1930s, all the major powers were rebuilding their armed forces, including their navies.

If nothing else, the naval diplomacy of the 1920s marked the halting transition from a world in which Great Britain was the dominant naval power to an uncertain new maritime order. Their expansive view of belligerent rights notwithstanding, the British had for more than a century championed a system of open maritime commerce. As the dominant maritime power, the British had also advanced a rudimentary model of ocean governance that they saw as consistent with freedom of the seas. Through unilateral action and bilateral treaties, Britain established the norm that slave trading was an unacceptable use of ocean freedom. British domestic regulation on shipping had also been deeply influential across the globe and had spawned early international instruments for ocean safety.

Most important, London had staunchly opposed national attempts to claim areas of the oceans by expanding their territorial seas. The British decline would render that basic ocean regime vulnerable. The changing alignment of the major powers was not the only factor pressuring the status quo on the oceans. Britain's relative decline coincided with an upsurge in curiosity about uses of the oceans beyond their long-established functions as fishing grounds, conduits for commerce, and forums for conflict.

Expeditions and Conservation

In July 1923, the German scientist Fritz Haber embarked on the passenger liner *Hansa,* bound for New York. The recipient of the 1918 Nobel Prize for his work in synthesizing ammonia, Haber enjoyed international renown. His role during the war as architect of Germany's chemical weapons program added an aura of intrigue and even menace to his reputation. Haber and his team of assistants tried to disguise their presence on board the *Hansa.* Designated as members of the crew, their names did not appear on the passenger manifest.

Yet Haber's notoriety ensured that word of his presence spread. A journalist who happened to be on board even filed a dispatch speculating on the scientist's activities. His account noted that Haber and his collaborators seemed to have a full laboratory on the vessel. Perhaps, the correspondent wrote, he was engaged in a "search for hidden force in salt water" that could propel ships. When questioned by the journalist, Haber almost impishly declined to clarify his mission. "At least the waters of the ocean are free for all men to experiment in. We are working as we did work in the laboratory and whether a discovery of value will be made is to be seen."[29]

The scientist's actual aim was not propelling ships but distilling gold from seawater. Relying on a set of calculations by a Swedish chemist, Haber had convinced himself that large amounts of gold could be extracted from the oceans. (He apparently hoped that doing so might help his country pay the onerous reparations imposed by the Versailles Treaty.) His onboard laboratory included a custom-made extraction machine, and throughout the *Hansa*'s voyage the device dutifully filtered seawater sucked into the vessel through special tubing. Eager to sample a variety of ocean regions, Haber and his team repeated the exercise on other voyages over the next three years.[30]

The mission failed. The amount of gold in seawater turned out to be a small fraction of what had been anticipated. But Germany's interwar bid to better understand the sea was not over. In 1925, it began one of the most notable oceanographic expeditions of the period. Facing the Versailles Treaty's severe restrictions on naval activities, the German navy endorsed an oceanography project as a way of reasserting the country's maritime standing. Rampant inflation and a growing economic crisis scuttled several attempts at a research mission, but the government finally cobbled together the necessary funds. *Meteor*, a specially outfitted ship with an early version of sonar, cruised the South Atlantic for two years, collecting data through thousands of soundings. *Meteor*'s mission significantly advanced understanding of the ocean floor, most notably by confirming that the ridge already discovered in the middle of the Atlantic extended all the way south.

If the properties of seawater and the shape of the major ocean basins were coming into clearer focus, the public was also getting new glimpses of undersea life. With the backing of several wealthy donors, the American naturalist William Beebe conducted expeditions off the coast of Africa and to the Galapagos Islands. His dispatches, which included sightings of dwarf sharks with green eyes and other curiosities, appeared regularly in major American newspapers and excited the public imagination. Frustrated by the limitations of his diving suit, Beebe teamed up with the engineer Otis Barton to design what they called a bathysphere, a spherical capsule that could ferry one or two people to unprecedented depths. In 1934, Beebe reached a depth of half a mile. He even conducted a national broadcast from the bathysphere while submerged, and media accounts of his descents included sketches of some of the fantastic creatures that he observed.[31]

Beebe relied almost entirely on private funding, and there was little official support for US oceanographers during this period. The one notable step
toward creating an infrastructure for US oceanography during the interwar
period came through private sources. In 1930, the Rockefeller Foundation
committed several million dollars to establish a new oceanographic institution at Woods Hole on Cape Cod, Massachusetts. The institute's first building
appeared later that year, and a modest research vessel began operations the
following summer.[32]

Meanwhile, far to the north, the Soviet government had begun sustained exploration of the Arctic. In 1932, the icebreaker *Sibiryakov* completed the Northern Sea Route in one season, the first time a Soviet vessel
had done so. The voyage, which nearly failed at several junctures, secured
for the crew a laudatory telegram from Soviet leaders, including Josef
Stalin. "The success of your expedition, which has overcome incredible
difficulties, proves once again that there are no strongholds which cannot
be taken by Bolshevik courage and organization."[33] Like the voyages
through the Northwest Passage that began in the 1850s, the icebreaker's
trek along Russia's Arctic fringe hinted at possible shipping through the
far north.

A few years later, several Soviet pilots made flights around and to the
North Pole, in the process becoming national celebrities. Relying again
on aircraft, the Soviets in 1937 established the first floating scientific station in the Arctic—designated North Pole 1. For almost a year, four Soviet
scientists manned the station as it drifted hundreds of miles. They took regular soundings along the way, and their research confirmed that there were
no large land masses in the vicinity of the North Pole. The Arctic, in contrast to Antarctica, should properly be considered ocean space. And that in
turn meant that future negotiations on how to govern the oceans would have
enormous implications for the region.

The German and Soviet oceanographic activity during this period
illuminates the tight link between the desire to understand the oceans and
the impulse to exploit them for national advantage. Powerful states—and,
in some contexts, *only* these states—had the necessary resources to explore
the oceans. As Haber pointed out to the prying journalist, all countries were
free to conduct any experiments they desired on the high seas. In the coming
decades, the often faint line between scientific ocean research and strategic
economic and military activity would emerge as a recurring irritant both at
sea and in negotiating rooms.

As interest in the undersea world increased, there were also stirrings of a marine conservation movement. When the League of Nations took up maritime issues in 1926, the Argentine delegate, a law professor named Jose Leon Suarez, made repeated calls for international cooperation to conserve maritime resources. Warning that "certain species were being exterminated," he pleaded for negotiations to regulate fishing and exploitation of resources beyond the three-mile limit.[34] His passionate interventions elicited polite expressions of concern from other delegates, but his fervor was not widely shared. The conference eventually tasked a subcommittee to study the issue, but there was little support for anything beyond that.

In certain quarters, there was more acute worry and even a sprinkling of coordinated action. The beleaguered fur seals of the Pribilof Islands—the subject of the 1893 arbitration—received some belated protection through a 1912 treaty signed by the United States, Great Britain, and Japan. A decade later, the United States and Canada signed a treaty to protect the halibut populations in the north Pacific. Canada pushed for a similar treaty to protect salmon populations, insisting that fishermen in Washington state were using purse seines to deplete salmon migrating back from the open ocean. Alaskan salmon fishermen were also aggressive about protecting their operations, and they soon perceived an even more distant foreign threat. Even though there was scant evidence for it, they claimed repeatedly that Japanese vessels were fishing in the waters off Alaska and exhausting the salmon stock. Their call for action was taken seriously in Washington, and officials proposed a conference with Japan to address the issue. US officials even considered unilaterally asserting the right to manage salmon stocks beyond US territorial waters.[35]

International regulation moved fastest, although hardly fast, when it came to whaling. The emergence of steam-powered vessels led to a rapid expansion of whaling activities in the early 1900s. Cannon-powered harpoons—sometimes equipped with grenades that exploded inside the animal—allowed hunters to hit their prey more routinely and with greater effect. Air pumps ensured that the whale carcass did not sink before it could be harvested. By 1925, some vessels were equipped with "slipways" that allowed crews to winch harpooned whales directly onto the deck.[36] In 1929, a leading Norwegian maritime researcher described excitedly the revolution in whaling created by "factory" whaling ships capable of harvesting whales without any recourse to land. "The fact that the floating factories have been equipped with a slip for hauling the entire whale aboard has more than anything else contributed to the expansion of pelagic whaling," he wrote. "The whale can consequently be treated aboard instead of at the side of the ship, and this not only in smooth water but in fairly rough seas."[37]

The toll of these newly efficient fleets on whale populations, particularly around Antarctica, was nearly catastrophic. In 1931, most major whaling nations agreed to limit their operations in "all the waters of the world, including both the high seas and territorial and national waters."[38] Another treaty followed in 1937. Several leading whaling nations chose not to participate, however, and the impact of these novel international regulations was not dramatic. They did at least establish the precedent of managing marine resources through multilateral negotiations, however, and one scholar at the time described them as "the beginning of a new era of cooperation."[39] For the whales, the outbreak of the Second World War was more effective protection than treaties. As the world's major nations directed their resources toward hunting each other, the whale populations began to recover.

Circumnavigating Regulation

Protecting marine life was only beginning to be an international concern, but regulation of life and activities on board the growing number of vessels plying the oceans was more developed. In the late 19th century, national legislation had significantly altered the functioning of the maritime industry. Britain was the locus of much of this activity, and Plimsoll's "coffin ship" campaign was carried on by new generations of reformers. British legislation on the maritime industry often "became the blueprint for legislation in most of the maritime countries of the world."[40] As enthusiasm for drafting multilateral agreements rose, maritime regulations appeared in international form as well as domestic law. In 1930, a new International Load Line Convention created international standards for how heavily ships could be loaded. A few years later, diplomats drafted additional treaties on the rights of seamen and minimum qualifications and age for those working at sea. Because these international agreements almost always lacked enforcement power, however, only national governments could ensure compliance.

Many in the shipping industry viewed the expanding web of national and international regulations as increasingly burdensome. US shipowners, who faced difficult market conditions between the wars, were particularly concerned. The vessels that had poured out of US shipyards during World War

I created a glut of capacity in its aftermath, even as the government extended certain Progressive-era protections to those in the maritime industry.[41] This combination of market and regulatory pressure indirectly produced one of the most notable developments in contemporary ocean governance: the "flag of convenience."

Since at least the early 19th century, an oceangoing merchant vessel had typically carried the flag of the country where it had its home port, and that port was normally in the home country of the ship's owners. Several important maritime countries required that ships flying the national flag be owned by nationals. A smaller number of states mandated that ships flying the flag be built in national shipyards or have a certain percentage of their nationals as crew. These requirements were a matter of national discretion, but all vessels on the high seas were expected to have a connection to and be governed by the laws of some country. Bilateral treaties often stated that each country recognized the vessels flying the other's flag.

Controversy occasionally arose over whether states were too promiscuously allowing vessels to fly their flag. In 1905, the new Permanent Court of Arbitration considered a British complaint that France was improperly allowing vessels owned by the Sultan of Muscat to fly the French flag. The British contended that the practice was facilitating the trade in slaves and questioned the French right to confer its flag on the sultan's vessels. The court responded with a ringing affirmation of each country's right to decide which vessels can fly its flag. "It belongs to every sovereign to decide to whom he will accord the right to fly his flag and to prescribe the rules governing such grants."[42] In 1927, in a case involving a deadly collision between French and Turkish vessels, the Permanent Court of International Justice reaffirmed the basic principle that vessels on the high seas

> are subject to no authority except that of the State whose flag they fly. In virtue of the principle of the freedom of the seas, that is to say, the absence of any territorial sovereignty upon the high seas, no State may exercise any kind of jurisdiction over foreign vessels upon them.[43]

Shortly after the First World War, moreover, most members of the League agreed that even landlocked states had the right to flag vessels at sea and that they also enjoyed the freedom to navigate on rivers to reach the sea.[44]

The clarity that was emerging about the exclusive rights of the flag state to govern vessels on the high seas should not obscure the long and colorful history of chicanery with national flags at sea. To avoid privateers and pirates, some merchant vessels carried multiple national flags and deployed them strategically to minimize their exposure. In the late 17th century, ships in the Indian Ocean wary of Captain Kidd flew British flags in the hopes of avoiding his attentions. One of the US Navy's first victories at sea resulted from similar deception. In 1801, during the campaign against the Barbary states, the US warship *Enterprise* lured a vessel from Tripoli into proximity by flying the Union Jack. Only when the vessels closed did the *Enterprise* reveal its true identity and open fire.[45] Fishing vessels, too, sometimes deployed national colors not their own in order to fish in restricted zones. But this kind of national subterfuge at sea was intermittent and opportunistic.

The more regular practice of flying a flag of convenience emerged in the 1920s, as the US government searched for a way to dispose of vessels seized during the war without harming their own shipping companies, already under severe strain as industry prices plummeted. The solution was to sell the ships but to require that they be transferred to foreign flags not competing directly with US vessels. Shipowners quickly realized that transferring vessels to a foreign flag carried substantial benefits. By law, US-flagged vessels had to employ a mostly American crew and comply with an increasingly elaborate set of rules regarding inspections and safety. Those requirements vanished once the vessel no longer flew the stars and stripes.

Panama emerged as an appealing alternative. The country had close links to the United States, a currency pegged to the US dollar, and a privileged location astride the canal. American shipowners flying the Panamanian flag could still benefit to a degree from American protection and influence while evading its increasingly onerous maritime safety regulations. The shipping companies did not hide their principal motive. A senior official from Pacific Freighters was candid in a 1922 interview with a New York newspaper:

> The chief advantage of Panamanian registry is that the owner is relieved of the continual but irregular boiler and hull inspections and the regulations as to crew's quarters and subsistence. We are under absolutely no restrictions, so long as we pay the $1 a net ton registry fee and 10 cents yearly a net ton tax.[46]

Several passenger liners, originally constructed for use in Germany, were also flagged in Panama, although the US owner of those vessels may have been motivated by evading Prohibition as much as inspection (the Justice

Department then interpreted Prohibition as preventing US-flagged vessels from serving alcohol). By 1925, Panama realized that ship registration offered significant revenue and amended its national laws to make the process simpler and more attractive. In the early 1930s, European shipowners began to follow Americans in transferring ships to Panamanian registry. The outbreak of civil war in Spain created an additional incentive for the move. A number of major countries, including the United States, enacted neutrality legislation to prevent their nationals from trading with belligerents. Panama enacted no such measures, and shipowners who switched to Panamanian registry could freely engage in the lucrative (if often dangerous) business of shuttling material and weapons to the Spanish combatants.

The emerging flag of convenience system—and the governance problems it would cause—was not the direct result of freedom of the seas. As the international court pointed out, however, the two were related. Freedom of the seas required that vessels on the high seas be left alone, subject only to the authorities of the flag state. That principle then combined with the commercial incentives of major shipowners and certain smaller governments to produce a system in which a vessel's flag often became as much a shield from effective oversight as a signal of it.

Grounded on the Territorial Sea

As diplomats debated the future of warfare at sea and shipowners experimented with switching flags, the question of the appropriate breadth of territorial waters emerged as a major point of contention. Britain had long helped check moves by certain countries to expand their national waters, but the realization that Britain's power was waning created space for those eager to challenge the three-mile tradition. In 1930, the League of Nations convened a group of experts to cut through the uncertainty. Spain's representative urged the group to simply let each country decide on the extent of its own territorial sea. But the British delegate warned that such a system would "produce a state of chaos."[47]

That point at least seemed to generate broad agreement; most governments represented at the conference professed to see value in setting some international standard, although several argued that individual circumstances had to be considered. A few delegates floated the idea of separate maritime zones—a territorial sea and then some kind of adjacent

zone within which states had more limited rights. But that seemed unnecessarily complicated to many delegates, and Czechoslovakia's ambassador
presciently warned that a new zone of limited jurisdiction might morph
into something like territorial waters. "You know how easy it would be
for a state to abuse [adjacent zones] and to create a kind of de facto sovereignty over the adjacent zone."[48]

The conference revealed that a bare majority of the forty states in attendance supported the traditional three-mile limit, including leading maritime
powers Great Britain, Japan, and the United States. The few landlocked countries at the conference also backed a three-mile zone, on the theory that their
interests were best served by the smallest possible coastal zone. But several
European countries, with Italy and Portugal in the lead, resisted any suggestion that the three-mile limit constituted existing international law. Portugal's
envoy advocated a territorial sea of 12 miles, emphasizing repeatedly that
50,000 people in his country relied on fishing for their livelihood. A narrow
territorial sea, he worried, would leave local fish stocks vulnerable to foreign
exploitation. Latin American countries also advocated an expanded territorial sea. Norway and Sweden insisted that their own long-standing four-mile
boundary had at least as much historical grounding as the three-mile limit.
For his part, Italy's envoy had little patience for excursions into past practice.
"History . . . does not count," he insisted; "it is the actual current needs that
count."[49]

There seemed to be no principled way for the three-mile camp to convince
the dissenters that its proposal was superior. The British negotiator did his
best, advocating a general policy of modesty in ocean claims that Grotius
would have appreciated. "When we are asserting sovereignty over a portion
of the high seas, which are the common highway of all the world, it behooves
us to be as limited in our demands of sovereignty as it is possible to be."
Japan's representative echoed that view, arguing that the negotiators should
"make the breadth as small as is consistent with the use of the high sea, which
is so important for all nations."[50]

With Japan and the United States in its corner, the British also pointed out
that nearly all major maritime powers supported the narrow three-mile limit.
"Nations which own over 70 percent of the world's tonnage have declared
themselves in favour of the three-mile limit unconditionally."[51] That argument cut little ice with Italy's increasingly vexed ambassador, who reminded
the British that negotiations were being conducted on the basis of the sovereign equality of states and that the largest maritime powers had no special

influence. "Here, we believe in the equality of States, so that the British case is worth no more than my own."[52] He and the Portuguese ambassador labored to show that changes in technology had rendered a three-mile limit obsolete. "It is out of touch with the requirements of modern life."[53] The conference ended amicably enough, but without any resolution on the breadth of the territorial sea.

Two months after the conference closed, President Herbert Hoover signed into law the Smoot-Hawley tariff legislation that would deepen the world economic crisis. A few months later, the Nazi party's representation in the *Reichstag* jumped from 12 seats to more than 100. The world would look very different the next time international diplomats took up the territorial sea question in earnest.

Sinking Freedom of Navigation

As Europe and Asia moved toward conflict in the 1930s, a key question was whether the maritime dynamics in the First World War—including unrestricted submarine warfare and expansive maritime "war zones"—would reappear. Through a variety of agreements negotiated after the war ended, the leading naval powers had attempted to stitch back together the traditional rules of naval combat. But the fabric was torn again just a few weeks after war broke out in Europe. On the night of September 3, 1939, a German submarine torpedoed the merchant vessel *Athenia*, which the U-boat commander apparently mistook for a British navy vessel. Within days, the British responded by arming its merchant vessels. That gave the Germans a pretext to treat all merchant vessels as hostile, and the path to unrestricted submarine warfare was all but assured.

Watching from across the Atlantic, President Franklin Roosevelt was determined to preempt the threat. At a conference in Panama, US and Latin American diplomats designed a maritime "zone of security." The vast area, within which the signatories said they would not tolerate belligerent activity, extended 300 miles to the east of the South American coast.

As a measure of continental self-protection, the American Republics, so long as they maintain their neutrality, are as of inherent right entitled to have those waters adjacent to the American continent, which they regard as of primary concern and direct utility in their relations, free from the commission of any hostile act by any non-American belligerent nation, whether such hostile act be attempted or made from land, sea or air.[54]

The protection zone was a curious construct from the perspective of traditional ocean freedom. It claimed to be a measure designed to protect freedom of navigation. After all, how could ships bound for or traveling from ports in the Americas navigate safely with commerce raiders and submarines lurking nearby? But the zone also gave a new twist to the perennial question of belligerent rights at sea. Instead of restricting *what* belligerents could do (seemingly a lost cause at that point), it restricted *where* they could be. In so doing, it arguably extrapolated from one of the original rationales for the territorial sea: giving coastal states a maritime buffer from conflicts that did not involve them. However, it also created a precedent for much larger territorial seas (a precedent that several Latin American states would draw on after the war ended) or perhaps even oceanic demilitarized zones.

In the deliberations that preceded the announcement of the security area, both the US State Department and the British government worried that the zone fell afoul of international law. A US law professor acknowledged that it might be best seen as a "legal innovation demanded by self-preservation."[55] Roosevelt, a dedicated pragmatist, argued that traditional territorial waters were inadequate to protect neutral states and their commerce. He and the other leaders initially left vague what precisely they would do if belligerents took hostile acts within the area. As new Axis attacks occurred in the area, however, Roosevelt's rhetoric hardened. In September 1941, he pledged that the US Navy would seek out and engage Axis vessels operating in the maritime zone without waiting for them to strike.

> My obligation as President is historic; it is clear. It is inescapable. It is no act of war on our part when we decide to protect the seas that are vital to American defense. . . . From now on, if German or Italian vessels of war enter the waters, the protection of which is necessary for American defense, they do so at their own peril.[56]

In practice, there were few attempts to enforce the security zone. Congress was doing its best to avoid the kind of maritime confrontations that had pulled the country into the First World War. In that effort, it enacted a series of neutrality measures designed to minimize the exposure of Americans to warfare at sea. Legislation forbade US vessels from carrying weaponry to the combatants and even prohibited individual Americans from traveling on belligerent ships into war zones. Senior officers in the US Navy strenuously objected to these measures, which they saw as abandoning the traditional US defense of free navigation.

Actions at sea were scarce, but the rhetorical broadsides from the White House continued. Like Wilson before him, Roosevelt seized on attacks on merchant shipping as evidence of German perfidy and inhumanity. He called Nazi submarines "the rattlesnakes of the Atlantic" and a "menace to the free pathways of the high seas." He warned that the Nazis aimed "to abolish the freedom of the seas, and to acquire absolute control and domination of these seas for themselves."[57] In the face of these threats, the president cast the neutrality zone as part of a tradition of American resistance to disorder on the seas. The theme of the United States as a champion of ocean freedom appeared widely. A poster exhorting American shipbuilders to speed up their work cast them as defenders of "freedom of the seas." (See Figure 3.2)

But what appeared to the United States as disorder—indiscriminate attacks by warships on merchant shipping—was viewed in a different light when the country shifted from neutral to combatant. In the hours after the Japanese attack on Pearl Harbor, the Navy directed its submarines to carry out unrestricted submarine warfare in the Pacific. The United States in effect declared an enormous free-fire zone, in which US ships would sink without warning any merchant vessels deemed to be supporting Japan. The initial US attacks had limited success due to faulty torpedoes, timid tactics, and inexperienced commanders, but the toll on Japanese merchant shipping became severe as the war progressed. In 1944 alone, US submarines sank more than 500 merchant vessels accounting for 2.5 million tons of cargo.[58] Certain US commanders who ran out of larger targets even sank small fishing junks in Japanese-controlled waters. At the Nuremberg trials, German admiral Karl Doenitz successfully used the US practice as part of a defense of his own policy of unrestricted submarine warfare. A US naval officer and historian has concluded:

Until the U.S. decision, unrestricted submarine warfare remained illegal and constrained to acts of reprisal. By conducting unrestricted submarine warfare without provocation, the United States implicitly legitimized the entire German unrestricted submarine campaign and irrevocably tore away the noncombatant status of civilian sailors. Henceforth, civilian sailors on merchant ships would be legitimate targets.[59]

Figure 3.2 US propaganda poster during World War II; image courtesy of Bancroft Library, University of California Berkeley.

The Second World War shattered interwar hopes that even the limited form of freedom of navigation during wartime could endure. In times of war, at least war of sufficient severity and scope, belligerents that had the means and motive would cut off maritime commerce that might benefit adversaries. The years immediately after the war would test whether an even more fundamental aspect of maritime freedom—narrowly limited territorial waters—would survive.

4

Adrift

(1945–1970)

In the summer of 1945, the Truman administration was in the midst of a massive effort to structure the postwar world. On August 8, 1945—as a US warplane prepared to drop an atomic bomb on the Japanese seaport of Nagasaki—the president signed the United Nations Charter. He thereby committed the United States to an ambitious collective security structure designed to prevent another global conflagration. The US-led campaign to build a multilateral architecture extended to other realms. With strong support from Washington, the World Bank and the International Monetary Fund prepared to offer loans to countries shattered by the war. All these initiatives involved intense consultation and negotiation with other countries. US diplomacy was decisive in building a multilateral architecture that has endured and expanded.

Yet the world's new international edifices barely touched the oceans. Given the salience of ocean freedom as a theme during the war, the lack of attention was striking. The UN Charter did not explicitly reaffirm freedom of the seas and it said nothing about the oceans other than to make clear that the new Security Council could impose blockades and use force at sea as parts of its mandate to maintain international peace and security. No new international institutions arose to manage ocean affairs.

If there was little multilateral ocean activity, the character of US postwar diplomacy on maritime issues was also far less consultative than on other questions. Just three weeks after Japan's surrender, the Truman administration moved abruptly and all but unilaterally to expand its control of certain ocean space. On September 28, 1945, the White House issued two presidential directives, which became known as the "Truman Proclamations." The first of these asserted the right of the United States to control the continental shelf, which extended in many areas more than a hundred miles into the ocean. The proclamation made little attempt to square the move with existing international law, instead it justified the policy as borne of necessity:

Having concern for the urgency of conserving and prudently utilizing its natural resources, the Government of the United States regards the natural resources of the subsoil and sea bed of the continental shelf beneath the high seas but contiguous to the coasts of the United States as appertaining to the United States, subject to its jurisdiction and control.[1]

A second proclamation addressed fisheries and what the government described as the "inadequacy of present arrangements for the protection and perpetuation of the fishery resources contiguous to its coasts." While not quite asserting sovereign control over fish stocks beyond the traditional three-mile limit, the proclamation did claim the right to establish protective zones in contiguous areas of the high seas fished by US nationals. The government acknowledged that other countries would likely avail themselves of the same privilege. "The right of any State to establish conservation zones off its shores in accordance with the above principles is conceded, provided that corresponding recognition is given to any fishing interests of nationals of the United States which may exist in such areas."[2] While both proclamations stressed that they would not impact freedom of navigation, the sudden shift in US policy profoundly altered the international maritime order.

In many ways, these moves were perplexing. The United States had long insisted that freedom of the seas was vital to its interests. It had bridled repeatedly at what it saw as interference with free navigation. In the international negotiations of the 1930s, the United States had aligned itself with Britain's minimalist position regarding the breadth of the territorial sea. As the newly dominant maritime and economic power, postwar Washington might well have been persuaded by the logic that led London to oppose national claims to ocean space. The US merchant fleet crisscrossed the globe, and its companies were well positioned to access undersea resources around the world, not just in its own neighborhood. In short, the United States appeared poised to assume Britain's place as bulwark against national expansion into the oceans. And yet just days into the peace, the superpower advanced one of the most audacious claims since the Treaty of Tordesillas.

The explanation lies in the United States' dual personality as a maritime nation protective of its access to the oceans but also a resource-hungry coastal country. In the months before the proclamations were issued, those personalities clashed quietly within the US government. The Interior Department, led by the influential and determined Harold Ickes, had its eyes fixed on the potential resources of the continental shelf. When Ickes first wrote to

Roosevelt on the subject in 1943, he succinctly blended economic, strategic, and geological arguments:

> The Continental Shelf extending some 100 or 150 miles from our shores forms a fine breeding place for fish of all kinds; it is an excellent hiding place for submarines; and since it is a continuation of our continent, it probably contains oil and other resources similar to those found in our States.[3]

Ickes had a sympathetic interlocutor in the White House. Roosevelt endorsed the idea of extending control over offshore resources, along the way evidencing a characteristic flexibility about legal limits on government power. "I recognize that new principles of international law might have to be asserted but such principles would not in effect be wholly new, because they would be based on the consideration that inventive genius has moved jurisdiction out to sea to the limit of inventive genius."[4] For all his interest in developing a new international architecture after the war, Roosevelt seemed unconcerned about the foreign implications of moves to expand the country's ocean control.

The State Department was more sensitive to how assertions of US control would appear abroad. "The adoption of the foregoing policy with respect to fisheries by the United States could, if proper precautions were not taken, lead to misunderstanding, suspicion, and opposition on the part of many other countries," officials in the department's Office of Economic Affairs worried.[5] Secretary of State Edward Stettinius, who for several months resisted Ickes's pressure to approve the proclamations, warned that the proposed shift would complicate the broader US effort to encourage multilateralism in economic matters. The State Department successfully insisted on testing the idea on a few foreign governments. And in articulating a rationale for the planned policy change, US officials seemed to redefine the freedom of the seas. So long as freedom of navigation was preserved, US officials argued, exclusive control of undersea resources was inoffensive:

> The rationale of the open sea being free and forever excluded from occu-
> pation on the part of any state is that it forms an international highway
> connecting distant lands and securing freedom of communications and
> commerce between states separated by the sea. There is no reason for
> extending this concept of the freedom of the high seas to the sea bed and
> subsoil beneath its bed. In the case of the sea bed and subsoil there is no

reason to apply either the theoretical argument that occupation is impossible because it can take place only with respect to a determined thing, or the practical argument that the freedom of the waters of the open sea is essential to the freedom of intercourse between states.[6]

As some US diplomats well understood, this formulation could easily be used in ways the United States would oppose. Sovereign control of the seabed might, in fact, significantly impact management and use of the waters above, not least through the construction of installations and structures to exploit seabed resources. Countries eager to claim large territorial seas might use the new logic with which Washington was experimenting. So long as these governments kept their expanded national waters open to "communications and commerce between states," they might well argue, where was the harm?

A leading international law scholar in the period, Georg Schwarzenberger, argued that exclusive control of the continental shelf was in fact "the thin end of a dangerous wedge" that might shatter freedom of the seas. Claims to undersea territory, he wrote, "easily degenerate into still more anarchic aspirations to sovereignty over the surface of the whole of the high seas above the continental shelf."[7] But perhaps even more fundamental was the question of process. The US move amounted to a unilateral change to the understood rules for the oceans. If the United States could change the rules without negotiation, why should others not tinker as well?

The British and Canadian governments warned several times against announcing the moves unilaterally and urged regional or international talks to address US concerns. No doubt with the Nordic countries in mind, British officials fretted that the planned proclamations would encourage "certain European countries . . . towards claiming a controlling interest in the fisheries near their coasts." London pleaded with the US administration to delay the proclamations or to at least make them as narrow and regionally specific as possible.[8] A State Department official concurred, urging a United Nations process for broad negotiations.[9] These pleas were unavailing. Ickes continued to pester, and a harried and distracted State Department finally gave its consent.

The Truman Proclamations spurred almost immediate emulation, and the copycat measures were often more assertive than the original. Countries in the Americas took the lead. Mexico's president issued an almost identical proclamation regarding the continental shelf a month later, while also signaling an intent to claim additional rights to the waters in the area. In the summer of 1947, both Chile and Peru asserted 200-mile maritime zones within which they could exercise sovereignty and control natural resources. (In searching for outer limits to their zone, Chilean experts considered the precedent of the wartime neutrality zone.)[10] With their enormous coastlines, those countries thereby put thousands of square miles of ocean space under greater national control. Three Central American states—Costa Rica, El Salvador, and Honduras—followed suit.

The United States, often linking arms with the United Kingdom and a handful of other countries, struggled to put the genie back in the bottle. In a series of diplomatic demarches, US diplomats argued that the nuances of the Truman Proclamations had been lost, and that foreign states had gone too far. The US ambassador in Peru complained that Peru's declaration of sovereignty out to 200 miles "appears to contravene the freedom of the high seas."[11] The United States had a point, but its credibility was thin. In the face of US opposition, Chile, Ecuador, and Peru banded together. In the 1952 Santiago Declaration, the three governments "proclaim[ed] as a norm of their international maritime policy that they each possess exclusive sovereignty and jurisdiction over the sea along the coasts of their respective countries to a minimum distance of 200 nautical miles from these coasts."[12]

The acquisitive trend continued outside of the Americas. Saudi Arabia expanded its territorial sea to six miles in 1949. Iran, Lebanon, and Syria also opted for six miles. The Soviet Union went even farther. Beginning in the late 1940s, Soviet officials and academics more consistently asserted 12-mile territorial waters. At sea, the Soviets stepped up seizures of foreign fishing vessels, including Swedish and Japanese boats that it claimed were operating within its waters.[13] A 1951 study found that a total of 19 countries claimed a territorial sea wider than the traditional three miles.[14] The cannon-shot rule was in tatters.

In the Pacific, China (still governed by the Nationalist government of Chiang Kai-shek) made its own bid for broader maritime influence, although in an indirect fashion. In 1947, China first publicly claimed the vast majority of the land features in the South China Sea, 159 in total. The government published a map with an enormous U-shaped area covering most of the South China Sea. The area was bounded by 11 dashes (later reduced to nine) that encompassed all the major features in the waters, including the Paracel Islands, the Spratly Islands, and Scarborough Reef. If realized and exploited—an outcome unlikely at the time, given China's debility and division—the claims would give China a dominant position in the South China Sea.

The Truman Proclamations were not the cause of all these moves. As the negotiations of the 1930s suggested, the desire of certain coastal countries for greater control of nearby waters had been building for decades. The Chinese move in the South China Sea, moreover, seems to have been about securing control of the (scant) land in the South China Sea rather than its waters. Scholars who have scoured the diplomatic archives have found little evidence that the now famous U-shaped line was meant to imply control of the large maritime spaces between the various South China Sea islands or that it was somehow designed to mirror the Truman Proclamations.[15]

But the unilateral US assertions undoubtedly accelerated the broader process of maritime expansionism. "Had the US government proceeded on a multilateral, negotiated basis to lay claim to its offshore resources, the ensuing rash of unilateral coastal State claims might not have occurred," the historian Ann Hollick concludes. "At least the United States would have had a firmer basis from which to protest the extensive claims of others."[16]

"The More Fish We Take"

Most of the countries claiming broader ocean control cited the desire to protect fisheries and other marine resources. For some, the professed concern was little more than a pretext. But others had genuine reason to fear for the health of the fish stocks and other marine resources near their shores. The increasing range and capacity of industrialized fishing fleets rendered even remote waters susceptible to exploitation. In 1947, the US trawler *Deep Sea*, fitted out with onboard freezing and packing equipment, began her maiden voyage to the Bering Sea.[17] In 1953, a "super trawler" was launched in Scotland. Carrying enormous nets and equipped with blast freezers, the new vessels could haul, freeze, and transport much larger quantities of fish than any of their predecessors.[18]

Even as these newly proficient fishing fleets worked the oceans, influential voices insisted that overfishing was not a problem. As late as 1951, a former government fisheries expert named Harden Taylor wrote, "The yield of these fisheries as a whole or of any considerable region has not only been sustained, but has generally increased with increasing human populations. . . . No single species so far as we know has ever become extinct, and no regional fishery in the world has ever been exhausted."[19]

But the inexhaustibility thesis itself was becoming endangered. In 1918, a young Russian fisheries expert named Fedor Baranov had published what would become a seminal work. His conclusion was simple: "The more fish we take from a body of water, the smaller is the basic stock remaining in it . . . [a]nd the less fish we take, the greater is the basic stock."[20] Over time (and after translation), Baranov's analysis became highly influential in the small scientific community engaged in fisheries research. Meanwhile, world events provided powerful anecdotal evidence of the human impact on fish stocks. The revival of several key fisheries during the war years—when fishing activities were dramatically reduced—caught the attention of experts and fishing communities alike.

Coastal countries seeking greater control of fisheries in contiguous waters felt they had all the justification they needed. But where did the spate of new national regulations leave countries whose fishing fleets sailed far afield? In Washington, the realization was hitting home that US companies had much to lose from expanded coastal state regulation. During a congressional hearing, Senator Theodore Green (from seafaring Rhode Island) worried that the Truman Proclamations had set in motion a process that was now harming US industries:

The [fisheries] proclamation was misinterpreted by several nations, which assumed it to mean that the United States would accept the extension of the sovereignty of those nations over the high seas off their coasts. The United States is strongly opposed to such extension of sovereignty on several grounds. The result of such extension of sovereignty out into the high seas could very well be disastrous to our interests in a number of high seas fisheries.[21]

In 1949, the United States announced a policy distinctly friendly to high seas fishing. "It would be morally as well as legally unjustifiable for a resource of the high seas to be fenced off and not fished to the full extent that is needed to produce the maximum sustained harvest from the resource."[22] The policy's author was Wilbert Chapman, an imposing and energetic fisheries expert who had worked inside and outside of government. He emerged as a leading advocate for "maximum sustainable yield" as the guiding principle of international fisheries regulation. Unlike Harden Taylor, Chapman conceded that stocks could be overfished, but he argued that regulation only became necessary when that tipping point had been reached, and not before. After several frenetic years in Washington, Chapman left government to work for the tuna industry, and he remained for the next decade an influential advocate of open high seas fishing.

The high seas fishing industry soon had to worry about international judges as well as national legislators. The setting for judicial intervention was the rich fishing grounds off Norway's coast, an area sprinkled with fjords, rocks, and bays. British fishing vessels worked the area periodically in the early 20th century, and their presence angered the Norwegian fishing community. When British vessels reappeared in the winter of 1947–1948, Norwegian politicians bemoaned the "trawler plague" and pledged to protect their traditional fishing grounds. To do so, Norway relied on maritime "baselines" originally drawn in the 1930s. These lines connected various points on the country's highly irregular coastline. Waters to the landward side of the lines were deemed internal—within which foreign vessels had no rights at all. The generous baselines also pushed the country's territorial waters farther out to sea, giving Norway's fishing community a precious additional margin of protection from foreign competition.

Determined to police these lines, Norwegian patrols periodically arrested British fishing crews in 1948 and 1949. The British government contemplated sending navy vessels to protect the trawlers, but London and Oslo ultimately agreed that an international court could handle the dispute. And in December 1951, the International Court of Justice ruled that Norway's baselines were consistent with international law, a narrow but important victory for coastal countries seeking greater control of nearby waters. The British judge on the court filed a vigorous dissent, warning that the decision would "injure the principle of freedom of the seas and . . . encourage further encroachments upon the high seas by coastal states."[23]

A few years later, an international fisheries conference convened in Rome to help untangle the increasingly confusing web of national fishing regulations. With diplomats from 45 countries in attendance, experts presented more than two dozen papers on fisheries science and regulation. They canvassed the various ways that countries had attempted to regulate fishing, including by mandating certain gear (such as nets that allowed younger fish to escape), limiting fishing catch, and restricting access to fisheries. The delegates considered the experience of the dozen international fishing arrangements that had been devised since the early 20th century. Two distinct models had emerged: regionally focused fishery organizations that covered a certain section of the ocean and other structures designed to deal with the complexities of a particular marine species, such as tuna, salmon, and the fur seal. Even the sanitized conference record makes clear that negotiations were fractious. The delegates were almost evenly divided between those supporting coastal country rights to regulate nearby fisheries (even beyond territorial waters) and those more protective of freedom to fish anywhere on the high seas.

The frigid and turbulent waters off Iceland soon confirmed that the Rome conference had resolved little. In September 1958, Iceland declared a 12-mile exclusive fishing zone, and a reprise of the 1893–1901 crisis unfolded. The British government protested and dispatched warships to protect its fishing trawlers. Over the next several months, fishing trawlers and naval vessels clashed periodically. In early November, an Icelandic patrol boat approached a British trawler and fired several shots at it. Only after the intervention of Royal Navy vessels did Iceland's patrol retreat.

In the end, it was British determination that crumbled. The navy patrols to Icelandic waters were expensive and dangerous. In August 1959, the *Economist* recommended that the government recognize Iceland's claims. "The three-mile convention, which this country still officially upholds, is no longer practical politics," the editors wrote. "Whether it was ever international law is open to dispute. It is simply no use going back to Grotius."[24] Soon thereafter, the British acquiesced to Iceland's claims. The contrast with the resolution of the 1890s dispute, when Iceland had reluctantly yielded, reflected the altered international environment: momentum was now on the side of the countries claiming more of the oceans.

Containment and Conflict

In late April 1956, a small group of observers gathered at the main port in Newark, New Jersey, to watch a curious operation. Swinging back and forth every seven minutes, a large crane loaded metal boxes onto a waiting vessel, the *Ideal X*. Stacked one on top of another, the boxes soon filled the vessel's hold. Once embarked, the lumbering *Ideal X* transported the containers to Houston, where they were loaded onto trucks. This system of "container shipping" was the brainchild of Malcom McLean, a trucking magnate from North Carolina who had grown frustrated as his trucks idled in line at ports. Pushing and prodding reluctant regulators and suspicious unions, McLean devised the system that increased the payload of cargo ships and, critically, slashed the time and manpower required to load and unload vessels. After the *Ideal X* experiment, container shipping spread to the US West Coast, and then eventually to Japan and other parts of the world.[25]

This container revolution took place in the context of a revival of ocean shipping after the Second World War. By the late 1950s, global shipping had surpassed pre-war levels.[26] Shipping to and from Asia and Africa, in particular, increased markedly. And a series of postwar international agreements sought to make ocean shipping ever more routine. Diplomats crafted a new safety convention, updating the one drafted after the *Titanic* disaster. By the late 1940s, governments recognized that a permanent international infrastructure was necessary to help regulate increasingly crowded international shipping lanes. The Inter-Governmental Maritime Consultative Organization (IMCO)—forerunner of today's International Maritime Organization—took shape a decade later. Increasingly detailed international supervision and the logistical breakthrough of containerization would usher in a new boom in ocean shipping.

Yet ocean commerce always had a political context, and the temptation for political leaders to interfere with it occasionally became overwhelming. The leading maritime power, the United States, engaged in several high seas maneuvers during the 1950s that encroached on freedom of navigation. One such foray came in 1954, as the Eisenhower administration sought to pressure the left-leaning government of Jacobo Arbenz in Guatemala. Alarmed that Soviet-aligned Czechoslovakia was shipping arms to Guatemala, Secretary of State John Foster Dulles pushed for a naval blockade of the Central American nation. To heighten its effect, Dulles importuned Britain and other European allies to permit unannounced inspections of their commercial vessels on the high seas. The request unsettled London, and one British diplomat privately wondered whether Dulles was "going fascist."[27] There were concerns inside the US government as well. The State Department's press secretary confided to his diary:

> I think the State Department made a very bad mistake, particularly with the British, in attempting to search ships going to Guatemala. This was done obviously in an attempt to stop arms shipment to the country, but somebody in the State Department (maybe Dulles) forgot that the right of search of neutral vessels on the high seas is one which we ourselves oppose.[28]

Events soon rendered the dispute moot; a CIA-backed force of rebels unseated Arbenz in June 1954. A few months later, the United States again tested legal boundaries in the Taiwan Straits, where a dangerous confrontation had developed between the nationalist forces on Taiwan and the communist mainland government. Soviet-bloc ships were regularly ferrying supplies to the communist government, and the Eisenhower administration was determined to impede the flow. Doing so with US vessels or aircraft was deemed too risky, operationally and legally. Instead, Washington funneled surveillance information to Nationalist forces, who then stopped and searched the vessels. Dulles confided to Eisenhower that the Guatemala and Taiwan Straits tactics were "a little illegal, but no one so far has picked it up." These moves were an early indication that the United States, like Great Britain before it, could be tempted to use its maritime muscle in ways that cut against its professed respect for high seas freedom.[29]

A much more substantial threat to free commerce emerged just a few months after the *Ideal X*'s first voyage as a container ship, when Egyptian president Gamal Abdel Nasser delivered a speech in the port city of Alexandria. For months, Nasser had been feuding with Western leaders about funding for a proposed dam project, and an open break between the nationalist leader and Western governments appeared imminent. His Alexandria speech was anticipated, but few knew what he was planning. By prearrangement, when Nasser uttered the name of the Suez Canal's creator—Ferdinand de Lesseps—Egyptian officials across the canal zone took control of the waterway, which to that point had been managed by the British-dominated Suez Canal Company. Nasser promised the world that the canal would remain open for business, but that business would now be in Egyptian hands.

The legality of the Suez nationalization was complex, and the move did not directly implicate the law of the sea; the canal was squarely in Egyptian territory and therefore generally not treated as international waters. Legalities aside, Nasser's move provoked alarm in Britain and France, where leaders feared that control of the canal would allow Nasser to throttle their economies at will; by 1955, most of Europe's oil supply passed through the canal. British and French leaders convinced themselves that Nasser was a new Mussolini—or even an Arab Hitler, set to embark on a campaign of regional conquest.

The stage was set for the Suez Crisis. After several months of desultory diplomacy, the British and French hatched a plan to wrest back control of the canal that involved interposing Anglo-French "peacekeeping" forces. Israel privately agreed that its forces would advance down the Sinai Peninsula, giving the British and French the pretext they needed for intervention. The operation—launched in October 1956—was a military success but a diplomatic catastrophe. Spurned by Washington, condemned by much of the world, and isolated at the United Nations, the former colonial powers finally withdrew and a UN peacekeeping force replaced their troops. Egypt retained control of the canal, which was littered with ships sunk during the conflict (Figure 4.1).

The confluence of container shipping's birth with these events highlighted the sharp divide between the commercial and political dimensions of ocean governance. Containerization was clearing obstacles to the flow of goods and imposing sometimes brutal new efficiencies in the maritime industry (which would shed thousands of jobs). Yet commercial pressure for ever more seamless and efficient ocean transport was running alongside a persistent sovereign demand for control, including over vital maritime waterways. The two trends were not necessarily in conflict. But as Suez demonstrated, sovereignty struggles over waterways could quickly jam the gears of commerce.

Figure 4.1 Ship sunk to block the Suez Canal; photograph courtesy of United Nations.

"Colonialism of the High Seas"

Two years after the imbroglio at Suez, delegates assembled in Geneva to attempt a diplomatic rescue of the relationship between the oceans and sovereign governments. The conference featured its share of predictable Cold War rhetoric. Soviet-bloc countries chastised Western militaries for conducting large-scale military exercises at sea (Western diplomats were able to point out that the Soviets had done the same). The Soviet-bloc countries had more support when they condemned US nuclear testing in the Pacific, which they characterized as a violation of high seas freedom. "There could be no freedom of the high seas while maritime areas and the air space above them were used for experiments resulting in the destruction of life and resources," said the delegate from Sri Lanka.[30] The concern was not hypothetical. In 1954, radiation from a US atomic test coated a Japanese fishing vessel, the *Lucky Dragon*, and sickened members of its crew.[31]

Changes in the international system since the 1930 conference were evident at this 1958 session. More countries participated and many more came from outside Europe. They brought a new anti-colonial tone, and the defenders of the traditional freedom of the seas found themselves on the defensive. While the 1930 League of Nations conference had featured heated disagreement about the three-mile zone, delegates then generally accepted that maintaining freedom of the seas was for the common good. Some diplomats from the developing world now portrayed the entire edifice of ocean freedom as rotten. What the doctrine of freedom of the seas had actually facilitated, Peru's representative argued, was not freedom but colonial subjugation. The ocean had been free really only for those with the power to take advantage of that freedom. It was "inadmissible that a sort of colonialism of the high seas should be allowed in the name of the freedom of the seas."[32]

Other governments joined the chorus, and some framed the conspicuous wealth divide between maritime powers and others as a product of past maritime freedom. "It was not the fault of the non-maritime states that they did not have large fleets," the Iranian delegate argued. "The reason was that they were under-developed in every way as a result of the policy of colonialism followed by the states which benefited from the freedom of the seas."[33] Pushed onto the defensive, the US delegation tried to recast a Grotian structure as "one of the major equalizing influences in the community of nations, since smaller and less wealthy states were given an opportunity to offset some of the advantages of states with extensive or more productive land areas."[34] In an internal cable to the State Department, the US delegation conceded that their arguments were making few inroads:

> Freedom of the high seas . . . .is regarded as a legal fiction invented by the maritime powers or their lawyers in order to rob the populations of the newly created nations who, since there is no more land, wish to annex the high seas as their lawful right and who is to say to them nay except the greedy maritime powers. It is readily apparent that a new social revolution is bursting forth and burgeoning among the peoples of the newly created states who will insist on re-examining all laws, customs and mores adopted by older civilizations before their birth as a nation and who now proclaim whatever is new is better than the old.[35]

Notwithstanding these tensions, the delegates were productive, at least as judged by the volume of paper they generated. In the space of two weeks, they finalized four distinct treaties and a handful of other documents. The agreements clarified several oceans issues, including the right of coastal states to exploit the resources of the continental shelf. In little more than a decade, the US claims to the continental shelf had gone from a unilateral assertion to a widely accepted international principle. On the question of the ocean's living resources, the conference yielded a separate treaty that struck a delicate balance between the right of coastal states to regulate nearby fisheries and the interests of maritime nations in fishing distant waters. It accorded coastal states a special role in enacting regulation, but insisted (as had the Truman Proclamation) that coastal countries do so in coordination with other states exploiting the fishery. The treaty leaned heavily on a proposed system of international arbitration to resolve the disputes that would inevitably emerge.

In yet another treaty, the delegates outlined the legal rules for the high seas. It defined the high seas as "all parts of the sea that are not included in the territorial sea or in the internal waters of a State" and affirmed that "the high seas being open to all nations, no State may validly purport to subject any part of them to its sovereignty."[36] In these waters, countries had the right to navigate, fish, and lay submarine cables. Alongside these rights, the treaty acknowledged a few responsibilities on the open ocean, including navigating safely and assisting vessels in distress. But the provisions on protecting the ocean's natural environment were skeletal: countries were forbidden to dump oil or radioactive waste but had few other obligations.

This 1958 Convention on the High Seas featured the most explicit international legal elaboration of freedom of the seas. Ironically, it came as the doctrine of high seas freedom faced ever more concentrated criticism. And the frenzy of treaty drafting still left unclear the limits of the territorial sea—and therefore the extent of the high seas themselves. On that issue, the delegates could not produce an answer that commanded sufficient support. Another attempt to define the limits of the territorial sea two years later failed, and the chances of a comprehensive agreement on the limits of national control appeared slim.

The Radicalization of Rachel Carson

Like diplomats, writers in the 1950s were paying increased attention to the oceans, and books on maritime themes appeared frequently on bestseller lists. Herman Wouk's *The Caine Mutiny*, the story of a navy crew ousting a neurotic captain, was a hit in 1952. A few years later, Nevil Shute's *On the Beach* was a top seller. The post-apocalyptic novel featured a US Navy submarine stranded in Australia after a devastating nuclear exchange. As the radiation inexorably spreads, the submarine's commander's final act is to sail his vessel beyond Australian waters and scuttle it on the high seas—a move he believes the US Navy's now silent high command would have approved.

The sea was even more impressively represented on nonfiction lists. In 1955, Anne Morrow Lindbergh secured the number one spot with *A Gift from the Sea*, an ocean-inspired rumination on life, meaning, and the role of women in modern America. Danish explorer and celebrity Peter Freuchen scored two bestsellers in 1958, his *Book of the Seven Seas* and a separate autobiographical account of a year spent in the Arctic. Other well-read maritime books included a British diplomat's diary of his sea voyage to Java, an account of the harrowing sinking of the *USS Indianapolis* during World War II, and a memoir by the captain of the first US submarine to sail under the North Pole.

Yet the author with the strongest claim to literary dominion over the ocean was Rachel Carson. From childhood, Carson had been fascinated with nature, and especially the sea. Her entries in children's essay contests featured marine creatures. A biology major in college, Carson's first extended contact with the sea came during a summer at Woods Hole, Massachusetts, in 1928. She later recalled that trips on boats dredging samples from the sea bottom were "when I first began to let my imagination go down under the water and piece together bits of scientific fact until I could see the whole life of those creatures as they lived them in that strange sea world."[37] Carson's writing first reached large audiences while she was working full time at the US Bureau of Fisheries. In a short 1937 piece in the *Atlantic*, she homed in on the beauty and mystery of the oceans.

> Neither you nor I, with our earthbound senses, know the foam and surge of the tide that beats over the crab hiding under the seaweed of his tide-pool home; or the lilt of the long, slow swells of mid-ocean, where wandering shoals of fish prey and are preyed upon, and the dolphin breaks the waves to breathe the upper atmosphere.[38]

Carson's first book, *Under the Sea-Wind*, told the story of the ocean from the perspective of several inhabitants—a sanderling, a mackerel, and an eel. A decade later, in 1951, she published *The Sea Around Us*, a magisterial account of the oceans that moved from luminous descriptions of the ocean's beginnings to meticulous—and carefully illustrated—descriptions of modern sea life. By the early 1950s, the increasingly successful and influential Carson had purchased a cottage on Maine's Southport Island, where she spent hours exploring the coast, collecting specimens, and turning her discoveries into bestselling prose. In 1955, Carson built on her runaway success with *The Edge of the Sea*, an exploration of creatures that populate the complex world between land and sea (Figure 4.2).

The sense that most animated Carson's work on the oceans was wonder. She said little if anything about politics and diplomacy; her relentless focus was the nature of the oceans and the ubiquity of ocean life, which she found in tide pools "no larger than a teacup."[39] The little that can be gleaned of her view of the ocean's political meaning was vaguely Grotian. She noted that distant and disparate civilizations can be made one by "the unifying touch of the sea."[40] In her early works, Carson also appeared influenced by the Grotian assumptions about the inexhaustibility of ocean resources. In *The Sea Around Us*, she expressed interest in new technologies for tapping ocean riches and speculated without apparent alarm about mining the depths for minerals and fuel.

But human beings appeared in Carson's ocean books mostly as outsiders, only now struggling to understand the ocean that had created them and all life. Echoing Lord Byron from more than a century earlier, she viewed the ocean as essentially beyond human control. "He has returned to his mother

Figure 4.2 Rachel Carson at sea; courtesy of Linda Lear Center for Special Collections and Archives, Connecticut College.

sea only on her own terms," she wrote of mankind. "He cannot control or change the ocean as, in his brief tenancy of earth, he has subdued and plundered the continents."[41] The next stage of Carson's work would alter her view of man's relevance and transform her wonder into alarm.

By 1958, Carson had embarked on a quite different project, which she described to sometimes skeptical friends as "the poison book." From a variety of sources, the writer had heard disturbing anecdotes about the environmental impact of insecticides, and DDT in particular. With her customary tenacity, Carson spent four years sifting and compiling the evidence. The result was *Silent Spring*, now widely regarded as the spark for the modern environmental movement, certainly in the United States. She methodically presented the evidence of insecticides' dangers and offered readers a choice between a "smooth superhighway on which we progress with great speed" toward destruction or a difficult alternative path "that assures our preservation of the earth."[42]

Although *Silent Spring* referred to the oceans only fleetingly, Carson's new awareness of the human threat to the marine realm emerged in a foreword to the second edition of *The Sea Around Us*. Writing in 1961, she warned of the dangers of depositing radioactive waste in the oceans and the knock-on effects of nuclear testing. "It is a curious situation that the sea, from which life first arose, should now be threatened by the activities of one form of that life."[43] Carson had little time to apply her awakening directly to the oceans. By the time *Silent Spring* was published, she was in the grips of cancer. She mustered her strength to defend the book's conclusions against attacks by representatives of the chemical industry, one of whom labeled her "a fanatic defender of the cult of the balance of nature."[44] Carson succumbed in 1964.

In her wake came a new generation of environmental campaigners, many of whom adopted very different tactics. The oceans were a focus for only a subset of these activists, but they produced some of the most iconic scenes of protest against environmental degradation. In 1969, a small group of environmental campaigners in British Columbia, Canada, were casting about for ways to protest US underground atomic tests. Originally calling themselves the Don't Make a Wave Committee, they finally christened the group Greenpeace. The campaigners conceived a plan for an ocean voyage to Amchitka, in the Aleutian Island chain, where the US government had scheduled a test.

There was fresh precedent for protest at sea. In 1958, several Quaker activists aboard a yacht named *The Golden Rule* sailed toward a US atomic test site in the Pacific. Their voyage spurred the US government to quickly enact regulations making it illegal to enter a testing zone. When the Quakers stopped in Honolulu to reprovision, the crew was fined and (after refusing to pay) ultimately arrested. After a stint in a Honolulu jail, some of the crew again set sail for the testing zone. Laboring under a misapprehension about maritime rules, they assumed that the coast guard's jurisdiction over them ended at the three-mile mark. The crew exulted as their ship slipped from US territorial waters into the open ocean. In fact, the Coast Guard had the right to board and inspect any US-flagged vessel on the high seas. Back to Honolulu *The Golden Rule* went.[45]

Jim Bohlen, one of the Greenpeace founders, admired the early Quaker effort but thought limited press coverage had reduced its impact. Accompanied by a clutch of sympathetic journalists (and carrying a substantial quantity of marijuana), Bohlen and other campaigners set sail in 1971 from Vancouver aboard a well-worn fishing vessel. To limit US legal jurisdiction on the high seas, the campaigners sailed under the Canadian flag. But the *Greenpeace* was beset by engine troubles and eventually returned home before the test occurred. A failure in its stated goal, the mission still proved to be a public relations bonanza. As it limped home, the *Greenpeace* and its crew were greeted by hundreds supportive of their cause. Shortly after it docked, a newly acquired vessel, the *Greenpeace Too*, departed for the proposed test site. A tradition of regular resistance at sea was born.[46]

To this point, questions of ocean governance had been largely the province of diplomats, naval officers, and merchants. Activists had played a role; the 19th-century anti-slavery campaigners in Britain had helped forge the prohibition on trading slaves by sea. But the emergence of Greenpeace—and a group that would eventually split off from it, the even more confrontational Sea Shepherd—added something new to the seascape. There now existed a small but determined group of activists who claimed to speak on behalf of the environment, very much including the ocean, and who were willing to engage in direct action to make their point.

As protest at sea became a regular feature of environmental activism, its practitioners discovered that the law of the sea offered mixed blessings. On the one hand, protest vessels on the high seas enjoyed the protection from foreign interference afforded to all mariners other than pirates and slave traders. But that immunity had a vital prerequisite. It was well established that vessels on the high seas had to be flagged—and flagging could be done only by sovereign governments. Activists intent on making points at sea had to ensure that at least one national government was willing to tolerate their behavior. The environmental movement was fast becoming transnational, but the system governing vessels was not.

The Soviets Turn Blue

By the late 1960s, the kind of nuclear tests that the *Golden Rule* and the *Greenpeace* protested had become less frequent. In the early 1970s, the United States canceled its underground testing in Alaska and also curtailed tests in the Pacific (the French continued testing in the Pacific, and their test sites were stalked several times by Greenpeace vessels). But the nexus between the oceans and nuclear weaponry remained important and would ultimately contribute to the development of a comprehensive legal framework for the oceans.

An undersea revolution in nuclear weaponry became very public in June 1959, when dignitaries and high-ranking naval officers gathered in Groton, Connecticut, for the launch of the USS *George Washington*. At first glance, she looked like the dozens of other submarines the facility had built as the United States poured money into its Cold War navy. The *George Washington* featured something unprecedented though: behind her conning tower were 16 tubes, built to house and launch Polaris ballistic missiles with nuclear warheads. Just six weeks after her christening, the submarine successfully launched two missiles while submerged.

The Soviets were not far behind. In late 1961, the K-102 conducted the first ever nuclear test involving a submarine-launched missile. The warhead launched from somewhere in the Barents Sea detonated in a Soviet test range in the Arctic Ocean with more than a megaton of force (many times more powerful than the bomb dropped on Hiroshima). The age of the submarine-launched ballistic missile had begun. This new capability altered the nuclear balance of terror that the superpowers had been building since the late 1940s. In one sense, the existence of missile submarines constantly at sea and ready to launch on a moment's notice made the nuclear balance more stable by ensuring the possibility of retaliation and enhancing mutual deterrence.

But undersea arsenals had disruptive potential as well. It was relatively easy to monitor land-based missiles and even enemy aircraft, but the knowledge that enemy nuclear weapons might be lurking just miles from the coast generated new levels of fear and uncertainty. As submarine-based nuclear weapons moved off the drawing board and into the oceans, Washington and Moscow engaged in increasingly dangerous games of undersea cat-and-mouse. US submarine commanders doggedly tracked Soviet missile submarines, determined to sink them quickly in case of conflict. In 1969, the USS *Lapon* tracked a Soviet ballistic missile submarine for 47 consecutive days as the vessel and its deadly payload meandered a few hundred miles off the United States' eastern seaboard.[47]

The development of Soviet submarine capabilities was just one part of a broader transformation of the Soviet Union into a global maritime power. The ability of the United States to impose a naval quarantine around Cuba during the 1962 missile crisis had galvanized Soviet naval spending. While insisting on its legality, the US State Department's legal adviser acknowledged that the quarantine "involved the use of naval force to interfere with shipping on the high seas."[48] It was US naval superiority that made that interference possible, and Moscow became determined to field its own global navy. In the mid-1960s, the Soviets embarked on a significant expansion of their surface fleet. In 1967, a Soviet admiral declared that "the Soviet Navy has now become an ocean-going navy."[49] Soviet naval squadrons began operating in more distant regions. During the Middle East conflicts of 1967 and 1973, Soviet ships operated in sometimes perilous proximity to US vessels.

As the Soviet navy bulked up and reached out, the country's fishing fleet also transformed. Once focused on regional waters, Soviet fishing vessels moved to the open seas in large numbers. Many had refrigeration capacity, allowing them to store their catch during long-distance voyages. One study of the Soviet fishing industry found that fish caught outside local waters accounted for only about a quarter of the total catch in 1928. By 1960, open seas fishing accounted for more than 75 percent. A decade later, 86 percent of the total Soviet catch came from the high seas.[50]

The extension of Soviet maritime reach may have been a boon to the development of international law on the oceans. For all their animosity, the superpowers both now viewed ocean governance primarily from a global perspective. They shared a desire to stop coastal states from making expansive claims to the oceans. Of particular importance, an ocean increasingly under national control would complicate their ability to deploy missile submarines around the world. The world's major straits particularly preoccupied the superpowers. Gibraltar, less than 10 miles wide at some points, controls entry to the Mediterranean Sea from the Atlantic. The Strait of Hormuz, 29 miles wide at its narrowest point, offers access from the Persian Gulf to the open ocean. The Bab al-Mandeb, about 20 miles wide, guards entry to the Red Sea—and therefore access to the Suez Canal. Most of these throughways are narrow enough that a regime of expanded territorial seas would leave little or no high seas passage at all. And if critical straits were subsumed by territorial seas, the rules at the time dictated that submarines pass through on the surface.

One solution would have been for the superpowers to accept the broader territorial seas but quietly instruct submarines not to surface. The chances of discovery were slim; most coastal countries lacked the kind of sophisticated sonar and sensors necessary to detect increasingly quiet nuclear-powered submarines. As the Soviets and the Americans demonstrated in their interactions, there was nothing sacrosanct about territorial waters. In 1952, the Dominican Republic complained to the United Nations about Soviet submarines operating in their waters.[51] In the 1950s and 1960s, US submarines crept inside Soviet territorial waters as they eavesdropped on communications and analyzed Soviet radar systems. Perhaps the most daring mission took place in 1971, when the USS Halibut sneaked into the Sea of Okhotsk and disgorged divers, who placed a tap on an undersea

communications cable. But incursions into territorial waters carried substantial military and diplomatic risk. Both superpowers preferred that their
submarines be able to move as freely as possible without the risk of being
discovered trespassing. Washington and Moscow agreed on little about international politics, but when it came to maritime rules, common ground
was emerging.

Oil and Water

US and Soviet submarines searched for each other silently, and many of
their most dangerous encounters became known only decades later. By contrast, the business of hunting undersea resources was pursued openly. By
the 1940s, several dozen exploratory wells had been drilled in the Gulf of
Mexico, some more than a mile offshore. Oil prospectors achieved a mile-
stone in 1946 when they built the first offshore drilling rig more than three
miles from the coast. In the early 1960s, the Soviet Union experimented with
offshore drilling in the Caspian Sea.[52] The oil industry developed specialized
equipment that allowed drilling in deep waters.

As offshore oil became a reality, it seemed likely that mineral deposits
lying on the seabed might be next in line for exploitation. In 1965, a mining
engineer named John Mero published *The Mineral Resources of the Sea*.
The author devoted the bulk of the book to the manganese nodules that the
Challenger had documented in the 1880s. The *Challenger* team had seen the
nodules as curiosities, but Mero viewed them as by far the most lucrative
sediment of the deep-ocean floor. Mero presented a hopeful, even rosy, picture of how these nodules could be harvested by the world's nations. "One of
the advantages of many of the mineral deposits of the sea," he wrote, "is that
they are generally equitably distributed throughout the oceans of the world
and are available to most nations that might wish to mine them."[53] Gathering
steam, he predicted that the exploitation of undersea minerals would spread
not only wealth but peace. Mining nodules "could serve to remove one of
the historic causes of war between nations, supplies of raw materials for
expanding populations."[54] The book had an outsized impact and was quickly
translated into Russian, among other languages. "Mero's book launched, if
not a thousand ships, approximately 200 research cruises by the USA, France,
Germany, and the Soviet Union alone."[55]

Those research cruises were expensive to deploy and produced uncertain outcomes. Turning Mero's vision into reality would require overcoming multiple technical hurdles, including designing a collection device that could operate at great depths and devising ways to transport minerals to the surface. Building on some of the advances made in offshore oil drilling, engineers had sketched ideas for all these tasks, but they were in the early stages.

If seabed mining remained a distant vision, the business of transporting oil by sea was fast becoming routine. Every year, more and larger oil tankers plied the ocean. In the 1960s, the first Very Large Crude Carrier was launched, followed soon thereafter by an Ultra Large Crude Carrier. Turmoil in the Middle East, and uncertainty about passage through the Suez Canal, convinced some shipping companies to invest in tankers even larger than the canal could accommodate. The enormous carrying capacity of these vessels helped mitigate the costs of the longer ocean routes that would be required by avoiding the canal. Steady economic growth "enabled the shipyards in Japan and in Europe to press the upper limits of tanker size."[56]

The *Torrey Canyon*, a tanker built in 1959, reflected the intense pressure to maximize tonnage. As built, she had a capacity of 60,000 tons. But within a few years she was modified so that her cargo capacity ballooned to 110,000 tons. On the morning of March 18, 1967, this newly capacious tanker was sailing off the southwest coast of England. Having begun her voyage in the Persian Gulf, she was close to delivering more than 100,000 tons of crude oil to the port of Milford Haven, in Wales. The vessel's operations reflected the increasingly multinational character of the shipping industry. She flew a Liberian flag but carried an Italian crew. The vessel was operated by a US company based in Bermuda, but transported oil on behalf of British Petroleum.

The captain, a veteran mariner named Pastrengo Rugiati, was under pressure. He had been informed that if he did not reach his port that evening, he would have to wait for the next favorable tide, five days later. To trim precious minutes off the voyage, Rugiati ordered the vessel onto an aggressive course, close to the British coast. A series of mistakes put the tanker on a collision course with a notorious reef—the Seven Stones—that had been responsible for dozens of shipwrecks over the years. Just after nine in the morning, the harried captain began a series of belated and botched attempts to alter course. At one point, frustrated by what seemed to be a malfunctioning steering system, Rugiati grabbed the phone to call the engine room directly. He instead reached the galley and was informed that his breakfast was ready.[57]

When the vessel finally altered course, it was too late. The *Torrey Canyon* rammed a reef at a speed of more than 15 knots, and the impact gouged an enormous hole in her hull. When she hit, the tanker was more than 10 miles off the British coast, in what the United Kingdom had long insisted were international waters. Several attempts to move the beleaguered vessel off the reef failed as oil from the vessel's tanks began streaming into the ocean. Increasingly desperate, the British government cast about for ways to staunch the flow. But for the first several days, it was limited in its response because the vessel was stranded in international waters, and its owners were not ready to declare the vessel a complete loss.

The long-standing British insistence on a narrow territorial sea had come back to haunt it. Out of options, the prime minister ordered airstrikes on the disabled tanker, with the aim of sinking it and, it was hoped, igniting and burning away the enormous fuel slick. For hours, Royal Navy and Air Force planes bombed and fired rockets at the hapless ship. But the oil stubbornly refused to burn and, within a few days, it was washing up on both the British and French coasts. The environmental impact was devastating. More than 25,000 birds were killed and sea life was affected for decades. A columnist in the *Observer* saw in the incident the end of traditional ocean freedoms. "The *Torrey Canyon* disaster shows that we can no longer afford to allow seamen complete freedom of the sea—for their mistakes no longer affect only their own lives."[58] Several members of Parliament focused on Britain's ability to respond outside of its narrow territorial sea:

> One other serious gap in maritime law at present is that if there is an accident outside territorial waters there is no established code, as I understand it, which permits a State to take emergency measures to deal with a foreign ship which may be endangering the State concerned unless and until the shipowner waives his rights to the wreck. It seems to me that this is a matter which must be put right.[59]

In the face of criticism, the prime minister conceded that "the old concept of territorial waters is not enough."[60] If Rachel Carson and the first generation of environmental activists recognized that activities on land could threaten the sea, the *Torrey Canyon* disaster forced a reckoning with the potential of ocean activities to wreak havoc on the land. That insight was not entirely new. The three-mile territorial sea originally had defense of the land as part of its justification. But the insidious spread of oil spilled at sea suggested to many that the defensive cordon needed to be drawn much farther from land.

Canada needed little convincing. Just two years after the *Torrey Canyon* disaster, the US-flagged *Manhattan* became the first tanker to complete the Northwest Passage. Its journey, from east to west, was a little more than a proof of concept; the *Manhattan* unloaded a single barrel of oil when it arrived at its destination. But the voyage created enormous controversy in Canada, as environmental and sovereignty concerns mingled and reinforced each other. What would happen, Canadian lawmakers demanded to know, if a *Torrey Canyon*–sized disaster occurred in the Arctic?

Canadian diplomats traveled to Washington to brief their US counterparts on their possible responses, including declaring a portion of the Arctic waters as internal and designating a large "pollution control" zone. The Canadian ambassador conceded that the prime minister was under "enormous pressure" to act. A State Department memorandum described the unsurprising US determination to oppose any such Canadian assertions:

> Such acceptance would jeopardize the freedom of navigation essential for United States naval activities worldwide, and would be contrary to our fundamental position that the regime of the high seas can be altered only by multilateral agreement. Furthermore, our efforts to limit extensions of coastal state sovereignty over the high seas worldwide will be damaged when other nations see that a country—physically, politically and economically—as close to the United States as Canada, feels it can undertake such action in the face of United States opposition.[61]

Not yet willing to simply claim the Arctic waters, the Canadian parliament opted for the pollution control zone, which gave the government significant authority to regulate shipping out to 100 miles. The thousands of gallons spilled by the *Torrey Canyon*, as well as a succession of other ocean spills and near spills, had altered the tolerance for risk. In this sense, new environmental concerns reinforced the post-1945 trend toward greater sovereign control. If the oceans were going to be conduits for dangerous cargoes, rulers on land would demand more control of nearby waters.

There was another current of thought on how to respond to the menace of spillage at sea. Instead of expanding national control, why not beef up international mechanisms regulating ocean commerce? And the multinational maritime infrastructure did get a boost from *Torrey Canyon*. IMCO, the maritime shipping organization launched in 1959, took on new responsibilities as it attempted to improve the safety of tanker shipments. At Britain's request, its council convened in an emergency session in May 1967, and IMCO launched a new legal committee to consider the public and private international law questions raised by the *Torrey Canyon* disaster. Just two years later, a new treaty emerged requiring oil tankers to carry insurance for any damage caused by spills.

Even in the best of times, multilateral action was slow and deliberate, tending to produce incremental results. By contrast, national action to expand ocean control could be quick and decisive. Just as IMCO was gaining new authority, the largest country in South America moved to expand its territorial sea to 200 miles. For more than a decade after the landmark Santiago Declaration, Brazil had held off in asserting the massive territorial sea that several of its regional counterparts had claimed. Within the Brazilian government and public, opinion on the wisdom of a 200-mile sea was split. Several legislators spoke out in favor of expanding the country's waters, and the move had support in coastal communities eager to keep at bay foreign fishing vessels. But an influential contingent in the Brazilian navy was concerned that the country did not have the naval resources to police a territorial sea that large. Foreign ministry officials worried about the international reaction—and particularly the anger such a move would stoke in Washington. In 1970, those concerns finally gave way, and a new government declared a 200-mile territorial sea.[62]

The most serious maritime crisis of the period developed two years later, and the trigger was yet another country's desire to expand its control seaward. In September 1972, Iceland announced a 50-mile fishing exclusion zone, more than tripling the size of the zone announced in 1958. Just as during the earlier crisis, British trawlers tested Reykjavik's willingness to enforce its claim. Some trawlers painted over their names and registration numbers to ensure that Iceland could not pursue them. Others clashed directly with Icelandic patrol boats. The incidents had comic elements: several British fishermen blared *Rule, Britannia!* from their loudspeakers and hurled lumps of coal and other refuse at the patrols. But the gamesmanship eventually turned dangerous. Iceland deployed a special craft designed to cut the fishing lines of trawlers, and the British government sought to protect their trawlers, first by advising them of the location of Icelandic vessels and then by deploying the Royal Navy. The spat had strategic implications as it put in doubt, at least briefly, Iceland's participation in NATO.[63]

Taken together, the moves toward national enclosure of the oceans in the period were remarkable. "The speed and frequency with which nations asserted unilateral claims into ocean space were almost dazzling," one commentator wrote. "No less than 81 states asserted over 230 new jurisdictional claims of varying degrees of importance."[64] The proliferating claims exposed the fragility of international norms regarding the oceans. A veteran Canadian diplomat judged that by the late 1960s, "the law of the sea was in a state of disorder bordering on chaos."[65]

5

The Ocean Constitution

(1970–1982)

In 1964, a bespectacled international bureaucrat named Arvid Pardo received a major promotion: he was asked to serve as Malta's ambassador to the United Nations. The fifty-year-old was not that well acquainted with the country he would represent. Born in Rome to a Swedish mother and a Maltese father, Pardo had lost both parents at a young age. He was cared for by an uncle and educated in France and Italy. During the Second World War, a young Pardo worked for the Italian resistance and apparently attracted the attention of the Gestapo on several occasions. After the war, he made his way through the shattered continent to Britain, where he worked as a dishwasher. Pardo's linguistic talents eventually landed him a job as a junior clerk for the brand-new United Nations organization, which was headquartered in London before its move to New York.

As Pardo labored in the new multinational bureaucracy, his father's homeland was charting its political future. Under British control since 1800, Malta had served Britain during World War II as a listening post and submarine base. It came under sometimes intense Italian and German bombardment but never fell. "Malta stood alone and unafraid in the center of the sea," proclaimed a grateful Franklin Roosevelt, "one tiny bright flame in the darkness—a beacon of hope for the clearer days which have come."[1] Those clearer days produced a desire for independence, and in September 1964, Malta parted ways with Britain. The island-state was admitted to the United Nations a month later. As one of the world's newest (and smallest) nations, Malta needed to build a competent diplomatic corps fast. Arvid Pardo knew the United Nations, was fluent in several languages, and (through his deceased father) had a plausible connection to the island.

As a newly minted UN ambassador, Pardo advocated a major initiative on the oceans. His effort to place the new island nation at the forefront of maritime affairs culminated in an hours-long speech at the United Nations in

November 1967. He foresaw undersea mountain ranges becoming sites for missile silos and anti-ballistic missile systems. He described a rich and varied marine environment on the precipice of new forms of exploitation. Some of his visions bordered on the fantastic. He speculated about floating oceanic fish farms, bounded by walls of bubbles and tended to by dolphins.

Pardo may have been channeling recent science fiction as much as science. Notable writers in the genre, including Arthur C. Clarke (whom Pardo mentioned briefly in his speech), turned their attention to the deep ocean in the 1950s and 1960s. Most famous for his space novels, Clarke saw both the ocean and outer space as frontiers with untapped potential for human use. "The frontier analogy was particularly important for Clarke," writes the scholar Helen Rozwadowski. "[He] was among the first writers to elaborate on it to make sense of human interaction with both oceans and space."[2] In the *Deep Range*, a 1954 novel, Clarke conjured a world in which the oceans fed a human race that had outgrown the earth and colonized the moon and Mars. Marine farmers harvested plankton from vast ocean farms while mini-submarines shepherded whale herds. A decade later, Clarke returned to ocean themes with *Dolphin Island*, which featured a benevolent team of international scientists learning to communicate with the intelligent sea creatures.

The ambassador shared Clarke's fascination with future uses of the ocean, but he saw the human advance into the deep through a darker lens. Where Clarke envisioned mostly abundance and harmony, Pardo predicted a "competitive scramble for sovereign rights over the land underlying the world's seas and oceans, surpassing in magnitude and in its implication last century's colonial scramble for territory in Asia and Africa." The diplomat might have pushed back against this process with a renewed emphasis on the traditional doctrine of the freedom of the seas. After all, Grotius was the most venerable opponent of ownership of the oceans. But Grotius's aversion to appropriation, and the doctrine of freedom of the seas that developed from it, did not extend to marine resources. With respect to living resources, the Grotian framework allowed ocean users to possess what they found on or within the high seas. That "finders-keepers" logic would seem to apply just as well to valuable minerals on the ocean floor.

Malta's ambassador therefore elaborated a different strategy: he urged his fellow diplomats to conceive of the seabed, and even the oceans more broadly, as "the common heritage of mankind." He hoped this new formula would help resist national encroachments without leaning on the crumbling foundations of the traditional freedom of the seas, including the notion that the resources of the oceans were inexhaustible. As Pardo wrote later:

> Malta had become convinced that, because of a number of factors, including the increasing value of ocean space, a total division of ocean space among coastal states was ultimately unavoidable unless the international community replaced the principle of freedom of the high seas, which rested on obsolescent assumptions, with another universally accepted principle more appropriate to a time when ocean space was becoming increasingly used and exploited in all its dimensions.[3]

He urged states to consider "some form of international jurisdiction and control over the sea-bed and the ocean floor underlying the seas beyond the limits of present national jurisdiction, before events take an irreversible course." That international mechanism should wisely manage the seabed in the interest not of particular states but of humanity as a whole.[4] Once again, the diplomat and the science fiction novelist seemed to be drawing from a similar script. Clarke imagined benign, technocratic governance of the ocean provided by a world secretariat and assembly. Pardo believed that something similar was possible with the deep seabed, although he acknowledged that achieving it would require states to suppress their acquisitive instincts. If they could do so, he insisted, undersea wealth could produce a steady stream of funds for the betterment of people around the world.

Pardo's insistence that the world faced a stark choice between national appropriation of the oceans and international control ran parallel to an emerging stream of academic thought. A year after Pardo's UN speech, a microbiologist named Garrett Hardin published a short article in the journal *Science*.[5] Titled "The Tragedy of the Commons," it became one of the most influential and widely cited examinations of environmental policy. Hardin's particular focus was overpopulation, but he advanced the general idea that shared spaces would inevitably be exploited beyond their capacity. Using the analogy of a shared grazing pasture, Hardin insisted that common spaces like the oceans were doomed:

> The oceans of the world continue to suffer from the survival of the philosophy of the commons. Maritime nations still respond automatically to the shibboleth of the "freedom of the seas." Professing to believe in the

"inexhaustible resources of the oceans," they bring species after species of fish and whales closer to extinction.

Hardin saw only two paths to avoiding the tragedy: divvying up and parceling out common spaces, or placing them under some kind of central control with the power to police their use.

For Pardo, the United Nations was the obvious vehicle to provide international control and avoid a carve-up of the ocean by national governments. Concurrent changes in the world organization made many of its members receptive to his clarion call. Decolonization was in full gallop, and newly independent African and Asian countries—joined by a smattering of others, like Malta—were becoming a diplomatic force; their numbers alone guaranteed influence in diplomatic conferences. In 1958, a total of 30 states from Africa and Asia participated in law of the sea negotiations. Fifteen years later, that number had jumped to 82. Differences between the established and affluent countries and the new and often poor states—now sometimes referred to as the north-south divide—emerged as a potent new political dynamic.

A few years before Pardo's speech, the "global south" had coalesced diplomatically as the G-77. The bloc had no unified position on maritime issues, and its members included countries with large coasts, countries with limited coasts, and those with no direct access to the sea. But they shared a fear: that the wealthy countries would leverage their superior technology and resources to plunder the seabed's apparent riches. Malta's ambassador provided the developing world a conceptual tool for resisting that outcome. In raising the specter of a new round of colonialism and emphasizing an international distribution of revenue, Pardo's conception "was ideally tailored to the [G-77's] purposes, and provided a strong position around which its members could rally."[6]

The speech galvanized international negotiations about the seabed. "Few speeches heard at the [UN] General Assembly have triggered off as much activity as Pardo's address," one observer wrote later.[7] In the bustle of activity that followed, the Maltese diplomat had reason to assume that Washington was receptive to his ideas. In a speech aboard a new US ocean research vessel in 1966, US President Lyndon Johnson had also cautioned against "a race to grasp and to hold the lands under the high seas." Anticipating Pardo's formulation, Johnson even called for the deep seas and the seabed to be "the legacy of all human beings."[8] The receptivity from Washington turned out to be short-lived, but Johnson's openness and the relative novelty of the seabed issue allowed Pardo to advance discussions in ways that would have been impossible on issues with more established national positions.

A seabed committee convened in late 1967, and its members advanced a moratorium on seabed mining that narrowly passed the General Assembly. The United States, the Soviet Union, and a number of other industrialized countries opposed that measure (which, like all Assembly resolutions, was nonbinding).[9] The opposition to a moratorium foreshadowed bitter fights to come over mining, but common ground remained possible. In 1970, the Assembly overwhelmingly endorsed a set of broad principles for the use of the seabed.[10] These included that its exploitation should be for the benefit "of all mankind" and that uses of the deep seabed should be exclusively peaceful. Both superpowers voted for the resolution.

That resolution marked the beginning of a broader and more intricate negotiation. Within a few years, the international deliberations on the seabed merged with a renewed effort to resolve other ocean issues, including the breadth of the territorial sea. There was disagreement about whether it was wise to link traditional law of the sea issues with the more novel question of managing the seabed, and the large maritime powers would have preferred to keep the threads separate. But the developing world's interest in internationalizing seabed resources proved impossible to resist. In December 1970, the Assembly called for a new international conference to address seabed and other law of the sea issues. For the third time in a dozen years, the international community would try to structure comprehensive rules for the oceans.

Building the Blocs

By the time the Third UN Conference on the Law of the Sea convened in December 1973, the vagaries of Maltese politics had rendered Pardo himself a mere observer. The diplomat who could claim to be the godfather of the conference watched from the side as battle lines from earlier maritime negotiations reconstituted. In one camp were the coastal states, which possessed extensive coastlines but not large navies or merchant fleets. These countries thought primarily in regional terms and wanted to control as much ocean space as possible and reap the rewards in terms of resources. As in the past, the Latin American states were among the most aggressive, and several of them favored territorial seas that extended all the way to 200 miles.

The "broad margin" countries—whose continental shelves extended beyond 200 miles—formed a particular subset of the coastal state group. They advocated national jurisdiction over these prolonged shelf areas. If it had been accepted that countries should control the resources of their continental shelf, why should that principle not extend to the limits of the shelf rather than to an arbitrary line at 200 miles? Some of the most prominent broad margin states were Argentina, Brazil, Canada, and India.

The large maritime powers—the United States, the Soviet Union, Britain, France, and Japan—became known as the "group of five," and their representatives met intermittently throughout the conference to compare notes and, at certain moments, coordinate strategy. One journalist noted that the group "affected a certain secrecy about itself, which was designed to save the Communist delegates the embarrassment of public association with the capitalists."[11] These powerful states wanted to maintain broad freedom of navigation, including for warships, and opposed the expansion of territorial seas. For the superpowers, safeguarding the ability of their warships (and aircraft) to pass through strategic chokepoints, including straits, was pressing. One maritime corridor was of particular concern to Washington: the Strait of Gibraltar. Its importance was underlined during the 1973 Middle East war, when the United States funneled military supplies to Israel from bases in western Europe. Fearful that they would become targets of the Arab oil embargo, key European states refused to give overflight permission to US transport aircraft. That made the strait a vital conduit for what became a massive airlift. As Ann Hollick has argued, the episode accentuated US concern about the legal status of straits:

> The paramount lesson of the Middle East conflict, in Defense Department eyes, was the unwillingness of NATO allies to provide refueling and overflight rights in a conflict they did not support.... Defense concluded that an internationally guaranteed right of access through international straits was indispensable to the projection of U.S. force.[12]

Washington and Moscow may have been on opposite sides of the 1973 conflict, but their shared concern about expanding territorial seas and the possible absorption of key international straits endured.

One country outside the elite group of maritime powers was the People's Republic of China, which had just displaced Taiwan as the representative of China at the United Nations and was still shaping its diplomatic profile. In an early speech to the UN, China's ambassador called for each state to determine its own territorial sea "according to its geographical features and its needs of economic development and national security."[13] China itself had announced a territorial sea of 12 miles in 1958, but it robustly endorsed the right of other states to go much further, casting the issue as a lever against great-power domination. "We firmly support the just struggle initiated by [Latin] American countries in defense of the 200 nautical-mile territorial sea and their own marine resources, and resolutely oppose the maritime hegemony and power politics of the superpowers."[14]

An often-muted presence at the negotiating table, China did establish an important new reality in the South China Sea soon after the discussions began. In January 1974, Chinese forces seized the Paracel Islands from the beleaguered government of South Vietnam. The operation involved a brief but fierce battle between Chinese and Vietnamese naval and ground forces. South Vietnam pleaded for help from the US fleet in the region, but Washington demurred. "We have cautioned our forces not to get involved," a Defense Department spokesman said at the time.[15] At the next law of the sea negotiating session, five months later, South Vietnam's ambassador reminded the delegations of his country's plight, noting that a "neighboring power" had illegally seized the islands. He pledged that Vietnam would never relinquish sovereignty over them, which was essential "to fix the limits of its national jurisdiction over the contiguous ocean space."[16] The seizure of the Paracels was a footnote to the negotiating conference, but it foreshadowed regional struggles to come and the significance of even small islands to broader ocean claims.

Landlocked countries and those with limited coastlines formed another substantial group, eventually numbering more than 50 delegations. These countries were concerned that if coastal state rights expanded considerably, their own access to fishing and other maritime resources would diminish accordingly. Given that most fish live in shallow waters, expanded national control might leave them little access. Throughout the conference, they argued that their traditional rights to fish and use marine resources required protection, and some members of the group insisted on a "right to fish" in coastal waters on equal terms as the coastal state itself. In a sense, this bloc of states was a natural ally of the maritime powers in opposing excessive coastal claims. But fully landlocked states had a concern the maritime powers did not: securing the right to access the sea by navigating on rivers and crossing the territory of other states.

A host of other countries had unique interests, including archipelagic states such as Indonesia and the Philippines (which wanted to control the ocean separating their many islands), small island nations (eager to ensure that they acquired all the ocean privileges of other states), and countries whose territory abutted major international straits (concerned about preventing harm to their shores from use of the straits). As negotiations progressed, countries with significant land-based mining operations formed an ad hoc group to ensure that their own interests were protected as seabed mining was negotiated. Other delegations had even more specific concerns. Canada wanted to ensure that the environmental measures it had just enacted to prevent pollution in the Arctic comported with the new treaty, and Turkey worried about what increased territorial seas would mean for Greek influence in the Aegean.

Overlaying all these alignments and particular interests was the evolving and often bitter divide between the developed and developing world. The large and diverse G-77 struggled to form a coherent position at the conference. "The number of cross-cutting interests among G-77 nations is astounding," two observers wrote.[17] But developing countries were unified in their skepticism about freedom of the seas, at least as defined by traditional maritime powers. Mexico's president acknowledged in a 1974 session that the doctrine might not have been invidious in intent, but he insisted that it had been in practice:

> While it is true that when the major Powers had established the basic principle of the freedom of the seas some three centuries before, they had not done so with the deliberate intention of subjugating or exploiting the smaller Powers, far less those States which did not then exist, it could not be denied that the developing States that now expected to be able to exploit the marine resources off their coasts were frequently prevented from doing so by obstacles and situations which derived from the principle of the freedom of the seas.[18]

Others were even less charitable, directly linking freedom of the seas with colonial occupation and domination. Indonesia's representative, who sought to designate the ocean between his country's various islands as internal waters, described his country as a victim rather than a beneficiary of ocean freedom:

> The waters and passage routes between our islands which have been an essential factor in unifying our country were transformed by outside Powers

into avenues for conquest. Thus, from our point of view, we have suffered from the consequences of the freedom of the seas expounded by Grotius.[19]

Ivory Coast's representative painted a similarly bleak picture of historic ocean freedoms. "From the beginning this doctrine was an instrument for the maintenance of the predominance of the most powerful maritime nations. . . . Thus it comes as no surprise that the new nations, discovering the considerable role of the sea in their development process, rejected . . . this pseudo-freedom of the seas which really served only to maintain their dependence."[20] Against these protests, the traditional maritime powers again attempted to defend the concept. The British ambassador insisted that freedom of the seas had "served the international community well" but noted that it had never been an unqualified freedom and should not be such now.

As these debates played out, a small but vocal group of activists roamed the hallways and meeting rooms. Largely from the United States, activists split into several distinct camps. Environmental groups, with the Sierra Club in the lead, formed one pole. Global environmentalism had received a major boost in 1972 when hundreds of diplomats, scientists, and activists gathered in Stockholm for the United Nations' first International Conference on the Human Environment. Transferring that momentum to the ocean negotiations, environmentalists sought strong language protecting the ocean and its natural resources from pollution. The plight of the world's whales was a focal point for certain activists, and during the negotiations they circulated a petition with more than 20,000 signatures demanding additional protections for whale populations.

Another notable activist group focused more on building the international architecture for ocean governance than preserving marine species. These "global governance" advocates prioritized the development of international cooperation, organization, and law. Quaker and Methodist groups were the most prominent in this category, and in both New York and Geneva their meetinghouses served as venues for strategy sessions. Miriam and Samuel Levering were central figures. "Sam's and my interest in environmental protection, though sincere, was definitely secondary," Miriam Levering recalled. "We were part of the Woodrow Wilson-Franklin Roosevelt generation of world order activists, not the more recent generation of environmental activists."[21]

The Leverings and the team they assembled came to be known as the "Neptune Group," and they divided their efforts between lobbying in

Washington and attending negotiating sessions in Geneva and New York. At the negotiations, the group published a newspaper that contained updates on various issues, interviews with delegates, and alternative solutions for negotiators. Sometimes at the request of diplomats, they brought in outside experts to brief them on technical topics, including how much revenue seabed mining might generate. At certain moments, and with mixed success, the group even served as an informal liaison between blocs of countries. Some of the attempted bridge-building was too ambitious; China and Vietnam—at loggerheads over the Paracel Islands—refused to attend a planned session on the South China Sea. Other efforts yielded better results, and diplomats credited the activists with improving the dialogue between developed and developing countries.

"Doodling on Documents"

There was ample time for bridge-building. Negotiations extended for almost a decade, as diplomats shuttled between Caracas, Geneva, and New York. In one key respect, the negotiators began handicapped. In many other multilateral negotiations, an expert body, often the UN's International Law Commission, presented a draft text as the basis for negotiations. In other contexts, subsets of states provided a draft. In the case of the United Nations Charter itself, for example, the leading allied powers—the United States, the Soviet Union, and Great Britain—had fashioned a draft in private and then presented it to the rest of the world for discussion and amendment.[22]

Neither option was viable in this context. Cautious states refused to delegate initial drafting, and so the negotiations began with many open questions but no provisional text. To help remedy this situation, an informal group arose in the conference's early days. Norwegian ambassador Jens Evensen recalled being approached in 1973 by several diplomats, including the US ambassador and a representative of the Soviet bloc. "[They] said we will never be able to succeed without a drafting group; would you be willing to form a very informal drafting group consisting of heads of delegations and experienced international lawyers?" The Evensen group, as it came to be known, met regularly during the conference, often funneling possible texts to the formal negotiating committees.[23]

If the lack of a formal text was an impediment to a rapid resolution of the conference, so were the negotiating rules that the states adopted.

A "gentlemen's agreement" urged negotiators to "reach agreement on substantive matters by way of consensus" and recommended against voting "until all efforts at consensus have been exhausted."[24] In the event of a deadlock, that agreement provided for a mandatory cooling off period and then two-days' notice before any votes would take place. This consensus arrangement was particularly important for larger powers, who worried about being outvoted by coalitions of smaller states. Decolonization had in key respects democratized international negotiations, and major powers found themselves increasingly outnumbered. As one legal scholar noted, "The consensus approach permits the maintenance of an egalitarian procedure which in practice may assure that multilateral negotiations reflect the real geopolitical power of the participating nations."[25] That informal agreement aside, the written rules for negotiations stipulated that a two-thirds majority would prevail, and the possibility of formal voting always loomed in the background.

To many participants, the negotiations seemed interminable. A 1976 dispatch from the *New York Times* noted that "the snail's pace leaves many negotiators grumbling, doodling on their documents or roaming restlessly around the crowded meeting rooms."[26] (Lead US negotiator Elliot Richardson was an accomplished sketch artist, and some of his drawings were later auctioned off.) Weary diplomats often decamped from the conference rooms for more informal meetings at nearby restaurants. Perle du Lac in Geneva was an especially popular retreat.[27]

Public and even governmental attention to the process waned as the years of negotiation accumulated. Using (and perhaps exceeding) his authority as president of the negotiations, Hamilton Shirley Amerasinghe finally urged the creation of a single draft negotiating text, which gave the sessions a focus they had lacked. The adroit Sri Lankan diplomat became an important engine of progress; his standing was such that when the Sri Lankan government removed him from his post as ambassador after a domestic political change, the negotiating states voted nonetheless to keep him as president of the conference. His untimely death in December 1980 complicated the already chaotic rush to finish the process.

Elements of the Deal

The decade-long deliberations ended with an elaborate compromise package. The fact that the negotiations produced one treaty—rather than a series of distinct agreements, as in 1958—was critical. Reduced to its barest essentials, the final agreement gave the powerful maritime states what they most wanted on freedom of navigation while a far larger group of countries, many of them from the developing world, secured what they most desired on seabed mining and control of nearby fisheries. That overarching compromise was embedded in a text that included dozens of other smaller compromises and accommodations designed to ensure broad support.

Finally resolving the long uncertainty about the extent of the territorial sea, the negotiators agreed that "every State has the right to establish the breadth of its territorial sea up to a limit not exceeding 12 nautical miles."[28] For the Latin American countries, that provision meant abandoning visions of full sovereignty out to 200 miles. But the agreement also represented a final defeat for the centuries-long British effort to hold the line at three miles. Within the territorial sea, the coastal state had broad powers to enforce safety and environmental regulations. The one significant limitation on the power of the coastal state over the territorial sea came through the venerable doctrine of "innocent passage." Unless something happening on board a vessel engaged in innocent passage directly affected the coastal country, it was urged not to interfere with shipboard activities. The Convention recognized that foreign warships have the right to innocent passage just as merchant ships do, although it established a variety of restrictions on their activities. Warships are not permitted, for example, to engage in weapons practice, dispatch or receive helicopters or other aircraft, collect information that might be harmful to the coastal state, or disrupt communications of the coastal state. Importantly, the Convention also required submarines to surface and show their flags in another country's territorial sea.

Coastal countries, the convention made clear, were free to enact certain basic rules about passage through the territorial sea. These might include establishing traffic lanes or other measures to protect marine resources. But the coastal state could not impose fees or taxes on ships passing through and it could not discriminate against the vessels of any particular state. While the coastal state might have criminal jurisdiction over foreign nationals on board vessels in territorial waters, the Convention urged coastal states not to exercise it unless the alleged crime had some direct bearing on their security. One question that the Convention did not resolve explicitly—and that has since emerged as a significant area of disagreement—is whether foreign warships must notify or seek authorization from the coastal state before proceeding with innocent passage.

The Convention's most significant innovation by far was the Exclusive Economic Zone (EEZ), a new maritime zone that could extend up to 200 miles from the coast (where most fish resided) (Figure 5.1). The Convention granted coastal states the right to manage the economic resources within this zone as well as to control the seabed under the water column. That right included the power to set regulations to protect marine resources. For countries watching their visions of a vast territorial sea disappear, the EEZ was a vital consolation. In a nod to the geographically disadvantaged states, the Convention urged coastal states to allow others access to the resources of their zone whenever possible, but it left it up to the coastal state to determine when to do so. Canada's delegation labored to ensure that there was a special provision recognizing the right of states dealing with "ice-covered areas" to enact regulations on shipping to protect the environment within the EEZ.

The negotiations struck a delicate compromise on the precise legal status of the EEZ; the final text simply left unclear whether it should be considered part of the high seas (as major maritime states preferred) or whether it represented its own distinct maritime zone (as coastal states wanted).[29] The ambiguity allowed maritime powers to argue that all traditional high seas rules applied in the EEZ, except for a limited set of exceptions regarding natural resources. For their part, coastal countries could plausibly assert that the zone out to 200 miles was somehow distinct. Differences on this point often centered on the right of foreign military vessels to operate freely in a country's EEZ. In an unusually frank 1976 meeting between Secretary of

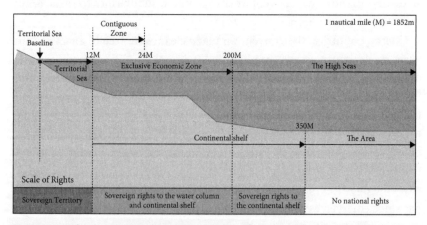

Figure 5.1 The Convention's new maritime zones; courtesy of Law of the Sea Primer Project, Fletcher School of Law and Diplomacy, Tufts University.

State Henry Kissinger and more than a dozen foreign ambassadors, Kenya's envoy insisted that the EEZ would inevitably evolve in a way that allowed for more restrictions:

> We have to take the exclusive economic zone as a fundamentally new concept, not just some rights from the territorial sea and the high seas. . . . Regarding military uses, it is not feasible in the future for coastal states to permit extensive maneuvers and weapons testing. The economic zone is completely new. Freedom of the seas must be changed. You should leave the law to develop.[30]

Other countries put on the record their own interpretations of the new ocean zone. In one of his closing interventions, Brazil's ambassador stated his country's view that "the provisions of the Convention do not authorize other States to carry out military exercises or manoeuvres within the exclusive economic zone, particularly when these activities involve the use of weapons or explosives, without the prior knowledge and consent of the coastal State."[31] The susceptibility of the EEZ to national regulation soon became a major point of contention between coastal countries and marine powers—one that still rankles today.

Another question that bedeviled negotiators was marine scientific research in the EEZ. Governments with active ocean research programs, led by the United States, wanted these areas to remain open for study. But many coastal states suspected that this research could be used to exploit ocean resources and wanted the right to approve any missions. The Chinese representative at one point made clear his view that ocean research was often little more than thinly veiled espionage:

> It was common knowledge that the same super-Power which [supports] "fundamental scientific research" or "freedom of scientific research," constantly sent large numbers of "research vessels" or "fishing fleets" equipped with electronic devices into the coastal waters of other countries or beneath those waters for the sole purpose of carrying on espionage activities.[32]

The final text required coastal state permission for research in the EEZ, but it also suggested that approval for research should be routinely granted. Geographically disadvantaged states secured a limited right to fish in nearby EEZs, but only when the coastal state determined there was a surplus of fish.

Beyond the expanded territorial sea and the EEZ lay a significantly diminished high seas. The 1958 High Seas Convention had defined that area as "all parts of the sea that are not included in the territorial sea or in the internal waters of a state." The innovation of the EEZ—and the ambiguity about whether it should be considered high seas—rendered a similarly concise definition in the new Convention impossible. That considerable ambiguity aside, the Convention reiterated the freedoms that ocean users had traditionally enjoyed in this realm: the right to navigate (by sea or overflight) and the right to fish. It also included other freedoms of more recent vintage: the right to lay submarine cables and pipelines, the right to construct artificial islands and structures (such as deep-sea oil rigs), and the right to conduct research. The high seas could not be appropriated by any state, and all states, whether coastal or landlocked, enjoyed access.

One of the most important pieces of the compromise package was its provisions for international straits. The innovative answer, apparently the brainchild of British negotiators, was to create a new type of "passage" to accompany the right of innocent passage in territorial waters. "Transit passage" gave all vessels and aircraft the right to navigate through recognized international straits so long as the transit did not threaten the countries that abutted the waterway. Unlike innocent passage, however, submarines were permitted to pass through straits while submerged and surface warships could engage in their normal activities. The coastal states could not suspend the right of passage through the straits—at least not legally. This regime gave the maritime powers the assurance they needed that their naval forces would be able to deploy around the globe.

Archipelagic countries also secured one of their principal objectives, acquiring the right to declare baselines conforming with the general shape of the archipelago and then declare the waters within those baselines to be their own. This structure gave countries that could meet the Convention's definition of an archipelagic state (including the Philippines and Indonesia) substantially more territorial water and eliminated the need for confusing rings of national waters around each island within the archipelago. Other countries retained the right to pass through these new archipelagic waters.

The Convention fully endorsed the unilateral Truman Proclamations of 1945 by recognizing the right of coastal states to control and exploit the resources of their continental shelves, out to a distance of 200 miles. And if a coastal state could demonstrate that its shelf extended beyond that point, it was eligible to claim rights on even more undersea territory, out to 350 miles or more. (Beyond 200 miles, however, states would be obligated to pay international royalties on drilling revenue.) These provisions opened the door for further national appropriation of the seabed, but they also created a complex process through which states should demonstrate empirically that their continental shelves extended beyond 200 miles.

Flags, Ports, and Courts

The Convention was most innovative in its elaboration of maritime zones: the territorial sea, EEZ, and international straits. When it came to regulation of shipping and other activities at sea, its ambitions were more modest. An array of international conventions, including many negotiated under the auspices of the International Maritime Organization, already covered international shipping. The long-established principle that, on the high seas, the flag state should have nearly exclusive control over vessels remained undisturbed. The only situations in which it was permissible for a state other than the flag state to detain a vessel on the high seas was when there was reasonable suspicion of piracy or slave trafficking, when a vessel was not flying a national flag, or when it was engaged in unauthorized broadcasting. The Convention added little to existing international law regarding piracy, and most of its provisions were identical to those in earlier treaties.

The continuing power of the flag state to govern high-seas activities raised the question of the identity of the flag state and its connection to the vessels flying its flag. The phenomenon of flags of convenience began in the 1920s, but it had mushroomed by the early 1960s. A UN report issued during the conference noted that tonnage sailing under flags of convenience now accounted for more than a quarter of total shipping. And the migration to flags of convenience accelerated during the decade-long negotiations. By 1979, more than 30 percent of global tonnage sailed under open registry (Figure 5.2). The basic criticism that the practice was little more than a circumventing of effective regulation remained potent:

A great many of the companies through which open-registry owners operate are merely "brass-plate" companies. Thus, repeated risk taking can be indulged in by unscrupulous shipowners, secure in the knowledge that a bad reputation can be erased by simply changing the name of their

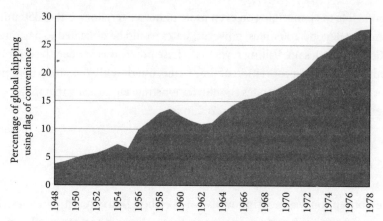

Figure 5.2 Growth in flags of convenience (1948–1978). From B. N. Metaxas, *Flags of Convenience: A Study of Internationalisation* (Aldershot, UK: Gower Publishing, 1985), 23.

company or ship. And the blame for a "missing" log-book can always be put onto the former owner, whose brass-plate company has been dissolved![33]

Events at sea ensured that the dysfunctionalities of the flag-of-convenience system got plenty of attention in the latter stages of Convention negotiations. In March 1978, the Liberian-flagged tanker *Amoco Cadiz* ran aground off the Britanny coast. The ship's rudder jammed during a storm, and the vessel began drifting toward the coast. A series of mishaps—plus the tanker's enormity—made arresting its drift almost impossible. The ship's anchor broke, and the lines that tugboats secured to the massive tanker would not hold. A few hours later, the tanker ran aground. More than 1.5 million barrels of oil poured into the sea, much of it washing up on French shores.

The French government responded by mandating that tankers remain farther from the coast, but French politicians also directed fire at the flag-of-convenience system. In truth, it was far from clear that lax regulation by Liberia was to blame for the disaster. The ship was no rustbucket; it had been built in Spain just four years before the accident and carried modern safety and navigation equipment.[34] Under the auspices of the Liberian government, a board of inquiry convened in the weeks after the disaster, and its deliberations focused on possible design and manufacturing defects in the ship's steering mechanism. In the face of complex evidence, French diplomats still pushed for what they viewed as a simple and elegant solution: phasing out flags of convenience. In that effort, they had support from a diverse group of countries, including Soviet bloc states and certain developing countries.[35]

But the leading-flag-of convenience countries—including Panama and Liberia—mounted a vigorous defense. A Liberian government minister chided the French for their accusations and insisted that "flags don't sink ships."[36] Most major maritime powers (including the United States) proved unwilling to force the issue and upset a system that benefited major shipping interests. In the end, the Convention nodded at the idea that there should be a relationship between the flagging state and the vessel—calling for a "genuine link." But it established no more clarity than that and no procedures for ensuring that such ties existed. That murky language ensured that the flag-of-convenience system emerged from the negotiations essentially unscathed.

Concern about unseaworthy vessels and ill-trained crews was not enough to overcome the flag-of-convenience system, but it did result in several innovative provisions in the Convention recognizing the right of port states to investigate dangerous vessels. "Prevention and punishment of marine pollution incidents left exclusively to the discretion of the flag state," one scholar wrote, "are now delegated to a truly universal system of control and surveillance."[37]

During the last years of the negotiations, countries worried about dangerous vessels collaborated to monitor vessel safety and help compensate for flag-state deficiencies. In the wake of the *Amoco Cadiz* spill, several European countries agreed to share information about safety violations on ships frequenting their ports. Participating countries committed to a regime of vessel inspections and to sharing their findings with other members. A few years later, an even more elaborate agreement (launched in Paris, fittingly) established procedures for how to ban problematic vessels from all participating ports.

As in so many areas, the Convention's provisions on the rights and responsibilities of flag states and port countries included vague formulations and complex language that would almost inevitably lead to disagreements. The emerging text was full of artful compromises designed to paper over differences that could not be resolved directly through the negotiations. Individual countries would naturally seek to interpret those provisions in a manner most favorable to them, and a mechanism was needed "to protect the agreed package of compromises against destruction through unchallengeable unilateral interpretations."[38]

The simplest answer for resolving future disputes would have been to hand them to an existing international court. The International Court of Justice (ICJ), launched in conjunction with the United Nations, had already developed a substantial track record on maritime disputes, including the 1949 *Corfu Channel* decision, which dealt with the status of international straits. The 1951 *Fisheries* case resolved the dispute between Norway and the United Kingdom and provided guidance on how states could draw maritime baselines. During the decade that the Convention was being negotiated, nearly a third of the court's docket touched on maritime matters. And as the negotiations concluded, the ICJ delivered a lengthy opinion about how to divide the continental shelf between Libya and Tunisia.

Yet not enough countries were comfortable with the ICJ to make it the sole venue for resolving disputes. Instead, the Convention allowed countries to choose from a menu of dispute resolution mechanisms. The ICJ was one option, but negotiators decided that the Convention should also have its own dedicated court—a new International Tribunal for the Law of the Sea. For those countries wary of formal international courts altogether, there was yet another choice: binding arbitration before an ad hoc group of experts. In a further nod to the sensitivities of sovereign states, the Convention allowed states to exclude certain kinds of disputes (including those involving military activities) from the mandatory dispute settlement process.[39]

The Mining Apparatus

These elements of the compromise had mostly come together by 1976, but hashing out seabed mining took much longer. On this issue, the tense relations between the poorer states and the developed world were fully on display, with the developing world concerned that rich countries were set to reap a lucrative undersea harvest. That concern was not groundless. The mining giant Kennecott Copper had conducted survey cruises for manganese nodules in the late 1960s. West German and Japanese conglomerates, with active government support, were also searching for appropriate concentrations of nodules. The French and the Soviets were in the hunt as well.

US intelligence agencies may have contributed to anticipation of a seabed bonanza through their own machinations. In 1968, a specially designed US submarine, the *Halibut*, located a Soviet missile submarine that had disappeared earlier that year in the Pacific. Realizing that it had a unique opportunity to explore a Soviet submarine and its missiles, the Central Intelligence Agency crafted a plan to recover it without Soviet knowledge. The plan involved constructing an enormous vessel able to lift the Soviet sub off the ocean floor without its haul being visible to satellites or other observers. The CIA teamed with Global Marine, a corporation specialized in deep-water drilling, and the billionaire Howard Hughes to make the ship a reality.

The elaborate project inevitably attracted attention, and the agreed-upon cover story was that the *Glomar Explorer* was being built for deep sea mining. As one of the industry officials involved pointed out, the undeveloped nature of the seabed mining industry helped render the story plausible:

> We liked the deep sea mining as a cover because, one, we knew a little something about it and really we had done a little bit of work in the mining business. . . . [I]t was a logical story and you could design a mining ship because who knew what a mining ship looks like?[40]

Certainly not the United Nations. In May 1974, the UN secretary general presented a report to the General Assembly on the economic implications of seabed mining. "By most estimates," it concluded, "nodule mining will prove to be a commercially profitable operation. Although the physical, technical and logistic problems are formidable, the existing technological capability can allow the industry to work." A key exhibit in the UN assessment was the *Glomar Explorer*. The report included schematics of the ship and a discussion of its likely mechanism for bringing nodules to the surface. The international media mostly mirrored the UN's credulity, reporting excitedly on the *Glomar Explorer*'s potential to vacuum riches up off the ocean floor.

While negotiators toiled in New York, the *Glomar Explorer* arrived at what intelligence officials had identified as the site of the Soviet submarine wreck. A Soviet vessel shadowed the US ship and inquired about its intentions, to which the crew dutifully responded "deep ocean mining." After several failed attempts, the crew succeeded in raising a portion of the doomed vessel off the seabed floor, up through nearly three miles of ocean, and into the vessel's hold. The operation was "unquestionably the most ambitious and the most audacious ocean engineering effort ever attempted."[41] The engineering was more competent than the cover story. By April 1975, several US newspapers reported on the real purpose behind the voyage.

The *Glomar Explorer*'s mission may have been a sham, but the West's determination to exploit undersea resources had, if anything, hardened in the years between Pardo's speech and the commencement of the Convention negotiations. In the United States, for example, Lyndon Johnson's conciliatory approach had yielded to a tougher line from his successors. One element driving this change was the shock of the oil embargo put in place by OPEC during the 1973 Middle East crisis. Its sharp economic impact reminded Western states of their economic vulnerability and the increasing importance of offshore resources. Potential mining states became "even less inclined than they had been before to accept a seabed regime that placed powers of production control in the hands of a developing country majority."[42]

Developing countries, for their part, mostly remained committed to international control of the seabed and to a mechanism for sharing the profits. After sometimes raucous debates within the G-77—during which some countries accused others of being tools of the Western powers—the bloc retreated from an insistence that all seabed mining occur under international control. A dual-track emerged in which both international authorities and private companies would have the right to mine. Even that dual-track was remarkably ambitious: it called for the creation of an International Seabed Authority (ISA) that would grant licenses for mining under the high seas. Countries or companies that wanted to mine in what was referred to as "The Area" would have to pay royalties and also designate a parcel of seabed of anticipated equal value for the ISA itself to mine, through an entity known as the "Enterprise." It was recognized that turning the ISA into a viable mining entity would require access to emerging technology, and so the Convention required seabed mining companies to sell technology to the ISA if it had no other way of obtaining it. The ISA would be able to generate revenue from its own mining operations and distribute them (through unspecified mechanisms) to the broader international community.

Most industry officials viewed the proposed apparatus with deep misgivings bordering on revulsion. The notion of being compelled to transfer technology they had labored to create was particularly galling. Northcutt Ely, a lawyer representing U.S. Steel, proved to be a particularly dogged opponent of the mining scheme emerging from the negotiations. He encouraged Congress to pass its own seabed mining legislation that would "assure continuing American access to the minerals of the seabed, as a freedom of the seas, and free of foreign domination, control, or veto."[43] The mining company Kennecott Copper hired one of the former US negotiators, Leigh Ratiner, and he helped stir congressional concern about the treaty process.

Washington Changes Tack

By 1980, the shape of a final treaty was becoming visible. The industrial-ized countries had at least secured the right for their companies to mine the seabed, although the ISA would still have significant control. Lead US nego-tiator Elliot Richardson made the case in a 1980 *Foreign Affairs* article that the draft convention achieved the vital US objective of ensuring mobility for its naval forces. He acknowledged persistent tensions on seabed mining but evinced optimism that the package might secure US support.[44] In August, Richardson even predicted that future historians would see the negotiation process "as the most significant development of the rule of law since the founding of the United Nations itself."[45] Richardson's sanguine appraisals appeared just as the Republican Party released its platform for the 1980 elec-tion. The document contained a warning about the state of the law of the sea negotiations:

> Too much concern has been lavished on nations unable to carry out sea-bed mining with insufficient attention paid to gaining early American access to it. A Republican Administration will conduct multilateral negotiations in a manner that reflects America's abilities and long-term interest in access to raw material and energy resources.[46]

When it took office, the administration of Ronald Reagan ordered US negotiators not to participate further in substantive talks until it could con-duct a full review of US policy. The US negotiating team also underwent major change, as the administration sought to ensure that its negotiators shared its more skeptical perspective. Opposition to the Convention was hardening in Congress as well as the White House. Treaty skeptics styled themselves the "seahawks" and they watched the negotiations suspiciously. John Breaux, a congressman from Louisiana, depicted the proposed Convention as nothing less than a decisive moment for the US position in the world:

> We will *not* meekly submit to the New International Economic Order; we will *not* mildly consent to the ruin of our system of values as a free enter-prise society.
> We will *not* quietly retreat from our rights and responsibilities as the leader of the Free World; we will *not* capitulate to our political and military adversaries.[47]

Conservative *New York Times* columnist William Safire described the negotiations as "history's greatest attempted rip-off."[48] Unsurprisingly, Ronald Reagan himself seemed persuaded that less regulation of the open ocean was better. A quote that leaked out of a National Security Council meeting suggested that the president was an instinctual Grotian. "We're policed and patrolled on land," the president reportedly said. "I kind of thought that when you go out on the high seas you can do what you want."[49] Reagan's anti-regulatory instincts contributed to a broader skepticism regarding what the Republican administration saw as the excesses and dysfunctionalities of many multilateral organizations.

In early 1982, US officials finally presented their counterparts with a 43-page document—known as the "Green Book"—outlining a variety of proposed changes to the text of the Convention, mostly focused on the seabed mining section. A group of 11 developed Western states, with Canada in the lead, gamely worked through the proposed changes to see what was achievable. But the moment was late and the gulf too wide. When it became clear that its proposed changes could not be implemented, the United States delegation called for a formal vote on the treaty text and was one of only four states (the others were Turkey, Venezuela, and Israel) to vote against it. A total of 130 countries voted for the treaty and 17 abstained.

If the Convention was too intrusive for Washington, it was not robust enough for Arvid Pardo, the intellectual godfather of the process. He viewed the end product mostly with dismay. Too much of the ocean had been pushed into sovereign hands, he worried:

> The magnitude of this appropriation, which has been carried out under a cloud of misleading rhetoric, is unprecedented in history, in terms both of the area and of the resources involved, and is grossly inequitable not only to landlocked and geographically disadvantaged states but also as between coastal states themselves.[50]

At the same time, the "common heritage" concept that he had championed had been only partially implemented. He was concerned that the International Seabed Authority was not strong enough to do its job.

These misgivings by Pardo and others mingled with relief and pride at the undeniable accomplishment. The final Convention text ran to 194 pages and included nine annexes. The conference organizers hurried to set a date to celebrate its completion and formally sign the document. But even that task involved last-minute drama. The ceremony had been slated to take place in Venezuela, where the negotiations had commenced nearly a decade before. Awkwardly, the Venezuelan government had soured on the treaty, because of long-standing maritime disputes with several neighbors. Jamaica, the future home of the International Seabed Authority, offered a solution. On December 10, 1982, at the Rose Hall International Hotel near Montego Bay, dozens of diplomats and ambassadors signed the Convention. The process had been under way for so long that public reaction was muted. China's *People's Daily* celebrated the signing primarily as a victory for the Third World. The Soviet news service TASS criticized "fierce attempts by the Reagan Administration to undermine the international accords."[51] US public opinion was divided, mostly along political lines, on the decision not to sign.

For some developing country diplomats, the Convention represented a decisive refashioning of the Grotian view for the purpose of achieving greater equity between states:

> Not since the work of Grotius, to whom all honour is due, will a text containing a comprehensive law of the sea wield such influence. *Mare liberum* was the result of one man's genius, sense of justice and imagination. The Convention, by contrast, is the work of hundreds of men and women, representing many millions of others. It is our earnest hope that the new Convention, being the result of our own collective and collaborative efforts and not merely the bequest of an era that has passed, will be applied so as to bring order and predictability to our use of the oceans and, *above all, to achieve a new distribution of the oceans' wealth, not as economic aid or charity but as a matter of legal right.*[52]

Just as the Dutch had sought to break the Portuguese monopoly on access to the rich Indian Ocean trade, the world's new countries saw themselves as loosening the grip of their powerful counterparts on marine resources and striking a blow against a version of ocean freedom that had facilitated exploitation. Freedom of the seas endured in parts of the Convention, but it was now more limited and accompanied by a formidable rival philosophy—the oceans as the common heritage of humanity.

The reality that the world's leading maritime power was not on board hung over the final ceremony. Certain diplomats, including India's ambassador, attempted a conciliatory tack, reminding US diplomats of how much they had contributed to the process. "The Conference has over a period of time not only benefited by the specialized knowledge and experience of the United States in several aspects of the subject-matter of its work, but also tried to accommodate the essential interests of that country in a fair and reasonable manner." Others gently but unmistakably warned the United States not to undermine the Convention. Nigeria's ambassador said the United States "cannot now afford the discomforts of isolation, especially over a treaty the negotiation of which accorded central priority to its declared vital interests."[53] Ambassador Tommy Koh of Singapore, serving as chair of the negotiation process, asked pointedly that "no nation put asunder this landmark achievement of the international community."[54]

6

Jockeying for Position

(1982–1995)

As the negotiations over the Convention neared their end, the first sustained naval combat since the Second World War erupted in a remote corner of the South Atlantic. The *casus belli* was the Falkland Islands, a British possession populated by about 1,800 people and many more sheep.[1] Situated fewer than 200 miles from Argentina's mainland, the islands had long been claimed by it. To Argentines, the islands were the Malvinas and continued British control was an offensive vestige of a bygone era. During the 1960s and 1970s, as colonial possessions around the world gained independence, London and Buenos Aires parleyed intermittently about a transfer of sovereignty. The talks stalled, however, not least because the islanders resisted any change in the status quo.

If the door of negotiated transfer appeared closed, Argentina's ruling generals decided that a window had opened for military action. British forces on the island were few, and the planned withdrawal of a British naval survey ship suggested that London lacked the means to defend its far-flung possession. Meanwhile, Argentina's leaders had ample domestic incentives to force the issue and distract the population from spiraling inflation and brutal repression of political opponents. The Argentine assault on the Falklands began on the evening of April 1, 1982. The badly outnumbered British contingent surrendered the next day.

Stung by the defeat, the government of Margaret Thatcher decided that it would not acquiesce to Argentine control. But the Royal Navy that the prime minister called on to lead Britain's response was far from the globe-straddling force it had once been. Navy budgets had been in decline since the 1960s, and the fleet had slowly shrunk. Writing just before the Falklands conflict, a former British minister warned that the failure to modernize ships was rendering the Royal Navy "increasingly obsolescent."[2] In the harried days after the invasion, the government pieced together a task force, partly by requisitioning several civilian cruise liners to serve as troop transports.

With nuclear-powered submarines in the lead, the faded naval power's armada began the almost 8,000-mile sprint to the South Atlantic.

The nature of naval conflict had changed dramatically in the decades since the Second World War. Both British and Argentine forces were equipped with missiles able to threaten opposing vessels from dozens of miles away. Recognizing the danger they would face, even from a distance, the British promptly declared a "maritime exclusion zone" of 200 miles around the islands. As the conflict unfolded, the British expanded this zone and made more draconian their restrictions, warning both military and civilian vessels that they could face military action if they entered. (The Argentines declared their own maritime zones, but their relative naval inferiority meant that these had less significance during the conflict.)

Not all the maritime zones declared during the Falklands imbroglio were exclusionary in nature; the combatants also created a "Red Cross box" in the ocean, a roughly 20-mile by 20-mile area north of the islands. The zone allowed hospital ships from both sides to operate in a safe, fixed, and widely known location. Shortly after the invasion, the British government outfitted a cruise ship, the SS *Uganda*, to serve as the first British hospital ship since the Korean War. To ensure that its neutrality would be respected, the ship sailed to the prescribed area unescorted, unarmed, and with visible Red Cross markings. Three smaller British oceanographic vessels served as "ambulances," ferrying wounded back to the *Uganda*. By most accounts, the system worked well, and British and Argentine ships even occasionally exchanged prisoners and patients.[3]

The hospital vessels were busy. On May 2, a British submarine sank the *General Belgrano*, a pre–World War II cruiser. More than 300 Argentine sailors died and dozens were wounded in the attack, which marked the most significant hostile sinking since World War II—and the first by a nuclear-powered submarine. The high death toll and the fact that the *Belgrano* had been several dozen miles outside Britain's 200-mile exclusion zone made the attack instantly controversial. The Argentine government decried the sinking as a "treacherous act of armed aggression," and less partisan observers wondered whether targeting the ship was necessary militarily. Necessary or not, the *Belgrano* sinking seems to have helped the British effort (Figure 6.1); the Argentine surface fleet essentially withdrew to port and played little role in the remainder of the conflict.

Britain's control of the oceans around the Falklands did not render its forces immune. Argentina's air force still posed a significant threat. A few

Figure 6.1 Britain's *Sun* celebrates the *Belgrano* sinking; courtesy of *The News*.

days after the *Belgrano* sinking, an Argentine Exocet missile ripped into the HMS *Sheffield*, killing 20 sailors. During the next several weeks, five more British vessels succumbed to aerial assault. But Britain eventually established enough sea and air control to place a substantial ground force on the islands. It advanced steadily toward the Argentine strongholds, which surrendered on June 14. A muscular British contingent remained in place as a deterrent.

The remoteness of the area limited the conflict's impact on civilian shipping, but on June 8 an aircraft bombed and strafed a Liberian-flagged tanker, the *Hercules*, which was sailing from the Virgin Islands to Alaska. The attack took place about 500 miles from the Falklands, well outside the exclusion zones created by the combatants. The *Hercules* limped into a Brazilian port but was eventually scuttled (in part because an unexploded bomb was lodged in its hold). It later became clear that Argentine aircraft had conducted the attack, perhaps thinking that the vessel planned to resupply British forces. For years after the conflict, the company that owned the ship sought compensation from the Argentine authorities, first in Argentina and then in the United States. After years of litigation, the case finally ended in the US Supreme Court, where the justices ruled that Argentina could not be sued in US courts.[4]

The Falklands War and the fate of the ill-starred *Hercules* served as reminders that the international community had never rebuilt effective protections for shipping during conflict; the legal wreckage of the world wars remained mostly untended. The naval technology on display in the conflict— some of it a generation behind what the superpowers' navies fielded—left little doubt that a major navy intent on disrupting shipping lanes could do so with even less difficulty than was the case during the Second World War. Freedom of navigation rested on the rarity of naval conflict, not the strength of international rules governing it.

Convention in Limbo

The Falklands War intruded only briefly on the final Convention negotiations; indeed, the hesitancy of many countries to ratify the laboriously negotiated document posed a more serious threat to it than military conflict. The Convention required 60 ratifications to enter into force, and the first years after the signing ceremony were not encouraging. A handful of countries ratified quickly, including Fiji, Zambia, Mexico, and Jamaica. But none of the major maritime powers appeared ready to follow their lead, and certainly not the United States. The US State Department's point person on ocean policy informed Congress that the agreement was fatally flawed. Publicly, the United States held out hope that the Convention would never come into force. In private communications, US diplomats were less sanguine. "In the absence of strong US diplomatic pressure, virtually all western countries are likely in time to join," a State Department memorandum to the National Security Council concluded. "Even with US pressure, many may participate in the Convention."[5]

The Reagan administration was determined at least to apply that pressure. Donald Rumsfeld, who had served as Gerald Ford's secretary of defense, toured Europe with the aim of "mov[ing] our allies away from early commitments to sign or ratify that treaty."[6] He presented a litany of complaints about the agreement's seabed mining arrangements. The mission produced an agreement among the United States, France, the United Kingdom, and West Germany to avoid disputes regarding seabed mining sites.[7] The Western powers pledged to coordinate on the designation of mining sites, raising the possibility of an international structure parallel to the Convention's envisioned International Seabed Authority.

As Rumsfeld's talking points indicated, US hostility to the treaty remained rooted in seabed mining. Washington was content with most of the other Convention provisions, including the new Exclusive Economic Zone. Indeed, in March 1983, Ronald Reagan proclaimed the United States' own EEZ, covering more than 7 million square miles. Pacific toeholds, including Hawaii, the Marshall Islands, and Guam, added tens of thousands of square miles. Only France, which benefited greatly from its own Pacific possessions (and French Polynesia in particular) could claim an EEZ of comparable size. In declaring its zone, the Reagan administration was careful not to endorse the idea that countries could restrict freedom of navigation in these areas. The EEZ, the proclamation said, "remains an area beyond the territory and territorial sea of the United States in which all States enjoy the high-seas freedoms of navigation, overflight, the laying of submarine cables and pipelines, and other internationally lawful uses of the sea."[8]

In some capitals, the spectacle of the United States taking advantage of the Convention's generous new maritime zones while refusing to join the agreement was too much to bear. "It is perfectly obvious," a Soviet spokesperson fumed, "the USA is now doing everything it can to impart a semblance of legality to its unilateral actions and try to legalize its absolutely illegal claims in relation to the world's oceans and their riches."[9] Discontent was not restricted to adversaries. As Washington worked to skirt the seabed mining structure through agreements with European states, Canadian and Japanese leaders fretted that Washington was undermining the Convention. Tommy Koh, the Singaporean diplomat who led the negotiating conference through its final stages, vented his frustration. "Reagan wants everything the Treaty gives," he said, "but not any of the obligations."[10] In 1985, the UN General Assembly urged all states to sign the Convention and asked states to desist from actions "undermin[ing] the Convention." Only Turkey and the United States opposed the resolution.[11]

The United States leaned on the notion of customary international law to claim the Convention's benefits without committing to it. The formal US position was that most of the Convention's provisions—on the territorial sea, innocent passage, and the EEZ—reflected the widespread practice of states and were therefore legally in force even for countries that chose not to join the Convention. The seabed mining regime, from Washington's perspective, was deeply controversial and therefore *not* part of customary law. It was a plausible argument in a few respects but strained in others. State practice on the breadth of the territorial sea had been inconsistent for years. How could the Convention's 12-mile rule be considered customary law so soon? And if it could, then why not the provisions on seabed mining?

For all the skepticism about the US position, even among close allies, Washington's opposition had an impact. As with most multilateral treaties, the Convention accorded states a limited window within which they could sign without ratifying it (when that window closed, states could join only by ratifying). For countries on the fence, that option was a valuable one, because it allowed them to express broad support for the treaty, participate in certain treaty processes, but not assume the full legal obligations of a treaty member. In December 1984, several governments that had not yet signed the treaty grappled with whether to do so. The debate was particularly acute in West Germany, which had already been designated as the home for the future Law of the Sea Tribunal. Washington made clear to German diplomats its strong preference that they not sign, and Germany had its own reasons to hesitate. Several German companies were pursuing seabed mining projects, and they disliked the Convention's provisions on sharing revenue, paying fees, and transferring proprietary technology. In late 1984, a divided German cabinet chose not to sign.[12] With less handwringing, Margaret Thatcher's British government also opted against signing.

Other maritime powers that had signed the Convention balked at ratifying. This group included Australia, China, Greece, France, Japan, the Netherlands, Spain, and South Korea. Indeed, by the end of 1984, only 14 states had ratified the Convention, with Egypt, Mexico, and the Philippines as the largest. The next year saw another smattering of ratifications, including Bahrain, Iraq, and Sudan. In 1985, a Western country finally ratified. Long wary of foreign fishing vessels, Iceland seized the chance to secure control over marine resources out to 200 miles. But by the end of 1985, the

Convention remained well short of the 60 ratifications needed to enter into force. It was far from certain the painstakingly crafted document would ever take legal effect. And even if it did, it might be crippled without the participation of so many powerful maritime players.

Enclosing the Northwest Passage

With the Convention's fate uncertain, the national enclosure of ocean space continued in certain areas of the world. In particular, a long-standing dispute between the United States and Canada over the status of the often ice-bound Northwest Passage grew more intense. In the 19th and early 20th centuries, dozens of explorers and sailors risked death attempting to complete the journey. The SS *Manhattan*'s controversial 1969 trip marked an important test of the Passage's commercial viability, however, and by the 1970s, icebreakers and research vessels were traversing the Passage on an almost annual basis.

Interest in the route was expanding beyond the shipping and research communities. In August 1984, the *Linblad Explorer*, a passenger ship designed by a Swedish-American entrepreneur, departed Newfoundland with the aim of becoming the first cruise ship to make it through. The ship carried 98 well-heeled passengers and 93 chilled bottles of Dom Perignon. Three weeks later, and with a bit of help from the Canadian Coast Guard and a commercial icebreaker, the ship arrived in Point Barrow, Alaska. "We found that small window of time during which waters in the region were free enough from ice to allow our passage," the captain reported.[13] The champagne was uncorked, and a luxury cruise route was christened.

Planning for a more sober passage began the next year, this time by the US Coast Guard's icebreaker *Polar Sea*. The United States informed Canada of the intended voyage but, critically, did not seek Canadian permission. That omission created a stir. "Those who would diminish Canada's Arctic presence by challenging our legal position in the Passage would take away some of our self-regard and distinctiveness," a Canadian maritime expert warned. "The Canadian Government that presided over a loss of jurisdiction in the Passage would have much to answer for."[14] Defensive government ministers noted that there would be Canadian government observers aboard the US ship, and that the two countries had "agreed to disagree" about the precise status of the Northwest Passage. However much Washington and Ottawa tried to finesse the voyage, the fundamental issue of sovereignty—crystal-lized in whether the United States needed to seek permission—would not go away. "It's a lousy piece of work by the [Canadian] government," thundered opposition leader Jean Chretien, who argued that Canada should insist on formal permission. As the *Polar Sea* began its journey, Canadian activists buzzed the ship in a rented plane and dropped on its deck a canister filled with Canadian flags.[15]

On this issue, Canadian public discontent was clearer than the government's legal position regarding the Passage. Successive governments had moved Canada closer to formally claiming the Northwest Passage while still leaving a measure of ambiguity. In the 1970s, Canada expanded the territorial sea it claimed around each of its Arctic islands from three to 12 miles and established its 100-mile environmental zone with special rules for the passage of ships (Figure 6.2). (Its diplomats labored to protect that latter provision during the Convention negotiations.)

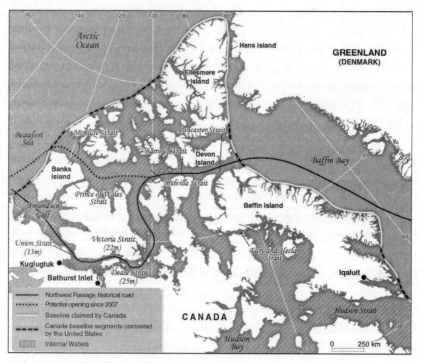

Figure 6.2 Canada's enclosure of the Northwest Passage; map courtesy of Frédéric Lasserre and the Quebec Council for Geopolitical Studies.

The *Polar Sea*'s controversial transit finally pushed Canada to take the next step. In 1986, Canada issued straight baselines in the Arctic that made parts of the Northwest Passage internal Canadian waters, subject to Canadian authority. The basis of the Canadian claim was its uncontested ownership of the Arctic archipelago north of the Canadian mainland. Canada's baselines meant that other nations might not have the right to pass through the area without permission. Washington stuck to its view that the Passage was an international strait, through which all ships enjoyed the right to navigate. The divergence emerged as "one of the most significant bilateral legal issues in the Canadian-United States relationship."[16]

The Canadian move was a window into how the Convention had changed—and not changed—the relationship between national governments and ocean space. The clarity about the new limits of the territorial sea meant that Ottawa felt unable to simply expand its territorial sea to claim the waters it wanted. Instead, Canada's desire for control was channeled through the Convention's framework, specifically by drawing maritime baselines that incorporated substantial ocean real estate. The fact that Canada, a country with a proud commitment to multilateralism, moved unilaterally on this front hinted at the pressures the Convention would face in containing national aspirations for ocean control.

Zone Defense

The process of negotiating the Convention had changed dramatically how countries interacted with the ocean. Most had welcomed the concept of the EEZ early in the negotiations, and the Convention's long gestation meant that the economic zone became part of international practice well before the treaty was completed. Many developing countries declared EEZs in the mid-1970s, including major coastal states India, Nigeria, Pakistan, and the Philippines. In 1982, the International Court of Justice declared that the EEZ "may be regarded as part of modern international law."[4] As the Convention waited in purgatory for the requisite number of ratifications, a group of additional states announced their own zones. The Soviet Union created an EEZ the year after the United States. Malaysia and Mexico soon followed suit. Turkey, one of the few states to vote against the Convention, declared its economic zone in 1986. Within the space of a decade, nearly a third of the world's oceans had come under a form of national jurisdiction.

Whether the new international lines would have meaning at sea depended largely on the ability of coastal countries to police their new ocean domains. Many countries lacked the means to monitor a large EEZ, let alone effectively confront trespassers. But some coastal states struck back against interlopers, with Argentina proving particularly assertive. Even during the Convention negotiations, it had forcefully challenged fishing vessels operating within 200 miles of its coast. In October 1977, its patrol boats fired on Bulgarian and Soviet trawlers and apprehended their crews. In 1986, Argentine patrol vessels confronted a fishing trawler from Taiwan. For several years, Thailand and Vietnam regularly seized each other's fishing crews when they crossed (or were accused of crossing) the new maritime boundaries. Longtime adversaries India and Pakistan did the same. Nicaragua arrested several dozen fishermen from Honduras operating in the former's EEZ. Those coastal states with the resources began beefing up their capabilities to monitor ocean space. Ireland in 1994 procured additional purpose-built aircraft to prevent intrusions in its EEZ by foreign vessels, primarily from Spain.

One of the most dramatic changes in fishing patterns occasioned by the EEZ occurred in the Grand Banks off Newfoundland. Long known for prodigious fishing yields, the area attracted vessels from around the world, many of which employed new trawling techniques. By strictly enforcing its EEZ in 1977, Canada ousted the polyglot fishing vessels from the cod-rich area. But the stocks of cod benefited little from the departure of international fishing vessels. Seeing an opportunity to bolster Newfoundland's weak economy, Canadian companies in the 1980s assembled a fleet of trawlers to take the place of the foreign ships. In short order, this all-Canadian fleet was pulling from the sea nearly as much fish as the multinational fleets had harvested. By the early 1990s, the cod all but disappeared.

If that experience demonstrated that national control did not necessarily produce enlightened stewardship, it at least showcased the ability of a national government to respond dramatically when disaster struck. The Canadian government in 1992 imposed a complete moratorium on cod fishing. Furious fishermen protested, and a near brawl broke out at one point as they challenged government officials. ("I didn't take the fish from the God damned water!" a frustrated government minister responded.)[17] Fish processing factories shut down and trawlers idled in port. Those whose livelihoods depended on cod set about waiting for their return.

The changed maritime disposition impacted other realms as well. Treasure hunters found that they had to be more cautious about the missions they planned. Outraged by the 1985 stripping of a sunken vessel, the Indonesian government much more aggressively monitored foreign diving trips. In 1988, Indonesian officials detained Australian and American divers who were searching for sunken treasure in Indonesia's EEZ.[18] Oceanographers were perhaps even more affected. The Convention's negotiators had haggled at length over what foreign scientific research would be permissible in the EEZ. Countries with active research communities sought to keep EEZs open for international research, but many poorer states viewed this research with suspicion, concerned that rich countries would figure out how to exploit their marine resources before they could.

> The prevailing image was of the developed states' fully equipped research vessels hovering off the coasts of developing countries struggling to become new nation-states under severe handicaps, including lack of essential knowledge about their patrimony. Developing states were particularly concerned about being placed at a competitive disadvantage in negotiations concerning offshore oil and gas fields or fisheries, if a distant state or multinational or state corporation . . . knew more about their EEZ than they did.[19]

In the end, the Convention required those conducting marine research to obtain the permission of the coastal state but made clear that refusals to grant permission should be exceptional. In some EEZs, approval turned out to be anything but routine. Oceanographers based at California universities, for example, sometimes struggled to get permission from the Mexican government to conduct studies inside that country's EEZ. In other places, researchers encountered long delays, last-minute withdrawals, and onerous requirements for conducting research (including, in some cases, taking on board observers or translating any findings into the language of the coastal state). "It's getting worse all over the world, not just with Mexico," a frustrated scientist complained. "Since countries have been claiming their 200-mile limits, the formality of the paperwork and the explanations needed beforehand become more and more detailed."[20] A State Department lawyer catalogued US complaints about how other countries were, in its view, abusing the Convention's provisions on marine research.[21] (To demonstrate its good faith, the United States allowed foreign scientists to conduct marine research in its own EEZ without seeking permission.)

More consequential to major navies were the Convention's ambiguities about what foreign military vessels could do in EEZs. While the United States and other maritime powers believed that EEZs remained the equivalent of the high seas when it came to naval activities, many coastal states disagreed. Several of these countries put laws on the books restricting foreign military activities in the EEZ. International law scholar Bernard Oxman, who had served as a US negotiator, asked, "If the economic zone is not high seas, does that open the door to gradual erosion of the rights and freedoms of all states in the economic zone?" He saw in these assertions signs that coastal states "have taken what they could get, waited a decent interval, and then struck out seeking more."[22] Writing in 1990, a US Navy officer expressed concern that national legislation constituted "potential time bombs . . . primed for use."[23] For the moment at least, the threat was latent. Coastal states rarely attempted to enforce their restrictions on foreign naval activity within their EEZs.

As with the EEZ, many countries adopted the new 12-mile territorial sea even before the Convention was finalized. After some hesitation, the United Kingdom and United States both yielded to the temptation of a larger territorial sea (in 1987 and 1988, respectively). Only a few countries claimed a smaller territorial sea than the Convention allowed. Singapore, the Asian trading hub, maintained a three-mile zone while Norway stuck to its four-mile sea. Japan and Korea both opted to keep three-mile territorial seas for certain areas in order to maintain high-seas shipping routes that would have otherwise been subsumed by territorial sea. In the Aegean Sea (although not in the Black Sea or the Mediterranean), Turkey kept a six-mile territorial sea, and it insisted that its nemesis Greece do the same. But these situations were unusual; most countries claimed as much sea as the Convention allowed.

The new 12-mile limit raised law enforcement issues as well as diplomatic ones. Because only the coastal state could legally take police action within the 12-mile zone, seaborne criminals needed to fear only one country's patrol forces. On the high seas, by contrast, any government had the right to stop and seize vessels suspected of engaging in piracy. A coastal state that could not police its own (expanded) national waters therefore created a potential safe haven for marauders. In the mid-1980s, maritime criminality was particularly prevalent in southeast Asia, where boats carrying refugees from Vietnam were often targeted.

A small group of countries, most in Latin America, maintained a territorial sea beyond 12 miles. Ecuador, El Salvador, Nicaragua, Panama, Peru, and Uruguay all stuck to their 200-mile territorial sea, at least until the

Convention came into force. On at least one occasion, their insistence proved deadly. In April 1992, a US C-130 transport plane was flying off the Peruvian coast, well seaward of the 12-mile mark. Several Peruvian fighter planes approached the US aircraft in an apparent attempt to enforce the country's claimed 200-mile sea. The fighters signaled for the US plane to land, and when it failed to do so, they strafed the plane twice. The pilots landed the crippled plane, but one crewman died in the incident.[24]

Other countries began exploring the Convention's more complicated possibilities for expanding their ocean rights. The most important of these was declaring an "extended continental shelf," which allowed a state to claim the seabed out to 350 miles (or even more, in certain circumstances). The Convention required countries to document their claim with scientific evidence about the nature of the seafloor in the area claimed. With that goal in mind, the Canadian government in 1984 committed millions of dollars to a seabed mapping project. Not all governments waited for the scientific evidence to arrive. Chilean dictator Augusto Pinochet announced in September 1985—on the anniversary of the coup that had installed him in power—that his country was claiming the maximum amount of seabed. "Today, on this patriotic anniversary," Pinochet said, "looking at the future and protected under the new international law that regulates the law of the sea, my Government has decided to proclaim our legitimate right over the continental shelf."[25]

Another way that coastal countries began tugging on the Convention's framework was in drawing the "baselines" that were the starting point for the new maritime zones. As Norway had demonstrated in the 1930s, plotting these lines was a particularly important (and complex) exercise for states with heavily indented or irregular coastlines. The Convention's rejiggering of ocean zones put new emphasis on the process. As discussed, Canada's claim to the Northwest Passage relied on baselines strung between its Arctic islands. For other countries eager to maximize their ocean realms, drawing long baselines between promontories on the coast was tempting. Doing so not only moved the territorial sea and EEZ seaward, but it also created potentially expansive internal waters to the landward side of the baseline within which other countries did not even enjoy the limited right of innocent passage. For these reasons, governments often kept a jealous eye on how their neighbors were drawing lines and whether their lines comported with the Convention's own criteria. In late 1985, Thailand objected to how Vietnam had established its baselines. Libya advanced one of the most aggressive baseline determinations, insisting that the entire Gulf of Sidra was internal waters.

The elbowing over baselines and rights within the new maritime zones could not obscure the remarkable progress many countries made in resolving potential areas of maritime friction. Around the globe, in pairs and sometimes in larger groupings, countries fashioned agreements to reckon with the pending reorganization of the oceans. Countries accustomed to fishing in what were now the EEZs of other countries often managed to negotiate access for their nationals and an array of bilateral fishing agreements appeared. The easing and then end of the Cold War created an even more conducive atmosphere for maritime negotiations. In 1987, Mikhail Gorbachev called for a détente in the Arctic. He envisioned a "zone of peace" and alluded to the potential for expanded foreign shipping via the Northern Sea Route, the maritime passage running near the Russian Arctic from the Barents Sea to the Bering Strait.

The superpowers also modeled effective maritime negotiations for the rest of the world. They agreed on a limited program of joint ocean research, and in 1988 a US oceanographic ship sailed into the Soviet EEZ in the Bering Sea to conduct research. Two Soviet scientists joined a US team from the Scripps Oceanographic Institution to survey the seabed in the area.[26] Two years later, Moscow and Washington made even more dramatic progress in that region, finalizing a maritime boundary in the Bering Sea (one of the world's longest) that resolved a long-standing irritant. In a hint of dynamics to come, however, Russian opposition figures protested that Gorbachev had ceded too much to the Americans.[27]

Crossing Lines to Make a Point

In March 1986, the US cruiser *Ticonderoga* and two destroyers operating in the Mediterranean steered south, in the direction of the Libyan coast. The ships soon crossed a point in the sea that Libya's ruler, Moammar Gaddafi, had deemed the "line of death." Libya was attempting to enforce a baseline that extended almost 300 miles, from one end of the Gulf of Sidra to the other. Gaddafi's government claimed that all waters to the landward side of the line were internal, within which no foreign ship had the right to navigate without explicit permission. The claim was excessive by almost any reading of international law, and the US Navy was intent on challenging it.

As US aircraft watched from above, the navy vessels readied themselves for a Libyan military reaction to their foray. It was not long in coming. The Libyan military launched several missiles toward the US ships, although none reached their target. Later in the day, Libyan fighter aircraft flew close to US planes, and several Libyan vessels headed out to challenge the Americans, drawing return fire. US aircraft sank two patrol craft and badly damaged another. By the end of the altercation, several dozen Libyan sailors had been killed.[28]

The US Navy's planned incursion into the Gulf of Sidra was part of a broader program. In 1979, even as the negotiations on the Convention were approaching their final phase, the administration of Jimmy Carter (a former naval officer) announced what it titled a "Freedom of Navigation" program. The new policy stipulated that the United States would routinely challenge maritime claims that it deemed "excessive."[29] Objections would first come through diplomatic channels, but the Carter administration made clear that the US Navy would be involved as well if states persisted in their claims. Nor would only US adversaries be the subjects of these freedom of navigation operations, which came to be known as FONOPs.

Two years after the Gulf of Sidra episode, the Black Sea hosted a naval confrontation with even higher stakes. The Soviet Union, which had decades before declared a territorial sea of 12 miles, had no issue with the Convention's framework of maritime zones. The Soviets did have a particular—although certainly not unique—interpretation of "innocent passage." To the United States, that venerable doctrine meant that all vessels, including warships, could pass through another country's territorial waters unannounced, so long as they did not engage in prohibited actions, such as weapons training and intelligence gathering. But the Soviets insisted on advance notice when foreign warships planned to transit their waters and required that foreign military vessels employ only designated lanes within the territorial sea. In the Black Sea, the Soviets had not even created those designated lanes, an omission implying that they did not permit innocent passage at all.

To challenge that interpretation, the United States dispatched the cruiser *Yorktown* and the destroyer *Caron* to the Black Sea in February 1988. On February 12, while on a straight-line route, the US ships briefly sailed within 12 miles of the Soviet coast. Almost immediately, Soviet vessels approached and warned their US counterparts to leave. The Americans politely refused, insisting that they were operating in accordance with international law. A second warning from the Soviets went unheeded. Moments later, the

Soviet vessels veered toward their American counterparts, sailing for several minutes within a few meters of each other. American crew members gathered at the railings and gawked at their opposites, who were standing at attention in dress uniforms. Then, as American sailors shouted in alarm, the Soviet vessels angled toward the Americans. For several harrowing moments, the warships rode hull-to-hull before the Soviets broke contact and turned away (Figure 6.3).

While physical damage to the ships was minimal, the danger posed by the incident was immediately apparent in Washington and Moscow, which were otherwise enjoying warmer relations. A Soviet diplomat insisted that the navy ships were gathering intelligence, which would have constituted a violation of innocent passage. US officials maintained that the operation was part of its broader freedom of navigation program and had no other purpose. "We cannot exempt the Soviets from the freedom of navigation program," said Secretary of State George Shultz. "To do so would accede to their illegal maritime claims."[30] In the end, the governments patched together a

Figure 6.3 US and Soviet warships collide in the Black Sea; photograph courtesy of US Department of Defense.

compromise. In September 1989, the US secretary of state and Soviet foreign minister signed an agreement at Jackson Hole, Wyoming, confirming that the Convention provided the rules for innocent passage and affirming that warships enjoyed that right. With these assurances in hand, the United States told the Soviets that it no longer planned to conduct freedom of navigation operations in the Black Sea. That accord minimized the chances of renewed incidents, but it was only a bilateral agreement.[31] A number of other coastal countries maintained that the original Soviet position was permissible under the Convention, and their interpretation meant that there was potential for future incidents.

Freedom of navigation deployments stirred controversy not only in some foreign capitals but at times within the US government. US diplomats often viewed the operations as unnecessarily provocative and ultimately counterproductive. Disagreements between the Defense Department and the State Department became a regular feature of internal deliberations about operations. "There are always reasons, raised by country desks and regional experts, not to conduct a FON exercise," two former Defense Department officials have noted.[32] These pressures aside, the Reagan administration mostly embraced the initiative its predecessor had launched. In a major speech in 1986, Assistant Secretary of State John Negroponte heralded the program as an effective use of US power to ensure wide access to the oceans. The United States had negotiated diligently for the Convention's text to reflect the American vision of freedom of the seas. On some issues, Negroponte wrote, the US view "may only be found by proper legal interpretation of subtle points and phrases."[33] The United States was prepared to expend resources—and even risk confrontation—to guarantee that its version of these fine points prevailed.

Flags and Reflags

In the years after the Convention was finalized, the practice of ships flying flags of convenience (FOC) endured and even expanded. The Convention's insistence that there be a "genuine link" between vessels and their flagging state proved mostly hollow. In 1986, a United Nations body endorsed a set of principles for ship registration that added detail to the "genuine link" concept, including that the flagging state be able to assess the conditions onboard flagged ships and that at least some members of the crew come from the flagging state.[34] With no mechanism for enforcing those admonitions, however, the guidelines had little impact. Panama and Liberia remained the leading flags of convenience. In 1991, vessels representing more than 90 million tons sailed under their flags. Cyprus, Honduras, and several other countries also flagged a substantial number of vessels. All told, nearly a third of global shipping operated under a flag of convenience.

New entrants tried to horn in on the action. In 1990, the US-based company that operated Liberia's open ship registry announced that it had struck a deal with the Republic of the Marshall Islands to provide similar services. Diminutive (and landlocked) Luxembourg announced that it would permit vessels to fly under its flag. A clutch of other states and entities, including the Bahamas, Bermuda, Singapore, and Hong Kong, provided what some referred to as "quasi flags of convenience." Their registries were not open to all vessels but were still quite lenient.

The system of flags of convenience had inveterate opponents in unions representing maritime workers from the developed world, who found themselves increasingly priced out of the maritime business. After a deadly fire aboard the Bahamas-flagged *Scandinavian Star*, a Swedish seafarers union directly blamed the flagging system for allowing lax safety conditions. "It's a bit like 19th-century slave vessels," a union official said, attributing the incident to "low-cost crews with poor education and low safety."[35] The International Transport Worker's Federation, which represented a range of maritime industry employees, even produced a film—*Runaway Flags*—to dramatize the dangers of the system.[36]

Lax safety standards and low wages were frequent criticisms, but another was the creation of zones of impunity at sea. Flag states had the first and strongest claim to jurisdiction over crimes committed on board their vessels. But flag-of-convenience countries often had little inclination—and few resources—to investigate and prosecute these crimes, which might not involve their nationals at all. In the mid-1990s, accounts trickled out of merchant ship crews ordering the marooning or even the murder of stowaways found on board. In part because port countries sometimes imposed fines on merchant ships that arrived with stowaways, a few captains decided instead to make the unwanted passengers disappear. In several of these cases, the culprits either got off entirely or received minimal punishment.[37]

Another consequence of the FOC system was that many merchant vessels could not count on their flag state to provide meaningful diplomatic and military support in the case of harassment. The vulnerability of these ships became particularly evident in the Persian Gulf during the long and bloody Iran-Iraq War, which began in 1980 and ground on until 1988. Several dozen large tankers normally transited the Gulf daily, ferrying oil around the world. Both belligerents showed some restraint toward international shipping in the conflict's early years. Almost inevitably, the restrictions fell away as the war continued, casualties mounted, and the desperation of the combatants increased. In 1984, the number of attacks on tankers transiting the Gulf jumped to 71 from 16 the previous year.[38] Just as the British and Argentines had done around the Falklands, the combatants declared large maritime exclusion zones. But international shipping was in far greater peril than during the South Atlantic conflict; Iran and Iraq each sought not only to control ocean space but to cripple the economy and fighting power of their adversary. Multiple tankers flying neutral flags were hit. Iranian Revolutionary Guard speedboats began attacking and detaining vessels thought to be carrying goods to or from Iraq.

The rights of neutral shipping during conflict—so central to 19th- and early 20th-century debates on freedom of the seas—reemerged as an urgent international issue. In 1983, the UN Security Council insisted that the combatants respect freedom of navigation in the area.[39] Diplomats floated the idea of using an international flag, either the UN flag or the flag of the International Committee of the Red Cross. But that proposal raised the question: if ships carrying an international flag were attacked, who would respond? A more realistic alternative was to "reflag" tankers in a way that offered some real-world protection. In 1987, Kuwait formally asked the United States to flag 11 of its tankers, and Washington agreed ("an unusual measure to meet an extraordinary situation," the State Department said).[40] To meet US legal requirements for flagging, the ships were transferred to a US company and then leased back to the original Kuwaiti owners. In the months that followed, the tankers transited the Gulf under the protection of the world's largest navy. On several occasions, navy vessels struck Iranian boats and ocean platforms being used as bases for attacks. Flags that were convenient for skirting national regulation were decidedly less so when shipping came under threat.

Island Hyping

As Iran and Iraq menaced tankers in the Persian Gulf, a tiny North Atlantic protrusion of windswept granite named Rockall broke into the news. In May

1985, the governments of Denmark and Iceland formally claimed the feature and the seabed around it. In doing so, they set up a confrontation with the United Kingdom, which had first claimed the spot in 1955. Britain's motivation at that time was strategic. London was planning a missile test in the area and apparently feared that the Soviets might use the rock to observe the launch. Battling strong winds, helicopter-borne Royal Marines were winched onto the outcropping. In their short time on Rockall, they cemented a plaque to the rock face, grabbed a few marine specimens, and conducted a hurried flag-raising ceremony.[41]

The Icelandic and Danish move on Rockall several decades later came with a distinct set of motivations. With the Convention completed, these countries were mulling their future ocean claims and, in particular, the possibility of drilling in areas well beyond their shores. They saw Rockall as part of a broader continental shelf belonging to them and rejected the notion that the tiny feature could give Britain any maritime rights. The British lodged a formal complaint with both governments, but a more audacious response came from a private citizen. Tom McClean, a British survival expert and former Special Air Service soldier, spent more than a month on Rockall in 1985. He lived in a specially designed crate, which was bolted to the rock to prevent his being swept off in a storm. When the weather permitted, McClean clambered outside and passed the time painting a large Union Jack onto the rock face.

The buzz of activity around Rockall reflected the newfound significance of even tiny maritime features. Sovereignty disputes over many islands (including the Falklands) long predated the Convention, but its provisions focused the attention of governments. Assuming that a maritime feature could qualify as an island, the Convention's rewards were bountiful; it granted islands not merely a 12-mile territorial sea but also an EEZ extending 200 miles in each direction. A speck in the ocean could therefore generate more than 120,000 square miles of potentially lucrative rights. As in the case of Rockall, however, there was sometimes dissension about whether a maritime feature constituted an island. The Convention required that islands be above sea level at all times and able to sustain human life or economic activity. Those criteria involved an element of subjectivity and created incentives for nationalist adventurers like McClean.

A few governments took heroic measures to ensure that patches of land remained above the waterline. The phenomenon of island-building has become well known because of China's recent enthusiasm, but the practice began long before. In the 1920s, Japan claimed an uninhabited atoll in the Philippine Sea, hundreds of miles from the main Japanese islands. Named Okinotorishima, it was placed under the administration of the Tokyo government. The United States assumed control of it and other islands after the war, and it reverted to Japanese administration only in the late 1960s. By the time the Convention was finalized, however, the winds and waves had taken a toll on Okinotorishima, which was gradually eroding. In 1987, the government of Tokyo dispatched work crews to bolster the coral outcropping with steel and concrete and ensure that it did not disappear entirely beneath the waves. "Our mission is to conserve Japanese territory," the engineer in charge of the project said.[42] The Japanese effort hinted at a difficult legal question: does a country lose its maritime rights if the island that was the basis for those rights is submerged? Japan was willing to spend millions to keep that question a theoretical one, but the rise in sea levels that scientists were already documenting promised it would become more salient in the years to come—particularly for island nations.

It was in the nearby South China Sea that the scramble for islands turned most fractious. As it emerged from the domestic upheaval of the Cultural Revolution, China more forcefully asserted claims in the waters to its east. For all its size, Beijing saw itself as an underdog in the South China Sea. "Even after consolidating control over the Paracels [in 1974], China's position in the South China Sea remained weak," the scholar Taylor Fravel writes. "[B]y the late 1970s, Taiwan, Vietnam, and the Philippines had occupied almost twenty islands and reefs between them."[43] China's position was particularly tenuous in the Spratly Island chain, where almost no usable land was left unclaimed by the 1980s. Given that reality, Beijing set its sights on several less than habitable reefs.

In January 1988, Chinese engineers oversaw an intense blasting and dredging effort that produced expanded, and now definitely usable, areas of land around several unoccupied features. Vietnam, which controlled most other features in the area, kept watch over the operation. The government in Hanoi was particularly concerned that China might take possession of Johnson Reef, a mostly submerged coral formation near the center of the Spratly Island chain. On March 14, tensions came to a head. Several dozen Vietnamese soldiers took up positions on the reef as Chinese vessels circled nearby. The men stood half submerged, in a ring around the Vietnamese flag. Then the Chinese vessels opened fire, and the line of men slowly collapsed into the water. According to the Vietnamese government, more than 60 soldiers died in the water that day.

Johnson Reef would stay under China's control, and China insisted that all the Spratly features should be Chinese. "The Spratly (Nansha) Islands have been an integral part of the territory of the People's Republic of China since ancient times," China's Central Committee statement insisted.[44] Even as it made these moves, China periodically reassured observers that it did not intend to interfere with the right of vessels to peacefully transit through these waters, and China's foreign minister pledged to settle any disputes about the South China Sea on the basis of international law.[45] But Beijing's willingness to use force rendered those reassurances hollow, and Chinese assertiveness was not limited to the South China Sea. In 1992, China enacted domestic legislation that identified the Senkaku/Diaoyu Islands, located in the East China Sea, as its own. That move set the Japanese on edge and set the stage for a slow-motion struggle over sovereignty.

Island disputes like these proliferated in multiple regions. The small island of Abu Musa sits in the middle of the Strait of Hormuz, through which enormous quantities of oil pass each year. The island's status generated persistent controversy between Iran and the emerging Arab kingdoms as Britain prepared to withdraw its forces from the region in the late 1960s. Iran dispatched forces but agreed in 1971 to share sovereignty with the new United Arab Emirates, and the island was effectively divided into Arab and Iranian halves. During the Iran-Iraq War, the island served as a useful base for Iranian naval forces. In 1992, Tehran tightened its grip by expelling United Arab Emirates (UAE) nationals and preventing others from arriving. Real estate in the middle of the straits, Tehran seems to have calculated, was too valuable to share.[46] Several other island disputes involved newly independent countries attempting to protect their nascent sovereignty. Eritrea, which gained independence from Ethiopia in the early 1990s, feuded with Yemen about the Hanish Islands in the Red Sea. That dispute turned violent in late 1995. In Eastern Europe, the newly independent countries of Estonia and Latvia butted heads over Ruhnu Island. And in the Black Sea, Snake Island became a point of contention between Ukraine and Romania.

Few patches of ocean are as thoroughly dotted with islands as the Aegean. Greece, which controlled the vast majority of islands in the area, including some only a few dozen miles from the Turkish coast, saw itself as a major beneficiary of the Convention's structure. With newly expanded territorial seas around each island, the prospect of the Aegean turning into a "Greek lake" was tantalizingly close. Turkey was well aware of that possibility and insisted that any move to expand the Greek territorial sea around the islands to 12 miles would be a cause for war. Turkey also proffered a claim of its own, insisting that the continental shelf in the Aegean was an extension of the Turkish land mass. The Greek and Turkish positions appeared irreconcilable, and the longtime adversaries lurched toward conflict in the spring of 1987 as Greece appeared poised to expand its ocean drilling activities. Turkey responded by dispatching its own oceanographic vessel to the area, accompanied by several warships. Energetic diplomacy by some of the world's biggest powers, and the intercession of NATO's secretary general, avoided open conflict. Greece did not (and has not to this day) asserted a 12-mile territorial sea in the Aegean.

Around the world, claims to often diminutive patches of land were producing outsized friction. "Because the possession of islands has become a crucial factor in determining the extent of a country's fishing and seabed mining rights," the editors of the *Financial Times* worried in 1995, "bitter international disputes are flaring over the ownership of obscure mid-ocean outcrops which would otherwise be of little interest."[47]

Mining on Hold

For all the controversy swirling over islands, US opposition to the Convention still rested almost entirely on its seabed mining provisions. Judged by their public statements, the US government and American companies still believed in the early 1980s that the industry was set to flourish. In December 1983, the United States Geological Survey announced that it had located a new source of cobalt, nickel, and manganese on the floor of the Pacific Ocean within the country's newly proclaimed EEZ. Meanwhile, the lead US agency for seabed mining, the National Oceanographic and Atmospheric Agency (NOAA), produced regulations for US companies interested in working in the deep seabed. US naval officers were also thinking about how the new industry might implicate its operations. A 1985 article in *Proceedings*, the influential magazine of the US Naval Institute, sketched a possible future in which US Navy hydrofoils patrolled sites where US companies were operating deep-sea mining rigs. (The author was then Lieutenant Commander James Stavridis, who would go on to serve as chief of naval operations and as NATO's top commander.)[48]

The expressed fear of the developing world during the Convention's nego-tiations was that wealthy countries would scoop up undersea riches, exac-erbating the divide between rich and poor. Determined to take advantage of the Convention structure, several non-Western countries readied them-selves for seabed activity. The Indian government prepared plans for mining and secured the status of a "pioneer investor" in seabed mining. By 1991, Cuba and the Soviet Union also won that recognition, conferred on them by the countries that had signed the Convention. These countries identi-fied specific areas for future mining operations, all in the so-called Clarion-Clipperton zone of the Pacific Ocean, thought to host significant quantities of manganese nodules.

As the competing plans for mining unfolded (almost entirely on paper), researchers in major maritime countries were cultivating new proficiency in operating at great depths. A French consortium developed prototypes of battery-powered underwater vehicles that could operate autonomously. A press account of its work speculated that the prototypes could be "invalu-able in France's dream to dominate ocean mining."[49] For its part, the British government signed a deal with a subsidiary of General Electric allowing the use of British government technology to survey the seabed. In 1986, the US submersible *Alvin* descended more than 13,000 feet to provide ghostly pictures of the *Titanic*'s wreckage, which had been located the previous year. Deep-sea vehicles like *Alvin* would be of little use in actual mining opera-tions, but they might be critical in servicing seabed mining equipment.

Technological vistas may have opened but the broader economic reali-ties in the years after the Convention was drafted were not kind to mining initiatives. Seabed mining was not nearly as close to being a viable com-mercial enterprise as had been thought. As the Convention was finalized, world copper prices began a long, steady decline that made the already tenuous economics of investing in seabed mining even more strained. Other mineral prices followed a similar trajectory. In late 1984, a mining industry official acknowledged that mining "will take place only if the oversupply of copper, which is contained in the nodules, is absorbed by the world market."[50]

The sluggish pace of seabed mining had implications for the broader evo-lution of ocean governance. It was the seabed mining provisions in the new Convention that most thoroughly embraced the oceans as the "common heritage" of humanity, and momentum for operationalizing that concept seemed to be dissipating. By contrast, many elements of the Convention that envisioned expanded national control—including the plumped up territorial sea and the new EEZ—had moved quickly into practice. And the nationalist competition for tiny islands revealed plenty of appetite for more ocean territory. Arvid Pardo's fears that the drafters had done too much carving up of the oceans between governments and not enough work building an international infrastructure seemed prescient.

Holes in the Ocean

The rapid acceptance of the EEZ meant that the great majority of fishing operations would now happen under the broad jurisdiction of some national government. For those worried about preserving fish stocks, this was potentially good news. The Convention changed the task of managing most fisheries from a complex collective action problem requiring cooperation among multiple states to a situation in which one government had clear responsibility. Yet the Convention was vague and elliptical on how countries should manage the fishing that still occurred on the high seas, as well as what to do about fish stocks that migrated between EEZs and the high seas or straddled different EEZs. The right of every state to fish on the open ocean had long been a core element of freedom of the seas, and the Convention endorsed it—to a point. It coupled the right to fish on the high seas with a duty to collaborate with other states to preserve the ocean's resources.

In the late 1980s, there were several indications that this duty was being ignored. The UN's Food and Agriculture Organization (FAO) reported that most of the world's fishing stocks were either fully exploited or in decline. The stress on fish stocks became particularly evident in an area of the frigid Bering Sea. When the Soviet Union and the United States declared their EEZs, in 1983 and 1984, respectively, these lines left a substantial patch of the high seas surrounded by EEZs. The area became known as the "Donut Hole," and it attracted a hungry crowd. Long-range fleets, including from China, Japan, Poland, and South Korea, descended on the area beginning in the early 1980s. One fisheries observer recalled a typical day in February 1986:

I counted 60 large factory trawlers around us belonging to four or five different nations. They lined up in a pattern of several rows to take turns dragging across a thin layer of Alaska pollock at about 400 [meters] depth, fishing with cavernous nets that opened 45 [meters] high for durations of several hours. That year, the Donut Hole sustained a "reported" winter catch of about 1 million tons.[51]

Negotiations to restrain rampant overfishing in the area began in the early 1990s and produced an agreement a few years later. The countries that fished in the area pledged to rely on scientific advice to establish a maximum catch for each country's fleet. To facilitate compliance, countries promised to notify other members when they planned to fish in the area. Their vessels would use satellite location technology and take on scientific observers from other countries. Even more notable, the countries fishing the area consented in advance to allow boarding and inspection by other government vessels. The agreement contained some notable innovations, but the damage had been done. Pollock populations in the area declined rapidly and showed few signs of recovery.[52]

Fears about pollock overfishing in the Donut Hole ran alongside long-standing US, Soviet, and Canadian concerns about Japanese salmon fishing in the broader north Pacific. Salmon and other anadromous fish posed a particular challenge for fisheries regulation given that they spawn in freshwater (squarely within national jurisdiction) but live most of their lives at sea. The Convention granted the country in whose waters anadromous stocks originated primary responsibility for maintenance of those stocks. Canada, the United States, and the Soviet Union realized that Japan's fishing fleet had developed techniques, including the use of "motherships" and drift nets, that boosted their efficiency. In theory, the Japanese vessels were pursuing "Asian" salmon but they of course caught salmon of other origins as well. The Japanese insisted that their haul of US and Canadian salmon was minimal, but North American fishing groups strenuously disagreed. These complaints merged with the concerns of environmentalists who opposed the Japanese use of drift nets, equipment they argued killed a large number of immature fish and other species.

Coastal countries' frustration about long-range fishing fleets hovering near EEZs and plundering migratory fish stocks crested not in the Pacific, but rather on Canada's eastern coast. Canadian fishermen complained bitterly to the government about the presence of foreign fishing vessels in the small portions of the Grand Banks that lie beyond Canada's 200-mile zone. On several occasions, Canadian patrol boats confronted foreign fishing vessels that it believed had crossed into Canada's waters. In May 1986, one such encounter took a bizarre turn. Canadian fisheries officials stopped two

Spanish trawlers to investigate whether they had crossed into the Canadian EEZ and fished illegally. At some point during the stop, the Spanish captain apparently panicked and took off toward the open ocean—with a catch that included four hapless (and unarmed) Canadian observers. Only after a 700-mile chase was the Royal Canadian Mounted Police able to secure the release of the observers and detain the trawlers.[53]

Disputes about whether vessels were respecting the new lines in the sea were sometimes dangerous, but at least they did not pose a threat to the basic compromises hammered out through the Convention. But those compromises came under increasing strain as fishing groups in Canada pressured the government to assert fisheries jurisdiction *beyond* the 200-mile limit of the EEZ. For months, the government resisted these pleas and instead attempted to work through a regional fisheries group, the Northwest Atlantic Fisheries Organization (NAFO). A Canadian official insisted that regional diplomacy of this sort was the only viable route and that unilateral action would pit the country against much of the international community:

> We would encounter massive resistance from all over the world. We would be all alone; there is no multilateral forum in which we could negotiate it, and there is no way we could impose it unilaterally even if we had a navy 10 times the size of the one we have right now.[54]

Yet Canadian efforts to work through NAFO left it frustrated. European members of the organization often held out against the view that Grand Banks fishing should be tightly restricted. One of the organization's negotiating sessions fell apart during the welcome dinner, at which a Canadian minister excoriated European delegates for what he described as stubborn and reckless overfishing.[55] Meanwhile, certain fishing vessels reflagged themselves in countries (including Panama) that were not NAFO members and had no legal obligations to obey its restrictions. By the early 1990s, the political pressure in Canada became too much to bear, and the government asserted a right not only to vigorously police its EEZ but also to unilaterally restrict certain fishing activities beyond it. This new policy was a jolt to the Convention's system, and the Canadian government struggled to defend its position.

At the international level, several initiatives sought to encourage greater respect for fish stocks on the high seas. In 1989, 15 countries signed an agreement to ban driftnet fishing in the South Pacific.[56] In 1993, the UN's Food and Agriculture Organization encouraged countries to ensure that any vessels they flagged be specifically authorized to fish on the high seas and encouraged flag states to cooperate with relevant regional fisheries organizations to implement restrictions. But it was becoming clear that the effort to preserve fisheries would succeed or fail at the regional level, through organizations like NAFO.

For some observers, the small scale of international efforts and the reliance on sluggish, consensus-driven regional organizations to preserve fish stocks was evidence that the "tragedy of the commons" remained an accurate description of ocean resource dynamics. Writing in the 1960s, Garrett Hardin had famously argued that the only avenues out of tragedy were divvying up common spaces or placing them under some form of centralized control with coercive power to enforce rules. The UN Convention had done some of the divvying up (through expanded EEZs) and a bit of the centralized control, but it had not fully embraced either of Hardin's solutions.

Even as concern grew about environmental pressure on the oceans, however, a new generation of scholars was challenging Hardin's dyspeptic view. Elinor Ostrom, a scholar at Indiana University, was the most prominent of the voices arguing that there might be other ways of preserving common resources. In 1990, she published *Governing the Commons*, which featured detailed accounts of several local communities successfully preserving common resources. Ostrom rejected the presumption that "individuals sharing a commons are inevitably caught in a trap from which they cannot escape."[57] Ostrom was no Pangloss; she acknowledged that tragic outcomes were possible, but she also outlined specific conditions that made effective management of common resources more likely.

Ostrom's case studies centered on domestic management of resources in countries as diverse as Canada, Sri Lanka, and Turkey. She was most interested in how individuals and local cooperatives interacted with each other and with local or national governments. Even when discussing fisheries, she made only passing reference to international agreements. Still, if extrapolated from the local to the international level, her broader insights offered glimmers of hope that groups of countries might be able to cobble together ad hoc solutions to address particular high-seas fisheries problems—even in the absence of a grand and centrally enforced multilateral solution. Ostrom's relative optimism would be tested in the years to come as new regional fisheries organizations formed and others expanded their activities.

"Did We Do This?"

As maritime actors adjusted to the Convention's implications for fishing, a more fundamental threat to the health of the oceans—and the planet—was already visible on the horizon. Scientists in the 1980s and 1990s turned their attention to how climate changes might affect processes such as ocean circulation and the upwelling of colder water from the sea bottom. Others examined how a rapid melting of icebergs would alter sea levels and the composition of sea water.[58]

If climate change endangered the health of the ocean, its potential as a part of the solution also began to attract scientific and commercial attention. In particular, several researchers advanced the notion that the ocean could become a receptacle for the excess carbon dioxide the world was producing. A major conference in 1990 considered seeding the ocean with iron to promote the blooming of phytoplankton and algae that might absorb carbon. "The urgency of the problem is such that we need to proceed with new ideas," said Francisco Ayala, chairman of a government workshop on how to implement such initiatives.[59]

The "Geritol solution," as some researchers called it, got one of its most significant tests in 1995. In May, a team of researchers boarded the vessel *Melville*. Already on board was a half-ton of iron ore. As the ship cruised back and forth over a predetermined patch of ocean, the researchers methodically dumped the iron into the water. The effect was dramatic. The patch of ocean turned from blue to green as phytoplankton bloomed and the chlorophyll levels in the water jumped. For some of those on board, the experience was unsettling:

> None of us was really prepared for what it would look or feel like. There were some of us who were quite pleased and others of us who would walk out to the fantail and burst into tears. It was a profoundly disturbing experience for me. We had deckhands come up to us and ask, 'did we do this?'[60]

By some estimates, an ambitious ocean seeding operation could remove as much carbon from the atmosphere as had been pumped in since the Industrial Revolution. The oceanographer John Martin, who had championed the seeding idea, once quipped, "Give me a half a tanker of iron and I'll give you the next ice age."[61] There were also potential environmental benefits beyond taming global warming; oceans with renewed algae might create more hospitable conditions for distressed fish stocks.

But the first experiments with ocean fertilization brought immediate warnings from environmentalists about the dangers of tinkering with the ocean on such a massive scale. There seemed certain to be unintended consequences. Still, those in favor of pursuing fertilization had a powerful response: the world was *already* experimenting on the climate (and on the ocean) every day through human activities. A colleague of Martin's described him as cynical in his view of human nature. "He felt . . . that humans should get their act together and stop emitting so much carbon dioxide. But he didn't believe that we would get our act together."[62]

The prospect of iron fertilization raised legal questions as well as ethical ones. Those conducting the fertilization experiments insisted that they were on solid ground. Just as Fritz Haber had defended his right to experiment freely on the open ocean in the 1920s, these scientists saw ocean research as a fundamental right. The new Convention did explicitly protect the right of countries to conduct scientific experiments on the high seas. But it also included (vague) requirements that states consider the environmental impact of their high-seas activities and not endanger the health of the ocean. A 1972 agreement provided its own restrictions on ocean dumping, although it clearly had in mind the jettisoning of waste material and left ambiguous the status of fertilization experiments. The scale of new environmental challenges was revealing the need for greater clarity about what kind of experimentation was permissible on the open ocean.

Rewriting the Convention

The Convention dramatically impacted national maritime practices well before it came into force. By the early 1990s, more than 120 coastal states had established a territorial sea of 12 miles and more than 100 countries had designated EEZs or special fishery zones to a distance of 200 miles. Yet the disaffection of the most powerful maritime states with the seabed mining arrangements remained. Even as the number of ratifying countries slowly ticked toward the required 60, it was uncertain whether the Convention would ever win the approval of leading maritime powers. "If we are not careful," the UN Secretary General warned, "these difficulties could steadily undermine the Convention itself, and everything would have to be redone from the start."[63]

As it happened, the political flexibility provided by the end of the Cold War and the dim prospects of seabed mining combined to free the Convention from the doldrums. Senior UN diplomats quietly negotiated with key states to see whether it would be possible to revisit the troublesome seabed mining architecture. One British newspaper described the talks as an effort to "re-open provisions over mining without appearing to surrender to what many developing countries see as American and British blackmail."[64]

The UN intermediaries found the national diplomats surprisingly open to compromise. Key developing state representatives realized that the Convention would be a shell of an agreement without the participation of major maritime powers. The fact that the West—with its emphasis on markets and free enterprise—was emerging victorious from the Cold War meant that the developing world position on seabed mining was vulnerable. As a US negotiator put it, "A fundamental shift toward the application of market principles to the management of deep seabed resources, and the declining near-term interest in commercial seabed mining are at the heart of the progress."[65]

Beginning in 1990, a small group of diplomats began meeting to hash out a compromise that would acknowledge these new realities while keeping alive the idea of international control of the deep seabed. In 1993, those consultations resulted in a draft, which was dubbed the "Boat Paper." It carried on board the elements of a potential compromise between developed and developing countries. Among other elements, it proposed increasing the influence of major powers in the planned International Seabed Authority, limiting the obligation of private companies to transfer technology, and reducing fees required for seabed mining applications. To reduce the procedural and political obstacles, this initiative was framed not as an amendment to the existing Convention but instead as an "implementing agreement" on seabed mining.

Parallel to the seabed mining discussions, another complex negotiation began in April 1993. These talks sought to clarify and sharpen the Convention's vague language on high-seas fishing. One diplomat acknowledged that these provisions had been "somewhat of an afterthought" during the original negotiations.[66] Two distinct fish populations now received sustained diplomatic attention. The first category was fish that migrated widely through the oceans ("highly migratory species"), such as tuna and swordfish.

The second was fish stocks that routinely moved beyond the 200-mile limit ("straddling stocks"). The Convention had done little more than encourage countries to negotiate about managing these fish populations. "Most states seemed to recognize that the legal framework provided by the [Convention] was in need of further clarification and development," wrote one scholar.[67] The willingness of a country like Canada to extend fisheries enforcement beyond 200 miles underlined the need for additional measures.

So even as national diplomats tinkered with the mining apparatus, they began drafting a new treaty that would require all countries to help sustain high-seas fish populations. When evidence was lacking about the health of a particular population, the document urged countries to follow a "precautionary" approach. It delegated the work of creating specific rules and quotas to regional fisheries organizations, several of which already existed. In regions where these organizations did not exist, the agreement urged relevant countries to form them. In their areas of responsibility, these cohorts of interested countries could impose restrictions on high-seas fishing. Critically, even countries that were not members of these regional organizations were obliged to comply with their rules (although a country that was not a member of the Convention *or* the fish stocks agreement would have no such legal obligation).

The successful revision of the seabed mining provisions and the progress toward the high-seas fishing agreement opened the floodgates to ratification of the Convention, particularly in the developed world. In 1995, 13 countries ratified and another several dozen more appeared ready to come on board. The "constitution for the oceans" was finally in force.

7

The Convention in Operation

(1995–2010)

In September 1996, the black metal sail of the USS *Pogy*, a nuclear attack submarine, broke through the Arctic ice. A crew member, clad in cold-weather gear, ascended the vessel's conning tower to assume lookout responsibilities. There was nothing odd about a US Navy submarine operating in the Arctic or even surfacing through the ice. For decades, submarines from several Western navies had prowled the area, often tracking increasingly quiet Soviet ballistic missile submarines. But the *Pogy's* mission on this occasion was unusual. It carried only half its normal complement of torpedoes; a dozen had been removed to make room for a group of civilian scientists and their equipment.

For the scientists operating where weapons once lay, the opportunity to conduct research via submarine was invaluable. "Alone among the vessels operating in the Arctic," several participants wrote, "the submarine can operate freely beneath the shifting pack ice."[1] The submarine's stealth—so important for avoiding detection by potential adversaries—made it ideal for hydrographic observations. *Pogy's* 1996 Arctic cruise took it along several undersea features, including the Lomonosov Ridge, which divides the Arctic Ocean into two main basins. The submarine surfaced at a half dozen locations to take additional measurements. The 45-day mission generated new data on water flows from the Atlantic Ocean and Bering Sea into the Arctic—including some showing that the ice in several parts of the Arctic was thinning.

A combination of factors produced the collaboration between the US Navy and civilian researchers. With the tempo of Russian submarine operations in the Arctic slowing, the *Sturgeon* class submarines that had been the US Navy's workhorses in the area enjoyed new operational flexibility. The Navy also benefited from data the scientists gathered on salinity, ice thickness, and currents, which were valuable for improving sonar performance. Public relations played a part as well. Demonstrating its broader utility was important for a submarine force reorienting after the collapse of its principal adversary.

While the US Navy deployed its largesse to assist Arctic scientists, the Russian government was struggling with what one minister described as a "catastrophic" situation in the region. After the dissolution of the Soviet Union, supplying fuel and food to Russia's Arctic cities and towns had become increasingly difficult. The winter of 1995–1996 was particularly trying, and some communities reportedly subsisted on canned food from the 1970s. A series of deadly airplane crashes in the region added to the sense of gloom. Russian president Boris Yeltsin promised to address the deprivation, but the economy was in tatters. The plight of Russia's Arctic communities was yet another sign of the country's transformation from superpower to supplicant.

Russia's struggles helped produce a diplomatic thaw in the region, as the country's need for cooperation increased and its suspicion of the West eased. In 1990, the United States and the Soviet Union had finalized years of work on a maritime boundary agreement that included contested areas of the Arctic. For their part, Denmark, Norway, and Iceland negotiated continental shelf divisions and fishery zones in the region in 1996 and 1997. As Arctic countries sorted out portions of their maritime boundaries, only one traditional territorial dispute in the region remained: Canada and Denmark disagreed (rather politely) over ownership of the uninhabited and desolate Hans Island, situated between Canada's Ellesmere Island and northern Greenland.

Multilateral breakthroughs accompanied these encouraging bilateral moves. In 1991, Arctic countries pledged to pay special attention to the region's environmental health, and that agreement foreshadowed an even more ambitious undertaking. In 1996, eight countries—Canada, Denmark, Finland, Iceland, Norway, Russia, Sweden, and the United States—established an Arctic Council to serve as an "international forum for cooperation" on common regional issues related to environmental protection and sustainable development.[2] The Council included permanent representation (although without formal voting rights) for indigenous groups, a first for intergovernmental forums of this sort. The level of enthusiasm varied among the members. Canada led the push to create the Council, and the Nordic states also favored an active body. By contrast, Russia and the United States were hesitant to give the Council significant authority, particularly on security issues. Still, the Arctic Council was born in an atmosphere of substantial optimism.

There were other manifestations of Arctic solidarity, some aimed at ameliorating past abuses. The newly transparent Russian government exposed the Soviet Union's decades-long practice of dumping radioactive material into its Arctic waters. Moscow detailed how the Soviet military had, over several decades, jettisoned more than a dozen failed or antiquated nuclear reactors. Beginning in 1992, joint teams from Russia, Norway, and the International Atomic Energy Agency visited the dumping sites, where they located the discarded reactors and conducted tests for radiation leakage. Given its proximity, Norway had a particular interest in ensuring the safety—and the perceived safety—of the waters. "If the rumor gets around that Norwegian and Russian fish are contaminated with radioactivity," worried the country's defense minister, "we aren't going to sell many fish."[3]

For the moment, commercial motives like those ran parallel to the broader political current of increased cooperation in the far north. The Arctic in the mid-1990s offered a broadly optimistic picture of what ocean governance might look like in the post–Cold War era. Countries in the region were resolving bilateral disputes, negotiating maritime boundaries, inaugurating new and innovative multilateral structures, and remedying at least a few of the region's environmental challenges. This was all being accomplished in the context of the Convention's ambitious new compromise for the oceans, which provided for expanded national control and new mechanisms of international management.

Building the Ocean Bureaucracy

The launch of the Arctic Council added a new contour to ocean multilateralism. A central feature of the international architecture remained the London-based International Maritime Organization. Born in the 1950s as the International Maritime Consultative Organization, the organization streamlined its name in the early 1980s. (The formal name change was delayed by several years, in part because Japan worried that if the initials "I-M-O" were sounded out as one word, it sounded like "hot potato" in Japanese.)[4] The renamed organization took up residence in a $50-million headquarters building in London's Albert Embankment, facing the River Thames. Membership expanded from 31 countries in the 1950s to more than 130 in 1995, and the organization's permanent staff swelled to include more than 200 professionals from several dozen countries. In 2001, an enormous bronze memorial depicting a lone seafarer on the bow of a cargo ship was placed in front of its headquarters (Figure 7.1).[5]

As the memorial implied, ensuring safe and orderly trade at sea remained the IMO's core mission. The organization devised and disseminated sea routes and adopted other regulations to avoid maritime collisions. It helped draft international standards for training maritime personnel and conducting search and rescue operations. Working with the International Chamber of Commerce, the IMO encouraged the creation of an International Maritime Bureau to track piracy and other criminality at sea.

Figure 7.1 Seafarers' Memorial at the International Maritime Organization; photograph courtesy of the International Maritime Organization.

While its focus remained maritime commerce, the IMO was not indifferent to the growth of a global environmental movement. In the wake of the 1967 *Torrey Canyon* disaster, the organization devoted increasing attention to the health of the ocean itself, and it facilitated several agreements designed to prevent pollution by ships. By the 1980s, the organization had refined its mission statement to promoting "safer shipping *on cleaner oceans*." In the 1990s, the IMO helped facilitate limits on air pollution from ocean-going ships and revised a long-standing agreement prohibiting dumping on the oceans.

Across the North Sea from Britain, the Hague-based International Court of Justice played its own role in ocean governance. In the late 1990s, it considered a maritime boundary dispute between Senegal and Guinea-Bissau and a fisheries controversy emanating from Canada's 1995 seizure of a Spanish fishing vessel. Inside the main UN bureaucracy in New York, the Division for Ocean Affairs and the Law of the Sea served primarily as a repository for information regarding ocean boundaries. The UN Commission on Trade and Development (UNCTAD) engaged with shipping issues beginning in the late 1960s. If the IMO was seen as favorable to shipping interests and the major maritime powers, UNCTAD was often a vehicle for developing countries to challenge—or at least bring attention to—what they perceived as unfair major-power dominance of the world's shipping industry.

To these established institutions, the UN Convention added several new multilateral structures. The planned International Seabed Authority (ISA) was the most controversial. The 1994 "implementing agreement" had altered the ISA's mandate and powers in an attempt to bridge the divide between developed and developing countries. But friction persisted as the new organization took shape. In 1995, the ISA member countries feuded for several months about how to apportion seats on the organization's executive board. Several European members finally broke the deadlock by agreeing to share a seat, and the Convention's member states then selected Satya Nandan, Fiji's lead maritime negotiator, as the ISA's first secretary general.

With an initial budget of just $5 million, Nandan had the task of assembling an international staff ready to process national requests for licenses to explore and mine the seabed under international waters. In a limited sense, the small team at the ISA thereby exercised control over more territory than almost any head of state. And through the fees the ISA would charge for mining permits and royalties from any eventual profits, the authority also had the potential to generate revenue directly, an unusual ability for intergovernmental organizations. Even after the 1994 tweaks to its powers, the ISA remained an audacious experiment in international governance.

Yet the organization was also fragile and operating in an uncertain political and economic climate. The United States remained outside the Convention and suspicious of the ISA. Through domestic legislation, Washington had already granted licenses for several deep-sea mining sites, which raised the prospect of a collision between the superpower and the international body. As the ISA began its work, however, tepid interest in mining made such a clash unlikely. There was plenty of seabed real estate to go around and not all that many customers. With mining activity mostly confined to research and planning, the seabed authority had the luxury of establishing itself without being immediately buffeted by demand for its services or friction between members and nonmembers. With little public attention, the ISA quietly set about developing the regulations it would use to manage future mining operations.

On the opposite side of the Atlantic, the Convention's other organizational innovation sprang into being. The International Tribunal for the Law of the Sea (ITLOS) became one of the first UN agencies headquartered in Germany. Judges from 17 different countries took up their posts, ready to rule on maritime disputes from around the world. In October 1996, dignitaries placed a foundation stone for the new court near the banks of the Elbe River. UN Secretary General Boutros Boutros-Ghali traveled to Hamburg for the occasion and declared, "With the establishment of this Tribunal we enter a new era."[6]

In another speech during his German trip, however, Boutros-Ghali acknowledged that the United Nations and the broader project of multilateralism faced headwinds. The near euphoria prompted by the end of the Cold War, particularly around the world organization, was dissipating into a cloud of recrimination. The large UN peacekeeping operations in Somalia, the Balkans, and Rwanda had ended catastrophically. Even as Boutros-Ghali traveled to Germany, US officials were ensuring that he would not enjoy a second term as secretary general; the Clinton administration repeatedly vetoed Boutros-Ghali's reappointment, and the United Nations in December selected Kofi Annan as its next leader.

The new maritime tribunal faced particular challenges of its own. To become a decisive voice on the law of the sea, it needed cases; the judges could issue binding rulings only in response to concrete disputes. While maritime squabbles were not in short supply, it seemed unlikely that many would make their way to Hamburg. On joining the Convention, countries selected from several options for resolving maritime disputes, including the Tribunal, the older and more established International Court of Justice, or some form of arbitration. For cautious governments, arbitration and the better known ICJ were often more appealing than the new court. Fewer than a third of UNCLOS members ultimately designated the Tribunal as their choice for resolving disputes. But the Tribunal did have an area of exclusive competence: the Convention made it the court of first resort when countries believed that one of their vessels had been unlawfully seized.

Just that sort of incident brought the Tribunal its first business. In October 1997, the *Saiga*, an oil tanker sailing under the flag of St. Vincent and the Grenadines, was operating off the coast of West Africa. The *Saiga* had been chartered by a Swiss company to refuel fishing vessels in the area. A practice known as bunkering, the provision of fuel at sea allowed fishing crews to work for longer periods without having to refuel at local ports. According to one crewmember, the *Saiga* was going about its business when it was suddenly approached:

> Approximately at 8 o'clock I have a rest because my watch is from 0000 till 0400. I heard [a sound] like hitting nuts but I heard automatic firing and then in two or three minutes later . . . I heard the announcement of the Captain that there is a piracy attack of the vessel and all the crew should proceed downstairs to the engine room.[7]

In the melee, two *Saiga* crewmembers—Ukrainian and Senegalese nationals—were injured by bullet fragments and flying glass. The "pirates" turned out to be armed Guinean officials, and their account of the incident was quite different. They alleged that the *Saiga* had operated not merely in the country's exclusive economic zone but inside its territorial waters. Guinea insisted that the vessel refused to heed calls to be inspected and instead sped off toward the waters of neighboring Sierra Leone. The crew was brought to shore and charged with illegally reselling oil within Guinea's EEZ.

St. Vincent, the *Saiga*'s flag state, promptly complained to the Tribunal. A few weeks later—light speed by the standards of international justice—the judges ruled that Guinea must release the *Saiga* and its crew. Several months later, the judges issued a full ruling on the merits of the case. Ambiguity in the Convention about how countries may regulate activities in their EEZs was a central issue. Guinea claimed that the Convention gave it the right to control commercial operations like bunkering. For its part, St. Vincent insisted that coastal state regulations in the EEZ had to be directly related to the preservation of marine resources. A few of the international judges worried that Guinea's interpretation could significantly expand the coastal state's powers in the EEZ and erode freedom of navigation, but there was no unanimity on that point. And in a foreshadowing of disputes to come, the Chinese judge, Zhao Lihai, insisted that coastal states had legal space to regulate activities in the EEZ:

> The exclusive economic zone, as a zone with its own legal status, is neither a part of the high seas, nor the territorial sea. Uses of the sea with regard to which the Convention has not expressly attributed rights or jurisdiction in the exclusive economic zone to the coastal State do not automatically fall under the freedom of the high seas. Therefore bunkering must not be regarded as falling within the high seas freedom of navigation or related to it.[8]

Zhao, one of China's leading authorities on the law of the sea, believed that "freedom of the seas" deserved no special deference and should not limit coastal state authority.[9] Ultimately, the judges deferred a decision on the limits of national power in the EEZ. Instead, they concluded that whatever its rights in the EEZ, Guinea had acted improperly because it apprehended the *Saiga* on the high seas, where forcible boarding is allowed only in exceptional circumstances. Boarding might have been acceptable if Guinea had been continuously following the *Saiga*—an exercise of "hot pursuit"—but the judges found no evidence that it had done so.

The *Saiga* case was a mixed blessing for the young Tribunal. It handled the case efficiently, in part by saving for later some of the thorniest issues. Yet there were troubling hints that countries might not abide by its rulings. Guinea did not promptly release the vessel, as the Tribunal had demanded. And for several months, the government continued its legal case against the *Saiga*'s crew. The sluggish compliance raised questions about what would happen if international judges tried to alter the maritime behavior of more powerful countries.

Assembling the Shelves

With new headquarters and grand titles, the International Seabed Authority and the Tribunal for the Law of the Sea were the Convention's marquee creations. Yet the more humbly titled and housed United Nations Commission on the Limits of the Continental Shelf could claim to be as significant, at least in the short term. Operating from spare offices inside the aging UN headquarters building in New York, the Commission would help apportion rights to thousands of square miles of undersea territory.

The Convention permitted countries to extend control of the continental shelf beyond 200 miles, out to 350 miles (or even more, in certain situations). This allowance reassured coastal states—in particular, the "broad margin" countries—that they might eventually secure large oil and gas reserves beyond their 200-mile zones. To avoid a spree of new sovereign expansion, however, the negotiators created the Commission as a watchdog. Countries seeking rights on additional undersea territory would have to demonstrate to Commission members that the seabed in question was actually a continuation of their continental shelf. Doing so would involve substantial effort and expense. The Convention's definition of what constituted an extended shelf— laid out in Article 76—relied on factors including the sedimentary thickness of the seabed and the gradient of the slope. As one observer commented, "Article 76 relies on hard-to-obtain and even-harder-to-decipher submarine data, which states must input into a complex formula that bases outer limits on undefined terms and confusing measurements."[10] Assessing the evidence compiled by states would be the task of 21 Commission members, including experts in geology, geophysics, and hydrography.

National assertions that lacked the Commission's blessing could be contested by other countries, whereas a submission that bore its imprimatur would be "final and binding" for all the Convention's member countries. The Convention therefore created significant technical impediments to asserting additional undersea rights and incentives not to do so outside its processes. What's more, the procedure came with a deadline. The Convention gave countries a decade after ratification to make submissions. As a whole, the extended continental shelf process would be a test of how well the expansion of the territorial sea and the creation of the EEZ had slaked sovereign appetites for ocean and undersea space.

Unsurprisingly, affluent countries with plausible claims to extended shelves moved first. Even these wealthy countries wrestled with whether the anticipated benefits of additional seabed claims justified the cost of the mapping effort.[11] In almost all areas, existing surveys of the seabed were preliminary and incomplete, and only expensive techniques like multi-beam sounding could provide clarity about the contours of the ocean floor. "All we've really done is a gross, crude first look," a Canadian scientist said. "What we need to do is go back and fill in some details."[12]

In the late 1990s, Australia, Canada, and Japan decided to invest in gathering those details of the seabed. In 1998, Australia surveyed its waters near Antarctica, and several optimistic scientists predicted that the country's undersea realm might become larger than its territory above sea-level. The imaging effort yielded some revelations. Australia's researchers discovered a previously unknown undersea mountain almost 15,000 feet in height.[13] A few years later, the Japanese government committed more than $90 million to its own undersea mapping effort and encouraged major private-sector players to get involved. A Japanese government spokesperson expressed confidence that the boost in research funding would be well received domestically. "The topic of expanding national territories is easy to understand for the public."[14]

Countries with more modest means joined the effort as well. In 1999, India's Department of Ocean Development announced surveys to determine the depth of sediment in the Bay of Bengal, the Arabian Sea, and the Indian Ocean. "This seabed project will mean a long-term strategic gain for India," a government minister said. "Our continental shelf will be for our exclusive use."[15] As the costs of such projects became apparent, some developing countries agitated in international meetings for financial assistance and a relaxation of the Convention's deadlines. Responding to that pressure, the UN General Assembly in 2000 established trust funds to help cash-strapped countries compile the necessary undersea evidence. The next year, the Convention's members extended by several years the deadline for submissions.[16]

As the continental shelf process unfolded, the few countries that had decided against joining the Convention found themselves in a curious position. As nonmembers, should they make submissions to the Commission regarding their own claims? Doing so might imply that they needed its approval, yet failing to go through the process could leave legal doubt about their claims. The question was acute for the US government. A preliminary survey in 2002 found that the United States might have rights to nearly a million square miles of undersea territory, twice the land area of California. The most promising areas were the Arctic Ocean, the Atlantic seaboard, and a stretch of the Pacific near Guam. The National Oceanographic and Atmospheric Agency (NOAA), working together with the coast guard, the navy, and the Interior Department's US Geologic Survey, designed research missions to generate detailed information about the seabed in these areas. In the summer of 2003, the coast guard ship *Healy* used an echolocation system to provide a detailed map of the Arctic floor.[17] Undecided about whether to file a submission with the Commission, Washington was at least ensuring that it had the evidence to do so.

Russia, which ratified the Convention in 1997, moved more quickly. In late 2001, it made the first ever submission to the Commission, outlining areas of extended shelf in the Arctic and Pacific. Russian government officials worried that the West was leaping ahead in oil and gas extraction and hoped that a continental shelf bid might bolster its energy claims in the Arctic.[18] The hurriedly compiled Russian file prompted objections. The United States charged that it had "major flaws" and released a paper criticizing several aspects of the submission. Canada, Japan, and Norway also complained. Moscow's haste had consequences; the Commission politely rebuffed the submission and encouraged Russia to gather additional evidence.

The suspicion that greeted Russia was replicated in other regions. In early 1997, Thailand's prime minister, returning from a trip abroad, was met at the airport by five foreign ambassadors eager to register their disapproval with Thailand's recently announced continental shelf submission.[19] Canada worried that France would use its islands of St. Pierre and Miquelon, situated less than 20 miles from Newfoundland, to gain undersea rights on Canada's doorstep and thereby "leapfrog" Canada's exclusive economic zone. Britain and Argentina exchanged bitter words as London prepared the portions of its own extended shelf submission that relied on ownership of the Falkland Islands.

The Convention had been designed in large part to end the turbulence associated with competing ocean claims. But the extended shelf process was perpetuating discord, albeit on a more limited scale. The race for undersea territory was particularly complicated near Antarctica. The 12 countries that had formed the Antarctic Treaty system in the 1950s agreed at that time to freeze their territorial claims to the continent. But did that understanding extend to the undersea shelf around the continent? Competing shelf submissions might unravel the compromise that had prevented a land rush on the frozen continent. Conscious of that danger, Australia threaded the needle when it filed its paperwork with the commission in 2004. It included information on the Antarctic continental shelf but requested the Commission "not to take any action for the time being."[20]

As thick files landed at the Commission's offices, it became evident that more countries than expected were taking advantage of the process. Russia's unsuccessful 2001 submission was the first, but Australia and Brazil filed submissions soon thereafter. Then came Ireland, New Zealand, and Norway. France, the United Kingdom, and Spain collaborated on a submission regarding an area in the Celtic Sea and Bay of Biscay. Several large developing countries, including Namibia, were preparing submissions, and the Commission hosted training seminars for interested countries. By 2007, nine states had prepared complete or partial submissions, and a substantial queue of countries was readying the paperwork. The Commission made pleas for additional personnel and resources as it struggled through the mountain of documentation.

More fundamental than the bureaucratic challenges were the conceptual implications of the scramble for undersea territory. Every square mile of seabed that moved into national hands moved out of international control. And any resources on the newly nationalized seabed would belong exclusively to the coastal country. The vision of undersea resources benefiting humanity as a whole was not gone, but it was fading. Canadian scholar Ted McDorman described the trend:

> No coastal state wants to be in the position in 50 years of looking back and seeing that because they were not aggressive in their assertion of the outer limit of the shelf, a valuable mineral resource is not within their sovereign control. The ethos of the 1970s when there was the international political will to accept the Common Heritage concept and a degree of global sharing increasingly appears to have been a blip on the historic law-of-the-sea radar.[21]

Facing a limited window for acquiring new undersea rights, some of the developing countries that had strongly advocated a "common heritage" approach proved decidedly acquisitive. If the extended shelf process was a meaningful indication, the national appetite for undersea territory remained healthy, and the potential for future friction was real.

On Board, with Baggage

The strong interest in making continental shelf submissions to the UN commission was part of a broad embrace of the Convention that followed the supplemental negotiations of the early 1990s. Twenty-seven countries ratified in 1996, more than double the previous year's total. The United Kingdom, the erstwhile maritime hegemon, joined in 1997. Like the United States, the British government had qualms about the seabed mining structure but it determined that the 1994 changes made the Convention acceptable. Announcing plans to join, Britain's foreign secretary described the agreement as "of crucial importance in the maritime field and very favourable to Britain."[22]

Ratification did force one bitter pill on the British. Rockall, that lonely spot of granite in the North Atlantic, was downgraded. Because it manifestly did not meet the Convention's definition of an island, the British government accepted that Rockall could not generate the 200-mile EEZ that the United Kingdom had previously claimed. When the government acknowledged that reality, British fishing interests fumed at the surrender of exclusive fishing grounds. "The whole principle of giving up an area of that size is something we cannot support," a fisheries association representative said.[23]

Several key developing countries ratified the Convention as well, including India and South Africa. Yet the most significant ratification came in May 1996, when the People's Republic of China announced that it would join the Convention. The Asian giant had been a marginal diplomatic player at the time the negotiations commenced. Throughout the 1970s, Chinese diplomats often positioned themselves as protectors of the developing world and staunch adversaries of both superpowers. China's foreign policy became more pragmatic in the years after the text was finalized, but China remained vague about its ratification plans. The 1996 decision therefore marked a significant acceptance of the international rules governing the ocean and a potential boon for stability in contested Asian waters. Joining the Convention suggested that China accepted its basic framework and would resolve disputes in accordance with its procedures.

The region was in need of reassurance. China's ratification came on the heels of a tense standoff with Vietnam about waters near Vanguard Bank, a submerged feature in the South China Sea. In 1992, China claimed drilling rights in a block of ocean within Vietnam's declared EEZ. Several close encounters at sea ensued. When Chinese vessels approached the area to begin operations, Vietnamese patrol craft fired warning shots. China responded a few months later by preventing supplies from getting to Vietnam's own drilling operation, eventually forcing its closure. In the Spratly Islands as well, China was altering the status quo. In February 1995, the Philippines discovered that China had stealthily occupied and built installations on Mischief Reef, complete with satellite dishes. Chinese explanations for the move were evasive and contradictory, deepening suspicion about Beijing's intentions. "After the Chinese move, not just the Philippines but Malaysia, Brunei, and Indonesia felt directly threatened."[24]

Hopes that Chinese ratification implied a more conciliatory approach were short-lived. Even as it joined the Convention, China announced a view of innocent passage very different from the one endorsed by Washington. Innocent passage, its government insisted, "shall not prejudice the right of a coastal state to request . . . a foreign state to obtain advance approval from or give prior notification to the coastal State for the passage of its warships through the territorial sea."[25] China was far from alone in that interpretation, but Beijing's view created immediate potential for friction with the United States. In 1988, Washington had challenged Moscow's interpretation of innocent passage with its risky Black Sea operation. China's announcement suggested that new iterations of that confrontation were likely.

Other Chinese assertions unnerved a broader group of countries. As it ratified, Beijing made public the baselines from which it would measure its territorial sea and exclusive economic zone. Using the familiar technique of "straight baselines," China significantly augmented the maritime space under its national jurisdiction. The baselines that China drew around the contested Paracel Islands were even more controversial than those for the mainland. They purported to create a large swath of Chinese waters in the middle of the South China Sea. The Philippines expressed alarm, and a Vietnamese official called the Chinese moves a "blatant violation" of international rules.[26] In July 1996, the Association of Southeast Asian States (ASEAN) urged restraint in maritime claims. Washington joined the chorus. The State Department criticized China's use of straight baselines and pointed out that enclosing whole island chains (rather than drawing a baseline around each individual island) was a technique available only to archipelagic states. China responded frostily. "The delimitation of baselines is in itself a sovereign act of the country," a spokesman said. "It is impossible to review it."[27]

At sea, the navies of the Asian countries most directly affected were no match for Chinese forces. China's navy—confusingly titled the People's Liberation Army Navy (PLAN)—had changed substantially since its founding in 1950. Early in its history, it was conceived of as little more than a coastal defense force. The development of Soviet and Japanese naval capabilities in the late 1960s and 1970s prompted a reconsideration. In 1997, Chinese president Jiang Zemin admonished the navy to "build up the nation's maritime Great Wall." Beijing purchased several new destroyers from Russia, armed with missiles able to hit targets dozens of miles away, while also producing new warships of its own design.[28] In 1997, a Chinese naval task force journeyed through the region and then as far afield as South America, "the widest-ranging Chinese naval deployment since the [15th century] voyages of Zheng He."[29]

That naval imbalance in the region produced some unorthodox maneuvers by the Philippines, which worried about Chinese intentions near the Spratly Islands. In May 1999, a Philippine navy vessel ran aground on Second Thomas Shoal, a teardrop-shaped atoll in the Spratly chain. The Philippines claimed that the grounding was an accident, but it was almost certainly a desperate attempt to claim ownership of the feature and preempt occupation by China. A small group of sailors remained on the grounded vessel, which was periodically resupplied by boat and air. Around the same time, a Philippine navy vessel sank a Chinese fishing boat during a chase near Scarborough Shoal, which was inside the Philippines EEZ but claimed by China.

Not all of the friction in Asian waters was generated by national governments. In September 1996, a group of nationalist citizens from Hong Kong set sail for the Senkaku Islands, claimed and controlled by Japan. The protesters reportedly planned to tear down a small lighthouse that a Japanese citizen group had installed on the islands a few months before. Carrying 18 protesters and more than 40 journalists, the vessel arrived near the Senkakus only to find a small flotilla of Japanese patrol boats awaiting them. The Japanese craft were able to prevent the ship from landing, and it eventually returned to Hong Kong. But the voyage was a vivid reminder that nationalist feelings in the region ran high on maritime disputes.

The most alarming moments in the region featured direct contact between US and Chinese military forces. In March 2001, the US hydrographic survey ship *Bowditch* was in the Yellow Sea conducting what the United States described as routine survey operations inside China's EEZ when it was "aggressively confronted" and instructed to leave by a Chinese frigate.[30] A more serious incident occurred a few weeks later. On April 1, a US EP-3 aircraft based on Okinawa headed out over the South China Sea. Commanded by Lieutenant Shane Osborn, the plane carried a crew of several dozen, including specialists in electronic warfare and surveillance. Several hours into the flight, the EP-3 was approached by Chinese fighter aircraft. At first, the fighters kept their distance and appeared content to monitor the US plane.

Then, according to the US account, one of the Chinese fighters rapidly closed the distance:

> The [Chinese fighter plane] pulled up just under [Lt. Shane] Osborn's left wing. To slow down further, the Chinese pilot, Wang Wei, pulled the nose of his aircraft up slightly. He fatally miscalculated the distance between the two aircraft. The main body of the fighter collided with the EP-3's number one rotary engine. The EP-3's propellers cut through the fuselage of the Chinese jet, severing it in half. The impact sheared the EP-3's nose cone clean off.[31]

The Chinese fighter plane spiraled into the ocean, and the larger US aircraft ended up in a nearly vertical dive. Osborn instructed his crew to prepare to bail, but the pilot was finally able to pull the plane under control. The only landing strip he could reach was on China's Hainan Island, and he pointed his wounded aircraft in that direction. As the crew hurriedly jettisoned classified material and smashed surveillance and cryptographic equipment, the EP-3 landed.

Chinese officials blamed the incident on the US plane, which they said was maneuvering erratically. More broadly, they criticized the US policy of flying reconnaissance missions over China's exclusive economic zone and demanded an apology. The Bush administration, which had taken office only a few months earlier, insisted on the prompt return of the crew and plane. To back up their claims of Chinese recklessness, US officials told reporters of previous risky intercepts by the Chinese pilot involved, including one when he reportedly came within 10 feet of a US aircraft and held up a sheet of paper with his email address printed on it.[32] Behind all the accusations and acrimony was the recurring dispute about the limits of national power in the EEZ—the same issue international judges grappled with inconclusively in the *Saiga* case. The United States believed its military had the right to operate freely in the Chinese EEZ, and China did not.

For more than a week, Washington and Beijing groped for a resolution to the crisis. In a painstakingly negotiated statement, the United States expressed regret over the incident and the loss of the Chinese pilot but never explicitly acknowledged that its aircraft was operating where it should not be. For its part, the Chinese government posthumously declared the lost fighter pilot a "Guardian of Territorial Airspace and Waters." The American crew finally returned to US soil in mid-April, but their plane stayed behind.

Chinese officials carefully inspected and then dismantled the aircraft, eventually shipping it back to the United States in pieces (and aboard a Russian
cargo plane).[33]

US protests after the *Bowditch* and EP-3 incidents centered on its rights
under international maritime law. And yet the world's leading maritime
power remained an outsider to the Convention, despite the efforts of the
Clinton and George W. Bush administrations. Both presidents became convinced that joining the Convention served US interests, not least by bolstering the credibility of complaints against China. "Refusal to ratify could
be a potential destabilizer in the United States' relationship with other
countries," one of the navy's top officers told senators in 1995.[34] Even as the
United States assumed the mantle of defender of the international rules for
the ocean, the US Senate continued to spurn the treaty that articulated those
rules most clearly.

Petro-Pirates and Ocean Peacekeeping

The increased friction over continental shelves in the Arctic and maritime
rights in the South China Sea were, in part, manifestations of a more complicated dynamic between the major powers. The relative harmony of the
early 1990s was yielding to a newly competitive dynamic. Even as this was
developing, a very old oceans problem reemerged. Pirate attacks in and
around Southeast Asia increased from 99 in 1998 to 257 in 2000, when the
region accounted for more than half of the reported worldwide total.[35] The
Straits of Malacca—the throughway for shipping between the Indian Ocean
and South China Sea—became the epicenter. Observers speculated that the
Asian financial crisis, which peaked in 1997, was encouraging violence at sea.
"Today's pirates are a troubling symptom of a new world order," a *New York
Times* correspondent wrote somewhat breathlessly, "one shaped by a fierce
Darwinian struggle in the feral markets of modern international trade."[36]
Even as it increased the incentives for piracy, financial turmoil tightened na-
tional purse strings and strained already limited resources for maritime law
enforcement.

As in centuries past, accusations circulated that some governments were
less than vigilant in dealing with pirate activity—and perhaps even com-
plicit in it. China received particular criticism for responding slowly to
requests for assistance and for repeatedly releasing apprehended pirates. "It

is unacceptable that China, a major maritime nation, has failed to take action against this type of criminal activity where local government officials are clearly involved," the International Maritime Bureau complained in 1998.[37] Those tracking the piracy boom insisted that certain local Chinese officials were in league with crime syndicates. The problem was not just in China; Indonesian customs officials apparently supplemented their income by occasional freebooting as well.[38]

The most audacious pirate attacks took place in the late 1990s. In May 1998, a dozen pirates in a speedboat clambered aboard the *Petro Ranger* not long after it left the relatively well-policed waters of Singapore. Once on board, the pirates subdued and locked up the tanker's crew, repainted the ship's superstructure, and assigned it a new name. After the purloined vessel had spent a few days at sea, smaller boats pulled alongside to siphon off the liquid cargo: 11,000 tons of diesel and kerosene. In October 1999, another group of pirates seized the Japanese-owned *Alondra Rainbow* off the coast of Indonesia, eventually setting its crew adrift on a lifeboat. Eleven days later, with flares and water nearly exhausted, the Japanese and Filipino mariners were rescued by a Thai fishing boat.[39]

Shipping industry representatives agitated for increased sovereign attention to law and order at sea. "Governments should be made aware that ship owners are bringing economic benefits to their countries and if nothing is done about it, shipping and trade will suffer," the head of an Asian shipping federation warned.[40] Frustrated shipowners experimented with solutions that did not rely on governmental action. Larger companies considered new technologies that would alert them whenever a vessel deviated from its planned course. They also tried old-fashioned muscle. A group of maritime security firms hired former British special forces soldiers to assist in the protection of large merchant ships.

Larger countries in the region were not entirely passive. The *Petro Ranger* seizure eventually ended when a Chinese maritime patrol became suspicious and boarded the vessel. The pirates tried to convince the Chinese that they were the legitimate crew, but the ruse eventually fell apart. India also played a part in pressuring pirates. Acting on a tip from a patrol aircraft, an Indian navy ship chased down the renamed and reflagged *Alondra Rainbow*.[41] But the government in the region best motivated and equipped to combat piracy was Japan's. Dependent on fuel and foodstuffs shipped through the Strait of Malacca, Japan saw suppressing maritime violence as a vital national security issue. The Japanese press reported in detail on the marooning of the *Alondra*

Rainbow's crew—coverage that helped focus the attention of policymakers. With a well-equipped Coast Guard and Maritime Self-Defense Force, Japan had the wherewithal to engage in regional patrols.

Averse to unilateral action, Tokyo advanced several multilateral plans for confronting piracy. The most far-reaching was an "ocean peacekeeping" force that would be authorized by the United Nations and operated jointly by countries in the region.[42] The plan proved too ambitious. Malaysia and Indonesia, in particular, resisted such an institutionalized structure. Their history made them skeptical of major-power initiatives for preserving freedom of navigation. "Malaysia has been colonized four times, three times by Europeans, and in all cases they arrived under the pretext of fighting piracy," a Malaysian vice admiral said. "So you can understand why we are particularly sensitive to these issues."[43]

Within a few years, piracy in the region ebbed as economic conditions improved and as Indonesia, Malaysia, and Singapore cobbled together resources to improve maritime security. Its visions of multilateral maritime security rebuffed, Japan still provided aid and training to regional coast guards seeking to improve their skills. While there were new dynamics at work and emerging technologies in the mix, the response to the rise in piracy in the 1990s was not so dissimilar from the past. Sometimes sluggishly, merchants and sovereign states with an interest in maintaining open commerce tamped down the violence. For the most part, the existing international law framework proved workable. Japan's unsuccessful bid for a more comprehensive solution demonstrated how potent historically driven concerns about sovereignty could be in thwarting maritime multilateralism. The refusal of the United States to ratify the Convention was the most obvious and consequential elevation of sovereignty over shared ocean governance, but plenty of other countries had motives to resist internationalized management of the seas.

Boarding Up

The phenomenon that most strained the rules concerning maritime law enforcement was not piracy but terrorism. In the wake of the attacks on September 11, 2001, US officials scrambled to plug multiple security gaps at once. One of these was the possible transfer of terrorists or weapons of mass destruction by sea. Security reviews after the terrorist attacks repeatedly identified maritime commerce as a likely conduit. The 9/11 Commission report detailed a plot by Al Qaeda associates to bomb ships and emphasized the vulnerabilities of the international shipping system. Malcom McLean's container revolution had been a boon for commerce, but tracking millions of containers was a nightmare for security officials. Efforts to ensure the security of container shipping, the 9/11 report warned, "have just begun."[44] In 2002, the IMO adopted regulations requiring ports and shipowners to assess their vulnerability and designate officials responsible for security. But any more robust measures would be a matter for national navies.

In late 2002, US intelligence agencies learned that a freighter, the *So San*, had taken on cargo in North Korea and was sailing toward the Middle East. Concerned that the vessel might be carrying weapons of mass destruction components to Iraq, US officials coordinated an interception. The warships in closest proximity were a pair of Spanish frigates, and hurried communication between Washington and Madrid resulted in a plan to stop and board the *So San*. Because the vessel did not appear to be flying a national flag, the Spanish had the legal toehold they needed. After firing shots across the ship's bow, Spanish sailors boarded and searched the vessel. In its hold, hidden among hundreds of bags of cement, lay 15 Scud missiles with conventional warheads.

The intelligence had been correct that the vessel was transporting arms from North Korea. But the *So San* was not carrying weapons of mass destruction and it was not headed to Iraq. Yemen's government announced that it had purchased and paid for the missiles and demanded that they be handed over. Nor was the *So San* actually stateless; the crew produced papers indicating that it was registered in Cambodia, and the Cambodian government confirmed their validity. Because there was nothing necessarily illegal about the shipment or the ship, the Spanish decided they were bound to let the *So San* proceed. President Bush was reportedly livid, and the incident convinced his administration that controlling the transfer of dangerous weapons at sea required more flexible rules for when boarding and seizure of vessels was permissible.[45]

The eventual result was the Proliferation Security Initiative (PSI), announced by President Bush in May 2003. At the heart of the initiative was a commitment by participating countries to board suspicious vessels within their own waters and—even more important—to consent to a search of their vessels if other members sought to board them on the high seas. Under heavy pressure, several leading flag-of-convenience countries, including Panama and Liberia, joined the initiative. In pushing PSI, the United States was emulating the approach employed by the British in their 19th-century anti-slavery patrols. And like the British program, the PSI received pointed criticism from countries suspicious of the maritime hegemon's motives.

China and India were particularly skeptical of the PSI's boarding provisions, and both countries declined to join the initiative. A Chinese official warned that PSI interdictions "might go beyond the international law."[46] One scholar summarized Indian concerns about the unfolding initiative and its potential to alter international rules:

> In this way, the apparently voluntary PSI which professes to target terrorist groups and supporting regimes becomes legalized, and consequently relegates crucial freedoms for maritime trade like the freedom of innocent passage in territorial waters and freedom of navigation in the high seas by allowing coastal States and participating States to interdict all suspected ships for inspection, search and seizure within territorial waters and in the high seas.[47]

Disagreements surrounding the program came to a head during 2004–2005 negotiations at the International Maritime Organization. Usually placid affairs, the sessions turned fractious as countries disagreed about the limits of boarding operations. The United States pushed for a "tacit consent" rule that would allow boarding of a suspicious vessel if the flag state did not respond to requests for permission within a short window of time. That was a step too far for many delegates, who regarded explicit flag state permission as an essential principle safeguarding the freedom of navigation. The US delegation ultimately dropped its proposal.[48]

The debate over boarding highlighted the distinct ways in which claims about ocean freedom intersected with politics. When it came to maritime zones, the United States saw itself as a principled and determined defender of maritime freedom, while other powers insisted that the prerogatives of coastal states be taken seriously. But in the terrorism context—as with the anti-communist struggles of the 1950s—the United States was willing to squeeze traditional freedom of navigation to grapple with what it perceived as existential threats. By contrast, China and India, both of whom believed in the right of coastal states to impose restrictions on innocent passage and EEZ use, could be purists about free navigation on the high seas.

The Flight of the *Viarsa*

In the mid-1990s, the old phenomenon of vessels fishing where they should not received a new name. The term "illegal, unreported, and unregulated fishing" first appeared in 1997, and IUU fishing soon became a catch-all category for everything from outright poaching within national waters to irresponsible (although not always illegal) high-seas fishing that was not reported to relevant regional fishing organizations. By some estimates, IUU fishing accounted for 10–20 percent of the total global catch. The World Bank estimated the annual economic losses to coastal states from IUU fishing at $50 billion.[49]

The heightened concern about rogue fishing came in the context of repeated warnings about the health of fisheries. In 2003, the UN's Food and Agriculture Organization warned that "too many vessels [are] chasing too few fish." In its annual review of world fisheries, the organization reported that more than two thirds of high-seas fish stocks were either depleted or at high risk of collapse.[50] Straddling stocks that moved between national waters and the high seas and migratory fish populations, including Atlantic bluefin tuna and southern bluefin tuna, seemed to be in particular peril.

There were at least two distinct challenges involved in combatting IUU fishing. First, national governments had to effectively supervise their EEZs. Even large countries with significant naval resources struggled with the task of monitoring ocean space out to 200 miles. But new technology could help: Canada signed a deal with Raytheon to provide a long-range surface radar to help monitor its EEZ. Vessel monitoring systems (VMS) could also paint for coastal states an electronic picture of nearby maritime activities. Namibia's government claimed significant success in rejuvenating the country's waters through an effective monitoring system. Some governments saw the new technology not only as a means for securing their own maritime zones but also as a way to ensure that their nationals did not provoke disputes with neighbors. Taiwan's prime minister publicly urged fishermen to use GPS systems in order to avoid wandering into the Japanese EEZ.[51]

Even as technology provided new ways of tracking fishing vessels, countermeasures appeared. In 2001, officials monitoring fishing in the Southern Ocean reported strange readings from VMS systems. As they sorted through the data, they concluded that certain fishing vessels had figured out how to send false readings, thereby frustrating monitoring.[52] As the incident suggested, the Southern Ocean attracted some of the most sophisticated IUU fishing. The incentive was the meaty and lucrative tooth-fish, marketed in the United States and elsewhere as Chilean sea bass. Profits from a successful toothfish haul made elaborate subterfuge worth the effort. A multinational group of experts described some of the tactics employed:

> The movements of patrol boats are monitored by spies and reported to the illegal fleet. Communication between vessels of the same fleet is kept to a minimum to avoid detection. If an interdiction is inevitable, older, less valuable, vessels are sacrificed to protect more valuable ones. Ownership structures involving multiple front companies are used to keep details from boat crews as well as authorities. Operational instructions for the illegal fleet are passed down through front companies with vessel masters often not knowing who their real employers are.[53]

An encounter with one of these "toothfish pirates" produced perhaps the most protracted attempt to protect a national EEZ. In early August 2003, an Australian patrol vessel was cruising the southern Indian Ocean. Two Australian possessions in the area, the sparsely populated Heard and McDonald Islands, created a large area of exclusive economic zone, and the Australian government had become increasingly committed to protecting it from unauthorized foreign fishing. On August 7, the Australian patrol caught sight of a trawler that appeared to be fishing inside the EEZ.

That vessel, the *Viarsa 1*, was under the command of a Spanish captain and had a crew drawn from Spain, Portugal, and several South American countries. The vessel was flagged by Uruguay but the owner was in Spain and in radio contact with his ship. Apparently on his instructions, the *Viarsa 1* resisted the Australian patrol's call to stop and be boarded. For its part, Uruguay refused the Australians permission to board and instead instructed the fishing vessel to return to its home port. For the next three weeks, the Australians trailed the *Viarsa 1* into the Southern Ocean, perilously close to Antarctic icebergs, and then on a more northerly course toward South America.[54]

On the high seas and without Uruguay's permission, a boarding operation was complex practically and legally. Australia insisted that it was in "hot pursuit," and therefore within its rights to pursue a violator into the open ocean. To avoid the abuse of vessels on the high seas, however, the right of hot pursuit comes with strict conditions. In the *Saiga* case, for example, the Guinean government could not demonstrate that it had maintained an uninterrupted chase from its waters, and so the Tribunal deemed its boarding illegal. Determined to avoid that outcome, the Australian commander struggled to maintain nearly constant radar contact with the fleeing vessel.

Finally, as the fishing vessel neared Uruguay's territorial waters, the Australians cobbled together a motley boarding party composed of South African and British men armed mostly with sawed-off shotguns. They clambered aboard, helped arrest the crew, and collected evidence. The still defiant Spanish captain and several officers were flown to Australia to stand trial. Several years later, an Australian jury failed to convict the men, but the country's fisheries minister was undaunted. "I would repeat the exercise tomorrow if a foreign fishing vessel is sighted by an Australian patrol vessel inside the Australian Fishing Zone," he insisted.[55]

Some countries without the means to effectively patrol their waters— let alone conduct dramatic, long-range operations like the *Viarsa 1* chase— reached out to private businesses and non-governmental organizations for assistance. During the late 1990s, Sierra Leone and Liberia both contracted with private security firms to patrol their maritime zones and deter unauthorized fishing.[56] These fragile governments gave private firms permission to monitor fishing, issue fines, and detain poachers. In 2001, the government of Ecuador struck a deal with the Sea Shepherd Conservation Society, led by the controversial Paul Watson, to help patrol the waters around the Galapagos Islands.

Expelled by Greenpeace in the late 1970s, Watson bought a vessel and built his own protest organization. One of the organization's first operations was to chase down and ram a vessel notorious for illegal whaling.[57] Throughout the 1980s and 1990s, Watson regularly confronted seal hunters and whaling ships, several times stalking vessels he believed were engaged in unlawful operations. Arrested for short periods by several different governments, Watson persisted and Sea Shepherd expanded. Along the way, the renegade captain clashed bitterly with Greenpeace, the organization he had helped found but whose more restrained methods he now rejected.

Watson cultivated relationships with celebrities (several of whom contributed significantly to the organization's coffers) and penned multiple books about his maritime battles (Figure 7.2). In addition to Greenpeace's spinelessness, a recurring theme in Watson's work was the international lawfulness of his efforts. The organization viewed itself as defending international

Figure 7.2 Captain Paul Watson and actress Darryl Hannah on a Sea Shepherd vessel; photograph courtesy of Eric H. Cheng.

agreements on fishing and whaling. And Watson often cited a (nonbinding) 1982 resolution passed by the UN General Assembly to claim international legal authority for confrontations at sea:

> We intervene against illegal activities, and we are simply upholding interna-
> tional conservation law, and the United Nations World Charter for Nature
> allows for us to do that. It says that any nongovernmental organization, or
> individual, is empowered to uphold international conservation law. That's
> why I've sunk ten whaling ships and destroyed tens of millions of dollars'
> worth of illegal fishing gear, and I'm not in jail.[58]

Watson's reading of international law was idiosyncratic, but the relationship that he had developed with the Ecuadorian government expanded. "We
are officially an environmental law enforcement agency," he exulted.[59] For
governments like Ecuador's that were struggling to monitor large maritime
realms, outsourcing sovereign powers to private actors was tempting. But the
tactic also risked recreating the privateering dynamic that had proven so destructive in the 17th and 18th centuries. The governments that had clashed

with Sea Shepherd in the past could only grimace at the sight of a newly dep-
utized Paul Watson.

Collective Action Problems

For coastal countries in need of assistance, private companies and crusaders
like Watson represented possible answers to poaching. On the high seas,
hopes for restraining overfishing rested mostly on less colorful actors. The
1995 Fish Stocks Agreement made "regional fisheries management organizations" (RFMOs) the frontlines in the battle against high-seas overfishing. By
the late 1990s, they had emerged as "the management mechanism of choice
through which the principles of conservation and cooperation . . . are to be
achieved."[60] Sea Shepherd was bold, brash, and staffed by idealists. For their
part, RFMOs were cautious, consensus-driven, and populated mostly by
anonymous government bureaucrats.

Several of these organizations focused on particular highly migratory
species, including tuna. Other organizations had cross-species regional
mandates, such as for the northeast Atlantic, the northwest Atlantic, the
South Pacific, or the southern Indian Ocean. Collectively, the world's more
than a dozen RFMOs claimed a role in managing most fish on the high seas.
Two marine biologists argued that this network of multinational supervision
had eviscerated one element of freedom of the seas:

> Steeped in the antiquated dogma of Hugo Grotius' 'The Free Sea' from the
> early 17th century, fishers have long considered the high seas as open-ac-
> cess, meaning anyone and everyone had rights to fish there. This perception,
> however, is obsolete today: regional fisheries management organizations
> (RFMOs) are currently the only legally mandated fisheries management
> bodies on the high seas. . . . In other words, 'The Free Sea' is no more.[61]

The Grotian ideal was certainly fading, but that particular obituary was pre-
mature. Countries that chose not to sign the Fish Stocks Agreement or join
relevant RFMOs were still within their rights to continue fishing on the high
seas. As had happened in the Grand Banks during the 1980s, certain fishing
vessels shifted flags precisely in order to evade regulation. Vessels "have been
deliberately deregistered from [RFMO] member states and reregistered
in non-member states in order to avoid application of conservation and

management measures adopted by those organizations."[62] High-seas fishing companies based in Spain, Taiwan, Korea, and the United States sometimes flagged their fishing vessels in countries like Belize, St. Vincent, and Honduras. The flag-of-convenience system had spread from the shipping industry to the world of high-seas fishing, and it brought with it a welter of governance problems.

Even when RFMOs did have clear jurisdiction, the means to enforce their regulations were often absent. Observers identified major holes in their ability to monitor and report reliably on the waters under their jurisdiction.[63] Environmentalists charged that the scientific advice these organizations received was often more about justifying high catch allowances than effectively conserving fish stocks. Analyses of the work of these scientific advisory bodies found that they were highly susceptible to political pressure from member states. When scientists did challenge the policy consensus, they sometimes found their analyses trimmed or omitted entirely. "Controversial material is omitted from reports and in turn are reduced to their lowest acceptable, (negotiated and politically influenced) common denominator."[64]

Still, there were bright spots. The North Pacific Anadromous Fish Commission showed particular promise. Canada, Japan, Korea, Russia, and the United States created the organization in the early 1990s with a mandate to conserve salmon and steelhead trout stocks on the region's high seas. The organization had a banner month in April 1999. In mid-April, a Canadian surveillance plane spotted a vessel suspected of driftnet fishing about 500 miles south of Alaska. The information was passed to the US Coast Guard, which boarded the Russian-flagged vessel the next day and handed over the vessel and crew to Russian authorities. A week later, the same US Coast Guard cutter saw a Chinese-flagged vessel engaged in prohibited salmon fishing with drift nets. With the assistance of a Chinese liaison official on board the coast guard ship, a team boarded and searched the *Ying Fa*.[65]

But that kind of coordinated and energetic monitoring on behalf of regional fisheries organizations was the exception. In most regions, the means were only slowly emerging to enforce new limits on high-seas fishing.

The Garbage Patch

If fish stocks in many places were in decline, the ocean's supply of certain inorganic material was abundant. In 1997, a Long Beach, California, native named Charles Moore was on his way back from a yachting race off the Hawaiian Islands. A sailor since boyhood, Moore had sold his furniture repair business and devoted himself full time to maritime pursuits. On the return from Hawaii, he and his crew passed through a remote area of the Pacific well off normal shipping routes. What Moore saw astounded him:

> As I gazed from the deck at the surface of what ought to have been a pristine ocean, I was confronted, as far as the eye could see, with the sight of plastic. It seemed unbelievable, but I never found a clear spot. In the week it took to cross the subtropical high, no matter what time of day I looked, plastic debris was floating everywhere: bottles, bottle caps, wrappers, fragments.[66]

The yacht was traversing what oceanographers refer to as a gyre, an area of broadly circular ocean currents. Floating debris that wanders into the gyre tends to remain there for long periods, and the buoyancy and durability of plastic ensure that it does not readily sink or disintegrate. Moore's discovery was eventually dubbed the "Pacific garbage patch," a moniker that resonated with the public and conjured up images of an actual island of trash. In the next few years, Moore returned to the area several times to sample the water and measure the plastic content. These and other subsequent observations confirmed that much of the plastic collected in the gyres was in small pellet form and hovered below the surface; the area was more a plastic soup than an island of plastic.

Moore had never completed college, but he immersed himself in the literature on marine plastic and presented his findings in peer-reviewed articles. Meanwhile, more conventional researchers attempted to understand the impact of accumulating ocean plastic on marine life. Their inquiries extended beyond the Pacific gyre that Moore had discovered. Similar collections of plastic were located in the Atlantic, Indian, and southern Pacific Oceans. Evidence emerged that a variety of sea creatures—including seabirds, otters, and some species of fish—were ingesting plastic. Birds proved particularly fond of discarded butane lighters, which may have appeared to them as food. Advocacy groups, including Greenpeace, used images of dead seabirds with various forms of plastic in their stomachs in public campaigns.

In a few contexts, floating debris proved an unexpected boon for understanding the ocean. For several years, the oceanographer Curtis Ebbesmeyer meticulously tracked the path of Nike sneakers and toy rubber ducks that were thrown from cargo ships during Pacific storms. He placed advertisements in local newspapers seeking information on washed up items that could be traced to the cargo vessels. Once he had verified the identity and location of the detritus, he logged the resulting data, and used a computer simulation to map the likely path of the debris. The resulting study helped refine understandings of ocean currents.[67]

To this point, international rules to protect the ocean environment had focused on managing behavior on the seas: fishing, dumping, and weapons testing. And those transiting the oceans had certainly contributed to the plague of ocean plastic. In the early 1990s, cruise ship passengers videotaped crew members hurling bags of trash into the ocean under cover of darkness.[68] Oceangoing fishing vessels often discarded or lost vast plastic drift nets, trawls, and longlines, which trapped marine life for years. Haltingly, countries put in place international agreements to address plastic pollution from vessels. In 1988, a new annex to a long-standing marine pollution agreement, originally negotiated in 1973, prohibited the dumping of all plastic waste and required large vessels to document and track waste disposal. In 1992, the UN General Assembly called for a moratorium on certain large drift nets. Rebuffing opposition from their own fishing industries, Japan and South Korea pledged not to use them.[69]

For all the sins of certain mariners, however, studies pinned most blame on land-based consumers. One study estimated that more than 80 percent of ocean plastic arrived via rivers, streams, and sewer systems. In 1995, governments took the first halting step toward stopping the migration of plastic from land to the ocean. A declaration finalized in Washington encouraged all countries to prevent the flow of harmful material into the ocean.[70] Grappling with the maladies afflicting the modern ocean, it was becoming clear, would require efforts that went well beyond supervising behavior at sea.

Hard to Port

In November 2002, an aged and rusting tanker, the *Prestige*, departed St. Petersburg, Russia, carrying nearly 80,000 tons of heavy oil. The vessel flew the flag of the Bahamas, but it was owned by a Greek conglomerate registered in Liberia. The vessel had a Greek captain and a mostly Filipino crew. On November 13, off the coast of Spain and in the midst of a gale, the ship's hull fractured. Rescue helicopters managed to evacuate most of the crew, but the captain and a few officers stayed with the ship. In an effort to get the stricken

vessel as far from the coast as possible, the Spanish government flew an experienced mariner onto the ship to work with the *Prestige*'s own captain. For
hours, the two men feuded. The Greek captain wanted to bring the wounded
vessel into port, but Spain's official insisted that the ship move out to sea and
hinted that the Spanish navy stood ready to enforce that demand.[71]

For several days, the *Prestige* was towed gingerly away from the Spanish
coast. "We're going to try to get it out at least 120 miles from Spain," a government spokesperson said. "Where it goes after that is not our responsibility."[72]
Neighboring Portugal watched the drama closely, and its government made
clear it wanted no part of the *Prestige*. A Portuguese warship sailed to the
boundary of its EEZ to ensure that the stricken tanker did not enter. Together,
Spain and Portugal had once claimed most of the ocean. Their ambitions now
were more modest: keeping one damaged vessel out of their waters.

Denied access to nearby ports, the ship wandered the Atlantic "like a
bomb ready to explode."[73] On November 19, it finally detonated. The *Prestige*
split in half and sank, bleeding more oil as it did. The remaining officers were
pulled from the doomed vessel, but Spanish authorities promptly arrested
the Greek captain and charged him with disobeying orders to expeditiously
move the vessel away from the coast. For all its efforts to keep the *Prestige* at
bay, the Spanish coast was hit hard by the spill.[74] The government estimated
that 70 percent of the beaches in Galicia were impacted.

The dilapidated condition of the *Prestige* was a painful reminder of the
failure of many flagging countries to exercise effective oversight of vessels.
It later came to light that the previous captain of the vessel had made several
complaints about its condition but had been rebuffed by the owners. Two
sister vessels had already been scrapped because of hull failures almost identical to the one the *Prestige* suffered. Efforts to increase the effectiveness of
flag-state regulation since the 1950s had yielded only limited success. In the
case of the *Prestige*, the American Bureau of Shipping (ABS), an independent
classification society, had inspected the vessel and declared it seaworthy just
six months before the disaster. Groups like ABS had been part of the maritime governance ecosystem for several centuries, and many flag countries all
but outsourced their responsibility for ensuring the seaworthiness of vessels
to organizations like it. In the wake of the *Prestige* disaster, Spain attempted
to hold ABS legally accountable. The litigation dragged on for several years
before US courts ruled that the organization was not liable.

For some European countries and European Commission officials, the
logical response to the dilemma of unsafe ships transiting near vulnerable

coastlines was to expand the ability of coastal countries to regulate those waters. In deference to freedom of navigation, the Convention gave coastal countries only limited power to regulate navigation through their EEZs. As outrage about the spill simmered, the European Commission proposed amending the Convention to permit more expansive regulation of tankers and other potentially dangerous vessels passing through national maritime zones. That initiative set off alarm bells in the shipping industry and in certain national capitals, which feared a new threat to free navigation. In the end, the idea of formally amending the Convention proved too ambitious, but the incident highlighted the continued incentive of coastal countries to protect themselves by bolstering their control of offshore areas.[75]

If the *Prestige* incident highlighted once again the deficiencies of flag-state governance, it also showcased the power of ports to deny entry. The refusal of the Spanish and Portuguese governments to allow the *Prestige* access was controversial. Several experts argued that granting the ship permission early in the crisis would have mitigated the environmental damage by allowing salvage crews to safely remove the stricken vessel's remaining oil. In the wake of the disaster, the International Maritime Organization took up the question of whether and when ports had an obligation to accept a vessel in distress. The resulting guidelines labored to balance a port's interest in keeping hazardous ships away with long traditions of offering shelter to ships in danger. The IMO emphasized that coastal states had no legal obligation to grant access but urged ports to "weigh all the factors and risks in a balanced manner and give shelter whenever reasonably possible."[76]

In these deliberations, many governments were keen to avoid any weakening of the various international agreements that had sprung up to foster cooperation between ports. These "port state control" measures relied ultimately on a port country's refusal to accept vessels, and they had emerged as an important, if not foolproof, alternative to relying on flag countries to effectively regulate vessels. Coordinated port-state regulation had begun as the Convention was being finalized, and in 1982 14 European countries launched the groundbreaking Paris Memorandum of Understanding. By the late 1990s, similar initiatives were under way in Asia, the Mediterranean, and the Indian Ocean. Working together, port authorities more regularly conducted vessel inspections, occasionally detaining or denying access to those failing the relevant international standards. Scofflaw vessels risked finding themselves on multinational watchlists and being denied entry to multiple ports.

Port-state cooperation originated to deal with deficiencies in merchant shipping, but it became evident that the strategy might also help control IUU fishing. In 2009, the UN's Food and Agriculture Organization advanced a new set of guidelines for port states to help ensure they were not receiving hauls of illegally caught fish. The proliferating port initiatives were an acknowledgment of the failures of flag-state regulation, but they also marked a continuing effort to build a governance system around those dysfunctionalities.

Flag Planting

On August 2, 2007, a Russian submersible descended slowly toward the bottom of the Arctic Ocean, almost 14,000 feet below the surface. Covered live by major Russian media outlets, the dive was more about politics than oceanography. In addition to the normal crew, two Russian members of parliament were on board. Once the submarine was in position, a mechanical arm reached out and placed a titanium Russian flag on the seabed. "If a hundred or a thousand years from now someone goes down to where we were, they will see the Russian flag," one of the parliamentarians said afterward. The crew received a congratulatory phone call from Russian president Vladimir Putin and a message of support from the Russian crew of the International Space Station.[77]

Aside from stoking national pride, the specific Russian aim was to dramatize its claim that the Lomonosov Ridge was an extension of the Russian continental shelf. After being rebuffed by the UN Commission in 2001, Russia was determined to bolster its case for extended seabed control. If Russia could demonstrate adequately that the ridge was a natural prolongation of its territory, it could secure rights on a substantial portion of the polar seabed. The Arctic flag-planting came amid increased Russian attention to the Northern Sea Route, which Moscow claimed passed through its internal waters.

Russia's Arctic assertiveness suggested that the country's profile on maritime issues might be in flux. The Soviet Union's development into a major maritime power in the 1960s had shifted Moscow's perspective on the oceans. As its field of view expanded from regional to global, Moscow worried less about ensuring local control and more about protecting freedom of navigation and access around the world. But the collapse of the Soviet Union in 1991 had almost overnight turned a global naval power back into one focused primarily on nearby waters. During the 1990s, a cash-hungry Russia hurriedly sold off or scrapped multiple warships, and the operational reach of the Russian navy contracted dramatically. Under Vladimir Putin, the Russian navy received some new resources and attention, but Moscow was still far from reassuming a global maritime posture. And as a regional player, Russia appeared increasingly focused on securing rights in adjacent waters.

Other Arctic states dismissed the Russian flag-planting operation as little more than a stunt. "This isn't the 15th century," the Canadian foreign minister said. "You can't go around the world and just plant flags and say 'We're claiming this territory.'"[78] Understandably, Canada's minister did not acknowledge that his own country had recently engaged in some notable maritime unilateralism. Canada had not planted flags exactly, but it had driven foreign fishing vessels away from waters beyond its exclusive economic zone and drawn controversial baselines that encompassed the Northwest Passage. The Russian foray to the Arctic seafloor may have been theatrical, but continued pressure to expand national control into the oceans was real and emanated from many different capitals.

Meanwhile, the prospects for internationalization of the oceans were mixed—and less promising than they had appeared in the mid-1990s. The notion of the oceans as the common heritage of humanity had mostly faded from diplomatic discussions. Regional fisheries organizations had managed limited success but did not yet appear up to the task of conserving high-seas fisheries. The International Seabed Authority was still in the experimental phase, and the Tribunal for the Law of the Sea had adjudicated only a handful of cases. Multilateral efforts to counter unsafe vessels and ocean plastic showed promise, but they struggled with the scale of the problems they confronted. The international community had staked a tentative claim to ocean governance, but the sovereign instinct to seek greater maritime control endured.

8

System Under Strain

(2010–Present)

One oddity of the Convention's first full decade in force was the near disappearance of the most controversial issue in its creation: seabed mining. The proto-industry that had bedeviled negotiators showed few signs of life in the 1990s and early 2000s. By 2005, however, market conditions finally produced a revival in its prospects. Nickel, manganese, and several other minerals jumped in value. "With the prices of some metals . . . more than doubling in the past three years," an industry reporter noted, "modern prospectors are defying investor skepticism, untested gear and a history of failed ocean ventures to mount the first commercial exploration in a generation."[1]

The logistics of pulling minerals from the deep seabed had always been daunting, but mining companies saw promise in electric-powered and remotely operated vehicles that could scour the seafloor and vacuum material to the surface for processing. A Canadian company, Nautilus Minerals, attracted investment for a project in the Bismarck Sea (inside Papua New Guinea's EEZ). Flush with cash and optimism, Nautilus ordered a custom mining vessel, to be named the *Jules Verne*.[2] In 2010, a Hong Kong company ordered a research vessel of its own to explore mineral deposits in the Pacific. India's National Institute of Ocean Technology reported success with an underwater robotic crawler.[3]

If the technology of mining was changing, so was the potential yield. It had long been assumed that the polymetallic nodules discovered in the 1870s by the *Challenger* expedition would be the main haul. As undersea knowledge grew, however, other features proved equally attractive. Researchers came to understand that when superheated water from deep-sea vents meets cold ocean water, substantial deposits of minerals often form. These "seafloor massive sulfides" could be rich sources of gold, copper, zinc, and other minerals.[4] And there were other tantalizing finds. In 2011, Japanese researchers reported concentrations of "rare earth" minerals in mud from the deep seabed. "Just one square kilometer of deposits will be able to provide one-fifth of the current global annual consumption," a Japanese scientist assured the BBC.[5] The discovery had potentially important strategic consequences, as China had long dominated the production and export of rare earth minerals.

As interest in seabed mining grew, activity at the Jamaica-based International Seabed Authority increased. The ISA finalized regulations for nodule mining and then released draft rules for mining sulfide deposits. ISA licenses to explore the seabed became a hotter commodity. From 2001 through 2010, the ISA signed only eight seabed exploration contracts. From 2011 through 2018, 19 were completed. These included a Russian explor-atory project in the mid-Atlantic and a Chinese venture in the Western Pacific.[6] Political leaders took note of the potential windfall. In 2013, British Prime Minister David Cameron pledged to put Britain at the forefront of the new industry.[7] Britain's involvement featured a new partnership with a British subsidiary of the US-based defense contractor Lockheed Martin. The company dispatched several research cruises to the nodule-rich Clarion-Clipperton zone of the Pacific.[8]

The collaboration between Lockheed Martin and the British government highlighted the obstacles US companies faced as they contemplated seabed mining. Absent a decision to ratify the Convention, US companies had to work through other governments to secure internationally recognized access to the deep seabed. Dissatisfaction with that reality became evident in 2012 when the Obama administration pushed once more for Senate ratification of the Convention.

Organized by Senator John Kerry, the hearings featured a star-studded parade of US navy, Coast Guard, and Marine Corps admirals and generals urging ratification. US business interests joined the procession, and their en-thusiasm marked an important change. During the negotiations in the 1970s and early 1980s, key US mining and energy companies vociferously opposed the Convention's seabed provisions and helped galvanize political opposition. At these new Senate hearings, the president of the Chamber of Commerce argued that widespread ratification of the Convention had changed business incentives. "Only by joining the Convention will the US secure its rights to vast mineral deposits on the US [extended shelf], and perhaps even more important, be able to sponsor companies to mine the deep seabed in the area beyond any national jurisdiction."[9] The CEOs of ExxonMobil, Lockheed Martin, and several other major US companies concurred.

Big business had climbed on board, but the requisite two-thirds of the Senate had not. Conservative legislators worried that the convention would open the United States to environmental challenges through the Law of the Sea Tribunal. As in previous years, opponents focused on what they viewed as the seabed authority's excessive powers. Senator James Inhofe, one of the treaty's most vocal opponents, insisted that the ISA represented an unprecedented international taxation scheme. Former Defense Secretary Donald Rumsfeld—a veteran of the Reagan administration's battles against the Convention—warned against "endors[ing] a treaty that makes it a legal obligation for productive countries to pay royalties to less productive countries based on rhetoric about 'common heritage of mankind.'"[10]

Skepticism about the ISA and its plan for internationalized mining was growing in a very different quarter. The shift from experimentation to actual mining—which appeared close—would test the ISA's ability to balance commercial and environmental pressures. As activists well understood, the ISA's relevance depended on a viable mining industry. In that sense, the organization was both a promoter of seabed mining and its regulator. In its draft regulations, the ISA included provisions admonishing would-be seabed miners to care for the environment as they hunted. "Each prospector shall take necessary measures to prevent, reduce and control pollution and other hazards to the marine environment arising from prospecting, as far as reasonably possible," the code for mining polymetallic nodules stipulated.[11]

The experience of the Papua New Guinea project suggested that these kinds of precautions would not forestall environmental challenges. Pledges to care for the environment notwithstanding, the government's contract with Nautilus Minerals sparked a vocal opposition movement. Local activists linked arms with more experienced and well-resourced international advocacy networks, including the veterans at Greenpeace. Campaigners arranged local protests but also appeared at international conferences. The opposition movement highlighted diverse dangers, including contamination of traditional fishing grounds and even the possible seismic impact of mining. Their arguments often boiled down to an insistence that there were too many unknowns to allow mining to proceed. Opponents could point to new research that bolstered the case for caution. A team of scientists dredged a portion of the seabed and then monitored how long it took for the original ecosystem to restore itself. The results, published in 2017, showed that some deep-sea fauna struggled to reestablish themselves even two decades after the initial seabed disturbance. "The effects of polymetallic nodule mining," the researchers concluded, "are likely to be long term."[12]

For a variety of reasons (many unrelated to the opposition), the Papua New Guinea mining project foundered, and Nautilus Minerals filed for bankruptcy in 2018. Activists saw in the company's plight a reprieve. "The longer Nautilus is delayed and tied up in protecting itself from bankruptcy," one anti-mining campaigner said, "the closer we are to stopping the project and protecting our livelihoods and seas."[13] Yet investor interest in mining remained strong. By the middle of 2019, another Canadian company, DeepGreen, had raised more than $150 million to pursue commercial mining in the Clarion-Clipperton Zone in the Pacific.

The environmental challenges to mining were serious, but equally important was whether the Convention's plan for international revenue sharing would function once profits appeared. The notion of the international seabed as the "common heritage of all mankind" still undergirded the Convention's mining mechanism, but the international atmosphere had changed dramatically since the 1970s. The collapse of the Soviet bloc and the triumph of the West had given free market forces a major boost, and the "New International Economic Order" proposed by the developing world in the 1970s was a mostly faded memory. The countries who planned to engage in deep-sea mining and those who hoped to see its benefits shared remained far apart on the financial details. A group of African countries proposed that the ISA should recover at least 40 percent of the profits from any seabed mining. The companies most likely to do the mining—and the countries sponsoring them—wanted to pay much less. There was little sign that compromise was imminent.[14] The real test for internationalized management of undersea territory was just beginning.

Inside the Territorial Sea

The challenge on the deep seabed was making operational a new and innovative international governance structure. On the ocean surface, there was also building pressure for greater multilateral management. The law of the sea had long provided that coastal states could control the waters adjacent to their coasts, and flag states should be responsible for regulating the conduct of their vessels on the high seas. By 2010, events were putting increased pressure on both of those pillars. The period saw novel attempts by the international community to conduct enforcement inside territorial waters as well as new efforts by both national governments and multilateral organizations to regulate activities on the high seas.

It was piracy that drew outsiders into territorial waters. The maritime lawlessness in the Straits of Malacca, so alarming in the late 1990s, had declined significantly by 2005. Off the coast of East Africa, however, a new threat to shipping was forming. This wave of maritime violence emanated from Somalia, which had descended into a state of near anarchy in the early 1990s. A US-led intervention designed to alleviate an ensuing famine ended disastrously in 1994, when dozens of Pakistani peacekeepers and US soldiers were killed in clashes with a warlord's forces. The Clinton administration chose to withdraw, and the UN peacekeepers followed the Americans to the exits.

Because there was no authority to challenge them, some foreign fishing vessels felt free to fish in Somali waters. A few Somalis apparently took matters into their own hands, driving off, firing on, and occasionally seizing foreign vessels. "We don't consider ourselves sea bandits," one Somali told a journalist. "We consider sea bandits those who illegally fish in our seas and dump waste in our seas and carry weapons in our seas. We are simply patrolling our seas. Think of us like a coast guard."[15]

Whatever the initial motivations, the maritime seizures off the coast of Somalia soon took on a different character. Clans and criminal syndicates realized that more lucrative targets than fishing boats plied the waters every day off the coast. Shipping coming from or heading to the Suez Canal was obliged to pass through the Gulf of Aden, between the coasts of Somalia and Yemen. As the business of Somali piracy grew, new tactics extended the range of marauders farther into the Gulf. Sometimes disguised as fishing trawlers, "mother ships" would shelter and supply the speedboats that conducted the actual attacks. By 2008, pirate attacks originating from Somalia accounted for close to half of all documented cases worldwide.

The increasingly brazen attacks finally sparked coordinated international action. Several countries, including the United States, stepped up naval activities. But foreign navies countering the threat faced an important legal limitation—they lacked authority to operate inside Somali territorial waters. The Somali state might have been a fiction, but other governments still took seriously its maritime rights. Marauders who could make it back inside territorial waters were usually off the hook. A US admiral recalled his exasperation in 2007 when a navy ship ended pursuit of a pirate vessel at the 12-mile mark:

Never mind that there was no effective government in that country. Never mind that there was really no one to ask for permission. Never mind that our warship was in hot pursuit. It was just like that damned kid's game, olly olly oxen free! They got past the line without being tagged. They're free to go.[16]

In June 2008, that legal impediment prompted the UN Security Council to make one of its most robust interventions into maritime security. A resolution authorized foreign naval forces to "enter the territorial waters of Somalia for the purpose of repressing acts of piracy and armed robbery at sea."[17] The Council members emphasized that the counter-piracy operations it was endorsing did not alter the basic maritime rights enjoyed by coastal states and pointed out that Somalia's (mostly ineffectual) transitional government had endorsed the move. Together, these special circumstances reassured nervous coastal states that the Council was not setting a precedent for international control of national waters. But the resolution *did* constitute a precedent. It meant that coastal state rights could, in certain circumstances, be taken from them. The governmental collapse in Somalia was unusually severe, but plenty of coastal countries had weak governance that might invite international intervention.

The UN's move to police territorial waters was part of a broader trend of international intervention to address civil conflicts, the spread of weapons of mass destruction, and international terrorism. With mandates from the Security Council, thousands of UN peacekeepers in multiple countries took on an array of complicated tasks, including protecting civilians, strengthening weak governments, and helping organize national elections.[18] The Council imposed a raft of new international sanctions and arms embargos, several of which impacted shipping operations. The Somalia piracy resolutions were therefore a reminder of the potential maritime implications of the powers bestowed on the Security Council decades before. So long as its members could agree, the Council could declare insecurity on national and international waters a matter of international concern. And in responding, the Council could strip away, modify, or suspend longtime legal doctrines.[19]

As the legal obstacles to an active naval response were cleared, a multinational flotilla assembled in the region, following in the wake of generations of pirate hunters. In December 2008, the European Union launched a naval operation to protect ships carrying supplies for the World Food Program and other multilateral activities in East Africa. (The operation constituted the EU's first major naval undertaking.) In April 2009, a US Navy admiral took command of a separate multinational task force. NATO initiated its own closely related naval operation. A Russian destroyer arrived to protect its country's merchant vessels. Several Chinese vessels deployed, a move that a Chinese official described as "showcas[ing] China's positive attitude in fulfilling its international obligations and the country's image as a responsible power."[20] The overlapping operations spawned a variety of coordinating mechanisms—and yielded some surprising goodwill. The US admiral commanding the international task force exchanged friendly visits with his Chinese counterpart, and a US navy ship rescued a North Korean vessel from pirates, prompting a rare expression of gratitude from Pyongyang.[21]

The robust international presence did not end the threat immediately; the ocean space off the Somali coast was too vast for even several dozen warships to effectively patrol. The seizure of the *Maersk Alabama* in April 2009—an episode later turned into a Hollywood film—evidenced the continuing peril. But that attack also showed how once soft merchant targets had been hardened. *Maersk Alabama's* crew had practiced piracy drills and it followed established procedures to disable the ship. Most of the crew sheltered in a reinforced safe room, and crew members even managed to capture one of the pirates. Unable to steer the ship, the Somalis settled for taking the captain hostage in one of the ship's lifeboats. (That kidnapping finally ended with the death of the pirates at the hands of US navy SEALs.) Other navies contributed to the show of international force. French naval forces captured a dozen pirates during a routine patrol, and an Indian warship clashed with several pirate vessels, sinking one.[22]

The Danish frigate *Absalon* saw as much action as any vessel in the anti-piracy campaign. Spurred by the 2007 seizure of a Danish merchant vessel, the government in Copenhagen made counter-piracy a focus for its small but proficient navy. Danish merchant ships accounted for around 10 percent of global tonnage, and the government saw its economic interests directly affected. The *Absalon's* encounters highlighted the continuing challenges to systematically confronting piracy. In September 2008, the ship broke up an attack and took on board 10 pirates. A Danish ambassador recalled confusion about what to do with the detainees. "We were looking at each other and asking, what is piracy from a legal perspective, and how do we deal with it. No one knew at the time."[23] Because Danish law did not clearly provide for prosecuting pirates—and because there was no appetite for bringing them to Denmark for trial—the men were eventually set free on a beach in Somalia.

Four months later, the *Absalon* took on board more pirates after another failed hijacking. This time, the Somalis languished at sea for almost six weeks while authorities in Copenhagen hashed out a plan. The men were eventually transferred to Dutch custody and put on trial in the Netherlands.

As these incidents suggested, international forces may have welcomed the authority to operate inside Somali territorial waters, but they had no intention of becoming the Somali judicial system. The logistical and evidentiary challenges of prosecuting pirates detained hundreds or thousands of miles away from national courts were daunting. What's more, the pirates might ultimately claim political asylum, putting governments in an awkward position. Eventually, some of the countries most involved in maritime policing fashioned a solution: detained pirates would be sent to nearby Kenya for trial. European and US financial assistance helped make the arrangement attractive to the Kenyan government.[24]

Like the efforts that had finally restrained violence a decade earlier in southeast Asia, the international response to piracy off Somalia was belated, sometimes uncoordinated, and ad hoc. But it also featured substantial naval cooperation and relied on new international legal authority to at least temporarily expand the reach of the pirate hunters. As such, the effort offered a glimpse of more robust and systematic international maritime security.

Seizures on the High Seas

If piracy prompted international police action inside territorial waters, large-scale migration by sea led governments and regional organizations to extend their border control efforts onto the high seas. That push outward was most systematic and sustained in the Mediterranean. The civil war in Syria and continuing unrest in several Arab countries generated an unprecedented wave of seaborne migration, much of it emanating from Libya's shores. In October 2015 alone, more than 220,000 migrants tried to reach Europe by sea. Those fortunate enough to survive the passage landed on the Greek islands, as well as in Malta, Italy, and Spain. But hundreds drowned before they found land.

The issue of what countries could do on the high seas to prevent unauthorized immigration had been percolating for decades. For the United States, the question became acute in the early 1990s, when thousands of Haitians attempted to reach US shores. The Clinton and George W. Bush administrations intercepted dozens of vessels, either returning those on board to Haiti or, in some cases, sending migrants to processing facilities (including one at Guantanamo Bay, Cuba). In 2001, Australia grappled with a similar dilemma when a succession of vessels crammed with migrants tried to reach its ports. In August 2001, Australian authorities forcibly stopped one such ship from coming into port. In the wake of that incident, the country adopted a policy—dubbed the "Pacific Solution"—of routinely diverting ships carrying migrants to processing facilities in third countries or to remote Australian facilities.[25]

Like the Americans and Australians, European officials had a clear motive to interdict migrants on the high seas. The international legalities of doing so were complex, however. Migrant vessels that were not flagged or properly registered were subject to boarding and inspection. And patrol craft who encountered dangerously overloaded or otherwise unseaworthy migrant ships had not only the right but also an international obligation to provide assistance. Because international rules were vague about where rescued mariners should be deposited—one key treaty said merely that they should be left in a "place of safety"—that obligation to rescue often provided legal cover for returning migrants to their starting point.

In the absence of either statelessness or unseaworthiness, European authorities did not have the clear right to board ships carrying migrants on the high seas; the migrant vessels enjoyed a basic freedom to navigate, at least until they reached European waters. To help address that reality, Italy and Libya agreed in 2008 to work jointly to counter seaborne migration. Italy delivered several patrol craft to help bolster Libya's monitoring capacity, and the two countries even undertook occasional joint patrols. As Libya descended into civil war in 2011, however, the cooperation dried up even as the flow of migrants intensified.

Matteo Renzi, Italy's prime minister during the height of the migration crisis, often chafed at the legal limits on Italian efforts to push back migrants. He described those smuggling migrants as "the slave traders of the 21st century," a reference that linked Italy's anti-migration campaign with Britain's 19th-century anti-slavery patrols. Intended or not, Renzi's allusion carried a governance implication: if the British could carve out an exception to free navigation in order to combat slave trading, why not now craft one to fight illegal migration? European Union officials picked up on the analogy. "I don't believe that people are less slaves if they are stopped or kept somewhere during the journey or locked in [a] boat that sinks," the EU's top foreign policy official said.[26] The EU itself launched an expanded operation in the Mediterranean to divert migrant vessels and rescue would-be migrants.

In early 2015, European diplomats seeking comprehensive legal cover for their expanded operations turned to the UN Security Council. After months of wrangling, the Council in October passed a resolution on the migration crisis. It emphasized the right of countries to stop and search unflagged vessels that might be smuggling migrants on the Mediterranean. That provision was not particularly controversial; unflagged vessels had long been subject to boarding and inspection. But the Council went further, giving government vessels the right to stop even flagged vessels suspected of carrying migrants so long as the patrolling country had attempted to get the permission of the flag state. That authorization encroached on the power of flag states and cracked the door to more systematic international management of high-seas traffic.[27]

As with its resolution regarding Somalia's territorial sea, the Council described its maritime move as a unique response to an extraordinary situation. But in bits and pieces—through arms embargos and sanctions, as a response to piracy, and now in its effort to manage Mediterranean migration—the Council was fashioning new and more intrusive forms of maritime governance. As the Council punished North Korea for its nuclear program, for example, new international restrictions made it increasingly difficult for North Korean–flagged ships to operate. The resolutions, one expert concluded, all but "eviscerated [North Korea's] flag state status."[28] Council members still were wary about explicitly authorizing high-seas boarding, but the freedom to navigate the world's oceans and the privileged place of flag states were less certain than in the past.

Government vessels were not the only ones ramping up efforts to interdict vessels on the high seas. Sea Shepherd's fleet—which the activist organization often referred to as "Neptune's Navy"—had swelled to nine vessels. The organization's most extended feat of vigilantism occurred in the summer of 2015. The target was the *Thunder*, a well-worn vessel flagged by Nigeria. Over the years, it had developed a reputation for fishing illegally and had operated under the flags of at least seven different countries. In 2013, Interpol, the international body designed to facilitate cooperation among national law enforcement agencies, issued an alert for the vessel.

A year later, Sea Shepherd received a solid lead on its whereabouts and sent several ships to track it down. Three months and more than 10,000 miles later, the chase ended when the *Thunder* sank, likely in an attempt by the crew to destroy the evidence of their fishing activities.[29] The gambit failed: as the *Thunder*'s crew sheltered in lifeboats, a Sea Shepherd team boarded the doomed vessel and recovered logbooks, cell phones, and computers. That evidence made its way to prosecutors in the west African country of Sao Tome and Principe, where the *Thunder*'s captain was eventually convicted. The *Thunder* was a wanted ship, but Sea Shepherd's right to chase it across the ocean was still uncertain. International rules on high-seas interdiction were built around governmental authority, not nongovernmental activists.

Certain other boarding operations outside of territorial waters received clearer international legal backing. In August 2009, a patrol vessel from Guinea Bissau detained the Panama-flagged *Virginia G*, which was operating in Guinea Bissau's exclusive economic zone. As in the earlier *Saiga* case, the dispute centered on bunkering—the provision of fuel to fishing boats at sea—and the question was whether coastal states could regulate it. The Tribunal had ducked that question in the *Saiga* case but now faced it directly.

Panama argued that freedom of the seas should only be limited when the Convention clearly allowed it. Any ambiguity, its legal team suggested, should be resolved in favor of ocean freedom. Panama had grounds to hope that its reasoning might be persuasive; in the *Saiga* case, several judges had expressed concern about limiting freedom of navigation by expanding coastal state powers too much. But in 2014, the judges ruled unanimously that coastal states enjoyed the right to regulate ships providing fuel to fishing vessels.[30] The decision marked a narrow but important victory for coastal countries seeking to regulate activities in their exclusive economic zones. As such, it contributed to a long-term trend that many had predicted: the EEZ gradually transforming into an expanded territorial sea.

New Passages

For all the attention they generated, boarding operations like these were uncommon. The vast majority of ocean traffic passed safely and without interruption, a testament to improved technology and regulation by bodies like the International Maritime Organization. Maritime shipping slowly recovered from the global recession that had begun in 2008, and container shipping volume increased more than 45 percent from 2010 to 2019.[31] Even with an improved global economy, however, many shipping companies still struggled to turn a profit. The industry kept a watchful eye on the diminishing Arctic ice—and prospects for shorter and cheaper routes there.

There were encouraging signs. In 2010, the first fully loaded merchant vessel completed the Northwest Passage. In 2013, the Danish-operated *Nordic Orion* became the first bulk carrier to do so. Loaded with 15,000 tons of coal, it shaved 1,000 miles off the alternative route through the Panama Canal. The ship's owner boasted that using the passage would not only save time but reduce carbon dioxide emissions.[32] Accompanied by an icebreaker, the luxury cruise ship *Crystal Serenity* completed the passage in 2016, carrying more than 1,000 passengers at a price tag of at least $21,000 each. The next year saw a record-shattering 33 completed journeys through the Northwest Passage.[33]

Activity increased dramatically in the Northern Sea Route near Russian territory as well. The number of transits jumped from zero in 2007 to 46 in 2012. In August 2011, the Russian *Vladimir Tikhonov* became the first supertanker to run the route. By doing so, she saved at least seven days sailing from the normal trip through the Suez Canal.[34] Eager to capture economic benefits from the increased traffic, the Russian government developed plans to expand and refurbish infrastructure near the route.

This increased use of the Arctic shipping routes prompted new multilateral regulation. In 2014, countries working through the International Maritime Organization finalized the International Code for Ships Operating in Polar Waters (known as the "Polar Code"). It established new training, safety, and navigation requirements for ships operating in polar waters, including special protective gear for mariners who might need rescue. The new code was just the latest in a steady stream of regulations from the IMO and other bodies designed to improve the safety and reliability of international shipping.

But nothing in the Code's more than 50 pages touched on the deeper sovereignty questions surrounding the Arctic passages. For Canada and Russia, the status of the increasingly viable routes was clear: they passed through the internal waters of these countries, and the governments therefore had the power to regulate passage (and to deny passage when it wished). The United States—and, less vocally, several other countries—still insisted that both the Northwest Passage and the Northern Sea Route were international straits.

Within the US government, the question of how to challenge the Russian and Canadian claims arose several times. For the US Coast Guard, however, the prospect of a freedom of navigation exercise in the Arctic raised daunting operational concerns. The United States possessed only a few working icebreakers. One senior Coast Guard officer recalled resisting pressure from White House officials to more aggressively assert US rights:

> The National Security Council approached me and said, "Hey, we ought to send the *Polar Star* through the Northern Sea Route and do a freedom of navigation exercise." . . . I said, "Au contraire, it's a 40-year-old ship. We're cannibalizing parts off its sister ship just to keep this thing running, and I can't guarantee you that it won't have a catastrophic engineering casualty as it's doing a freedom of navigation exercise, and now I've got to call on Russia to pull me out of harm's way. So this is not the time to do it."[35]

These practical realities combined with political considerations to delay a direct reckoning with the status of the Arctic passages. But the gap between the US position and that of Canada and Russia was too large to obscure indefinitely, and the chances of an international adjudication of the dispute appeared remote. None of the countries most involved appeared willing to hand the sensitive question to international judges or arbitrators.

Scarborough Fair

Disputes over diminutive islands and other maritime features had been simmering since the Convention made clear how much ocean real estate islands could generate. And nowhere were the frictions as intense as in the South China Sea. By 2010, China's economic growth and expanding maritime capabilities were turning these recurrent tensions into a geopolitical drama. Washington was a treaty ally of Japan and the Philippines and was enjoying warmer relations with other South China Sea claimants, including Vietnam. These military and diplomatic linkages meant that gambits over reefs or shoals often seemed to pit a rising China against the reigning superpower.

Alongside this geopolitical undercurrent was a legal and institutional one. China's assertion of broad rights in the South China Sea—seemingly based on the nine-dash line—was a potential threat to the Convention. Whether China was in fact challenging the maritime legal order depended on what the nine-dash line meant. The line might represent a straightforward sovereignty claim to all the islands and other features in the South China Sea. However offensive to other claimants, that assertion would not itself violate the Convention, which says nothing about sovereignty over land features. But China's words and actions kept open the possibility that the line implied something more: special maritime rights in a vast area of ocean.

The unexpectedly high number of extended continental shelf applications and Canadian and Russian claims to the Arctic passages had already signaled the continuing national pressure to control ocean space and access to resources. But those claims were at least grounded in the Convention. If Beijing could make its more nebulous assertions stick, other countries might be tempted to follow suit, thus threatening the Convention's fragile compromise. In 2009, the Chinese government crossed an important threshold when it published the nine-dash line in a filing with the United Nations (Figure 8.1). China once again chose its words carefully, and the filing did not clear away the legal fog surrounding the nine-dash line.[36]

Three years later, however, a confrontation at sea set in motion a legal reckoning for China's controversial maritime demarcation. On April 8, 2012, a

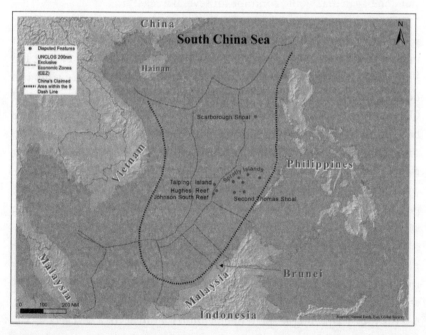

Figure 8.1 Lines in the South China Sea; map courtesy of Law of the Sea Primer Project, Fletcher School of Law and Diplomacy, Tufts University.

patrol plane from the Philippines spotted Chinese fishing boats anchored in the shallow waters off Scarborough Shoal. The shoal is a triangular collection of reefs and rocks that lies north of the Spratly Islands, east of the Paracels, and about 120 miles from the Philippine island of Luzon. At high tide, much of the feature is submerged, and its highest point is a mere six feet above the water. Because the shoals are within 200 miles of the main Philippine islands, Manila believes that they are squarely within its EEZ and that it has clear authority to regulate fishing and other activities there.

Alerted to the presence of Chinese fishing vessels at Scarborough, the Philippine government dispatched the pride of its small navy, the *Gregorio del Pilar*. A retired US Coast Guard cutter, the vessel had been commissioned into the Philippine navy only the previous year. When it arrived, Philippine marines boarded the Chinese boats and discovered fish, giant clams, live sharks, and coral—the fruits of what the Philippines considered illegal fishing. As the marines returned to their ship to prepare paperwork for arrests, however, the Chinese fishermen apparently made a distress call. Two Chinese government vessels promptly sailed into the area and stationed themselves between the fishing boats and the *Gregorio del Pilar*. A tense standoff began that would continue for several weeks.[37]

In Beijing and Manila, senior officials defended what they viewed as their sovereign rights. The shoal, declared the Philippine foreign minister, "is an integral part of Philippine territory."[38] A Chinese general warned that the Philippines was underestimating "the strength and willpower of China to defend its territorial integrity."[39] Ominously, by late April, the number of Chinese vessels at the shoals increased dramatically, and their maneuvers became more aggressive; a Chinese cutter reportedly raced toward two Philippine vessels at more than 20 knots before veering away at the last moment.[40]

Hopeful that the world would be sympathetic as it confronted a much more powerful state, the Philippines called for international action to resolve the standoff. For its part, China used its enormous economic leverage. In early May, shipments of bananas from the Philippines were held up at Chinese ports, ostensibly because they had failed inspections. Most observers saw the move as a signal to the Philippines about the dangers of its stubbornness at Scarborough. Behind the scenes, US diplomats struggled to tamp down a crisis they feared might spark open conflict. In that, they succeeded. The Philippines withdrew its vessels from the shoal in mid-June, apparently with an understanding that the Chinese would reciprocate. But by the time the standoff ended, the Chinese were in effective control. A chain hung across the entrance to the shoal's inner lagoon, and a Chinese vessel prowled the area. Filipino fishing boats that attempted to enter were chased away, sometimes with water cannons.[41]

The Philippines had run out of attractive options at Scarborough, but The Hague was a different matter. Since 2011, the idea of seeking an international ruling had circulated in Philippine legal and governmental circles. One of the country's most prominent jurists, Antonio Carpio, doggedly advocated the international option. He consulted widely with experts and petitioned relevant officials in the government. But there was plenty of skepticism. Could the Philippines actually initiate a legal process without China's consent? If so, how good were the odds of winning? And what exactly would a favorable ruling give Manila?

Questions like these made resorting to international adjudication a gamble. According to the journalist Marites Vitug, government officials often viewed the idea of resorting to an international tribunal as radical. For his part, Carpio insisted that establishing legal rights in the South China Sea should be seen as a decades-long effort:

> [He] kept telling everyone that this was not going to be a quick, short-term battle but a "multi-generational struggle." This was a constant message of Carpio's, [who explained] it this way in an interview: "This generation will get the ruling. The next generation will convince the world to support us, and maybe the generation after that will convince China."[42]

The Scarborough confrontation made Carpio's radical idea appear more reasonable. Like the Dutch in the early 1600s, the Philippines faced a much more powerful adversary and saw value in presenting their maritime arguments to the world. The Dutch had turned to a young Hugo Grotius; officials in Manila reached out to several white-shoe law firms. Paul Reichler, a veteran attorney at the law firm Foley Hoag, emerged as the most attractive candidate. In addition to familiarity with maritime issues, Reichler had experience battling Goliaths in international courtrooms. In the mid-1980s, he had served as counsel to Nicaragua, arguing that US efforts to unseat the Nicaraguan regime violated the United Nations Charter. After initially defending itself, the United States refused to participate further in the case. The legal process went ahead anyway, and the judges eventually delivered a stinging rebuke to Washington. "The Nicaragua case caused [the Philippine team] to trust us," Reichler recalled. "They knew that we had the fortitude to fight against big, powerful countries and not allow ourselves to be intimidated and back down."[43]

Reichler and his small team built on and refined the strategy that Carpio had begun. On January 22, 2013, the Philippines formally notified China that it was initiating the case. A few weeks later, Beijing's ambassador in the Philippines returned the documentation to the Philippines foreign ministry, declaring that the case was "incorrect."[44] Other countries in the region mostly stayed silent, wary of China's wrath. Yet Manila's move won cautious support in the United States. John Kerry, now serving as the secretary of state, urged China to "see the wisdom" of a judicial resolution.[45] That admonition had no effect, and in the months that followed Chinese officials reiterated their refusal to participate. But the wheels of international justice were turning.

Because China had years before designated arbitration as its preferred mechanism for resolving disputes related to the Convention, the Philippines case went not to the tribunal in Hamburg or the International Court of Justice but instead to an ad hoc panel of experts convened under the auspices of the Permanent Court of Arbitration (PCA) in The Hague. Per the rules, the Philippines nominated one arbitrator. Because China was boycotting, the president of the Law of the Sea Tribunal then designated the other arbitrators. When the Tribunal convened for the first time in a Hague courtroom, the polished wood table assigned to China sat empty (Figure 8.2) while the Philippines' legal team prepared to make its case.

Capturing the *Sunrise*

In Arctic waters, another major power was testing the Convention's system for resolving disputes. In September 2013, a group of Greenpeace activists set sail from Norway on board the *Arctic Sunrise*, an ice-strengthened vessel purchased by the organization in 1995. (In a double dose of irony, the vessel had previously served two longtime Greenpeace adversaries—seal hunters and the French government.) Flagged in the Netherlands, the ship was bound for a Russian drilling platform in the Arctic, inside Russia's EEZ. While Russia was within its rights to drill there, Greenpeace and other activists insisted that doing so endangered a fragile ecosystem.

Figure 8.2   China's empty table at the South China Sea Arbitration; photograph courtesy of the Permanent Court of Arbitration.

The mission had been in the works for months, and the plan was for several activists to attach themselves to the platform as an ongoing protest. Greenpeace's technological savvy had grown considerably in the decades since its founding. The team had constructed a high-tech capsule that would shelter the activists and allow them to remain on the Russian structure for weeks. Off the coast of Norway, the Greenpeace members had repeatedly practiced their technique for securing lines to the platform and attaching the capsule. They knew they would have only a few moments to do so before Russian patrols arrived.

In the predawn darkness of September 18, a small team of activists clambered aboard Zodiac boats and sped toward the platform, their survival capsule in tow. The plan fell apart almost immediately. The capsule detached from the boat towing it, and several campaigners resorted to hooking themselves to the rig and unfurling a large banner. Russian security forces blasted them with freezing water and quickly apprehended those who had climbed on board. Meanwhile, the Russian coast guard demanded to board the *Arctic Sunrise* itself. The tense exchange between the activists and the coast guard recorded by Greenpeace—raised the same legal issue that the *Saiga* case and several South China Sea incidents had: how broad were coastal state rights in the EEZ?

RUSSIAN PATROL: "Heave to and take on board our inspection team."
Arctic Sunrise: "We have absolutely no reason to let you on board. We're in international waters, you have no jurisdiction here."
RUSSIAN PATROL: "You are in Russia's Exclusive Economic Zone."
Arctic Sunrise: "Well, that's right. So if you suspect us of illegal fishing, please let us know. Because that's the only reason you can legally come on board our ship. Unless you think we're pirates."
RUSSIAN PATROL: "If you do not submit to inspection, we will use all means at our disposal."
Arctic Sunrise: "You are not allowed on board. We are in international waters."
RUSSIAN PATROL: "We will use all means at our disposal, including warning shots at your vessel."[46]

The next day, helicopter-borne Russian commandos rappelled onto the *Arctic Sunrise*, arrested the crew, and towed the vessel into port. Russian officials announced plans to charge the protesters with piracy. The charge was soon reduced to "hooliganism," but the government still pledged to prosecute. After unsuccessful diplomatic overtures, the Dutch government asked the Law of the Sea Tribunal to order the crew's release. "I feel responsible for the ship and its crew because it's a ship that sails under the Dutch flag," the foreign minister said.[47] The Dutch argued that the Russians had no right to board the main vessel, which had been outside of Russian territorial waters and beyond the small exclusion zone that Russia had established around the drilling rig. Because two British nationals were part of the crew, the United Kingdom's foreign minister, William Hague, applauded the legal challenge. "Russian officials will now be called to explain their actions before an international court of law," he said.[48] But Moscow dismissed the international tribunal and defended its right to seize the ship and put the crew on trial. "Everything that happened with the *Arctic Sunrise* was pure provocation," a Russian diplomat said. "I would say we have more questions for the Dutch than they can have for us."[49]

By late 2013, China and Russia, both permanent members of the UN Security Council, found themselves accused of flouting maritime rules. The contexts were very different, but Beijing and Moscow were both claiming the freedom to exclude others from waters they viewed as being under their jurisdiction. As important, both governments had signaled their intent to ignore the Convention's dispute resolution system. Their defiance marked one of the most serious tests yet for the still new maritime governance system.

Judgment Day

Just before Christmas Day 2013, Russia announced that it was dropping charges against one of the detained Greenpeace crew members from the *Arctic Sunrise*. The rest of the crew was released soon thereafter. Moscow insisted that the reprieves were an act of mercy rather than legal obligation, and Russia still refused to participate in the Tribunal's proceedings or to recognize its decision. The *Arctic Sunrise* itself remained in Russian hands for another six months; it finally sailed from Murmansk in August 2014. As it approached Amsterdam, 15 of the original crewmembers and dozens of others gave the ship a festive homecoming. The vessel's celebratory return echoed that of the *Greenpeace* to Canada in 1972. In both cases, the vessels had failed in their ostensible missions, but the activist group had reaped significant publicity for its cause. A few months later, the *Arctic Sunrise* was back at work, challenging a Spanish drilling operation near the Canary Islands.[50]

It was an open question whether the Convention's dispute resolution system would be as resilient as Greenpeace's protest ships. The Russian refusal to engage with the Law of the Sea Tribunal played out as the South China Sea arbitration moved toward its own denouement. In 2015, the appointed international arbitrators heard arguments about their jurisdiction. While China had still made no formal submissions, it did circulate a position paper that rejected the Tribunal's jurisdiction and what it termed the Philippines' "abuse" of the Convention's procedures. "The unilateral initiation of the present arbitration by the Philippines," it claimed, "will not change the history and fact of China's sovereignty over the South China Sea Islands and the adjacent waters."[51]

Undaunted, the judges unanimously decided to proceed, dashing Chinese hopes for an early end to the case. That decision allowed them to consider the substance of the Philippines' complaint—including its argument that China's nine-dash line violated the Convention. The Philippines legal team, which had expanded to include several renowned international experts, ultimately filed a 300-page brief and dozens of annexes stuffed with maps, expert reports, and testimony.

The formal hearings commenced in November 2015 and lasted for almost a week. Former US negotiator Bernard Oxman, one member of the Philippines' legal team, put the case in historical context. China's nine-dash line, he argued, was just the latest in a long line of presumptuous sovereign claims to the oceans that must be discarded. "From the time of Grotius through the widespread acceptance of the United Nations Convention on the Law of the Sea," he argued, "international law has not preserved, admitted, or accepted claims to control vast areas of the sea in derogation of either the freedom of the seas or the rights of the immediately adjacent coastal state."[52]

Another long presentation addressed whether any of the more than two dozen features in the Spratly chain could sustain human habitation and therefore be considered islands. Paul Reichler engaged in some rhetorical flourishes as he argued that the spits of land did not merit that status:

> I will now provide you with a complete history of human settlement on all 28 of these features, from the beginning of time to World War II. I ask that you please listen carefully. [Pause] That was it. In case you missed it, I will go over it again a bit more slowly. [Pause] I have now covered it in its entirety twice. . . . The comprehensive historical and anthropological evidence that is before you shows you that there was no human settlement on any of these features—none at all—between the first chapter of Genesis and the middle of the 20th century. This is particularly compelling evidence of their non-habitability.[53]

By the summer of 2016, the Tribunal members were prepared to rule. They released an almost 500-page decision on July 12, and even a cursory glance revealed a sweeping victory for the Philippines. The decision flatly rejected China's nine-dash line as a basis for determining maritime rights in the South China Sea. What's more, it cited ample evidence that China itself had treated the waters as part of the high seas in the past, undercutting the argument that they were historically Chinese:

> For much of history . . . China's navigation and trade in the South China Sea, as well as fishing beyond the territorial sea, represented the exercise of high-seas freedoms. China engaged in activities that were permitted to all States by international law, as did the Philippines and other littoral States surrounding the South China Sea. Before the Second World War, the use of

the seabed, beyond the limits of the territorial sea, was likewise a freedom open to any State that wished to do so.[54]

The decision went much further. Systematically reviewing the characteristics of the various land features in the Spratlys, the judges declared that none were islands and that they could therefore not generate EEZs. Even Itu Aba, the largest feature in the chain, could not sustain habitation on its own and was a rock rather than an island. Taken together, the rejection of the nine-dash line as a basis for maritime rights and the downgrading of the South China Sea features constituted a devastating setback for China's pretensions to special rights in the South China Sea.

The decision got even worse for Beijing when the arbitrators turned to environmental questions. Relying on expert assessments, the Tribunal found that Chinese activities in the area were despoiling the marine environment. The ruling cited the harvesting of endangered species, blast fishing, and the use of cyanide as particularly destructive. But the bulk of the environmental section focused on the impact of China's extensive island-building campaign. The Tribunal described the environmental destruction wrought by the Chinese technique of grinding up coral reefs and then sucking up the resulting fragments to help expand the territory above the water line. All this activity violated the Convention's (rudimentary) standards of care toward the maritime environment. China's activities, the Tribunal concluded, "have caused devastating and long-lasting damage to the marine environment."

The victory produced pockets of jubilation in the Philippines, but the official response was restrained, not least because the country was in the midst of a tumultuous presidential transition. A month before the Tribunal's decision, a controversial former mayor named Rodrigo Duterte was elected president. He assumed office just weeks after the ruling, determined to mend relations with China and, as a consequence, downplay the country's sweeping victory.

For the international legal community, however, there was no minimizing the ruling. Decisive international legal decisions against major powers are rare, and lawyers described the decision as one of the most significant in decades. Substantively, the ruling bolstered at least one pillar of the otherwise teetering doctrine of freedom of the seas. National appropriation of ocean space without some basis in the Convention, the Tribunal insisted, was unacceptable. Through its interpretation of the Convention's spare environmental provisions, the Tribunal fleshed out considerably the obligations that countries have to protect the high-seas environment—including through environmental impact assessments and continuous monitoring of the effects of high-seas activities.[55] The Tribunal rebuffed any Chinese sovereign claim to open waters, but it also made clear that all countries have meaningful obligations to protect what they do not own.

Unsurprisingly, Beijing responded coldly to the ruling. *People's Daily,* the Communist Party newspaper, warned, "The Chinese government and the Chinese people firmly oppose [the ruling] and will neither acknowledge it nor accept it."[56] A longtime Chinese diplomat described the ruling as "waste paper."[57] That initial defiance did not foreclose the possibility that China might eventually accommodate itself to the decision. There was sufficient ambiguity in China's ocean claims that it could perhaps square the ruling with its own policies in a way that saved face. That course would require a major shift in China's political approach, however, and there were few signs Beijing was ready for that.

Rise of the FONOPs

The Philippines' international legal challenge produced victory in court but little change in the South China Sea. At least for the moment, pushing back against China's maritime claims would depend more on ships at sea than lawyers in courtrooms. The decision had generated quiet satisfaction in much of the region, including in Japan, Vietnam, and Indonesia. Yet welcoming the ruling was quite different from confronting the growing Chinese navy and coast guard. The US navy was the only force with the means and motive to do so, and the US freedom of navigation program was a ready-made vehicle.

Attention to that program, which was launched in the late 1970s, had fluctuated over the decades. The 1986 US foray into Libya's claimed waters and the 1988 Black Sea bumping incident with Soviet ships were dramatic, but the program mostly faded from view as the Cold War ended. Still, its basic design endured: Washington was committed to challenging what it viewed as excessive maritime claims, including through freedom of navigation operations (FONOPs) by naval forces. The United States had long insisted that the Convention's basic provisions regarding maritime zones were part of customary international law, and it wanted to ensure that coastal countries did not gradually alter those rules through their claims.

As controversy over China's South China Sea activities grew, the freedom of navigation program moved to center stage. With operations in Iraq and Afghanistan consuming military resources, the US navy did not conduct any operations to rebut Chinese maritime claims from 2004 through 2006. In 2007, the navy challenged China's restrictions on operations in the EEZ. The next year, it contested two different Chinese claims, and by 2011 Washington was challenging four distinct Chinese maritime assertions, including EEZ restrictions, straight baselines, and limitations on innocent passage.[58] The US government did not always announce these operations, but one expert compilation showed a marked increase in South China Sea FONOPs from 2015 to 2019.[59]

The United States was unique in the emphasis it placed on rebutting Chinese claims through naval operations. A few allied countries, including Australia and the United Kingdom, pitched in on occasion, although neither government formally labeled their maneuvers as "freedom of navigation" operations. Most other countries in the region watched the drama play out from a distance. Japan's government announced that it "strongly support[ed]" US operations, but constitutional and political restrictions on the use of its military made it infeasible for Japanese ships to join US FONOPs or conduct their own.[60]

Designing an appropriate naval response to distinct Chinese claims involved legal, political, and operational considerations. To challenge the Chinese insistence that foreign military vessels could not conduct surveillance in its EEZ, a US warship or aircraft could transit through China's zone at a convenient time and place and simply ignore Chinese demands to leave. As the 2001 EP-3 incident demonstrated, these operations carried risk, but the choreography was at least straightforward.

More specific Chinese claims, particularly those associated with rocks and reefs, required greater precision, as they involved sailing close to Chinese installations with limited room for maneuver. In October 2015, USS *Lassen* passed within 12 nautical miles of several Spratly Island features. To contest the straight baselines that China had drawn around the Paracel Islands, the USS *Decatur* made a U-shaped transit through the area enclosed by China's baselines (but outside each island's 12-mile territorial sea) (Figure 8.3).

Washington's increased pressure on China's claims culminated in a July 2020 statement by Secretary of State Mike Pompeo, which emphasized US support for the South China Sea arbitral ruling and rejected China's bid for

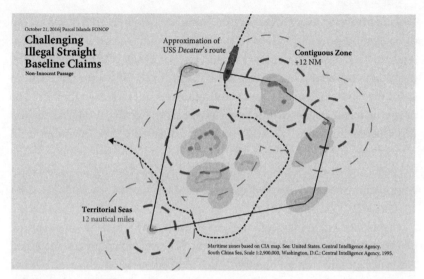

Figure 8.3 Challenging Chinese claims around the Paracel Islands; illustration courtesy of Asia Maritime Transparency Initiative.

"maritime empire." The United States, Pompeo insisted, "stand[s] with the international community in defense of freedom of the seas and respect for sovereignty and reject[s] any push to impose 'might makes right' in the South China Sea or the wider region."[61]

As the US navy ramped up its activities in the South China Sea, it increased the scope of freedom of navigation operations in other maritime domains as well (although, as we have seen, it hesitated to do so in the Arctic). Navy ships contested claims by Venezuela, Iran, and Russia, but the operations were not limited to US adversaries. The United States challenged the maritime assertions of a range of other countries, including Brazil, the Dominican Republic, India, Saudi Arabia, Taiwan, and Vietnam. The revived program signaled a redoubled effort by the leading maritime power to advance its interpretation of maritime freedom (Figure 8.4).

In so doing, the United States saw itself providing a global public good. Yet the program had a more limited appeal than its advocates sometimes acknowledged. Washington was focused on the ability of its large and advanced navy to operate freely—and as close to other countries' shores as the Convention permitted. A few other countries, particularly those in security relationships with the United States, shared Washington's desire to ensure maximum freedom of action for naval and air forces.

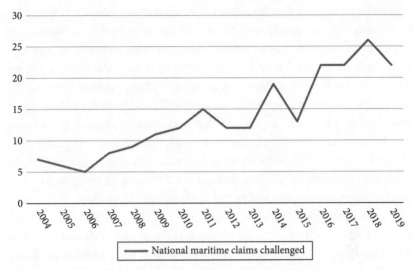

Figure 8.4 Expanding freedom of navigation operations; US Department of Defense.

But it was easy to view the program as the niche project of a maritime super-power. Most national naval forces and coast guards operated close to home and had no need or desire to conduct operations in other countries' exclusive economic zones or to pass through their territorial seas without advance notice. The unilateralism of the exercises added to doubts about it. The United States decided on its own which maritime assertions were excessive and made no effort to involve international courts or arbitrators. When it came to FONOPs, "the United States acts as accuser, judge, jury, and executioner," one scholar wrote. "It knows what the law is and has taken it upon itself to enforce it."[62]

When faced with indifference or opposition, US advocates of the program argued that unchecked coastal state restrictions would spread seaward and ultimately threaten everyone's interests, particularly if national restrictions started to impinge on commercial navigation. That logic was plausible but far from airtight. Why did a country's refusal to allow foreign warships to conduct exercises in its EEZ or transit unannounced through its territorial sea necessarily have implications for commercial shipping? During the Convention negotiations, Kenya's ambassador had bluntly informed Henry Kissinger that coastal countries would not long tolerate military activity in their EEZs and that the law of the sea would evolve to accommodate their concerns. More than four decades later, the tug of war between the maritime power and coastal claimants continued.

Assessing trends in that usually quiet struggle is not easy. Over the years, US pressure has convinced a few coastal countries to rescind what Washington viewed as an excessive maritime claim. Yet many other coastal countries kept restrictions on the books. At least 40 countries restrict the right of foreign warships to conduct innocent passage and almost 20 impose some limits on foreign military activities in the EEZ. The stretch of coast from the Indian Ocean toward the South China Sea has been fertile ground for national restrictions. Iran, Pakistan, India, Thailand, and Malaysia all limit military activities in their EEZs and the right of foreign warships to conduct innocent passage.[63] These countries have rarely resisted the occasional US freedom of navigation operation, but they have also declined to alter their national legislation.

At certain moments, this tacit agreement to disagree has come under strain. In April 2021, the US navy announced that one of its warships, the USS *John Paul Jones*, had passed through India's EEZ without notifying or seeking permission from the Indian government. The Indian foreign ministry protested to Washington, and a prominent Indian naval expert warned that "such operations normalise military activism close to India's island territories [and] encourage other regional navies to violate India's domestic regulations."[64] The historical overtones were hard to ignore. Vasco da Gama and later generations of Westerners had used their superior naval forces to dominate trade routes, force open ports, and occasionally bombard resisters into subjugation. Modern governments in the region preferred to keep foreign naval forces as far from their shores as possible.

There were important differences, but the United States in the 21st century was playing a role similar to that taken on by the British in the 18th and 19th centuries, when London tried to keep territorial seas from swelling beyond the customary three miles. For decades, the British gamely rebuffed attempts by several countries to expand their maritime domains, and they employed diplomatic, economic, and occasionally military pressure. That effort ultimately failed, and it was not clear that the US campaign would be any more successful in the long run.

Negotiating the High Seas

The low-level struggle between the United States and certain coastal countries over freedom of navigation was playing out against the backdrop of multiple efforts to preserve the health of the ocean. For decades, fisheries negotiations had been the focal point of international oceans diplomacy. Alarming new research and reporting on ocean health were now generating pressure for comprehensive international regulation that went beyond simply managing fish stocks.

One sprawling scientific effort, the Census of Marine Life, wrapped up in 2011. It drew on the work of hundreds of researchers in more than 80 countries and territories. "Life astonished us everywhere we looked," said Myriam Sibuet, one of the project's scientific advisers. "In the deep sea we found luxuriant communities despite extreme conditions."[65] The evidence of human impact was also substantial. In one part of the Mediterranean, researchers found that accumulated garbage was outcompeting marine life. The project also explored the seeming disappearance of many mollusk species and the struggles of sea turtles to avoid extinction.[66]

Evidence of accelerating ocean acidification made concerns about the loss of marine life acute. "Known to only a small number of researchers ten years ago," several scholars wrote, "the issue of ocean acidification has developed into one of the fastest growing fields of research in marine sciences."[67] Scientists presented evidence that acidification was weakening the shells of mollusks and other hard-shelled marine life. Coral reefs also appeared to be frequent victims, as more acidic ocean water bleached the reefs and destroyed fragile ecosystems. "If we don't take action on this issue very rapidly, coral reefs—and everything that depends on them, including both wildlife and local communities—will not survive into the next century," one researcher warned.[68]

In this context of mounting environmental alarm, freedom of the seas remained part of the ocean discourse, but it was often viewed as an awkward vestige of the past. That approach was apparent in the work of the Global Ocean Commission, launched in 2013 by the Pew Charitable Trusts and Oxford University. Led by several former national leaders and senior ministers, the Commission sought to highlight the plight of the open ocean. Its first report, released in 2014, warned of a "cycle of decline" in ocean health. For the Commission, the high-seas freedoms outlined in the original Convention were now an impediment to sensible policy. "The concept of the 'freedom of the high seas' guaranteed in the Convention once conjured up images of adventure and opportunity, but it is now driving a relentless 'tragedy of the commons,' characterised by the depletion of fish stocks and other precious marine resources."[69]

A new mechanism emerged for trying to break the cycle of degradation. Within their territorial waters and exclusive economic zones, several countries created "marine protected areas" (MPAs) to safeguard ocean ecosystems and marine resources. The power that coastal states have to protect their waters placed those innovations on solid legal ground. In the United States, successive administrations used powers derived from the Antiquities Act of 1906 to protect undersea space. The George W. Bush administration established several marine national monuments. In 2016, the Obama administration quadrupled the size of the existing marine monument around the Hawaiian Islands, placing more than 580,000 square miles under the federal government's protection.[70]

Much more ambitious was the idea of creating similar protected areas on the high seas. The concept was similar in design to regional fisheries organizations. As in that context, groups of countries using a certain ocean space would agree to limit their activities in the area. Unlike most fisheries organizations, however, the goal of high-seas MPAs would be conservation of marine resources broadly rather than just ensuring a sustainable fishing yield. MPAs could employ a range of possible restrictions to that end, including local fishing bans and limitations on other ocean activities such as drilling or cable-laying.

In 2009, diplomats discussed the idea of an MPA entirely within international waters at meetings of the regional organization devoted to managing the waters near Antarctica. The remoteness of the area and the mostly untouched nature of these waters were principal arguments for preservation. A collection of ocean experts, including famed oceanographer Sylvia Earle and the son of the oceanographer Jacques Cousteau, backed the project of declaring an MPA. As activists sought to generate public pressure, the member countries methodically deliberated. Russia and China proved particularly reluctant, and their representatives questioned the legal and scientific basis for an MPA. Year after year, the negotiations continued. Finally, in 2017, after a few last-minute concessions to the holdout countries, the Ross Sea Marine Protected Area was born. Covering nearly a million square miles, it was the largest MPA created to that point. Member countries agreed not to fish at all in most of the area.

By 2020, more than 20 MPAs existed that incorporated areas of the high seas. For all the publicity that surrounded these projects, the real-world impact was not always clear. The countries that helped create MPAs usually did not commit additional resources to monitor or enforce restrictions on the use of these areas. As important, high-seas MPAs faced the same legal limitations that bedeviled regional fisheries organizations: a club of countries—however well-intentioned—could not forbid a nonmember country from using an area of the high seas.

Even the most enthusiastic advocates of new high-seas protected zones acknowledged that they were a stopgap measure. For those most concerned about the health of the oceans, a more comprehensive solution was essential. In a variety of international forums and at the United Nations itself, Australia, Canada, and a group of mostly European countries explored the diplomatic possibilities—including a new treaty or some kind of binding addendum to the Convention. There was precedent for modifying or supplementing the Convention. In the mid-1990s, diplomats agreed to alter the seabed mining arrangements and drafted an agreement to manage high-seas fish stocks. Why not now add substance to the Convention's thin provisions on protecting the high seas?

There was broad support, but the process was slow. In 2015, the UN General Assembly voted to convene formal negotiations, and they finally began in 2018. Environmental nongovernmental organizations (NGOs) followed the diplomacy closely and depicted it as vital to ensuring the health of the oceans. "A new treaty for high-seas protection will be a game changer for the future of our ocean and the millions dependent on it for their survival," an influential coalition of NGOs insisted.[71] A Greenpeace representative declared that "a global network of marine reserves is urgently needed to bring life back into the ocean—this new treaty should make that happen."

As the negotiations began, a number of these voices advocated a simple but dramatic move: a ban on high-seas fishing. In 2014, two scientists attempted to model the impact of such a ban and concluded that in most cases, it would improve overall fishing yield. The logic was straightforward enough: with fishing outlawed, the high seas could become a sanctuary for the replenishment of many stocks of fish and other marine animals.[72] That idea proved too ambitious, but the negotiations did reveal substantial agreement that remaining high-seas freedoms needed to be adapted. Even skeptical countries could agree to negotiate about possible environmental impact statements for high-seas activity and a process to facilitate further environmental protection zones.

Alongside the general concern for the high-seas environment, many developing countries had a distinct goal: ensuring that the benefits of marine genetic resources were shared internationally. In this respect, there was a striking parallel between these new high-seas negotiations and the

Convention process of the 1970s and early 1980s. In both contexts, developing countries feared that the rich world would reap the rewards of ocean research and thereby deepen global inequities. That concern was not theoretical. A promising anti-cancer drug, trabectedin, had been derived from sea squirts. A group of anti-viral medications had roots in research conducted on sea sponges. That category included remdesivir, later identified as potentially effective in treating COVID-19.[73]

Assuming that genetic resources harvested from the high seas produced profitable drugs in the future, should the proceeds be shared among the international community? It was on this question that the sharpest philosophical divide emerged. Developing countries revived the "common heritage of mankind" language and argued that it applied just as much to genetic resources as it did to undersea minerals. Many developed countries, with the United States among them, saw the harvesting of genetic resources as squarely within the freedom of the high seas. They argued that marine genetic resources were quite different from seabed minerals. Unlike minerals, which have inherent value, a piece of genetic material taken from a living organism is essentially worthless. Only through the application of extensive (and expensive) research can that genetic material become valuable. Given this reality, they argued, any benefit sharing would have to be substantially different from the mining structure.

Even if that philosophical divide were overcome, there was sharp disagreement about the appropriate methods for overseeing new high-seas regulations. At one end of the spectrum of possible solutions stood the International Seabed Authority—a permanent international structure with a standing bureaucracy. For many developing countries, something similar (and perhaps even an expanded and newly empowered ISA) made sense. In most rich countries—and certainly in Washington—there was no appetite for creating a new international bureaucracy or expanding the ISA's remit. As the negotiations dragged on, delegates struggled with how to implement new restrictions on high-seas activities—but there was little doubt that new international regulation was on the way.

Boyan Slat's Voyage

Not everyone was waiting for the diplomats to act. Four hundred years after a Dutch prodigy made the case for a free sea, another overachiever from

Holland tried to clean up some of the mess that free use of the oceans had produced. Like Grotius, Boyan Slat hailed from the city of Delft. While Grotius's talents lay in the humanities, Slat's mind was drawn toward engineering challenges. At age 14, he organized the simultaneous launch of 213 water rockets, securing a place in the Guinness Book of World Records. Slat planned to focus his university studies on aerospace, but a personal encounter drew him to the oceans. While diving near Greece during a family holiday, the teenager encountered plastic in the waters and on the beach. Marine plastic's ubiquity galvanized him much as it had Charles Moore, the sailor who discovered the Pacific "garbage patch."

In 2013, Slat recorded a TED talk that featured photographs from holiday dives, a jar of plastic fragments he collected, and images of dead birds that had ingested plastic. A shaggy-haired and nervous Slat recounted how he and fellow engineering students had tested a trawl net to capture plastic in the ocean. He outlined a design for a plastic collection device with long arms that could be anchored to the seabed inside one of the ocean gyres. Ocean currents were helpfully gathering ocean plastic. Why not now scoop it up? The student argued that the whole effort could even make money, as the collected plastic was recycled and resold.

Slat's talk went viral, and the school project morphed into a multi-million dollar organization titled The Ocean Cleanup. It attracted funding from hundreds of individual donors, including celebrities and corporate executives. Slat put his university studies on hold and added dozens of employees and volunteers to the project. The United Nations designated Slat a "Champion of the Earth" and he was named the Young Entrepreneur of 2017.[74] But the project attracted withering criticism as well as accolades. One ocean conservation expert called the project "a fool's errand."[75] Scientists worried that the effort might do more environmental harm than good, by disturbing the organisms that had taken up residence on the floating plastic. International lawyers had their own concerns. Would the plastic collection device be a vessel? If so, what national flag would it fly? They also worried that the device might impede navigation and violate international agreements designed to protect the world's shipping lanes.

Objections like these—together with the engineering challenge of turning a concept into a functional prototype—forced multiple revisions to the original plan. The designers struggled to match the device's pace with that of the floating plastic. In June 2018, a vessel towed the first prototype into a gyre in the Pacific. But the mechanism had trouble holding onto the plastic it encountered. Then a piece of the device detached. Four months later, and with no plastic removed, the prototype was towed back to port. Slat and his team retooled and tried again, but a new realism was reflected in the organization's statements. "If the journey to this point taught us anything, it is that it's definitely not going to be easy," Slat conceded.[76]

In December 2019, the group was finally able to showcase its first catch. A vessel journeyed to the gyre, collected 60 bags of plastic retrieved by the contraption, and ferried it to Vancouver (Figure 8.5). At a rainy press conference, surrounded by recovered ocean plastic, Slat announced plans to refashion the refuse from the Pacific into collector's items that would help generate a regular stream of income for the cleanup effort. He encouraged the organization's supporters to sign up for some of the first ocean pollution mementos. "It's plastic that has a story," Slat said.[77]

Even as the first haul of ocean plastic was being unloaded, the organization had shifted substantial energy and resources toward land. In late 2019, it launched a new prototype: a solar-powered barge that could be stationed inside or near the outlet of major rivers, poised to collect plastic before it drifted out to sea. Riverine interception dispensed with many challenges of

Figure 8.5 Boyan Slat with ocean plastic; photograph courtesy of The Ocean Cleanup.

working on the high seas. But it also meant that the organization would be working squarely within national jurisdiction and thus would have to strike deals with governments before deploying the collectors. A project that began with visions of using high-seas freedom to cleanse the oceans was being pulled ineluctably toward waters under national control.

Conclusion
Sea Changes

In the summer of 2020, the United States navy positioned three of its aircraft carriers in the western Pacific Ocean. Each of the massive vessels housed thousands of sailors and marines and could launch dozens of combat aircraft. The accumulation of firepower was designed to maintain maritime freedom in the region. "Only the U.S. Navy can integrate a carrier strike force on this scale and consistently project power to protect freedom of the seas," a US admiral insisted.[1]

In describing the United States as the protector of ocean freedom, the admiral was echoing countless other assertions by US politicians, military officers, and commentators. On this telling, the disputes unfolding in Asian waters are a contest between China's desire for maritime domination and the US determination to protect access to the oceans by defending international rules. That narrative connects with a powerful current in US diplomatic history. Today's American officials echo earlier generations of leaders who inveighed against Barbary piracy, British impressment, boarding agreements to counter the slave trade, privateering restrictions, and German submarine attacks. The style of political rhetoric has changed in the intervening decades, but few modern American politicians would quibble with Woodrow Wilson's insistence that ocean freedom was "sacred" or Franklin Roosevelt's contention that "all freedom depends on freedom of the seas." The modern Democratic and Republican parties disagree on many things, but they share a conviction that protecting ocean freedom is a vital national interest.

The contest over maritime rights in Asia is therefore easy to view as the latest iteration of a long-running contest between the desire of certain rulers to control the ocean and the insistence of others that the oceans must be open to all. Just as the English challenged Spanish dominance and the Dutch protested against the Indian Ocean claims of the Portuguese, smaller countries in East Asia, backed by the United States, are resisting the maritime pretensions of a new world power. More than 400 years after Hugo Grotius declared the sea open for all, warships sailing through waters claimed by China can plausibly claim to be following in his wake.

The apparent historical continuity can be deceptive, however. Asia's contemporary maritime disputes are in fact layered over a slow-motion revolution in how humans interact with the oceans and what rules govern their use. One would not know it from the press releases and the proclamations, but events in the last century have greatly undermined the Grotian idea of "freedom of the seas," which had as its pillars free navigation, freedom to exploit ocean resources, and minimal national jurisdiction over ocean space. A United States that claims to be the concept's most robust and consistent defender has in fact played a more complicated role.

As this account documents, the dismantling of freedom of the seas has occurred in several phases, not always related to each other. As submarines began to stalk the seas, the world wars of the 20th century all but destroyed the idea that free navigation could be maintained during conflict. As a noncombatant, the United States argued against blockades, unrestricted submarine warfare, and other blockages of open waters. As a combatant, it found those tactics impossible to resist. When the Second World War ended, the United States then led the hunt for ocean resources on the continental shelf, setting in motion a process that badly strained the idea that the open ocean should be beyond national control. The process of national expansion into ocean space eventually produced the UN Convention on the Law of the Sea, which quadrupled the traditional size of the territorial sea and created a large new maritime economic zone.

The consequences of those changes are still playing out across the globe, as governments seek to ensure that outsiders respect their maritime rights. Given the ubiquitous rhetoric about maritime freedom, it is easy to forget that most disputes in the South and East China Seas and in the Mediterranean are not really about freedom of ocean access; they are about which nation should be able to control the waters in question. The standoff between the Philippines and China that produced the 2016 international ruling, for example, centered on whether Beijing or Manila had the right to manage fishing near Scarborough Shoal; neither country was arguing that all ocean users should have access. Similarly, the choice in the increasingly dangerous waters around the Senkaku Islands is between Japanese and Chinese dominion.

Military technology and hunger for ocean resources have challenged freedom of the seas, but so has a new perspective on the past. The decolonization that began in earnest in the 1950s gave voice to new countries, many of whom viewed Grotius's legacy with deep skepticism. In international conferences, diplomats from these new governments argued with increasing vehemence that freedom of the seas had been little more than a means for maritime powers to exercise their will. That current of thought remains relevant, and Chinese officials have tapped it as they respond to US naval deployments. Rhetoric about ocean freedom, they have argued, is a pretext for domination. "In the guise of 'freedom of navigation', [the United States] has frequently approached and illegally entered waters and airspace of China near the relevant reefs in South China Sea," a Chinese diplomat argued. "It is quite clear who is seeking to build a 'maritime empire' and playing power politics in the South China Sea."[2] Chinese actions have been too brazen and its claims too extreme for that argument to change many minds in the region, but the rhetoric is a reminder that the legacy of "freedom of the seas" is complex and that its appeal is more limited than its advocates sometimes acknowledge.

A belated reckoning with the environmental consequences of free ocean use has added to the pressure on freedom of the seas. The story of that realization passes through the squabbles of fisheries experts, attempts in the 1930s to restrain the industrialized slaughter of whales, Rachel Carson's mounting alarm, and modern-day research into ocean plastic and acidification. International scrutiny of all manner of high-seas activities is increasing. The headlines generated by the 2016 South China Sea decision understandably focused on the finding that China's maritime claims were unlawful, but the ruling also advanced the idea that all countries have substantial obligations to the ocean environment. Ongoing diplomatic negotiations aim to provide even more substance to those duties.

If the health of the oceans has made freedom to exploit maritime resources increasingly untenable, the response to ocean-borne threats has periodically put pressure on the freedom to navigate, even during peacetime. On the high seas, governments with the resources to do so are devising new ways to confront perceived threats, including drugs, unwanted migrants, and dangerous weapons. In so doing, they often strain traditional notions of free navigation. The United States is a purist about territorial claims to the oceans, but it has proved much more pragmatic when it comes to interdiction operations aimed at heading off these threats.

Taken together, these various trends have produced a new approach to the oceans, which is more complex than rhetoric about ocean freedom often suggests. US concern about freedom of action for its naval forces is an important issue, but it is just one slice of modern ocean governance (and not one that matters greatly to most countries). The broader maritime compromise—embodied in the UN Convention and emerging international jurisprudence—provides for both increased national control and new forms of international governance.

The idea of the high seas as an unowned and minimally regulated space remains relevant, but it is far weaker than in the past. The world still mostly treats the oceans as a common space but one that is significantly reduced in size and subject to multiple and sometimes overlapping new forms of regional and international rules. An array of different regional and international organizations helps manage ocean use.

***

Can this complex, hybrid model of ocean governance endure? There are some grounds for optimism, both from theoretical and diplomatic perspectives. Distinct groups of scholars have arrived at the conclusion that intricate compromises like the current ocean governance arrangement can function effectively. Specialists in the study of common resources have built on the work of Elinor and Vincent Ostrom to explore how "polycentric" governance of common spaces and resources is possible. Having multiple sources of governance, it has been argued, may help "strik[e] a balance between centralized and fully decentralized or community-based governance."[3] The crude logic of the "tragedy of the commons"—which demanded either full privatization of common spaces or centralized control—is no longer satisfying.

For their part, international relations scholars have focused on the phenomenon of "regime complexity," which two scholars have described as "a set of overlapping and perhaps even contradictory regimes that share a common focus."[4] That concept is particularly apt for contemporary ocean governance, which includes important roles for unilateral action (such as freedom of navigation operations), regional diplomacy (including fisheries groups and new marine protected areas), multilateral treaties, and rulings from several different international courts and tribunals. Working from multiple different angles, scholars have acknowledged that the future of international governance may be more about complexity than clarity.

From a diplomatic perspective, there is also reason to think that the compromise on the oceans can survive. The vast majority of countries—and almost all coastal states—have joined the UN Convention, accepted the maritime zones it creates, and committed to abide by its procedures for resolving disputes. The refusal of the United States to join the Convention is a blow, but it is mitigated by broader US advocacy for most of the Convention's rules. China's claims have emerged as the most consequential challenge to the Convention, but they remain ambiguous and potentially reversible. When Antonio Carpio championed the Philippines challenge to China's nine-dash line, he argued that rebuffing China at sea might take decades, and long-term optimism of that sort remains tenable.

China's perception of itself and its relationship with the ocean could change in the coming years. Paradoxically, increasing maritime power may encourage Beijing to slowly back away from its maritime claims. As described in Chapter 2, Great Britain in the 19th century abandoned its claims to nearby waters as it became a global maritime power. The Soviet Union became much more friendly to ocean freedom in the 1960s as its naval and maritime reach expanded (an evolution covered in Chapter 5).

The Chinese challenge to the Convention may therefore subside, and existing maritime rules might also avoid the worst outcomes for the marine environment. With some tweaks, addenda, and a dose of enlightened self-interest, the Convention's basic compromise could manage and protect the oceans for future generations. Often ineffective regional fisheries organizations might slowly improve, as new technologies on land and at sea allow for better monitoring of even large areas of the ocean. Entrepreneurs and maritime experts are experimenting with crowd-sourcing to boost the monitoring capacity of coastal countries. Unmanned ocean drones may eventually prove an even more effective tool. Seaborne activists will continue to expose and harass those who abuse the oceans, perhaps goading sluggish governments into action. Future inventors may follow Boyan Slat's lead and devise ingenious new mechanisms for remediating some of the damage that has been inflicted on the high seas.

Confronting violence at sea is always a challenge, but doing so likely does not require radical change to ocean legalities. In the last several decades, governments and merchants collaborated to subdue flares in piracy in the Straits of Malacca and off the coast of Somalia. In extreme cases, the UN Security Council has used its wide legal powers to bolster international maritime security efforts.

As recent reporting has documented, forced labor and other human rights abuses at sea remain a daunting problem, but they also could be addressed without fundamental change to ocean rules. Many abuses at sea are more a manifestation of weak national governance than a failure of the international

architecture. Governments that struggle to stop human trafficking and abusive labor conditions on their territory have trouble doing so on vessels
they flag. The flag-of-convenience phenomenon exacerbates the problem
by allowing countries to flag many more vessels than they are able to regulate effectively. Yet international rules already provide a potential solution
by requiring a "genuine link" between the flag state and the vessel. If that requirement were finally taken seriously, the capacity of major maritime countries to enforce their national rules could be deployed to address crime and
abuses at sea.

***

A version of the status quo could therefore endure, but it is not hard to
imagine scenarios in which the tentative compromise on the oceans
changes significantly—or falls apart entirely. Open conflict about Asian or
Mediterranean waters would have unpredictable consequences and might
prompt massive closures of contested waters and perhaps a new spate of
line-drawing. Turkey's government has never accepted the Convention and
it recently embraced a "blue homeland" concept that imagines expanded
maritime rights in the Mediterranean. Several countries in Latin America
still harbor visions of extended maritime control. The refusals of China and
Russia to abide by the Convention's dispute resolution system (described in
Chapter 8) could encourage more open defections.

A terrorist attack employing merchant vessels would likely lead to new
restrictions on commercial navigation and expanded boarding and inspection rights. Arvid Pardo's fears about a destabilizing rush for undersea
minerals (discussed in Chapter 5) may still prove prescient. The international mechanism for managing deep-sea mining has barely been tested, and
competition for profits could create more pressure than it can bear. As we
have seen, multinational management of fisheries is lackluster, and coastal
countries worried about fishing fleets hovering outside their waters may be
tempted to extend their maritime boundaries, as a few have already done.

The fragility of the current maritime status quo is in part a product of its
uncertain conceptual foundation. For all its defects, freedom of the seas had
a coherent philosophical foundation that today's hybrid model lacks. The
clearest conceptual alternative to Grotian freedom is the idea of the oceans as
humanity's "common heritage." Yet that vision has never fully taken hold, and
confusion about how to conceive of the ocean renders the current compromise vulnerable. If encouraged by politicians, the public in many countries

248 THE POSEIDON PROJECT

will need little convincing that they deserve greater ocean real estate. As they have reached for rights on extended continental shelves (a process described in Chapter 7), leaders have employed nationalistic arguments that might easily be deployed for even more grandiose claims.

In the face of confusing, sluggish, and often frustrating multilateral management of the oceans, unilateral national expansion will therefore remain an alluring alternative. China's ocean claims are significant not just for the immediate frictions they create but also as a potential precedent for other coastal countries. There is a conceit that the world has evolved past unilateral ocean claims, and Russia's 2007 flag planting at the bottom of the Arctic aroused as much derision as alarm. Yet there is a robust history of unilateral action to alter maritime rules (including by Great Britain and the United States), and China's assertions could simply be the next iteration of that pattern.

Whether the way forward is incremental and negotiated or more erratic and unilateral, one thing is certain: the future ocean will feature less traditional freedom than ever before. Grotius may have prevailed in the "battle of the books" that played out in the 17th century—but he is on course to lose the war.

Notes

Introduction

1. Nao Arakawa and Will Colson, "The Japan Coast Guard: Resourcing and Responsibility" (Asia Maritime Transparency Initiative: April 1, 2015), https://amti.csis.org/author/wcolson.
2. Center for New American Security, "A Deadly Game: East China Sea Crisis 2030," July 22, 2020, https://www.cnas.org/publications/video/a-deadly-game-east-china-sea-crisis-2030
3. Jessica Paga and Margaret M. Miles, "The Archaic Temple of Poseidon at Sounion," *Hesperia: The Journal of the American School of Classical Studies at Athens* 85, no. 4 (2016), 657–710.
4. Michael Birnbaum, "Russian Submarines Are Prowling Around Vital Undersea Cables," *Washington Post*, December 22, 2017.
5. Ian Urbina, *The Outlaw Ocean: Journeys Across the Last Untamed Frontier* (New York: Knopf Doubleday, 2019).
6. William Langewiesche, *The Outlaw Sea* (New York: North Point Press, 2004), 3.
7. Targeted News Service, "Anarchy on the High Seas: Global Ocean Commission Calls for an Ocean Sustainable Development Goal," February 4, 2014.
8. Senate Commerce, Science and Transportation Committee Hearing, "Our Blue Economy: Successes and Opportunities," Testimony by Michael Conathan, Executive Director, Aspen Institute, Aspen High Seas Initiative, *Congressional Documents and Publications*, March 27, 2019.
9. *The Simpsons*, "The Mansion Family," Season 11, Episode 12.
10. John D. Negroponte, *Who Will Protect Freedom of the Seas?* (Washington, DC: US Department of State, Bureau of Public Affairs, 1986).
11. Hugo Grotius, *The Free Sea* (Indianapolis, IN: Liberty Fund, 2012).
12. Franklin D. Roosevelt, "Radio Address Announcing an Unlimited National Emergency," May 27, 1941. Online by Gerhard Peters and John T. Woolley, *The American Presidency Project*, http://www.presidency.ucsb.edu/ws/?pid=16120.
13. "Royal Caribbean-International Names Much Anticipated Ultra-Voyager," PR Newswire (November 9, 2004).
14. Pittman B. Potter, *The Freedom of the Seas in History, Law, and Politics* (New York: Longmans, Green, 1924).
15. United Nations Conference on Trade and Development, *Review of Maritime Transport 2017*, https://unctad.org/system/files/official-document/rmt2017_en.pdf.
16. Food and Agriculture Organization, *State of the World's Fisheries 2018*, http://www.fao.org/family-farming/detail/en/c/1145050/.

17. Daniel Patrick O'Connell, *The International Law of the Sea* (Oxford: Clarendon Press, 1982), 1.

18. Bethan O'Leary et al., "The First Network of Marine Protected Areas (MPAs) in the High Seas: The Process, the Challenges and Where Next," *Marine Policy* 36, no. 3 (2012), 598–605; Marta Chantal Ribiero, "'The 'Rainbow': The First National Marine Protected Area Proposed Under the High Seas," *International Journal of Marine and Coastal Law* 25, no. 2 (2010), 183–207.

19. For a discussion of the expanded continental shelf and exclusive economic zone (EEZ) issues, in particular, see Scott Shackelford, "Was Selden Right: The Expansion of Closed Seas and Its Consequences," *Stanford Journal of International Law* 47 (2011), 1.

20. Arvid Pardo, "United Nations Speech," *The Common Heritage: Selected Papers on Oceans and World Order* (Valletta: Malta University Press, 1975).

21. See Crow White and Christopher Costello, "Close the High Seas to Fishing?" *PLoS Biology* 12, no. 3 (2014), e1001826; U. Rashid Sumaila et al. "Winners and Losers in a World Where the High Seas Is Closed to Fishing," *Scientific Reports* 5 (2015), 8481.

Chapter 1

1. Ibn Jubayr, *The Travels of Ibn Jubayr*, trans. R. J. C. Broadhurst (London: J. Cape, 1952), 26.

2. Jubayr, *The Travels of Ibn Jubayr*.

3. Martin W. Lewis, "Dividing the Ocean Sea," *Geographical Review* 89, no. 2 (April 1999), 190.

4. Lincoln Paine, *The Sea and Civilization: A Maritime History of the World* (New York: Knopf, 2013), 77.

5. Callum Roberts, *The Unnatural History of the Sea* (Washington, DC: Island Press, 2007), 18.

6. For a skeptical account, see Loren J. Samons, "Kimon, Kallias and Peace with Persia," *Historia: Zeitschrift für Alte Geschichte* H. 2 (1998), 129–140. For a defense of the treaty's existence, see George Law Cawkwell, "The Peace Between Athens and Persia," *Phoenix* 51, no. 2 (1997), 115–130.

7. Egidia Occhipinti, "Historiography and Hegemony," in *The Hellenica Oxyrhynchia and Historiography* (Leiden: Brill, 2016), 141–161.

8. Quoted in Ian Maxwell, "Seas as Places," *Shima: The International Journal of Research into Island Cultures* 6, no. 1 (2012), 27–29.

9. Chester G. Starr, *The Roman Imperial Navy, 31 B.C.–A.D. 324* (Ithaca, NY: Cornell University Press, 1941), 168.

10. Quoted in Jonathan Ziskind, "International Law and Ancient Sources: Grotius and Selden," *Review of Politics* 35, no. 4 (1973), 550–551.

11. Quoted in Pitman B. Potter, *The Freedom of the Seas in History, Law, and Politics* (New York: Longmans, Green, 1924).

12. Paine, *Sea and Civilization*, 317–318.

13. David Abulafia, *The Boundless Sea* (Oxford: Oxford University Press, 2019), 155.

14. Hassan S. Khalilieh, *Islamic Maritime Law: An Introduction* (Boston: Brill, 1998), 133–141.

15. Khalilieh, *Islamic Maritime Law*, 104.

16. J. Kathirithamby-Wells and John Villiers, eds., *The Southeast Asian Port and Polity: Rise and Demise* (Singapore: Singapore University Press, 1990), 154.

17. R. P. Anand, "Maritime Practice in South-East Asia until 1600 A.D. and the Modern Law of the Sea," *International and Comparative Law Quarterly* 30, no. 2 (April 1981), 444.

18. Geoff Wade, "The Zheng He Voyages: A Reassessment," *Journal of the Malaysian Branch of the Royal Asiatic Society* 78, no. 1 (288) (2005), 51.

19. Nicholas A. M. Rodger, *The Safeguard of the Sea: A Naval History of Britain, 660–1649*, vol. 1 (New York: Norton, 1998), 4.

20. Elmer Belmont Potter, ed., *Sea Power: A Naval History*, 2nd ed. (Annapolis, MD: Naval Institute Press, 1981), 15.

21. Hasan S. Khalilieh, *Admiralty and Maritime Laws in the Mediterranean Sea (ca. 800–1050): The Kitāb Akriyat al-Sufun* vis-à-vis *the Nomos Rhodion Nautikos* (Leiden: Brill, 2006), 250–251.

22. Laws of Oléron Art. 6, xiv, http://www.admiraltylawguide.com/documents/oleron.html.

23. S. Raffles, "The Maritime Code of the Malays," *Journal of the Straits Branch of the Royal Asiatic Society*, no. 3 (July 1879), 63.

24. Philip de Souza, *Piracy in the Graeco-Roman World* (Cambridge: Cambridge University Press, 2002), 50.

25. Allen M. Ward, "Caesar and the Pirates," *Classical Philology* 70, no. 4 (1975), 267–268.

26. Josiah Osgood, "Caesar and the Pirates: or How to Make (and Break) an Ancient Life," *Greece and Rome* 57, no. 2 (2010), 319.

27. Alex Mallett, "A Trip Down the Red Sea with Reynald of Châtillon," *Journal of the Royal Asiatic Society* 18, no. 2 (2008), 141–153.

28. Peter D. Shapinsky, "Japanese Pirates and the East Asian Maritime World, 1200–1600," in *Oxford Research Encyclopedia of Asian History* (Oxford: Oxford University Press, 2016).

29. De Souza, *Piracy in the Graeco-Roman World*, 193–212.

30. Quoted in Andrew Palmer, *The New Pirates: Modern Global Piracy from Somalia to the South China Sea* (London: I.B. Tauris, 2014), 2.

31. Philip de Souza, "'They Are the Enemies of All Mankind': Justifying Roman Imperialism in the Late Republic," in Jane Webster and Nicholas J. Cooper. *Roman Imperialism: Post-Colonial Perspectives* (Leicester: University of Leicester,1996), 125–134 [emphasis added].

32. Frederic L. Cheyette, "The Sovereign and the Pirates, 1332," *Speculum* 45, no. 1 (January 1970), 47.

33. James E. Wadsworth, *Global Piracy: A Documentary History of Seaborne Banditry* (London: Bloomsbury Publishing, 2019).

34. Thucydides, *History of the Peloponnesian Wars*.

35. Stella Xu, "The Guardian of the Maritime Network in Premodern East Asia: Contested History and Memory of Chang Pogo," *Korean Studies* 40, no. 1 (2016), 119–139.

36. Ernst Daenell, "The Policy of the German Hanseatic League Respecting the Mercantile Marine," *American Historical Review* 15, no. 1 (October 1909), 50.

37. Samuel Eliot Morison, *Admiral of the Ocean Sea: A Life of Christopher Columbus* (Boston: Little, Brown, 1942).

38. Sanjay Subrahmanyan, *The Career and Legend of Vasco da Gama* (Cambridge: Cambridge University Press, 1997), 112.

39. William J. Bernstein, *A Splendid Exchange: How Trade Shaped the World* (New York: Grove Press, 2008), 103.

40. Abdul Sheriff, "Navigational Methods in the Indian Ocean," *Ships and the Development of Maritime Technology on the Indian Ocean* 2 (2002), 219.

41. Quoted in Luis Madureira, "The Accident of America: Marginal Notes on the European Conquest of the World," *CR: The New Centennial Review* 2, no. 1 (Spring 2002), 136.

42. Ruby Maloni, "Control of the Seas: The Historical Exegesis of the Portuguese 'Cartaz,'" in *Proceedings of the Indian History Congress*, vol. 72 (New Delhi: Indian History Congress, 2011), 476–484.

43. Treaty between Spain and Portugal concluded at Tordesillas, June 7, 1494, https://ava lon.law.yale.edu/15th_century/mod001.asp.

44. For more on this point, see Philip E. Steinberg, "Lives of Division, Lines of Connection: Stewardship in the World Ocean," *Geographical Review* 89, no. 2 (1999), 254–264.

45. Thomas Suárez, *Early Mapping of the Pacific: The Epic Story of Seafarers, Adventurers and Cartographers Who Mapped the Earth's Greatest Ocean* (North Clarendon, VT: Tuttle, 2004), 49.

46. Quoted in Thomas Wemyss Fulton, *The Sovereignty of the Sea* (Edinburgh: William Blackwood and Sons, 1911), 107.

47. Hugo Grotius, *The Free Sea* (Indianapolis, IN: Liberty Fund, 2004), 11.

48. Grotius, *The Free Sea*, 31.

49. R. P. Anand has argued that Grotius drew heavily on the example of freedom of the seas that was practiced in the Indian Ocean. "His genius lies not only in observing that practice, but in systematically presenting it as a principle or doctrine relying on the ever-respected Roman law, and recommending it to Europeans as the most sensible practice." "Maritime Practice in South-East Asia until 1600 A.D. and the Modern Law of the Sea," *International and Comparative Law Quarterly* 30, no. 2 (April 1981), 448.

50. Grotius, *The Free Sea*, 116.

51. John Selden, *Mare Clausum: The Right and Dominion of the Seas in Two Books* (London: Printed for A. Kembe and E. Thomas, 1663).

52. Pieter Geyl, "Grotius in *Transactions of the Grotius Society*," 12, "Problems of Peace and War," Papers Read before the Society in the Year 1926 (1926), 81–97.

53. Hugo Grotius, *The Free Sea*, trans. Richard Hakluyt (Indianapolis, IN: Liberty Fund, 2004), 32–33.

54. Benjamin Redding, "A Ship 'For Which Great Neptune Raves': The Sovereign of the Seas, La Couronne and Seventeenth-Century International Competition over Warship Design," *Mariner's Mirror* 104, no. 4 (2018), 402–422.

55. Jonathan R. Dull, *The Age of the Ship of the Line: The British and French Navies, 1650–1815* (Lincoln: University of Nebraska, 2009), 1.

56. Paul M. Kennedy, *The Rise and Fall of British Naval Mastery* (London: Macmillan, 1983), 78.

57. Martin Robson, *A History of the Royal Navy: The Seven Years War* (London: I.B. Tauris, 2016), 4 [internal quotations omitted].

Chapter 2

1. Cornelius van Bynkershoek et al., *De Dominio Maris Dissertatio*, ed. James Brown Scot (New York: Carnegie Endowment for International Peace, 1923), 43–44.

2. Lori Fisler Damrosch and Sean D. Murphy, *International Law, Cases and Materials*, 6th ed. (St. Paul, MN: West Academic Publishing, 2014), xxii.

3. Emer de Vattel, *The Law of Nations* (Indianapolis: Liberty Fund, 2008), 255.

4. Letter from Benjamin Franklin to Charles Dumas (December 19, 1775), in Francis Wharton, *The Revolutionary Diplomatic Correspondence of the United States*, vol. 2 (Washington: US Government Printing Office,1889).

5. Paine, *Sea and Civilization*, 489.

6. Lance Davis and Stanley Engerman, *Naval Blockades in Peace and War: An Economic History Since 1750* (New York: Cambridge University Press, 2006), 28.

7. See, for example, Eli Filip Heckscher, *The Continental System: An Economic Interpretation* (Oxford: Clarendon Press, 1922); Joel Mokyr and N. Eugene Savin, "Stagflation in Historical Perspective: The Napoleonic Wars Revisited," *Research in Economic History* 1 (1976), 198–259; Reka Juhász, "Temporary Protection and Technology Adoption: Evidence from the Napoleonic Blockade," *American Economic Review* 108, no. 11 (2018), 3339–3376.

8. A. D. Harvey, "European Attitudes to Britain During the French Revolutionary and Napoleonic Era," *History* 63, no. 209 (1978), 356–365.

9. Quoted in Harvey, "European Attitudes to Britain."

10. "From John Adams to Benjamin Rush, 31 August 1808," *Founders Online*, National Archives, https://founders.archives.gov/documents/Adams/99-02-02-5250.

11. Bruce Redford, *Venice and The Grand Tour* (United States: New Haven, CT: Yale University Press, 1996), 63.

12. Andrew Lambert, "'Now Is Come a Darker Day': Britain, Venice, and the Meaning of Sea Power," in Miles Taylor, ed., *The Victorian Empire and Britain's Maritime World, 1837–1901: The Sea and Global History* (New York: Springer, 2013).

13. Lord Byron, *Childe Harold's Pilgrimage* (New York: HarperPerennial Classics, 2014).

14. Christopher Lloyd, *The Nation and the Navy: A History of Naval Life and Policy* (London: Cresset Press, 1954), 223.

15. Quoted in Bernstein, *A Splendid Exchange*, 259.
16. Because incoming vessels did not face this crew requirement, the system yielded a surplus of Indian seaman in British ports. See Michael H. Fisher, "Working Across the Seas: Indian Maritime Labourers in India, Britain, and in Between, 1600–1857," *International Review of Social History* 51, no. S14 (2006), 21–45.
17. Thomas Wemyss Fulton, *The Sovereignty of the Sea: An Historical Account of the Claims of England to the Dominion of the British Seas, and of the Evolution of the Territorial Waters* (Prague: Good Press, 2019), 537.
18. Michael Lewis, *The History of the British Navy* (London: Penguin Books, 1957), 22, quoted in Kennedy, *The Rise and Fall of British Naval Mastery*, 193.
19. Janice Thomson, *Mercenaries, Pirates, and Sovereigns: State-Building and Extraterritorial Violence in Early Modern Europe* (Princeton, NJ: Princeton University Press, 1994), 54.
20. For an account of Kidd's career, capture, and legacy see C. Robert Ritchie, *Captain Kidd: And the War Against the Pirates* (New York: Barnes & Noble, 1998).
21. *Treaties and Engagements with Native Princes and States in India 1817 and 1818* (and anterior), United Kingdom: n.p., 1824.
22. Ota Atsushi, ed., *In the Name of the Battle Against Piracy: Ideas and Practices in State Monopoly of Maritime Violence in Europe and Asia in the Period of Transition* (Leiden: Brill, 2018).
23. "The Duties of The Government in the Event of War," *Economist*, January 14, 1854.
24. Quoted in Thomson, *Mercenaries, Pirates, and Sovereigns*, 72.
25. Jan Martin Lemnitzer, "'That Moral League of Nations against the United States': The Origins of the 1856 Declaration of Paris," *International History Review* 35, no. 5 (2013), 1068–1088.
26. *A Digest of the International Law of the United States: Taken from Documents Issued by Presidents and Secretaries of State, and from Decisions of Federal Courts and Opinions of Attorneys-General* (Washington: US Government Printing Office, 1887), 487.
27. See John G. Clark, "Marine Insurance in Eighteenth-Century La Rochelle," *French Historical Studies* 10, no. 4 (1978), 575.
28. Paine, *Sea and Civilization*, 473.
29. Stephen D. Behrendt, "The Annual Volume and Regional Distribution of the British Slave Trade, 1780–1807," *Journal of African History* 38, no. 2 (1997), 187–211.
30. James Oldham, "Insurance Litigation Involving the Zong and Other British Slave Ships, 1780–1807," *Journal of Legal History* 28, no. 3 (2007), 299–318.
31. Keith Hamilton, "Zealots and Helots," in Keith Hamilton and Patrick Salmon, eds., *Slavery, Diplomacy, and Empire* (Brighton: Sussex Academic Press, 2009), 20.
32. Quoted in Holger Lutz Kern, "Strategies of Legal Change: Great Britain, International Law, and the Abolition of the Transatlantic Slave Trade," *Journal of the History of International Law* 6, no. 2 (2004), 233–258.
33. Final Act of the Congress of Vienna, Act XV, "Declaration of the Powers, on the Abolition of the Slave Trade" (February 8, 1815); see also Suzanne Miers, "Slavery and the Slave Trade as International Issues 1890–1939," *Slavery and Abolition* 19, no. 2 (1998), 16–37.

34. "Quintuple Treaty—Its Effect on American Commerce," *Democratic Free Press (1842–1848)*, June 14, 1843.

35. "The Hero of the Freedom of the Seas," *Detroit Free Press*, September 30, 1848.

36. *Treaty between United States and Great Britain for the Suppression of the Slave Trade.* Concluded at Washington, D.C., April 7, 1862.

37. Suzanne Miers, *Britain and the Ending of the Slave Trade* (London: Longman, 1975), 15.

38. Quoted in Christopher Lloyd, *The Navy and the Slave Trade: The Suppression of the African Slave Trade in the Nineteenth Century* (London: Taylor & Francis, 2012), 243.

39. The provision was not tested for more than four decades, however, and no one was punished under its terms until the middle of the Civil War, when the United States executed Nathaniel Gordon. He had been arrested after a search of his vessel revealed 897 people crammed into the hold, almost half of them children. See James A. Rowley, "Captain Nathaniel Gordon, the Only American Executed for Violating the Slave Trade Laws," *Civil War History* 39, no. 3 (1993), 216–224.

40. See Leslie Bethell, "The Independence of Brazil and the Abolition of the Brazilian Slave Trade: Anglo-Brazilian Relations, 1822–1826," *Journal of Latin American Studies* 1, no. 2 (1969), 115–147.

41. Gold, *Maritime Transport*, 80–81.

42. See generally Charles Wright and Charles Ernest Fayle, *A History of Lloyd's from the Founding of Lloyd's Coffee House to the Present Day* (London: Macmillan, 1928).

43. Nicolette Jones, *The Plimsoll Sensation: The Great Campaign to Save Lives at Sea* (London: Hachette, 2013).

44. *Protocols of Proceedings of the International Marine Conference*, vol. 1, (Washington, DC: Government Printing Office), 1890.

45. *Protocols of Proceedings*, vol. 2, 350.

46. *Protocols of Proceedings*, vol. 2, 984.

47. Bill Hayton, *The South China Sea: The Struggle for Power in Asia* (New Haven, CT: Yale University Press, 2014), 43–44.

48. Lloyd A. Brown, *The Story of Maps* (New York: Dover, 1979), 282.

49. Kennedy, *The Rise and Fall of British Naval Mastery*, 193.

50. For a discussion of the organization and Beaufort's role, see Mead T. Cain, "The Maps of the Society for the Diffusion of Useful Knowledge: A Publishing History," *Imago Mundi* 46, no. 1 (1994): 151–167.

51. Charles King, *The Black Sea: A History* (Oxford: Oxford University Press, 2005), 154.

52. The Constantinople Convention (October 29, 1888).

53. Quoted in John Bastin, "Raffles and British Policy in the Indian Archipelago, 1811–1816," *Journal of the Malayan Branch of the Royal Asiatic Society* 27, no. 1 (1954), 84–119.

54. Bastin, "Raffles and British Policy."

55. Henry Keppel, *The Expedition to Borneo of HMS Dido for the Suppression of Piracy: With Extracts from the Journal of James Brooke, Esq., of Sarāwak*. vol. 18 (New York: Harper & Brothers, 1846), 250.

56. Helen Rozwadowski, *Fathoming the Ocean: The Discovery and Exploration of the Deep Sea* (Cambridge, MA: Harvard University Press, 2009), 57–59.

57. M. F. Maury, *Explanations and Sailing Directions to Accompany the Wind and Current Charts* (Philadelphia: Biddle, 1855), 154.

58. Douglas R. Burnett, Robert Beckman, and Tara M. Davenport, eds., *Submarine Cables: The Handbook of Law and Policy* (Leiden: Brill, 2013), 20–23.

59. Myres McDougal and William T. Burke, *The Public Order of the Oceans: A Contemporary International Law of the Sea* (Dordrecht: M. Nijhoff, 1987), 781.

60. Julian Anthony Koslow, Kristina Gjerde, and Tody Koslow, *The Silent Deep: The Discovery, Ecology and Conservation of the Deep Sea* (Chicago: University of Chicago Press, 2007), 23.

61. Charles Wyville Thomson et al., *Report on the Scientific Results of the Voyage of H.M.S. Challenger During the Years 1872–76: Under the Command of Captain George S. Nares and the Late Captain Frank Tourle Thomson: Deep-sea deposits* (London: H. M. Stationery Office, 1891), 341.

62. Alan Grosbard, "Treadwell Wharf in the Summerland, California Oil Field: The First Sea Wells in Petroleum Exploration," *Oil Industry History* 3, no. 1 (2002), 1–18.

63. "Oil Prospects in Deep Seas," *Oil & Gas Journal*, June 24, 1915, 3.

64. *Toronto Leader* article quoted in "Fisheries: The Supply in Canada and Newfoundland Waters," *Detroit Free Press*, November 28, 1872.

65. Edwin Ray Lancaster et al., *The Scientific Memoirs of Thomas Henry Huxley*: Supplementary Volume (London: Macmillan, 1903),

66. *Fur Seal Arbitration* (Washington, DC: US Government Printing Office, 1895), 228.

67. *Convention Between the Governments of Denmark and the United Kingdom Of Great Britain and Northern Ireland For Regulating The Fisheries Of Their Respective Subjects Outside Territorial Waters In The Ocean Surrounding The Faroe Islands* (June 24, 1901). *Laws and Regulations on the Regime of the High Seas*, vol. 1 (New York: United Nations, 1951), 232.

68. Alfred Thayer Mahan, *The Influence of Sea Power upon History, 1660–1783* (London: Sampson Low, Marston , 1892), 138..

69. Joseph S. Nye, "Ocean Rule Making from a World Politics Perspective," *Ocean Development & International Law* 3, no. 1 (1975), 32.

70. A. E. J. Went, *Seventy Years Agrowing: A History of the International Council for the Exploration of the Sea, 1902–1972.* Copenhagen: International Council for the Exploration of the Sea, 1972.

71. Hague Convention (VIII) Relative to the Laying of Automatic Submarine Contact Mines (January 26, 1910). One report to the assembled diplomats stated that "it can never fail to be present in the minds of all that the principle of the liberty of the seas, with the obligations which it implies on behalf of those who make use of this way of communication open to the Nations, is the indisputable prerogative of the human race." James Brown Scott, *A Survey of International Relations Between the United States and Germany, August 1, 1914–April 6 1917: Based on Official Documents* (Oxford: Oxford University Press, 1917), 243.

72. *International Convention for the Safety of Life at Sea*, Signed at London (January 20, 1914).
73. David McCullough, *The Path Between the Seas: The Creation of the Panama Canal, 1870–1914* (New York: Simon & Schuster, 2001).

Chapter 3

1. Pye's account, which came in correspondence, is available at https://catalog.archives. gov/id/833792.
2. Schweiger maintained a war diary, which was found and published after the war. War Diary of His Majesty's Submarine U-20; 1915; Naval Records Collection of the Office of Naval Records and Library, Record Group 45. [Online Version, https://www. docsteach.org/documents/document/war-diary-of-his-majestys-submarine-u20, September 1, 2020.]
3. Lawrence Sondhaus, *The Great War at Sea*, 149.
4. "Wilson's First Lusitania Note to Germany," https://wwi.lib.byu.edu/index.php/Wil son%27s_First_Lusitania_Note_to_Germany.
5. Declaration concerning the Laws of Naval War. London, February 26, 1909, https:// ihl-databases.icrc.org/ihl/INTRO/255.
6. "North Sea Closed by British Order," *New York Times*, November 3, 1914.
7. "Great Britain's Declaration of War Upon American Commerce," *Washington Post*, December 30, 1914.
8. Rolf Hobson, *Imperialism at Sea: Naval Strategic Thought, the Ideology of Sea Power, and the Tirpitz Plan, 1875–1914* (Netherlands: Brill Academic Publishers, 2002), 291.
9. John W. Coogan, *The End of Neutrality: The United States, Britain, and Maritime Rights, 1899–1915* (Ithaca, NY: Cornell University Press, 1981), 254.
10. Quoted in Erik Larson, *Dead Wake: The Last Crossing of the Lusitania* (New York: Crown, 2015), 330.
11. Andrew Lambert, "Great Britain and Maritime Law from the Declaration of Paris to the Era of Total War," in Rolf Hobson and Tom Kristiansen, eds., *Navies in Northern Waters* (London: Routledge, 2004), 23–50.
12. Woodrow Wilson, *War Messages*, 65th Cong., 1st Sess. Senate Doc. No. 5, Serial No. 7264, Washington, DC, 1917; 3–8.
13. Reginald R. Belknap, *The Yankee Mining Squadron; Or, Laying the North Sea Mine Barrage* (Annapolis, MD: United States Naval Institute, 1920), 17.
14. For an account of the clearing operation, see Noel Davis, *Sweeping the North Sea Mine Barrage* (United States: Annapolis, MD: The Detachment), 1919.
15. Walters, *History of the League of Nations*, 27.
16. Amos S. Hershey, "The German Conception of the Freedom of the Seas," *American Journal of International Law* 13, no. 2 (1919), 207–226.
17. Hershey, "The German Conception of the Freedom of the Seas."

18. President Woodrow Wilson's Fourteen Points, http://avalon.law.yale.edu/20th_cent ury/wilson14.asp.

19. Julian Stafford Corbett, *The League of Nations and Freedom of the Seas* (Oxford: Oxford University Press, H. Milford, 1918).

20. Covenant of the League of Nations, Art. 23(e).

21. Kennedy, *Rise and Fall of British Naval Mastery*, 325.

22. Phillips Payson O'Brian, "British and American Naval Power," *Politics and Policy* 9, no. 2 (1936), 125–126.

23. Christopher Bell and John Maurer, eds., *At the Crossroads Between Peace and War: The London Naval Conference of 1930* (Annapolis: Naval Institute Press, 2014), 202.

24. E. G. Trimble, "Violations of Maritime Law by the Allied Powers During the World War," *American Journal of International Law* 24, no. 1 (January 1930), 79–99.

25. Quoted in B. J. C. McKercher, *The Second Baldwin Government and the United States, 1924–1929: Attitude and Diplomacy* (Cambridge: Cambridge University Press, 1984), 93.

26. "Borah Is Seeking Parley of Nations on Maritime Law," *New York Times*, December 1, 1928, 11.

27. Herbert Hoover, *Public Papers of the Presidents of the United States: Herbert Hoover.* Washington: Office of the Federal Register, National Archives and Records Services, General Services Administration, 1974.

28. The parties to the Second London Conference reiterated Article 22 of the 1930 London treaty on "cruiser rules." See *Procès-verbal Relating to the Rules of Submarine Warfare Set Forth in Part IV of the Treaty of London of 22 April 1930*, London (November 6, 1936) https://ihl-databases.icrc.org/applic/ihl/ihl.nsf/Article.xsp?action=openD ocument&documentId=C103186F0C4291EEC12563CD00519832.

29. "Will Oceans Propel Ships?" *Los Angeles Times*, July 31, 1923.

30. See generally Morris Goran, *The Story of Fritz Haber* (Norman: University of Oklahoma Press, 1967).

31. For an account of Beebe's career, see Carol Grant Gould, *The Remarkable Life of William Beebe: Explorer and Naturalist* (Washington, DC: Island Press, 2012).

32. H. B. Bigelow, "The Progress of the Woods Hole Oceanographic Institution," *Eos, Transactions American Geophysical Union* 11, no. 1 (1930), 229–232.

33. William Barr, "The Voyage of Sibiryakov, 1932," *Polar Record* 19, no. 120 (1978), 253–266.

34. *League of Nations Committee of Experts for the Progressive Codification of International Law (1925-1928): Minutes* (Dobbs Ferry, NY: Oceana Publications, 1972), 34. *(1925–1928): Minutes* (United States: Oceana Publications, 1972), 34.

35. For a detailed account of interactions between US fishing interests and the State Department, see Jonathan G. Utley, "Japanese Exclusion from American Fisheries, 1936–1939: The Department of State and the Public Interest," *Pacific Northwest Quarterly* 65, no. 1 (1974), 8–16.

36. See Robert J. Hofman, "Sealing, Whaling and Krill Fishing in the Southern Ocean: Past and Possible Future Effects on Catch Regulations," *Polar Record* 53, no. 1 (2017), 88–99.

37. Gunnar Isachsen, "Modern Norwegian Whaling in the Antarctic," *Geographical Review* 19, no. 3 (July, 1929), 387–403.

38. *Convention for the Regulation of Whaling, Geneva* (September 24, 1931), published in League of Nations, Treaty Series, vol. 155, 351.

39. L. Larry Leonard, "Recent Negotiations Toward the International Regulation of Whaling," *American Journal of International Law* 35, no. 1 (1941), 90.

40. Edgar Gold, *Maritime Transport: The Evolution of International Marine Policy and Shipping Law* (Lexington, Mass : Lexington Books1981), 124.

41. In 1920, Congress passed the Jones Act, which declared it essential "that the United States shall have a merchant marine of the best equipped and most suitable types of vessels sufficient to carry the greater portion of its commerce and serve as a naval or military auxiliary in time of war or national emergency, ultimately to be owned and operated privately by citizens of the United States." *The Merchant Marine Act of 1920*.

42. Permanent Court of Arbitration, *Muscat Dhows Case (France vs. Great Britain)*, Award of the Tribunal (August 8, 1905). https://pca-cpa.org/en/cases/93/

43. Permanent Court of International Justice, S.S. *"Lotus," France v Turkey*, Judgment (1927). https://www.ilsa.org/Jessup/Jessup16/Batch%201/TheLotusCase.pdf

44. Convention and Statute on Freedom of Transit, *Barcelona* (April 20, 1921). https://treaties.un.org/doc/Publication/UNTS/LON/Volume%207/v7.pdf

45. Kraska and Pedrozo, *The Free Sea*, 39

46. Quoted in Rodney P. Carlisle, *Sovereignty for Sale: The Origins and Evolution of the Panamanian and Liberian Flags of Convenience* (Annapolis, MD: Naval Institute Press, 1981), 10.

47. League of Nations, Conference for the Codification of International Law—1930, First Meeting, 20.

48. Conference for the Codification of International Law, 127.

49. Conference for the Codification of International Law, 16.

50. Conference for the Codification of International Law, 21.

51. Conference for the Codification of International Law.

52. Conference for the Codification of International Law, 143.

53. Conference for the Codification of International Law, 135.

54. "Declaration of Panama," *Foreign Relations of the United States*, Diplomatic Papers, 1939, The American Republics, vol. V, Doc. 60. https://history.state.gov/historicaldocuments/frus1939v05/d60

55. William E. Masterson, "The Hemisphere Zone of Security and the Law," *American Bar Association Journal* 26, no. 11 (1940), 860–863.

56. Franklin D. Roosevelt, Fireside Chat. Online by Gerhard Peters and John T. Woolley, The American Presidency Project, https://www.presidency.ucsb.edu/documents/fireside-chat-11 .

57. Franklin Delano Roosevelt and Samuel Irving Rosenman, *The Public Papers and Addresses of Franklin D. Roosevelt: The Call to Battle Stations, 1941* (New York: Random House, 1938), 386.

58. Davis and Engerman, *Naval Blockades in Peace and War*, 423.

59. Joel Ira Holwitt, *Execute Against Japan: The U.S. Decision to Conduct Unrestricted Submarine Warfare* (College Station: Texas A&M University Press, 2009), 176.

Chapter 4

1. Presidential Proclamation No. 2667, September 28, 1945. https://www.presidency.ucsb.edu/documents/proclamation-2667-policy-the-united-states-with-respect-the-natural-resources-the-subsoil

2. Presidential Proclamation No. 2668, September. 28, 1945. https://www.archives.gov/federal-register/codification/proclamations/02668.html

3. The Secretary of the Interior (Ickes) to President Roosevelt, *Foreign Relations of the United States, Diplomatic Papers, 1945, General: Political and Economic Matters*, Vol. II., Doc. 760.

4. Ann L. Hollick, *U.S. Foreign Policy and the Law of the Sea* (Princeton, NJ: Princeton University Press, 2017), 30.

5. Memorandum by the Office of Economic Affairs (September 23, 1944), *Foreign Relations of the United States: Diplomatic Papers, 1945, General: Political and Economic Matters*, Vol. II., Doc. 766.

6. Memorandum by the Assistant Chief of the Division of British Commonwealth Affairs (April 26, 1945), *Foreign Relations of the United States, Diplomatic Papers, 1945, General: Political and Economic Matters*, Vol. II, Doc. 773.

7. Georg Schwarzenberger, *The Fundamental Principles of International Law* quoted in Shigeru Oda, *International Control of Sea Resources* (Leyden: A. W. Sythoff, 1963), 157.

8. *Foreign Relations of the United States: Diplomatic Papers, 1945, General: Political and Economic Matters*, Vol. II, Doc. 780.

9. *Foreign Relations of the United States: Diplomatic Papers, 1945, General: Political and Economic Matters*, Vol. II, Doc. 790.

10. Ann L. Hollick, "The Origins of 200-Mile Offshore Zones," *American Journal of International Law* 71, no. 3 (1977), 494–500.

11. The Ambassador in Peru (Cooper) to the Secretary of State (June 19, 1948), *Foreign Relations of the United States, 1948, The Western Hemisphere*, Vol. IX, Doc. 516.

12. Chile, Ecuador, and Peru, Declaration on the Maritime Zone (August 18, 1952). https://treaties.un.org/doc/publication/unts/volume%201006/volume-1006-i-14758-english.pdf

13. Some uncertainty remained regarding Soviet sea space, and that vagueness about the limits of the territorial sea had deadly consequences. In the early 1950s, the United States routinely engaged in aerial surveillance near the Soviet coast. In several instances, Soviet aircraft fired on US planes that Moscow believed had intruded into its airspace. See Norman Polmar, *Spyplane: The U-2 History Declassified* (Osceola, WI: MBI Publishing, 2001) MBI Publishing, 2001).

14. S. Whittemore Boggs, "National Claims in Adjacent Seas," *Geographical Review* 41, no. 2 (1951), 185–209.

15. For attempts to unravel the origins and intent of the map, see Chris P. C. Chung, "Drawing the U-shaped Line: China's Claim in the South China Sea, 1946–1974," *Modern China* 42, no. 1 (2016): 38–72; Bill Hayton, "The Modern Origins of China's South China Sea Claims: Maps, Misunderstandings, and the Maritime Geobody," *Modern China* 45, no. 2 (2019), 127–170.

16. Ann L. Hollick, "U.S. Oceans Policy: The Truman Proclamations," *Virginia Journal of International Law* 17, no. 1 (Fall 1976), 23–56.

17. "Ship Is Freezing Plant: Bering Sea Trawler Will Process Catch While on Cruise," *New York Times*, June 9, 1947.

18. Hector M. Lupin, Aurora Zugarramurdi, and Maria A. Parin, *Economic Engineering Applied to the Fishery Industry* (Rome: Food and Agriculture Organization of the United Nations, 1995), 9.

19. Quoted in *Classic Papers in Natural Resource Economics* (London: Palgrave Macmillan, 2000), 181.

20. Fedor Il'ich Baranov and William Edwin Ricker, *On the Question of the Biological Basis of Fisheries: On the Question of the Dynamics of the Fishing Industry* (Bloomington: Indiana University, 1945.)

21. Quoted in Charles B. Selak, "Recent Developments in High Seas Fisheries Jurisdiction under the Presidential Proclamation of 1945," *American Journal of International Law* 44, no. 4 (1950), 670–681.

22. Wilbert M. Chapman, "Report on Activities with Respect to High Seas Fisheries, 1949," quoted in Carmel Finley, *All the Fish in the Sea: Maximum Sustainable Yield and the Failure of Fisheries Management* (Chicago: University of Chicago Press, 2011).

23. International Court of Justice, *Fisheries Case* (United Kingdom vs. Norway) (December 18, 1951), Dissenting Opinion of Sir Arnold McNair, 185.

24. "Winning the Cod War," *Economist*, August 15, 1959, 435.

25. See Marc Levinson, *The Box: How the Shipping Container Made the World Smaller and the World Economy Bigger* (Princeton, NJ: Princeton University Press, 2008).

26. Gold, *Maritime Transport*, 245.

27. John W. Young, "Great Britain's Latin American Dilemma: The Foreign Office and the Overthrow of 'Communist' Guatemala, June 1954," *The International History Review* 8, no. 4 (1986), 573–592.

28. Excerpt from the Diary of James C. Hagerty, Press Secretary to the President, *Foreign Relations of the United States, 1952–1954, The American Republics*, Vol. 4, Doc. 474.

29. See John W. Young, "Great Britain's Latin American Dilemma: The Foreign Office and the Overthrow of 'Communist' Guatemala, June 1954," *The International History Review* 8, no. 4 (1986): 573–592; Memorandum of Telephone Conversation, Prepared in the White House, Foreign Relations of the United States, 1952–1954, China and Japan, Volume XIV, Part 1, Doc. 216.

30. United Nations Conference on the Law of the Sea, *Official Records* (Switzerland: United Nations, 1958), vol. 4, 12.

31. Susan Southard, *Nagasaki Deluxe: Life After Nuclear War* (New York: Penguin Publishing Group, 2015), 211.

32. A/CONF. 13/39, 5th meeting, par. 13.

33. *Official Records* (United States: United Nations, 1958), vol., 23.
34. United Nations Conference on the Law of the Sea, *Official Records* (New York: United Nations, 1958), vol., 15.
35. Telegram from the Delegation to the Conference on the Law of the Sea to the Department of State (April 21, 1958), *Foreign Relations of the United States, 1958-1960, United Nations and General International Matters*, Vol. II, Doc. 369.
36. Convention on the High Seas (April 29, 1958).
37. Quoted in Mark Hamilton Lytle, *The Gentle Subversive: Rachel Carson, Silent Spring, and the Rise of the Environmental Movement* (United Kingdom: Oxford University Press, 2007), 35.
38. R.L. Carson, "Undersea," *Atlantic Monthly*, September 1937, 322–325.
39. Rachel Carson, *The Edge of the Sea* (United Kingdom: Houghton Mifflin, 1955), 113.
40. Carson, *The Edge of the Sea*, 249.
41. Rachel Carson, *The Sea Around Us* (United Kingdom: Oxford University Press, 2003), 19.
42. Rachel Carson, *Silent Spring* (New York: Houghton Mifflin, 1962), 277.
43. *The Sea Around Us*, XIII.
44. John M. Lee, "Silent Spring is Now Noisy Summer," *New York Times*, July 22, 1962, 87.
45. For an account of the voyage, see Albert Bigelow, *The Voyage of the Golden Rule: An Experiment with Truth* (Garden City: Doubleday, 1959).
46. Frank Zelko, *Make It a Green Peace! The Rise of a Countercultural Environmentalism* (New York: Oxford University Press, 2013).
47. Christopher Drew, Sherry Sontag, and Annette Lawrence Drew, *Blind Man's Bluff: The Untold Story of American Submarine Espionage* (New York: PublicAffairs, 2008).
48. Abram Chayes, "Law and the Quarantine of Cuba," *Foreign Affairs* 41, no. 3 (April 1963), 550–557.
49. *Izvestia*, July 29, 1967, quoted in James Cable, *Gunboat Diplomacy: Political Applications of Limited Naval Force* (New York: Praeger, 1971), 144.
50. Jan J. Solecki, "A Review of the U.S.S.R. Fishing Industry," *Ocean Management* 5 (1979), 97–123.
51. "'Soviet' Submarines to Be Cited to U.N.," *New York Times*, March 5, 1952, at 6, cited in James Kraska, "Putting Your Head in the Tiger's Mouth: Submarine Espionage in Territorial Waters," *Columbia Journal of Transnational Law* 54 (2015), 164.
52. Stephen Lewarne, *Soviet Oil: The Move Offshore* (Boulder: Westview Press, 1988), 56.
53. John L. Mero, *The Mineral Resources of the Sea* (Amsterdam: Elsevier Publishing, 1965), 5.
54. Mero, *Mineral Resources*, 279.
55. Julian Anthony Koslow, Kristina Gjerde, and Tody Koslow, *The Silent Deep: The Discovery, Ecology and Conservation of the Deep Sea* (Chicago: University of Chicago Press, 2007), 166.
56. Andrew G. Spyrou, *From T-2 to Supertanker: Development of the Oil Tanker, 1940-2000* (Bloomington: iUniverse, 2011), 31.
57. Richard Girling, *Sea Change: Britain's Coastal Catastrophe* (London: Eden Project, 2008).

58. "Controlling the Masters of the Sea," *Observer*, April 2, 1967.

59. *The Parliamentary Debates (Hansard): House of Lords Official Report* (United Kingdom: H. M. Stationery Office, 1967), vol. 281, 1167.

60. *The Parliamentary Debates (Hansard)*, vol. 281, 877.

61. Memorandum from the Executive Secretary of the Department of State (Eliot) to the President's Assistant for National Security Affairs (Kissinger), (March 12, 1970), *Foreign Relations of the United States, 1969–1976, Vol. E–1, Documents on Global Issues, 1969–1972*, Doc. 367.

62. Michael A. Morris, *International Politics and The Sea: The Case of Brazil* (Boulder, CO: Westview Press, 1979). .

63. GuÐmundur J. GuÐmundsson, "The Cod and the Cold War," *Scandinavian Journal of History* 31, no. 2 (1996), 97–118.

64. John Temple Swing, "Who Will Own the Oceans?" *Foreign Affairs* 54, no. 3 (1976), 527–546.

65. Alan Beesley, "The Negotiating Strategy of UNCLOS III: Developing and Developed Countries as Partners: A Pattern for Future Multilateral International Conferences?" *Law and Contemporary Problems* 46, no. 2 (1983), 183–194.

Chapter 5

1. "Mr. Roosevelt Gives Scroll to People on Isle of Malta," Associated Press, December 10, 1943.

2. Helen M. Rozwadowski, "Arthur C. Clarke and the Limitations of the Ocean as a Frontier," *Environmental History* 17, no. 3 (2012), 578–602.

3. Arvid Pardo, "Before and After," *Law and Contemporary Problems* 46, no. 2 (1983), 95–105.

4. United Nations General Assembly, First Committee (November 1, 1967), A/C.1/PV1515. https://undocs.org/A/C.1/PV.1515

5. Garrett Hardin, "The Tragedy of the Commons," *Science* 162 (1968), 1243.

6. Barry Buzan, *Seabed Politics* (New York: Praeger, 1976), 128.

7. Antony J. Dolman, *Resources, Regimes, World Order* (New York: Foundation Reshaping the International Order/Pergamon Press, 1981), 225.

8. *Public Papers of the Presidents of the United States*, Lyndon B. Johnson, Book II, July 1 to December 31, 1966 (Washington, DC: US Government Printing Office, 1967), 724.

9. UN General Assembly Resolution 2574 D (1969). https://legal.un.org/diplomatic conferences/1973_los/docs/english/res/a_res_2574_xxiv.pdf

10. UN General Assembly Resolution 2749 (1970). https://digitallibrary.un.org/record/201718?ln=en

11. William Wertenbaker, "Law of the Sea—I," *New Yorker*, August 1, 1983, 50.

12. Ann L. Hollick, *U.S. Foreign Policy and the Law of the Sea*, 273.

13. Myron H. Nordquist, *United Nations Convention on the Law of the Sea, 1982: A Commentary* (Dordrecht: Martinus Nijhoff, 1985), 130.

14. U.N. Doc. A/AC. 138/SR. 72 (1972).

15. *New York Times*, "U.S. Cautioned 7th Fleet to Shun Paracels Clash," January 22, 1974.

16. *Third United Nations Conference on the Law of the Sea: Official Records* (New York: UN, 1975), 191, https://legal.un.org/diplomaticconferences/1973_los/docs/english/vol_1/a_conf62_sr22.pdf.

17. Alan G. Friedman and Cynthia A. Williams, "Group of 77 at the United Nations: An Emergent Force in the Law of the Sea," *San Diego Law Review* 16 (1979), 574.

18. Summary Records of Plenary Meetings, A/CONF.62/ SR.45, 45th meeting (July 26, 1974). https://legal.un.org/diplomaticconferences/1973_los/docs/english/vol_1/a_conf62_sr45.pdf

19. Third United Nations Conference on the Law of the Sea, 1973-82, vol. XVII, Verbatim Records of the Plenary, Resumed Eleventh Session and Final Part Eleventh Session and Conclusion: 186th Meeting, A/CONF.62/SR.186. https://legal.un.org/diplomatic conferences/1973_los/docs/english/vol_17/a_conf62_sr186.pdf

20. Third United Nations Conference on the Law of the Sea, 1973-82, vol. XVII, Verbatim Records of the Plenary, Resumed Eleventh Session and Final Part Eleventh Session and Conclusion: 186th Meeting, A/CONF.62/SR.186. https://legal.un.org/diplomatic conferences/1973_los/docs/english/vol_17/a_conf62_sr186.pdf

21. Ralph B. Levering and Miriam L. Levering, *Citizen Action for Global Change: The Neptune Group and Law of the Sea* (Syracuse, NY: Syracuse University Press, 1999), 78.

22. See generally David L. Bosco, *Five to Rule Them All: The UN Security Council and the Making of the Modern World* (New York: Oxford University Press, 2009).

23. Barry Buzan, "Negotiating by Consensus: Developments in Technique at the United Nations Conference on the Law of the Sea," *American Journal of International Law* 75 (1981), 324.

24. Myron Nordquist et al., *United Nations Convention on the Law of the Sea, 1982: A Commentary* (Dordrecht: Martinus Nijhoff, 1985), 101.

25. Jonathan Charney, "United States Interest in a Convention on the Law of the Sea: The Case for Continued Efforts," *Vanderbilt Journal of Transnational Law* 11, no. 39 (1978).

26. Kathleen Teltsch, "Delegates Doodle as Procedural Details Slow Down Progress at the U. N.'s Law of the Sea Conference," *New York Times*, March 28, 1976, 13.

27. William Wertenbaker, "The Law of the Sea—II," *New Yorker*, August 8, 1983, 60.

28. UN Law of the Sea Convention, Art. 3, https://www.un.org/Depts/los/convention_agreements/texts/unclos/unclos_e.pdf.

29. For a discussion of this ambiguity, see Philip Allott, "Power Sharing in the Law of the Sea," *American Journal of International Law* 77, no. 1 (January 1983), 1–30.

30. *Foreign Relations of the United States, 1969–1976*, Vol. E-3, *Documents on Global Issues, 1973–1976*, Document 42. https://history.state.gov/historicaldocuments/frus1 969-76ve03/d42

31. Robert W. Smith and Ashley J. Roach, *Excessive Maritime Claims* (Newport: Naval War College, 1994).

32. *Third United Nations Conference on the Law of the Sea: Official Records* (New York: UN, 1975).

33. I. M. Sinan, "UNCTAD and Flags of Convenience," *Journal of World Trade Law* 18 (1984), 95.

34. John Kifner, "Wreck of the Amoco Cadiz Revives Issue of Safety in Transporting Oil," *New York Times*, March 23, 1978.

35. Ebere Osieke, "Flags of Convenience Vessels: Recent Developments," *American Journal of International Law* 73, no. 4 (October 1979): 604–627.

36. "Captain Suffered Enough, Says Liberia, Restoring His License," *Associated Press*, March 5, 1981.

37. George C. Kasoulides, *Port State Control and Jurisdiction: Evolution of the Port State Regime* (Leiden: Brill Nijhoff, 1993), 126.

38. Louis B. Sohn, "Peaceful Settlement of Disputes in Ocean Conflicts: Does UNCLOS III Point the Way," *Law and Contemporary Problems* 46, no. 2 (Spring 1983): 195–200.

39. Law of the Sea Convention, Art. 298, https://www.un.org/depts/los/convention_agr eements/texts/unclos/closindx.htm

40. Norman Polmar and Michael White, *Project Azorian: The CIA and the Raising of the K-129* (Annapolis: Naval Institute Press, 2010), 71.

41. Polmar and White, *Project Azorian*, xi.

42. Buzan, *Seabed Politics*, 213.

43. Deep Seabed Hard Minerals Act: Joint Hearings Before the Committee on Commerce, Committee on Foreign Relations and the Committee on Armed Services, United States Senate, Ninety-fourth Congress, Second Session, on S. 713 . . . May 17 and 19, 1976. Washington, DC: U.S. Government Printing Office, 1976, 113.

44. Elliot L. Richardson, "Power, Mobility and the Law of the Sea," *Foreign Affairs* 58, no. 4 (1980), 902–919.

45. Paul Lewis, "After 6 Years, Law of Sea Parley Nears Mining Pact," *New York Times*, August 30, 1980, 4.

46. Republican Party Platforms, Republican Party Platform of 1980 Online by Gerhard Peters and John T. Woolley, The American Presidency Project https://www.preside ncy.ucsb.edu/node/273420.

47. Statement by the Honorable John B. Breaux before the Senate Sub-committee on Arms Control, Oceans and International Operations and Environment, Senate Committee on Foreign Relations, United States Senate, Ninety-seventh Congress, First Session, March 5, 1981 (Washington: U.S. Government Printing Office, 1981)., https://www.google.com/books/edition/Law_of_the_Sea_Negotiations/gIr6PRE1Z X4C?hl=en&gbpv=0

48. William Safire, "The Great Ripoff," *New York Times*, March 19, 1981.

49. Lou Cannon, "Public's Personality Seems Split in Its Perception of Reagan," *Washington Post*, July 12, 1982.

50. Arvid Pardo, "An Opportunity Lost," in Bernard Oxman, David Caron, and Charles L.O. Buderi, eds., *Law of the Sea: U.S. Policy Dilemma* (San Francisco: Institute for Contemporary Studies), 1983.

51. "Law of the Sea Convention: US Attitude Attacked," *BBC Summary of World Broadcasts*, December 8, 1982.

52. *Third United Nations Conference on the Law of the Sea: Official Records* (New York: UN, 1984), vol. 17, 49 [emphasis added].

53. *Third United Nations Conference on the Law of the Sea: Documents* (United Kingdom: Oceana Publications, 1988), vol. 18, 219.

54. *Third United Nations Conference on the Law of the Sea: Official Records* (United States: UN, 1984), vol. 17, 14.

Chapter 6

1. The 1980 census recorded 1,813 residents of the islands.

2. Keith Speed, "Royal Navy Cuts—Former Minister Comments," *Marine Policy* 6, no. 2 (1982), 150–151.

3. For accounts of the legal and operational context, see Arthur M. Smith, "Has the Red Cross-Adorned Hospital Ship Become Obsolete?" *Naval War College Review* 58, no. 3 (2005), 121; A. R. Marsh, "A Short but Distant War—the Falklands Campaign," *Journal of the Royal Society of Medicine* 76, no. 11 (1983), 972.

4. The case was *Argentine Rep. v. Amerada Hess*, 488 U.S. 428 (1989).

5. Memorandum from the Executive Secretary of the Department of State (Bremer) to the President's Assistant for National Security Affairs (Clark), *Foreign Relations of the United States*, 1981–1988, Vol. XLI, Global Issues II, Doc. 162.

6. Telegram from the Department of State to the Embassies in Japan, the United Kingdom, West Germany, France, Italy, Belgium, and the Netherlands, *Foreign Relations of the United States*, 1981–1988, Vol. XLI, Global Issues II, Doc. 179.

7. "Agreement Concerning Interim Arrangements Relating to Polymetallic Nodules of the Deep Seabed," signed by France, the Federal Republic of Germany, the United Kingdom, and the United States (September 1982). https://iea.uoregon.edu/treaty-text/3641

8. Proclamation 5030 of March 10, 1983. https://www.archives.gov/federal-register/codification/proclamations/05030.html

9. "Soviet Government Statement on US Refusal to Sign Law of the Sea Convention," *BBC Summary of World Broadcasts*, April 25, 1983.

10. "UN Sea Treaty Side Issue May Go to World Court, Singapore Aide Says," *Platt's Oilgram News*, February 1, 1983.

11. UN General Assembly Resolution A/RES/40/63 (December 10, 1985). https://undocs.org/en/A/RES/40/63

12. "Bonn Won't Sign Law of the Sea," *Associated Press*, November 27, 1984.

13. "First Passenger Ship Navigates the Northwest Passage," *United Press International*, Sept. 12, 1984, https://www.upi.com/Archives/1984/09/12/First-passenger-ship-navigates-Northwest-Passage/8564463809600/.

14. Franklyn Griffiths, "Arctic Authority at Stake," *Globe and Mail*, June 13, 1985.

15. Matthew Fisher, "Polar Sea Gets the Message as Plane Drops Flags on Deck," *Globe and Mail*, August 9, 1985.

16. Donald R. Rothwell, "The Canadian-U.S. Northwest Passage Dispute: A Reassessment, " *Cornell International Law Journal* 26, no. 2 (Spring 1993), 331–372.

17. "John Crosbie Was Known for His Wit and Straightforward Talk," *Hamilton Spectator* (Ontario, Canada), January 11, 2020.

18. "New Charges Brought Against Alleged Treasure Hunters," *United Press International*, June 10, 1988.

19. Robert L. Friedheim, *Negotiating the New Ocean Regime* (Columbia: University of South Carolina Press, 1993), 209.

20. Kristine Moe, "Conference May Calm Waters; U.S. and Mexico Hope to Iron out Sea Research Differences," *San Diego Union-Tribune*, September 30, 1985.

21. See J. Ashley Roach, "Marine Scientific Research and the New Law of the Sea," *Ocean Development and International Law* 27, no. 1–2 (1996), 59–72.

22. Bernard Oxman, "United States Interests in the Law of the Sea Convention," *American Journal of International Law* 88, no. 167 (1994), 170.

23. Stephen A. Rose, "Naval Activity in the EEZ-Troubled Waters Ahead," *Naval Law Review* 39 (1990), 67.

24. Eugene Robinson, "Peru Defends Firing on U.S. C-130; Washington Sources Acknowledge the Flight Plan Was Violated," *Washington Post*, April 28, 1992.

25. "Pinochet Speaks on Anniversary of 1973 Coup in Chile," *BBC Summary of World Broadcasts*, September 13, 1985. For an early analysis of that claim, see Kilaparti Ramakrishna, Robert E. Bowen, and Jack H. Archer, "Outer Limits of Continental Shelf: A Legal Analysis of Chilean and Ecuadorian Island Claims and US Response," *Marine Policy* 11, no. 1 (1987), 58–68.

26. "U.S. Ship in Soviet Waters Points to New Era," *New York Times*, August 16, 1988.

27. Valery Konyshev and Alexander Sergunin, "Russia's Policies on the Territorial Disputes in the Arctic," *Journal of International Relations and Foreign Policy* 2, no. 1 (March 2014), 55–83.

28. For a detailed account, see Joseph Stanik, *El Dorado Canyon: Reagan's Undeclared War with Qaddafi* (Annapolis, MD: Naval Institute Press, 2017).

29. "U.S. Will Challenge Coastal Sea Claims That Exceed Three Miles," *New York Times*, August 10, 1979, Al.

30. Quoted in John T. Oliver, *Freedom of Navigation, Rights of Passage, International Security, and the Law of the Sea* (Charlottesville, University of Virginia School of Law, 1993).

31. Lawrence Juda, "Innocent Passage by Warships in the Territorial Seas of the Soviet Union: Changing Doctrine," *Ocean Development and International Law* 21, no. 1 (1990), 111–116

32. James Kraska and Raul Pedrozo, *The Free Sea: The American Fight for Freedom of Navigation* (Annapolis, MD: Naval Institute Press, 2018), 191.

33. John D. Negroponte, "Who Will Protect Freedom of the Seas?" No. 855. (Washington, DC: US Department of State, Bureau of Public Affairs, 1986).

34. United Nations Convention on the Conditions for Registration of Ships (February 7, 1986). https://treaties.un.org/doc/Publication/MTDSG/Volume%20II/Chapter%20 XII/XII-7.en.pdf

35. "Flags of Convenience Issue Reviewed After Ferry Disaster," *Associated Press*, April 12, 1990.
36. Discussed in Clifford B. Donn, "Flag of Convenience Registry and Industrial Relations," *Maritime Studies* 1989, no. 47 (1989), 1–9.
37. The journalist Scott Malcomson documented one such case in "The Unquiet Ship: What Happened on Board the Freighter Dubai Which Turned Its Stowaways into Castaways?" *New Yorker*, January 20, 1997, 72.
38. Ronald O'Rourke, "The Tanker War," *Proceedings* 114, no. 5 (1988).
39. UN Security Council Resolution 540 (October 31,1983).
40. United States Department of State, *Current Policy* no. 958, "International Shipping and the Iran-Iraq War" (May 17, 1987), 2, quoted in Myron H. Nordquist and Margaret G. Wachenfeld, "Legal Aspects of Reflagging Kuwaiti Tankers and Laying of Mines in the Persian Gulf," *German Yearbook of International Law* 31 (1988), 138–164.
41. British Broadcasting Corporation, "1955: Britain Claims Rockall," http://news.bbc.co.uk/onthisday/hi/dates/stories/september/21/newsid_4582000/4582327.stm.
42. Clyde Haberman, "Japanese Fight Invading Sea for Priceless Speck of Land," *New York Times*, January 4, 1988.
43. Taylor M. Fravel, "China's strategy in the South China Sea," *Contemporary Southeast Asia* (2011), 292–319.
44. "Oil Prospective Spratlys Still a Flashpoint," *Oil & Gas Journal*, October 25, 1999.
45. "Alatas Cites Qian on Use of Laws to Solve Maritime Disputes," *BBC Summary of World Broadcasts*, July 31, 1995.
46. See generally Dan Caldwell, "Flashpoints in the Gulf: Abu Musa and the Tunb Islands," *Middle East Policy* 4, no. 3 (1996), 50–58; Thomas R. Mattair, *The Three Occupied UAE Islands: The Tunbs and Abu Musa* (Abu Dhabi, UAE: Emirates Center for Strategic Studies and Research, 2005).
47. "A Law Becalmed," *Financial Times*, October 21, 1996.
48. "Resource Wars," *Proceedings* 111, no. 1 (January 1985), https://www.usni.org/magazines/proceedings/1985/january/resource-wars.
49. Mark Newham, "France Digs Deep into the Ocean Bed," *Financial Times*, March 6, 1985.
50. "Prospects Dim for Mining of the Seabed, Delegates Say," *Globe and Mail*, September 25, 1984.
51. Kevin M. Bailey, "An Empty Donut Hole: The Great Collapse of a North American Fishery," *Ecology and Society* 16, no. 2 (2011).
52. The Convention on the Conservation and Management of Pollock Resources in the Central Bering Sea (June 16, 1994), https://www.state.gov/donut-hole-agreement; see also David A. Colson, "Current Issues in International Fishery Conservation and Management," *Department of State Dispatch* 6 (1995), 100.
53. Barbara Yaffe, "Spanish Trawlers Returning to Canada; High-Seas Chase Ends with Arrests," *Globe and Mail*, May 26, 1986.
54. Stephen Thorne, "Fishery Gone Astern Under Canada's Economic Zone 200-Mile Limit Designed to Stop Depletion of Fish," *Toronto Star*, December 29, 1986.
55. "Crosbie's Speech Sends Europeans on Angry Walkout," *Globe and Mail*, September 15, 1988.

56. The Convention for the Prohibition of Fishing with Long Driftnets in the South Pacific (1989), https://iea.uoregon.edu/treaty-text/3055

57. Elinor Ostrom, *Governing the Commons: The Evolution of Institutions for Collective Action* (Cambridge: Cambridge University Press, 1990), 14.

58. Wallace S. Broecker, "Massive Iceberg Discharges as Triggers for Global Climate Change," *Nature* 372, no. 6505 (1994), 421.

59. "Ideas for Making Ocean Trap Carbon Dioxide Arouse Hope and Fear," *New York Times*, November 20, 1990.

60. Megan Jacqueline Ogilvie, "Ocean Fertilization: Ecological Cure or Calamity," PhD diss., Massachusetts Institute of Technology, 2004.

61. Caroline Dopyera, "The Iron Hypothesis," *Earth* (October 1996), 26–33.

62. *Science News* 148 (September 30, 1995), 220.

63. *International Organizations and the Law of the Sea: Documentary Yearbook*, vol. 1 (1985) (Boston: Graham & Trotman/Martinus Nijhoff, 1994), 208.

64. "Turning the Tide on Abuse of the Sea," *The Guardian*, December 14, 1990.

65. John Norton Moore and Myron Nordquist, *Entry into Force of the Law of the Sea Convention* (The Hague: M. Nijhoff, 1995), 72–73.

66. Gudmundor Eiriksson, "Satya N. Nandan's Role in Drafting the Informal Single Negotiating Text: Aspects of the Preparatory Work for UNCLOS," in Michael Lodge and Myron H. Nordquist, eds., *Peaceful Order in the World's Oceans: Essays in Honor of Satya N. Nandan* (Leiden: Martinus Nijhoff Publishers, 2014).

67. James Harrison, *Making the Law of the Sea: A Study in the Development of International Law* (Cambridge: Cambridge University Press, 2011), 101.

Chapter 7

1. D. Rothrock, W. Maslowski, D. Chayes, G. Flato, and J. Grebmeier, *Arctic Ocean Science from Submarines. A Report Based on the SCICEX 2000 Workshop* (Seattle, University of Washington Seattle Applied Physics Lab, 1999).

2. "Declaration on the Establishment of the Arctic Council," Joint Communique of the Governments of the Arctic Countries on the Establishment of the Arctic Council, Ottawa, Canada (September 19, 1996), https://oaarchive.arctic-council.org/bitstream/handle/11374/85/EDOCS-1752-v2-ACMMCA00_Ottawa_1996_Founding_Declaration.PDF?sequence=5&isAllowed=y.

3. Patrick E. Tyler, "Soviets' Secret Nuclear Dumping Causes Worry for Arctic Waters," *New York Times*, May 4, 1992.

4. See Agustín Blanco-Bazán, "IMO-Historical Highlights in the Life of a UN Agency," *Journal of the History of International Law*, 6 (2004), 259.

5. "IMO Plans Seafarers' Memorial for London HQ," *IMO News* 2 (2000).

6. "Secretary-General Inaugurates Law of Sea Tribunal in Hamburg, as Trip to Germany Continues," *Federal News Service*, October 21, 1996.

7. International Tribunal for the Law of the Sea, Public Hearing Held on Thursday 27 November 1997, in the M/V "SAIGA" case (Saint Vincent and the Grenadines v. Guinea). https://www.itlos.org/fileadmin/itlos/documents/cases/1/pv_97_271197_pm_eng.pdf

8. International Law Reports (Cambridge: Cambridge University Press, 2002).

9. See Zou Keyuan, "A Tribute to Zhao Lihai," *Chinese Journal of International Law* 1 (2002), v–viii.

10. Anna Cavnar, "Accountability and the Commission on the Limits of the Continental Shelf: Deciding Who Owns the Ocean Floor," *Cornell International Law Journal* 42 (2009), 387.

11. Murray Hogarth, "Australia's Claims to Giant Area at Risk," *Sydney Morning Herald*, January 1, 1997.

12. Charles Mandel, "Map-makers Race to Divide Ocean Floor: Underwater Treasure: According to New UN Rules, Countries Have a Decade to Stake Their Claims," *National Post* (Canada), June 7, 2003.

13. Simon Benson, "A Part of Australia that Nobody Has Seen," *Daily Telegraph*, April 22, 2002.

14. Tetsuya Ennyu, "Proving Continental Shelf Claim Costly," *Daily Yomiuri* (Tokyo), July 16, 2003.

15. Uttara Choudhury, "India Plans Major Expansion of Maritime Boundary," *Agence France Presse*, November 23, 1999.

16. Decision Regarding the Date of Commencement of the Ten-year Period for Making Submissions to the Commission on the Limits of the Continental Shelf Set Out in article 4 of Annex II to the United Nations Convention on the Law of the Sea, SPLOS/72, May 29, 2001. https://undocs.org/SPLOS/72

17. Larry A. Mayer, James V. Gardner, "US Law of the Sea Cruise to Map the Foot of the Slope and 2500-m Isobath of the US Arctic Ocean Margin, Barrow to Barrow. Cruise Report" (2004) https://scholars.unh.edu/ccom/1264.

18. "Russia Seeks Legal Fixing of Outer Boundary of Its Continental Shelf in Arctic Ocean," *RIA Novosti*, September 11, 2001.

19. "Continental Shelf to Become Regional Controversy," *BBC Summary of World Broadcasts*, February 5, 1997.

20. Alister Doyle, "Claimants Tiptoe Around Lucrative Antarctic Rights," *Reuters*, January 29, 2008.

21. Ted L. McDorman, "The Continental Shelf," in Donald Rothwell et al., eds., *The Oxford Handbook of the Law of the Sea* (Oxford: Oxford University Press, 2015), 202.

22. "Foreign and Commonwealth Office: UK accession to the United Nations Convention on the Law of the Sea," *M2 Presswire*, July 22, 1997.

23. Stephen Breen and Bill Mowat, "Fishermen Attack Loss of Rockall Rights," *Scotsman*, July 28, 1997.

24. Bill Hayton, *The South China Sea: The Struggle for Power in Asia* (New Haven, CT: Yale University Press, 2014), 87.

25. Declaration of the People's Republic of China Upon Ratification of the UN Convention on the Law of the Sea, August 25, 2006, available via United Nations

Treaty Collection. https://treaties.un.org/doc/Publication/MTDSG/Volume%20II/Chapter%20XXI/XXI-6.en.pdf

26. Edward Luce, "Manila Rebuffs Territorial Claim by Beijing," *Financial Times*, May 18, 1996.

27. Johanna Son, "China Springs New Surprise in Territorial Tussle," IPS-Inter Press Service, July 31, 1996.

28. Bernard D. Cole, *The Great Wall at Sea: China's Navy Enters the Twenty-First Century* (Annapolis, MD: Naval Institute Press, 2001).

29. Cole, *Great Wall at Sea*, 167.

30. Jake Douglas, Zack Cooper, et al., *Countering Coercion in Maritime Asia: The Theory and Practice of Gray Zone Deterrence* (Washington, DC: Center for Strategic & International Studies, 2017), 54.

31. Robert T. Kline, "The Pen and the Sword: The People's Republic of China's Effort to Redefine the Exclusive Economic Zone through Maritime Lawfare and Military Enforcement," *Military Law Review* 216 (2013), 124.

32. Steven Lee Meyers and Christopher Drew, "Chinese Pilot Reveled in Risk, Pentagon Says," *New York Times*, April 6, 2001, A1.

33. "Russians to Fly Out Spy Plane," BBC News, June 10, 2001.

34. "US Congress Urged by Admiral to Ratify Law of the Sea Treaty," *Agence France Presse*, June 30, 1995.

35. International Chamber of Commerce, International Maritime Bureau, *Piracy Report 2000*.

36. Jack Hitt, "Bandits in the Global Shipping Lanes," *New York Times*, August 20, 2000.

37. Felix Soh, "Local Officials in Southern China Linked to Piracy," *Straits Times* (Singapore), February 1, 1998.

38. See Robert Go, "Customs Corruption Costing Indonesia Billions of Dollars," *Straits Times* (Singapore), September 17, 2002.

39. For a detailed account of the seizure and its aftermath, see William Langewiesche, "Anarchy at Sea," *The Atlantic*, September 2003.

40. "Report: Asian Ship Owners Urge Governments to Fight Maritime Piracy," *Associated Press International*, December 2, 1998.

41. Marcus Hand, "Indian Coast Guard Opens Fire to Seize Hijacked Ship," *Business Times* (Singapore), November 17, 1999.

42. Marcus Hand, "Set Up UN Coast Guard to Fight Piracy in Region," *Business Times* (Singapore), November 16, 1999.

43. Caroline Vavro, "Piracy, Terrorism and the Balance of Power in the Malacca Strait," *Canadian Naval Review* 4, no. 1 (2008), 13–17.

44. *The 9/11 Commission Report: Final Report of the National Commission on Terrorist Attacks upon the United States* (Washington, DC: US Government Printing Office, 2011), 391.

45. David E. Sanger and Thom Shanker, "Reluctant U.S. Gives Assent for Missiles to Go to Yemen," *New York Times*, December 12, 2002.

46. Jinyuan Su, "The Proliferation Security Initiative (PSI) and Interdiction at Sea: A Chinese Perspective," *Ocean Development and International Law* 43, no. 1 (2012), 96–118.

47. Ticy V. Thomas, "The Proliferation Security Initiative: Towards Relegation of Navigational Freedoms in UNCLOS? An Indian Perspective," *Chinese Journal of International Law* 8, no. 3 (2009), 657–680.

48. For a discussion of the negotiations, see Natalie Klein, "The Right of Visit and the 2005 Protocol on the Suppression of Unlawful Acts against the Safety of Maritime Navigation," *Denver Journal of International Law and Policy* 35 (2006), 287–332.

49. World Bank, Food and Agriculture Organization, Kieran Kelleher, Rolf Willmann, and Ragnar Arnason, *The Sunken Billions: The Economic Justification for Fisheries Reform* (Washington, DC: World Bank, 2009).

50. Food and Agriculture Organization, *State of the World's Fisheries* (Rome: FAO, 2003).

51. "Taiwan PM Urges Fishing Boats to Use GPS to Avoid Entering Japanese Waters," BBC Monitoring Asia Pacific, June 22, 2005.

52. Governments of Australia, Canada, Chile, Namibia, New Zealand, and the United Kingdom, WWF, IUCN and the Earth Institute at Columbia University, High Seas Task Force, *Closing the Net: Stopping Illegal Fishing on the High Seas* (2006), 28, https://www.oecd.org/sd-roundtable/papersandpublications/39375276.pdf.

53. *Closing the Net*, 25.

54. For a detailed account of the chase, see Bruce G. Knecht, *Hooked: Pirates, Poaching, and the Perfect Fish* (Emmaus, PA: Rodale Books, 2007). For an analysis of some of the legal implications, see Erik Jaap Molenaar, "Multilateral Hot Pursuit and Illegal Fishing in the Southern Ocean: The Pursuits of the Viarsa 1 and the South Tomi," *International Journal of Marine and Coastal Law* 19, no. 1 (2004), 19–42.

55. Robin Pash, "Foreign Fishermen Acquitted after Costly Pursuit," *Associated Press*, November 5, 2005.

56. Valentin J. Schatz, "Marine Fisheries Law Enforcement Partnerships in Waters under National Jurisdiction: The Legal Framework for Inter-State Cooperation and Public-Private Partnerships with Non-Governmental Organizations and Private Security Companies," *Ocean Yearbook Online* 32, no. 1 (2018), 329–375.

57. Claude Berube, "Sea Shepherd: The Evolution of an Eco-Vigilante to Legitimized Maritime Capacity Builder," *CIWAG Maritime Irregular Warfare Studies* 3 (Newport: US Naval War College, 2021).

58. Gerry Nagtzaam, *From Environmental Action to Ecoterrorism? Towards a Process Theory of Environmental and Animal Rights Oriented Political Violence* (Cheltenham, UK: Edward Elgar, 2017), 260.

59. Schatz, "Marine Fisheries Law Enforcement."

60. *Oxford Handbook of the Law of the Sea*, 440.

61. Sarika Cullis-Suzuki and Daniel Pauly, "Failing the High Seas: A Global Evaluation of Regional Fisheries Management Organizations," *Marine Policy* 34, no. 5 (2010), 1036–1042.

62. Rothwell, *The Oxford Handbook of the Law of the Sea*, 446.

63. See Cullis-Suzuki and Pauly, "Failing the High Seas."

64. Tom Polacheck, "Politics and Independent Scientific Advice in RFMO Processes: A Case Study of Crossing Boundaries," *Marine Policy* 36, no. 1 (2012), 132–141.

65. Ross Anderson, "Allied Effort Chased Down Salmon Pirates," *Seattle Times*, May 8, 1999.

66. Charles Moore, "Trashed: Across the Pacific Ocean, Plastics, Plastics, Everywhere," *Natural History*, November 2003.

67. See Curtis C. Ebbesmeyer and W. James Ingraham Jr., "Pacific Toy Spill Fuels Ocean Current Pathways Research," *Eos, Transactions American Geophysical Union* 75, no. 37 (1994), 425–430.

68. The U.S. Justice Department ultimately fined Princess and Royal Caribbean cruise lines for inadequate supervision. See David Holmstrom, "Video Helps Torpedo Trash Dumping at Sea," *Christian Science Monitor*, January 23, 1997.

69. These resolutions included UN General Assembly Resolution 46/215 (December 20, 1991).

70. UN Environment Programme, Global Programme of Action for the Protection of the Marine Environment from Land-based Activities, Washington Declaration on Protection of the Marine Environment from Land-based Activities (1995). https://nicholasinstitute.duke.edu/sites/default/files/coral-reef-policies/Washington_Declaration.pdf

71. "Spain: The Lawless Sea," *Frontline* (January 2004).

72. "Stricken Tanker Towed Out to Sea," BBC News, November 15, 2002.

73. Veronica Frank, "Consequences of the *Prestige* Sinking for European and International Law," *International Journal of Marine and Coastal Law* 20, no. 1 (2005), 3.

74. Chris Millar and Hugh Muir, "Worst Ever Oil Disaster; Stricken Tanker Sinks Off Spanish Coast," *Evening Standard* (London), November 19, 2002.

75. See Frank, "Consequences of the Prestige Sinking for European and International Law."

76. Guidelines in Places of Refuge for Ships in Need of Assistance, IMO Assembly Resolution A.949 (23), December 5, 2003. https://www.imo.org/en/OurWork/Safety/Pages/PlacesOfRefuge.aspx

77. C. J. Chivers, "Eyeing Future Wealth, Russians Plant the Flag on the Arctic Seabed, Below the Polar Cap," *New York Times*, August 3, 2007.

78. "Canada Mocks Russia's 15th Century Arctic Claim," *Reuters*, August 2, 2007.

Chapter 8

1. Peter Robison, "High Metals Prices Lead Miners Down to Seabed," *International Herald Tribune*, October 4, 2006.

2. "Nautilus Minerals Enters Into 'Jules Verne' Mining Ship Deal," *Mining Magazine*, November 2006.

3. "India Now Capable of Deep-Sea Mining," *Hindustan Times*, December 18, 2006.

4. Porter Hoagland, Stace Beaulieu, et al., "Deep-Sea Mining of Seafloor Massive Sulfides," *Marine Policy* 34, no. 3 (2010), 728–732.

5. "Japan Finds Rare Earths in Pacific Seabed," *BBC News*, July 4, 2011. Findings from their research can be found at Yasuhiro Kato, et al., "Deep-sea Mud in the Pacific Ocean as a Potential Resource for Rare-earth Elements," *Nature Geoscience* 4, no. 8 (2011), 535.

6. Stephen Chen, "China Enters Race with Foreign Rivals to Mine the Seabed for Valuable Minerals," *South China Morning Post*, September 4, 2013.

7. Terry Macalister, "David Cameron Says Seabed Mining Could Be Worth £40bn to Britain," *The Guardian*, March 14, 2013.

8. "UK Seabed Resources Joins Deep-ocean Mineral-mining Rush in Pacific," *PACNEWS*, March 15, 2013.

9. Senate Foreign Relations Committee Hearing, "The Law of the Sea Convention (T.Doc.103–39): Perspectives from Business and Industry," testimony by Thomas Donohue, president and chief executive officer, US Chamber of Commerce, Washington, DC, *Congressional Documents and Publications*, June 28, 2012.

10. Laura Litvan, "Rumsfeld Says Treaty Would Force U.S. to Share Wealth," *Bloomberg*, June 14, 2012.

11. International Seabed Authority, Regulation 5, "Regulations on Prospecting and Exploration for Polymetallic Nodules in the Area," https://www.isa.org.jm/files/documents/EN/Regs/MiningCode.pdf.

12. Daniel OB Jones et al., "Biological Responses to Disturbance from Simulated Deep-Sea Polymetallic Nodule Mining," *PLoS One* 12, no. 2 (2017): e0171750.

13. Andrew Thaler, "Is This the End of Nautilus Minerals?" *DSM Observer*, March 21, 2019.

14. International Seabed Authority, "African Group Submission of Two Payment Regimes for Consideration by the Council of the International Seabed Authority," July 2019. https://www.isa.org.jm/files/files/documents/agpaymentregimes.pdf

15. Jeffrey Gettleman, "Q. & A. with a Pirate: 'We Just Want the Money,'" *New York Times*, September 30, 2008. For analyses that address the linkage between illegal fishing and piracy, see Stig Jarle Hansen, "Debunking the Piracy Myth: How Illegal Fishing Really Interacts with Piracy in East Africa," *RUSI Journal* 156, no. 6 (2011), 26–31.

16. Michael Hirsch and Terry McKnight, *Pirate Alley: Commanding Task Force 151 Off Somalia* (Annapolis, MD: Naval Institute Press, 2012).

17. UN Security Council Resolution 816 (June 2, 2008), https://en.wikipedia.org/wiki/United_Nations_Security_Council_Resolution_816.

18. For a variety of perspectives on the Security Council's transformation, see David M. Malone, ed., *The UN Security Council: From the Cold War to the 21st Century* (Boulder, CO: Lynne Rienner, 2004).

19. For a discussion of the Council's maritime measures, see Brian Wilson, "The Turtle Bay Pivot: How the United Nations Security Council Is Reshaping Naval Pursuit of Nuclear Proliferators, Rogue States, and Pirates," *Emory International Law Review* 33 (2018): 1.

20. "China Navy 'Confident, Capable' in Somalia Piracy Mission," *Xinhua Economic News Service*, December 23, 2008.

21. "North Korea Offers Rare Thanks to U.S. for Help," Reuters, November 8, 2007, https://www.reuters.com/article/us-korea-north-pirates/north-korea-offers-rare-tha

nks-to-u-s-for-help-idUSSEO27491420071109. For a discussion of coordination efforts, see Douglas Guilfoyle, "Somali Pirates as Agents of Change in International Law-making and Organisation," *Cambridge International Law Journal* 1, no. 3 (2012): 81–106.

22. Hari Kumar and Alan Cowell, "Indian Navy Says It Sank Pirate Ship," *New York Times*, November 20, 2008.

23. Jessica Larsen and Christine Nissen, *Learning from Danish Counter-Piracy Off the Coast of Somalia*,, DIIS Report, no. 10 (2017), 29. https://www.econstor.eu/bitstream/10419/197616/1/1009488635.pdf

24. See James Thuo Gathii, "Kenya's Piracy Prosecutions," *American Journal of International Law* 104, no. 3 (2010), 416–436.

25. For discussion of the policy, see Tara Magner, "A Less than 'Pacific' Solution for Asylum Seekers in Australia," *International Journal of Refugee Law* 16, no. 1 (2004), 53–90.

26. Andrew Rettman, "Slaves and Terrorists? EU Rhetoric on Migrants Under Fire," *EU Observer*, May 22, 2015.

27. UN Security Council Resolution 2240 (October 9, 2015), https://www.securitycounci lreport.org/atf/cf/%7B65BFCF9B-6D27-4E9C-8CD3-CF6E4FF96FF9%7D/s_res_2 240.pdf.

28. Wilson, "The Turtle Bay Pivot," 53.

29. Ian Urbina, "A Renegade Trawler, Chased by Eco-Vigilantes," *New York Times,* July 28, 2015.

30. International Tribunal for the Law of the Sea, *The M/V "Virginia G" Case (Panama/ Guinea-Bissau)*, https://repository.law.miami.edu/cgi/viewcontent.cgi?article= 1421&context=fac_articles.

31. UN Conference on Trade and Development, *2020 E-Handbook of Statistics*, https://unctad.org/webflyer/handbook-statistics-2020.

32. "Northwest Passage Crossed by First Cargo Ship, the Nordic Orion, Heralding New Era of Arctic Commercial Activity," *Reuters*, September 27, 2013. https://nationalp ost.com/news/canada/northwest-passage-crossed-by-first-cargo-ship-the-nordic-orion-heralding-new-era-of-arctic-commercial-activity.

33. "A Year After Its Historic Voyage, the Crystal Serenity Is Preparing to Sail the Northwest Passage Again," *Arctic Journal*, May 24, 2017.

34. "Tanker Vladimir Tikhonov Completes Successful Northern Sea Route Transit in a Week," *Maritime Executive*, September 1, 2011.

35. Christopher Woody, "Coast Guard Passed on Arctic Exercise," *Business Insider*, December 14, 2018.

36. People's Republic of China, Note Verbale CML/17/2009 (May 7, 2009), https://www.un.org/depts/los/clcs_new/submissions_files/mysvnm33_09/chn_2009re_mys_vn m_e.pdf.

37. For a detailed account of the standoff, see Michael Green et al., *Countering Coercion in Maritime Asia: The Theory and Practice of Gray Zone Deterrence* (Washington, DC: Center for Strategic and International Studies, 2017).

38. "Tension Rises in S. China Sea over Chinese Actions in Philippine Waters," *Japan Economic Newswire*, April 11, 2012.

39. "China and Philippines in Standoff over Resource-Rich Islands," *International Business Times News*, April 11, 2012.
40. Asia Maritime Transparency Initiative, "Counter-Coercion Series: Scarborough Shoal Standoff" (May 22, 2017), https://amti.csis.org/counter-co-scarborough-standoff/.
41. For an in-depth account of the standoff, see Alan Dupont and Christopher G. Baker, "East Asia's Maritime Disputes: Fishing in Troubled Waters," *Washington Quarterly* 37, no. 1 (2014), 79–98.
42. Marites Vitug, *Rock Solid: How the Philippines Won Its Maritime Case Against China* (Quezon City: Ateneo de Manila University Press, 2018).
43. Author interview with Paul Reichler.
44. "China Rejects Philippine UN Mediation Effort," *Associated Press,* February 19, 2013.
45. Matthew Lee, "Kerry: US to Boost Support for Philippines Security Forces as South China Sea Tensions Rise," *Associated Press*, December 17, 2013.
46. Ben Stewart, *Don't Trust, Don't Fear, Don't Beg: The Extraordinary Story of the Arctic 30* (New York: New Press, 2013).
47. Toby Sterling, "Netherlands Seeks Return of Greenpeace Ship from Russia," *Prince George Citizen (British Columbia),* October 5, 2013.
48. Kunal Dutta, "Hague in Talks with Russia over Activists; Foreign Secretary Raises Concerns About Welfare of Arrested Greenpeace Britons," *The Independent*, October 5, 2013.
49. Peter Cluskey, "Russia Dismisses Dutch Action over Greenpeace Ship," *Irish Times*, October 8, 2013.
50. Greenpeace International, Press Release, "Greenpeace Ship Arctic Sunrise Detained in Spain Following Oil Protest," November 18, 2014, https://www.greenpeace.org/international/press-release/6829/greenpeace-ship-arctic-sunrise-detained-in-spain-following-oil-protest/
51. Ministry of Foreign Affairs of the People's Republic of China, "Position Paper of the Government of the People's Republic of China on the Matter of Jurisdiction in the South China Sea Arbitration Initiated by the Republic of the Philippines," December 7, 2014, https://www.fmprc.gov.cn/nanhai/eng/snhwtlcwj_1/t1368895.htm.
52. *In the matter of an arbitration under Annex VII of the United Nations Convention on the Law of the Sea,* Permanent Court of Arbitration Case No. 2013-19, Hearing on the Merits and Remaining Issues of Jurisdiction and Admissibility, Day 2, 87, https://pca-cpa.org/en/cases/7/.
53. *In the matter of an arbitration under Annex VII of the United Nations Convention on the Law of the Sea,* Permanent Court of Arbitration Case No. 2013-19, Hearing on the Merits and Remaining Issues of Jurisdiction and Admissibility, Day 2, 87, https://pca-cpa.org/en/cases/7/.
54. *In the matter of an arbitration under Annex VII of the United Nations Convention on the Law of the Sea,* Permanent Court of Arbitration Case No. 2013-19, Award of 12 July, para. 269, https://pca-cpa.org/en/cases/7/.
55. Yoshifumi Tanaka, "The South China Sea Arbitration: Environmental Obligations Under the Law of the Sea Convention," *Review of European, Comparative and International Environmental Law* 27, no. 1 (2018), 90–96.

56. Tom Phillips, Oliver Holmes, and Owen Bowcott, "Beijing Rejects Tribunal's Ruling in South China Sea Case," *The Guardian*, July 12, 2016.

57. Chun Han Wong, "Veteran Chinese Diplomat Warns on South China Sea Ruling," *Wall Street Journal* [ChinaRealTime blog], July 6, 2016.

58. US Department of Defense, *Freedom of Navigation Reports* (various years).

59. Collin Koh, Twitter post, August 27, 2020, https://twitter.com/collinslkoh/status/1299139214596960256.

60. Li Bao, "Japan's Naval Chief Rules Out Joint-US Freedom of Navigation Patrols," *Voice of America*, September 28, 2016.

61. US Department of State, "U.S. Position on Maritime Claims in the South China Sea," July 13, 2020, https://kh.usembassy.gov/u-s-position-on-maritime-claims-in-the-south-china-sea/.

62. Amitai Etzioni, "Freedom of Navigation Assertions: The United States as the World's Policeman," *Armed Forces and Society* 42, no. 3 (2016), 501–517.

63. National legislation imposing restrictions is collected in Department of Defense, *Maritime Claims Reference Manual* (2014), https://www.jag.navy.mil/organization/code_10_mcrm.htm.

64. Abhijit Singh, "Not on the Same Page at Sea," *The Hindu*, April 13, 2021.

65. "Census Charts World Beneath the Seas," *Agence France Presse*, Ocober 5, 2010.

66. *First Census of Marine Life 2010: Highlights of a Decade of Discovery*, http://www.coml.org/media-resources/reports-archive.html.

67. U. Riebesell and J. Gattuso, "Lessons Learned from Ocean Acidification Research," *Nature Climate Change* 5 (2015), 12–14.

68. Carnegie Institution, "Ocean Acidification Already Slowing Coral Reef Growth," February 24, 2016, https://carnegiescience.edu/news/ocean-acidification-already-slowing-coral-reef-growth.

69. Global Ocean Commission, *From Decline to Recovery: A Rescue Package for the Global Ocean* (June 2014), https://www.mckinsey.com/~/media/mckinsey/dotcom/client_service/sustainability/pdfs/from_decline_to_recovery_a_rescue_package_for_the_global_ocean.ashx.

70. The White House, Presidential Proclamation—Papahanaumokuakea Marine National Monument Expansion, August 26, 2016, https://obamawhitehouse.archives.gov/the-press-office/2016/08/26/presidential-proclamation-papahanaumokuakea-marine-national-monument.

71. "NGOs urge RIO+20 to Back New Treaty on Oceans Protection," *Agence France Presse,* June 17, 2012.

72. Crow White and Christopher Costello, "Close the High Seas to Fishing?" *PLoS Biol* 12, no. 3 (2014), e1001826.

73. See J. Monk et al., "Trabectedin as a New Chemotherapy Option in the Treatment of Relapsed Platinum Sensitive Ovarian Cancer," *Current Pharmaceutical Design* 18, no. 25 (2012), 3754–3769; Nakarin Suwannarach et al., "Natural Bioactive Compounds from Fungi as Potential Candidates for Protease Inhibitors and Immunomodulators to Apply for Coronaviruses," *Molecules* 25, no. 8 (2020), 1800.

74. "Dutch Ocean Crusader Awarded Top Global Environmental Prize from UN," *Federal NewsFeed Embassy of the Netherlands News* (November 19, 2014).

75. "Ocean Cleanup Array Critiqued," *ITWeb Online* (April 9, 2013).https://advance-lexis-com.proxyiub.uits.iu.edu/api/document?collection=news&id=urn:contentItem:5854-VN51-DXR5-F3KR-00000-00&context=1516831.

76. Shaun Milne, "Clean-up Efforts Under Way on Plastic Island Three Times the Size of France," *The Herald* (Glasgow), October 5, 2019.

77. Video of the press conference is available at https://www.youtube.com/watch?v=x_Jx IzjaySc.

Conclusion

1. "Nimitz, Reagan Team Up, Advance International Rules-Based Order," *Defense Department Documents and Publications*, June 28, 2020 https://www.navy.mil/Press-Office/Press-Releases/display-pressreleases/Article/2284555/nimitz-reagan-team-up-advance-international-rules-based-order/.

2. "Remarks by spokesperson of the Chinese Embassy to Malaysia on the statement of the US Department of State on the South China Sea," *The Star* (Malaysia), July 20, 2020.

3. Keith Carlisle and Rebecca L. Gruby, "Polycentric Systems of Governance: A Theoretical Model for the Commons," *Policy Studies Journal* 47, no. 4 (2019), 927. For more on polycentricity, see Michael Dean McGinnis, *Polycentric Governance and Development: Readings from the Workshop in Political Theory and Policy Analysis* (Ann Arbor: University of Michigan Press, 1999).

4. Karen J. Alter and Kal Raustiala, "The Rise of International Regime Complexity," *Annual Review of Law and Social Science* 14 (2018), 329–349.

Selected Bibliography

Articles

Allott, Philip. "Power Sharing in the Law of the Sea." *American Journal of International Law* 77, no. 1 (January 1983): 1–30.

Alter, Karen J., and Kal Raustiala. "The Rise of International Regime Complexity." *Annual Review of Law and Social Science* 14 (2018): 329–349.

Anand, R. P. "Maritime Practice in South-East Asia Until 1600 A.D. and the Modern Law of the Sea." *International and Comparative Law Quarterly* 30, no. 2 (April 1981): 440–454.

Bailey, Kevin M. "An Empty Donut Hole: The Great Collapse of a North American Fishery." *Ecology and Society* 16, no. 2 (2011).

Barr, William. "The Voyage of Sibiryakov, 1932." *Polar Record* 19, no. 120 (1978): 253–166.

Bastin, John. "Raffles and British Policy in the Indian Archipelago, 1811–1816." *Journal of the Malayan Branch of the Royal Asiatic Society* 27, no. 1 (May 1954): 84–119.

Beesley, Alan. "The Negotiating Strategy of UNCLOS III: Developing and Developed Countries as Partners: A Pattern for Future Multilateral International Conferences?" *Law and Contemporary Problems* 46, no. 2 (1983): 183–194.

Behrendt, Stephen D. "The Annual Volume and Regional Distribution of the British Slave Trade, 1780–1807." *Journal of African History* 38, no. 2 (1997): 187–211.

Berube, Claude. "Sea Shepherd: The Evolution of an Eco-Vigilante to Legitimized Maritime Capacity Builder." *CIWAG Maritime Irregular Warfare Studies* 3 (Newport, RI: US Naval War College Press, 2021).

Bethell, Leslie. "The Independence of Brazil and the Abolition of the Brazilian Slave Trade: Anglo-Brazilian Relations, 1822–1826." *Journal of Latin American Studies* 1, no. 2 (1969): 115-147.

Bigelow, H. B. "The Progress of the Woods Hole Oceanographic Institution." *Eos, Transactions American Geophysical Union* 11, no. 1 (1930): 229–232.

Blanco-Bazán, Agustín. "IMO-Historical Highlights in the Life of a UN Agency." *Journal of the History of International Law* 6, no. 2 (2004): 259–283.

Boggs, S. Whittemore. "National Claims in Adjacent Seas." *Geographical Review* 41, no. 2 (1951): 185–209.

Broecker, Wallace S. "Massive Iceberg Discharges as Triggers for Global Climate Change." *Nature* 372, no. 6505 (1994): 421–424.

Buzan, Barry. "Negotiating by Consensus: Developments in Technique at the United Nations Conference on the Law of the Sea." *American Journal of International Law* 75 (1981): 324–348.

Cain, Mead T. "The Maps of the Society for the Diffusion of Useful Knowledge: A Publishing History." *Imago Mundi* 46, no. 1 (1994): 151–167.

Caldwell, Dan. "Flashpoints in the Gulf: Abu Musa and the Tunb Islands." *Middle East Policy* 4, no. 3 (1996): 50–58.

Carlisle, Keith, and Rebecca L. Gruby. "Polycentric Systems of Governance: A Theoretical Model for the Commons." *Policy Studies Journal* 47, no. 4 (2019): 927-952.

Carson, Rachel. "Undersea," *Atlantic Monthly* 160, no. 3 (September 1937): 322–325.

Cavnar, Anna. "Accountability and the Commission on the Limits of the Continental Shelf: Deciding Who Owns the Ocean Floor." *Cornell International Law Journal* 42 (2009): 387-440.

Cawkwell, George Law. "The Peace Between Athens and Persia." *Phoenix* 51, no. 2 (1997): 115–130.

Center for New American Security. "A Deadly Game: East China Sea Crisis 2030." July 22, 2020. https://www.cnas.org/publications/video/a-deadly-game-east-china-sea-crisis-2030.

Charney, Jonathan. "United States Interest in a Convention on the Law of the Sea: The Case for Continued Efforts." *Vanderbilt Journal of Transnational Law* 11 (1978): 39-75.

Chayes, Abram. "Law and the Quarantine of Cuba." *Foreign Affairs* 41, no. 3 (April 1963): 550-557.

Cheyette, Frederic L. "The Sovereign and the Pirates, 1332," *Speculum* 45, no. 1 (January 1970): 40-68.

Chung, Chris P.C. "Drawing the U-shaped Line: China's Claim in the South China Sea, 1946-1974." *Modern China* 42, no. 1 (2016): 38–72.

Clark, John G. "Marine Insurance in Eighteenth-Century La Rochelle." *French Historical Studies* 10, no. 4 (1978): 572–598.

Colson, David A. "Current Issues in International Fishery Conservation and Management." *Department of State Dispatch* 6 (1995): 100–104.

Cullis-Suzuki, Sarika, and Daniel Pauly. "Failing the High Seas: A Global Evaluation of Regional Fisheries Management Organizations." *Marine Policy* 34, no. 5 (2010): 1036–1042.

Daenell, Ernst. "The Policy of the German Hanseatic League Respecting the Mercantile Marine." *American Historical Review* 15, no. 1 (October 1909): 47–53.

Donn, Clifford B. "Flag of Convenience Registry and Industrial Relations." *Maritime Studies* 1989, no. 47 (1989): 1–9.

Dopyera, Caroline. "The Iron Hypothesis." *Earth* (1996): 26–33.

Dupont, Alan, and Christopher G. Baker. "East Asia's Maritime Disputes: Fishing in Troubled Waters." *Washington Quarterly* 37, no. 1 (2014): 79–98.

Ebbesmeyer, Curtis C., and W. James Ingraham Jr. "Pacific Toy Spill Fuels Ocean Current Pathways Research." *Eos, Transactions American Geophysical Union* 75, no. 37 (1994): 425–430.

Etzioni, Amitai. "Freedom of Navigation Assertions: The United States as the World's Policeman." *Armed Forces & Society* 42, no. 3 (2016): 501–517.

Fisher, Michael H. "Working Across the Seas: Indian Maritime Labourers in India, Britain, and in Between, 1600-1857." *International Review of Social History* 51, no. S14 (2006): 21–45.

Frank, Veronica. "Consequences of the *Prestige* Sinking for European and International Law." *International Journal of Marine and Coastal Law* 20, no. 1 (2005): 3.

Friedman, Alan G., and Cynthia A. Williams. "Group of 77 at the United Nations: An Emergent Force in the Law of the Sea." *San Diego Law Review* 16 (1979): 555–574.

Gathii, James Thuo. "Kenya's Piracy Prosecutions." *American Journal of International Law* 104, no. 3 (2010): 416–436.

Grosbard, Alan. "Treadwell Wharf in the Summerland, California Oil Field: The First Sea Wells in Petroleum Exploration" *Oil Industry History* 3, no. 1 (2002).

GuÐmundsson, GuÐÐmundur J. "The Cod and the Cold War." *Scandinavian Journal of History* 31, no. 2 (1996): 97–118.

Guilfoyle, Douglas. "Somali Pirates as Agents of Change in International Law-Making and Organisation." *Cambridge International Law Journal* 1, no. 3 (2012): 81–106.

Hansen, Stig Jarle. "Debunking the Piracy Myth: How Illegal Fishing Really Interacts with Piracy in East Africa." *RUSI Journal* 156, no. 6 (2011): 26–31.

Hardin, Garrett. "The Tragedy of the Commons." *Science* 162, no. 3859 (1968): 1243–1248.

Harvey, A. D. "European Attitudes to Britain during the French Revolutionary and Napoleonic Era." *History* 63, no. 209 (1978): 356–365.

Hayton, Bill. "The Modern Origins of China's South China Sea Claims: Maps, Misunderstandings, and the Maritime Geobody." *Modern China* 45, no. 2 (2019): 127–170.

Hershey, Amos S. "The German Conception of the Freedom of the Seas." *American Journal of International Law* 13, no. 2 (1919): 207–226.

Hoagland, Porter, Stace Beaulieu, et al. "Deep-Sea Mining of Seafloor Massive Sulfides." *Marine Policy* 34, no. 3 (2010): 728–732.

Hofman, Robert J. "Sealing, Whaling and Krill Fishing in the Southern Ocean: Past and Possible Future Effects on Catch Regulations." *Polar Record* 53, no. 1 (2017): 88–99.

Hollick, Ann L. "The Origins of 200-Mile Offshore Zones." *American Journal of International Law* 71, no. 3 (1977): 494–500.

Hollick, Ann L. "U.S. Oceans Policy: The Truman Proclamations." *Virginia Journal of International Law* 17, no. 1 (Fall 1976): 23–56.

Ikenberry, G. John. "Why the Liberal World Order Will Survive." *Ethics & International Affairs* 32, no. 1 (2018): 17.

International Chamber of Commerce, International Maritime Bureau, *Piracy Report 2000*.

Isachsen, Gunnar. "Modern Norwegian Whaling in the Antarctic." *Geographical Review* 19, no. 3 (July 1929): 387–403.

Jones, Daniel O. B., et al. "Biological Responses to Disturbance from Simulated Deep-Sea Polymetallic Nodule Mining." *PLoS One* 12, no. 2 (2017): e0171750.

Juda, Lawrence. "Innocent Passage by Warships in the Territorial Seas of the Soviet Union: Changing Doctrine." *Ocean Development and International Law* 21, no. 1 (1990): 111–116.

Juhász, Reka. "Temporary Protection and Technology Adoption: Evidence from the Napoleonic Blockade." *American Economic Review* 108, no. 11 (2018): 3339–3376.

Kato, Yasuhiro et al. "Deep-Sea Mud in the Pacific Ocean as a Potential Resource for Rare-Earth Elements." *Nature Geoscience* 4, no. 8 (2011): 535–539.

Kern, Holger Lutz. "Strategies of Legal Change: Great Britain, International Law, and the Abolition of the Transatlantic Slave Trade." *Journal of the History of International Law* 6, no. 2 (2004): 233–258.

Keyuan, Zou. "A Tribute to Zhao Lihai." *Chinese Journal of International Law* 1 (2002): v–viii.

Klein, Natalie. "The Right of Visit and the 2005 Protocol on the Suppression of Unlawful Acts Against the Safety of Maritime Navigation." *Denver Journal of International Law and Policy* 35 (2006): 287–332.

Kline, Robert T. "The Pen and the Sword: The People's Republic of China's Effort to Redefine the Exclusive Economic Zone through Maritime Lawfare and Military Enforcement." *Military Law Review* 216 (2013): 124–169.

Konyshev, Valery, and Alexander Sergunin. "Russia's Policies on the Territorial Disputes in the Arctic." *Journal of International Relations and Foreign Policy* 2, no. 1 (March 2014): 55–83.

Kraska, James. "Putting Your Head in the Tiger's Mouth: Submarine Espionage in Territorial Waters." *Columbia Journal of Transnational Law* 54 (2015): 164–247

Kraska, James. "The Law of the Sea Convention and the Northwest Passage." *International Journal of Marine and Coastal Law* 22, no. 2 (June 2007): 257–282.

Langewiesche, William. "Anarchy at Sea." *The Atlantic* 292, no. 2, (September 2003): 50-80.

Lemnitzer, Jan Martin. "'That Moral League of Nations Against the United States': The Origins of the 1856 Declaration of Paris." *International History Review* 35, no. 5 (2013): 1068–1088.

Leonard, L. Larry. "Recent Negotiations Toward the International Regulation of Whaling." *American Journal of International Law* 35, no. 1 (1941): 90–113.

Lewis, Martin W. "Dividing the Ocean Sea." *Geographical Review* 89, no. 2 (April 1999): 188–214.

Maduriera, Luis. "The Accident of America: Marginal Notes on the European Conquest of the World." *CR: The New Centennial Review* 2, no. 1 (Spring 2002): 117–181.

Magner, Tara. "A Less Than 'Pacific' Solution for Asylum Seekers in Australia." *International Journal of Refugee Law* 16, no. 1 (2004): 53–90.

Malcomson, Scott. "The Unquiet Ship: What Happened on Board the Freighter Dubai Which Turned Its Stowaways into Castaways?" *New Yorker*, January 20, 1997.

Mallett, Alex. "A Trip Down the Red Sea with Reynald of Châtillon." *Journal of the Royal Asiatic Society* 18, no. 2 (2008): 141–153.

Maloni, Ruby. "Control of the Seas: The Historical Exegesis of the Portuguese 'Cartaz.'" *Proceedings of the Indian History Congress* 72 (2011): 476–484.

Marsh, A. R. "A Short but Distant War—the Falklands Campaign." *Journal of the Royal Society of Medicine* 76, no. 11 (1983): 972–982.

Masterson, William E. "The Hemisphere Zone of Security and the Law." *American Bar Association Journal* 26, no. 11 (1940): 860–863.

Maxwell, Ian. "Seas as Places." *Shima: The International Journal of Research into Island Cultures* 6, no. 1 (2012): 27–29.

Miers, Suzanne. "Slavery and the Slave Trade as International Issues 1890–1939." *Slavery and Abolition* 19, no. 2 (1998): 16–37.

Mokyr, Joel, and N. Eugene Savin. "Stagflation in Historical Perspective: The Napoleonic Wars Revisited." *Research in Economic History* 1 (1976): 198–259.

Molenaar, Erik Jaap. "Multilateral Hot Pursuit and Illegal Fishing in the Southern Ocean: The Pursuits of the Viarsa 1 and the South Tomi." *International Journal of Marine and Coastal Law* 19, no. 1 (2004): 19–42.

Moore, Charles. "Trashed: Across the Pacific Ocean, Plastics, Plastics, Everywhere." *Natural History* 112, no. 9 (November 2003): 46–51.

Moore, John Norton. "The Law of the Sea: A Choice and a Challenge." *Virginia Journal of International Law* 15, no. 4 (1974): 791–794.

Moore, John Norton. "The Regime of Straits and the Third United Nations Conference on the Law of Sea." *American Journal of International Law* 74 (1980): 77–121.

Nordquist, Myron H., and Margaret G. Wachenfeld. "Legal Aspects of Reflagging Kuwaiti Tankers and Laying of Mines in the Persian Gulf." *German Yearbook of International Law* 31 (1988): 138–164.

Nye, Joseph S. "Ocean Rule Making from a World Politics Perspective." *Ocean Development & International Law* 3, no. 1 (1975): 29–52.

O'Brian, Phillips Payson. "British and American Naval Power." *Politics and Policy* 9, no. 2 (1936): 125–126.

O'Leary, Bethan et al. "The First Network of Marine Protected Areas (MPAs) in the High Seas: The Process, the Challenges and Where Next." *Marine Policy* 36, no. 3 (2012): 598–605.

O'Rourke, Ronald. "The Tanker War." *Proceedings* 114, no. 5 (1988).

Oldham, James. "Insurance Litigation Involving the Zong and Other British Slave Ships, 1780–1807." *Journal of Legal History* 28, no. 3 (2007): 299–318.

Osgood, Josiah. "Caesar and the Pirates: or How to Make (and Break) an Ancient Life." *Greece and Rome* 57, no. 2 (2010): 319-336.

Osieke, Ebere. "Flags of Convenience Vessels: Recent Developments." *American Journal of International Law* 73, no. 4 (October 1979): 604–627.

Oxman, Bernard. "United States Interests in the Law of the Sea Convention." *American Journal of International Law* 88, no. 167 (1994): 167-178.

Paga, Jessica, and Margaret M. Miles. "The Archaic Temple of Poseidon at Sounion." *Hesperia: The Journal of the American School of Classical Studies at Athens* 85, no. 4 (2016): 657–710.

Pardo, Arvid. "Before and After." *Law and Contemporary Problems* 46, no. 2 (1983): 95–105.

Polacheck, Tom. "Politics and Independent Scientific Advice in RFMO Processes: A Case Study of Crossing Boundaries." *Marine Policy* 36, no. 1 (2012): 132–141.

Proelss, Alexander. "The Limits of Jurisdiction Ratione Materiae of UNCLOS Tribunals." *Hitotsubashi Journal of Law and Politics* 46 (2018): 47–60.

Raffles, S. "The Maritime Code of the Malays." *Journal of the Straits Branch of the Royal Asiatic Society*, no. 3 (July 1879): 62–84.

Ramakrishna, Kilaparti, Robert E. Bowen, and Jack H. Archer. "Outer Limits of Continental Shelf: A Legal Analysis of Chilean and Ecuadorian Island Claims and US Response." *Marine Policy* 11, no. 1 (1987): 58–68.

Redding, Benjamin. "A Ship 'For Which Great Neptune Raves': The Sovereign of the Seas, La Couronne and Seventeenth-Century International Competition Over Warship Design." *Mariner's Mirror* 104, no. 4 (2018): 402–422.

Ribiero, Marta Chantal. "'The 'Rainbow': The First National Marine Protected Area Proposed Under the High Seas." *International Journal of Marine and Coastal Law* 25, no. 2 (2010): 183–207.

Richardson, Elliot L. "Power, Mobility and the Law of the Sea." *Foreign Affairs* 58, no. 4 (1980): 902–919.

Riebesell, U., and J. Gattuso. "Lessons Learned from Ocean Acidification Research." *Nature Climate Change* 5 (2015): 12–14.

Roach, J. Ashley. "Marine Scientific Research and the New Law of the Sea." *Ocean Development and International Law* 27, no. 1–2 (1996): 59–72.

Rose, Stephen A. "Naval Activity in the EEZ-Troubled Waters Ahead." *Naval Law Review* 39 (1990): 67.

Rothwell, Donald R. "The Canadian-U.S. Northwest Passage Dispute: A Reassessment." *Cornell International Law Journal* 26, no. 2 (Spring 1993): 331–372.

Rowley, James A. "Captain Nathaniel Gordon, the Only American Executed for Violating the Slave Trade Laws." *Civil War History* 39, no. 3 (1993): 216–224.

Rozwadowski, Helen M. "Arthur C. Clarke and the Limitations of the Ocean as a Frontier." *Environmental History* 17, no. 3 (2012): 578–602.

Samons, Loren J. "Kimon, Kallias and Peace with Persia." *Historia: Zeitschrift für Alte Geschichte* H. 2 (1998): 129–140.

Schatz, Valentin J. "Marine Fisheries Law Enforcement Partnerships in Waters Under National Jurisdiction: The Legal Framework for Inter-State Cooperation and Public-Private Partnerships with Non-Governmental Organizations and Private Security Companies," *Ocean Yearbook Online* 32, no. 1 (2018): 329–375.

Schatz, Valentin J., Alexander Proelss, and Nengye Liu. "The 2018 Agreement to Prevent Unregulated High Seas Fisheries in the Central Arctic Ocean: A Critical Analysis." *International Journal of Marine and Coastal Law* 34, no. 2 (2019): 195–244.

Selak, Charles B. "Recent Developments in High Seas Fisheries Jurisdiction under the Presidential Proclamation of 1945." *American Journal of International Law* 44, no. 4 (1950): 670–681.

Shackelford, Scott. "Was Selden Right: The Expansion of Closed Seas and Its Consequences." *Stanford Journal of International Law* 47 (2011): 1–50.

Sinan, I. M. "UNCTAD and Flags of Convenience." *Journal of World Trade Law* 18 (1984): 95–109.

Smith, Arthur M. "Has the Red Cross-Adorned Hospital Ship Become Obsolete?" *Naval War College Review* 58, no. 3 (2005): 121–131.

Sohn, Louis B. "Peaceful Settlement of Disputes in Ocean Conflicts: Does UNCLOS III Point the Way?" *Law and Contemporary Problems* 46, no. 2 (Spring 1983): 195–200.

Solecki, Jan J. "A Review of the U.S.S.R. Fishing Industry." *Ocean Management* 5 (1979): 97-123.

Soons, Alfred HA. "The Effects of a Rising Sea Level on Maritime Limits and Boundaries." *Netherlands International Law Review* 37, no. 2 (1990): 207-232.

Speed, Keith. "Royal Navy Cuts—Former Minister Comments." *Marine Policy* 6, no. 2 (1982): 150–151.

Steinberg, Philip E. "Lives of Division, Lines of Connection: Stewardship in the World Ocean." *Geographical Review* 89, no. 2 (1999): 254–264.

Su, Jinyuan. "The Proliferation Security Initiative (PSI) and Interdiction at Sea: A Chinese Perspective." *Ocean Development and International Law* 43, no. 1 (2012): 96–118.

Sumaila, U. Rashid et al. "Winners and Losers in a World Where the High Seas Is Closed to Fishing." *Scientific Reports* 5 (2015): 1-6.

Suwannarach, Nakarin et al. "Natural Bioactive Compounds from Fungi as Potential Candidates for Protease Inhibitors and Immunomodulators to Apply for Coronaviruses." *Molecules* 25, no. 8 (2020): 1800.

Swing, John Temple. "Who Will Own the Oceans?" *Foreign Affairs* 54, no. 3 (1976): 527–546.

Tanaka, Yoshifumi. "The South China Sea Arbitration: Environmental Obligations Under the Law of the Sea Convention." *Review of European, Comparative & International Environmental Law* 27, no. 1 (2018): 90–96.

Thomas, Ticy V. "The Proliferation Security Initiative: Towards Relegation of Navigational Freedoms in UNCLOS? An Indian Perspective." *Chinese Journal of International Law* 8, no. 3 (2009): 657–680.

Trimble, E. G. "Violations of Maritime Law by the Allied Powers During the World War." *American Journal of International Law* 24, no. 1 (January 1930): 79–99.

Utley, Jonathan G. "Japanese Exclusion from American Fisheries, 1936–1939: The Department of State and the Public Interest." *Pacific Northwest Quarterly* 65, no. 1 (1974): 8–16.

Vavro, Caroline. "Piracy, Terrorism and the Balance of Power in the Malacca Strait." *Canadian Naval Review* 4, no. 1 (2008): 13–17.

Wade, Geoff. "The Zheng He Voyages: A Reassessment." *Journal of the Malaysian Branch of the Royal Asiatic Society* 78, no. 1 (2005): 37–58.

Ward, Allen M. "Caesar and the Pirates." *Classical Philology* 70, no. 4 (1975): 267–268.

White, Crow, and Christopher Costello. "Close the High Seas to Fishing?" *PLoS Biology* 12, no. 3 (2014): e1001826.

Wilson, Brian. "The Turtle Bay Pivot: How the United Nations Security Council Is Reshaping Naval Pursuit of Nuclear Proliferators, Rogue States, and Pirates." *Emory International Law Review* 33 (2018): 1–90.

Xu, Stella. "The Guardian of the Maritime Network in Premodern East Asia: Contested History and Memory of Chang Pogo." *Korean Studies* 40, no. 1 (2016): 119–139.

Young, John W. "Great Britain's Latin American Dilemma: The Foreign Office and the Overthrow of 'Communist' Guatemala, June 1954." *International History Review* 8, no. 4 (1986): 573–592.

Ziskind, Jonathan. "International Law and Ancient Sources: Grotius and Selden." *Review of Politics* 35, no. 4 (1973): 550–551.

Books and Reports

The 9/11 Commission Report: Final Report of the National Commission on Terrorist Attacks Upon the United States. Washington, DC: US Government Printing Office, 2011.

Abulafia, David. *The Boundless Sea: A Human History of the Oceans*. New York: Oxford University Press, 2019.

Alexandrowicz, C.H.. *An Introduction to the History of the Law of Nations in the East Indies*. Oxford: Clarendon Press, 1967.

Atsushi, Ota, ed. *In the Name of the Battle Against Piracy: Ideas and Practices in State Monopoly of Maritime Violence in Europe and Asia in the Period of Transition*. Netherlands: Brill, 2018.

Baranov, Fedor Il'ich, and William Edwin Ricker. *On the Question of the Biological Basis of Fisheries: On the Question of the Dynamics of the Fishing Industry*. Bloomington: Indiana University, 1945.

Barnes, Ruth and David Parker, ed., *Ships and the Development of Maritime Technology on the Indian Ocean*, vol. 2 (Abingdon: Routledge, 2002)

Belknap, Reginald R. *The Yankee Mining Squadron; Or, Laying the North Sea Mine Barrage*. Annapolis, MD: United States Naval Institute, 1920.

Bell, Christopher, and John Maurer, eds. *At the Crossroads Between Peace and War: The London Naval Conference of 1930*. Annapolis: Naval Institute Press, 2014.

Bernstein, William J. *A Splendid Exchange: How Trade Shaped the World*. New York: Grove Press, 2008.

Bigelow, Albert. *The Voyage of the Golden Rule: An Experiment with Truth*. Garden City: Doubleday, 1959.

Bosco, David L. *Five to Rule Them All: The UN Security Council and the Making of the Modern World.* New York: Oxford University Press, 2009.

Brown, Lloyd A. *The Story of Maps.* New York: Dover, 1979.

Brunsman, Denver Alexander. *The Evil Necessity: British Naval Impressment in the Eighteenth-century Atlantic World.* Charlottesville: University of Virginia Press, 2013.

Buck, Susan J. *The Global Commons: An Introduction.* Washington, DC: Island Press, 2012.

Burnett, Douglas R., Robert Beckman, and Tara M. Davenport, eds. *Submarine Cables: The Handbook of Law and Policy.*

Leiden : Martinus Nijhoff Publishers, 2014.

Buzan, Barry. *Seabed Politics.* New York: Praeger, 1976.

Byers, Michael. *International Law and the Arctic.* Cambridge: Cambridge University Press, 2013.

Lord Byron, *Childe Harold's Pilgrimage.* New York: HarperPerennial Classics, 2014 [originally published 1812].

Cable, James. *Gunboat Diplomacy: Political Applications of Limited Naval Force.* New York: Praeger, 1971.

Carlisle, Rodney P. *Sovereignty for Sale: The Origins and Evolution of the Panamanian and Liberian Flags of Convenience.* Annapolis, MD: Naval Institute Press, 1981.

Carson, Rachel. *The Edge of the Sea.* Boston: Houghton Mifflin, 1955.

Carson, Rachel. *The Sea Around Us.* New York: Oxford University Press, 1961.

Carson, Rachel. *Silent Spring.* New York: Houghton Mifflin, 1962.

Cole, Bernard D. *The Great Wall at Sea: China's Navy Enters the Twenty-First Century.* Annapolis, MD: Naval Institute Press, 2001.

Coogan, John W. *The End of Neutrality: The United States, Britain, and Maritime Rights, 1899–1915.* Ithaca, NY: Cornell University Press, 1981.

Corbett, Julian. *The League of Nations and Freedom of the Seas.* London: Oxford University Press, 1918.

Cushing, D. H. *The Provident Sea.* Cambridge: Cambridge University Press, 1988.

Damrosch, Lori Fisler, and Sean D. Murphy. *International Law, Cases and Materials*, 6th ed. St. Paul, MI: West Academic, 2014.

Davis, Lance, and Stanley Engerman. *Naval Blockades in Peace and War: An Economic History Since 1750.* New York: Cambridge University Press, 2006.

De Souza, Philip. *Piracy in the Graeco-Roman World.* Cambridge: Cambridge University Press, 2002.

De Vattel, Emer. *The Law of Nations.* London: J. Newbery, 1760.

Dolman, Antony J. *Resources, Regimes, World Order.* New York: Foundation Reshaping the International Order/Pergamon Press, 1981.

Drew, Christopher, Sherry Sontag, and Annette Lawrence Drew. *Blind Man's Bluff: The Untold Story of American Submarine Espionage.* New York: PublicAffairs, 2008.

Dull, Jonathan R. *The Age of the Ship of the Line: The British and French Navies, 1650–1815.* Lincoln: University of Nebraska, 2009.

Earle, Sylvia. *The World Is Blue: How Our Fate and the Ocean's Are One.* Washington, DC: National Geographic, 2009.

Elleman, Bruce A. *China's Naval Operations in the South China Sea: Evaluating Legal, Strategic and Military Factors.* Kent: Renaissance Books, 2018.

Feifer, George. *Breaking Open Japan: Commodore Perry, Lord Abe, and American Imperialism in 1853.* New York: HarperCollins, 2013.

Finley, Carmel. *All the Fish in the Sea: Maximum Sustainable Yield and the Failure of Fisheries Management*. Chicago: University of Chicago Press, 2011.

Friedheim, Robert L. *Negotiating the New Ocean Regime*. Columbia: University of South Carolina Press, 1993.

Fulton, Thomas Wemyss. *The Sovereignty of the Sea*. Edinburgh: William Blackwood and Sons, 1911.

Giraldez, Arturo. *The Age of Trade: The Manila Galleons and the Dawn of the Global Economy*. Lanham, Md.: Rowman & Littlefield, 2015.

Girling, Richard. *Sea Change: Britain's Coastal Catastrophe*. London: Eden Project, 2008.

Global Ocean Commission. *From Decline to Recovery: A Rescue Package for the Global Ocean*. Oxford: Global Ocean Commission, globaloceancomission.org, June 2014.

Gold, Edgar. *Maritime Transport: The Evolution of International Marine Policy and Shipping Law*. Lexington, Mass.: Lexington Books, 1981.

Goran, Morris. *The Story of Fritz Haber*. Norman: University of Oklahoma Press, 1967.

Gould, Carol Grant. *The Remarkable Life of William Beebe: Explorer and Naturalist*. Washington, DC: Island Press, 2012.

Closing the Net: Stopping Illegal Fishing on the High Seas. Governments of Australia, Canada, Chile, Namibia, New Zealand, and the United Kingdom, WWF, IUCN and the Earth Institute at Columbia University. High Seas Task Force. London: Department for Environment, Food and Rural Affairs 2006.

Green, Michael et al. *Countering Coercion in Maritime Asia: The Theory and Practice of Gray Zone Deterrence*. Washington, DC: Center for Strategic & International Studies, 2017.

Greenfield, Jeanette. *China's Practice in the Law of the Sea*. Oxford: Clarendon Press, 1992.

Grotius, Hugo. *The Free Sea*, translated by Richard Hakluyt. Indianapolis, IN: Liberty Fund, 2004 [originally published 1609].

Guilfoyle, Douglas. *Shipping Interdiction and the Law of the Sea*. Cambridge: Cambridge University Press, 2009.

Hamilton, Keith, and Patrick Salmon. *Slavery, Diplomacy, and Empire*. Brighton: Sussex Academic Press, 2009.

Harrison, James. *Making the Law of the Sea: A Study in the Development of International Law*. Cambridge: Cambridge University Press, 2011.

Hawksley, Humphrey. *Asian Waters: The Struggle Over the South China Sea and the Strategy of Chinese Expansion*. New York: Abrams, 2020.

Hirsch, Michael, and Terry McKnight. *Pirate Alley: Commanding Task Force 151 Off Somalia*. Annapolis, MD: Naval Institute Press, 2012.

Hobson, Rolf. *Imperialism at Sea: Naval Strategic Thought, the Ideology of Sea Power, and the Tirpitz Plan, 1875–1914*. Leiden: Brill, 2002.

Hobson, Rolf, and Tom Kristiansen. *Navies in Northern Waters*. Portland, OR: Frank Cass, 2004.

Hollick, Ann L. *U.S. Foreign Policy and the Law of the Sea*. Princeton, NJ: Princeton University Press, 2017.

Holwitt, Joel Ira. *Execute Against Japan: The U.S. Decision to Conduct Unrestricted Submarine Warfare*. College Station: Texas A&M University Press, 2009.

Ikenberry, G. John. *Liberal Leviathan: The Origins, Crisis, and Transformation of the American World Order*. Princeton: Princeton University Press, 2011.

International Law Reports. Cambridge: Cambridge University Press, 2002.

International Organizations and the Law of the Sea: Documentary Yearbook, vol. 1 (1985). London: Graham & Trotman/Martinus Nijhoff, 1994.

Jenner, C. J., and Tran Truong Thuy, eds. *The South China Sea: A Crucible of Regional Cooperation or Conflict-Making Sovereignty Claims?* Cambridge: Cambridge University Press, 2016.

Jones, Nicolette. *The Plimsoll Sensation: The Great Campaign to Save Lives at Sea*. London: Little Brown, 2006.

Jubayr, Ibn. *The travels of Ibn Jubayr, being the chronicle of a mediaeval Spanish Moor concerning his journey to the Egypt of Saladin, the holy cities of Arabia, Baghdad the city of the caliphs, the Latin kingdom of Jerusalem, and the Norman kingdom of Sicily*, trans. R.J.C. Broadhurst. London: J. Cape, 1952.

Kasoulides, George. *Port State Control and Jurisdiction: Evolution of the Port State Regime*. Dordrecht: Martinus Nijhoff, 1993.

Kathirithamby-Wells, J., and John Villiers, eds. *The Southeast Asian Port and Polity: Rise and Demise*. Singapore: Singapore University Press, 1990.

Kennedy, Paul. *The Rise and Fall of British Naval Mastery*.London: Penguin Books Limited, 2017.

Keppel, Henry. *The Expedition to Borneo of HMS Dido for the Suppression of Piracy: With Extracts from the Journal of James Brooke, Esq., of Sarāwak*, vol. 18. New York: Harper & Brothers, 1846.

Khalilieh, Hassan S. *Islamic Maritime Law: An Introduction*. Boston: Brill, 1998.

Khalilieh, Hassan S. *Admiralty and Maritime Laws in the Mediterranean Sea (ca. 800–1050): The Kitāb Akriyat al-Sufun vis-a-vis the Nomos Rhodion Nautikos*. Leiden: Brill, 2006.

King, Charles. *The Black Sea: A History*. Oxford: Oxford University Press, 2005.

Knecht, Bruce G. *Hooked: Pirates, Poaching, and the Perfect Fish*. Emmaus, PA: Rodale Books, 2007.

Koh, Tommy. *Building a New Legal Order for the Oceans*. Singapore: NUS Press, 2020.

Koslow, Julian Anthony, Kristina Gjerde, and Tody Koslow. *The Silent Deep: The Discovery, Ecology and Conservation of the Deep Sea*. Chicago: University of Chicago Press, 2007.

Kraska, James, and Raul Pedrozo, *The Free Sea: The American Fight for Freedom of Navigation*. Annapolis, MD: Naval Institute Press, 2018.

Lancaster, Edwin Ray et al. *The Scientific Memoirs of Thomas Henry Huxley: Supplementary Volume*. London: Macmillan, 1903.

Langewiesche, William. *The Outlaw Sea*. New York: North Point Press, 2004.

Larson, Erik. *Dead Wake: The Last Crossing of the Lusitania*. New York: Crown, 2015.

Levering, Ralph B., and Miriam L. Levering. *Citizen Action for Global Change: The Neptune Group and Law of the Sea*. Syracuse, NY: Syracuse University Press, 1999.

Levinson, Marc. *The Box: How the Shipping Container Made the World Smaller and the World Economy Bigger*. Princeton, NJ: Princeton University Press, 2008.

Lewarne, Stephen. *Soviet Oil: The Move Offshore*. Boulder: Westview Press, 1988.

Lloyd, Christopher. *The Nation and the Navy: A History of Naval Life and Policy*. Westport: Greenwood Press, 1961.

Lloyd, Christopher. *The Navy and the Slave Trade: The Suppression of the African Slave Trade in the Nineteenth Century*. Abingdon: Taylor & Francis, 2012.

Lodge, Michael, and Myron H. Nordquist. *Peaceful Order in the World's Oceans: Essays in Honor of Satya N. Nandan*. Leiden: Brill | Martinus Nijhoff, 2014.

Lupin, Hector M., Aurora Zugarramurdi, and Maria A. Parin, *Economic Engineering Applied to the Fishery Industry*. Rome: Food and Agriculture Organization of the United Nations, 1995.

Lytle, Mark Hamilton. *The Gentle Subversive: Rachel Carson, Silent Spring, and the Rise of the Environmental Movement*. Oxford: Oxford University Press, 2007.

Mahan, Alfred Thayer. *The Influence of Sea Power Upon History, 1660–1783*. London: Sampson Low, Marston , 1892.

Malone, David M., ed. *The UN Security Council: From the Cold War to the 21st Century*. Boulder, CO: Lynne Rienner, 2004.

Mann, Itamar. *Humanity at Sea: Maritime Migration and the Foundations of International Law*. New York: Cambridge University Press, 2016.

Marx, Jenifer. *Pirates and Privateers of the Caribbean*. Malabar, Fla: Krieger Publishing, 1992.

Mattair, Thomas R. *The Three Occupied UAE Islands: The Tunbs and Abu Musa*. Abu Dhabi: Emirates Center for Strategic Studies and Research, 2005.

Maury, M. F. *Explanations and Sailing Directions to Accompany the Wind and Current Charts*. Philadelphia: Biddle, 1855.

Mawani, Renisa. *Across Oceans of Law: The Komagata Maru and Jurisdiction in the Time of Empire*. Durham, NC: Duke University Press, 2018.

McCullough, David. *The Path Between the Seas: The Creation of the Panama Canal, 1870–1914*. New York: Simon & Schuster, 2001.

McDougal, Myres, and William T. Burke. *The Public Order of the Oceans: A Contemporary International Law of the Sea*. Dordrecht: Martinus Nijhoff, 1987.

McGinnis, Michael Dean. *Polycentric Governance and Development: Readings from the Workshop in Political Theory and Policy Analysis*. Ann Arbor: University of Michigan Press, 1999.

McKercher, B. J. C. *The Second Baldwin Government and the United States, 1924–1929: Attitude and Diplomacy*. Cambridge: Cambridge University Press, 1984.

Mero, John L. *The Mineral Resources of the Sea*. Amsterdam: Elsevier, 1965.

Metaxas, Basil N. *Flags of Convenience: A Study of Internationalisation*. Brookfield, Vt.: Gower, 1985.

Miers, Suzanne. *Britain and the Ending of the Slave Trade*. London: Longman, 1975.

Moore, John Norton, and Myron Nordquist. *Entry into Force of the Law of the Sea Convention*. The Hague: Martinus Nijhoff, 1995.

Morison, Samuel Eliot. *Admiral of the Ocean Sea: A Life of Christopher Columbus*. Boston: Little, Brown, 1942.

Morris, Michael A. *International Politics and the Sea: The Case of Brazil*. Boulder, CO: Westview Press, 1979.

Murphy, Martin N. *Small Boats, Weak States, Dirty Money: Piracy and Maritime Terrorism in the Modern World*. New York: Columbia University Press, 2010.

Nagtzaam, Gerry. *From Environmental Action to Ecoterrorism? Towards a Process Theory of Environmental and Animal Rights Oriented Political Violence*. Cheltenham: Edward Elgar, 2017.

Nandan, Satya N., Myron H. Nordquist, and James Kraska. *UNCLOS 1982 Commentary: Supplementary Documents*. Leiden: Martinus Nijhoff, 2012.

Negroponte, John D. *Who Will Protect Freedom of the Seas?* Washington, DC: US Department of State, Bureau of Public Affairs, 1986.

Nissen, Christine, and Jessica Larsen. *Learning from Danish Counter-Piracy Off the Coast of Somalia*. DIIS Report No. 2017:10. Copenhagen: Danish Institute for International Studies, 2017.

Nordquist, Myron H. *United Nations Convention on the Law of the Sea, 1982: A Commentary* [multiple volumes]. Dordrecht: Martinus Nijhoff, 1985.

Occhipinti, Egidia. *Hellenica Oxyrhynchia and Historiography: New Research Perspectives*. Leiden: Brill, 2016.

O'Connell, Daniel Patrick. *The International Law of the Sea*. Oxford: Clarendon Press, 1982.

Odell, Rachel Esplin. "Mare Interpretatum: Continuity and Evolution in States' Interpretations of the Law of the Sea." PhD diss., Massachusetts Institute of Technology, 2020.

Ogilvie, Megan Jacqueline. "Ocean Fertilization: Ecological Cure or Calamity." PhD diss., Massachusetts Institute of Technology, 2004.

Oliver, John T. *Freedom of Navigation, Rights of Passage, International Security, and the Law of the Sea*. Charlottesville: University of Virginia School of Law, 1993.

Ostrom, Elinor. *Governing the Commons: The Evolution of Institutions for Collective Action*. Cambridge: Cambridge University Press, 2015.

Ostrom, Elinor et al., eds. *The Drama of the Commons*. Washington, DC: National Academies Press, 2002.

Oxman, Bernard, David Caron, and Charles L. O. Buderi, eds. *Law of the Sea: U.S. Policy Dilemma*. San Francisco: Institute for Contemporary Studies, 1983.

Paine, Lincoln. *The Sea and Civilization: A Maritime History of the World*. New York: Knopf, 2013.

Palmer, Andrew. *The New Pirates: Modern Global Piracy from Somalia to the South China Sea*. New York: Bloomsbury, 2014.

Papastavridis, Efthymios. *The Interception of Vessels on the High Seas*. Portland, OR: Hart, 2013.

Pardo, Arvid. *The Common Heritage: Selected Papers on Oceans and World Order*. Valletta: Malta University Press, 1975.

Pedrozo, Raul, and James Kraska. *The Free Sea: The American Fight for Freedom of Navigation*. Annapolis, MD: Naval Institute Press, 2018.

Petrow, Richard. *In the Wake of Torrey Canyon*. New York: D. McKay, 1968.

Polmar, Norman. *Spyplane: The U-2 History Declassified*. Osceola, WI: MBI Publishing, 2001.

Polmar, Norman, and Michael White. *Project Azorian: The CIA and the Raising of the K-129*. Annapolis, MD: Naval Institute Press, 2010.

Potter, Elmer Belmont, ed. *Sea Power: A Naval History*, 2nd ed. Annapolis, MD: Naval Institute Press, 1981.

Potter, Pitman Benjamin. *The Freedom of the Seas in History, Law, and Politics*. New York: Longmans, Green, 1924.

Proelss, Alexander. *United Nations Convention on the Law of the Sea: A Commentary*. Germany: C. H. Beck, 2017.

Protocols of Proceedings of the International Marine Conference, vol. I. Washington, DC: Government Printing Office, 1890.

Redford, Bruce. *Venice and the Grand Tour*. New Haven, CT: Yale University Press, 1996.

Ritchie, Robert C. *Captain Kidd and the War Against the Pirates*. Cambridge, MA: Harvard University Press, 1986.

Roberts, Callum. *The Unnatural History of the Sea*. Washington, DC: Island Press, 2007.

Robson, Martin. *A History of the Royal Navy: The Seven Years War*. London: IB Tauris, 2016.

Rodger, Nicholas A. M. *The Safeguard of the Sea: A Naval History of Britain, 660–1649*, vol. 1. New York: W. W. Norton, 1998.

Roosevelt, Franklin Delano, and Samuel Irving Rosenman. *The Public Papers and Addresses of Franklin D. Roosevelt: The Call to Battle Stations, 1941*. New York: Random House, 1938.

Rothrock, D., W. Maslowski, D. Chayes, G. Flato, and J. Grebmeier. *Arctic Ocean Science from Submarines. A Report Based on the SCICEX 2000 Workshop*. Seattle: University of Washington Seattle Applied Physics Lab, 1999.

Rothwell, Donald et al., eds. *The Oxford Handbook of the Law of the Sea*. Oxford: Oxford University Press, 2015.

Rozwadowski, Helen M. *Fathoming the Ocean: The Discovery and Exploration of the Deep Sea*. Cambridge: Harvard University Press, 2009.

Rozwadowski, Helen M. *Vast Expanses: A History of the Oceans*. London: Reaktion Books, 2018.

Scott, James Brown. *A Survey of International Relations Between the United States and Germany, August 1, 1914–April 6 1917: Based on Official Documents*. Oxford: Oxford University Press, 1917.

Selden, John. *Mare Clausum*. Clark, NJ: Lawbook Exchange, 2004.

Shapinsky, Peter D. "Japanese Pirates and the East Asian Maritime World, 1200–1600." In *Oxford Research Encyclopedia of Asian History*. Oxford: Oxford University Press, 2019.

Sloggett, Dave. *The Anarchic Sea: Maritime Security in the Twenty-first Century*. London: Hurst, 2013.

Smith, Robert W., and Ashley J. Roach. *Excessive Maritime Claims*. Newport, RI: Naval War College, 1994.

Smith, Tim D. *Scaling Fisheries: The Science of Measuring the Effects of Fishing, 1855–1955*. Cambridge: Cambridge University Press, 1994.

Sondhaus, Lawrence. *The Great War at Sea: A Naval History of the First World War*. Cambridge: Cambridge University Press, 2014.

Southard, Susan. *Nagasaki Deluxe: Life After Nuclear War*. New York: Penguin, 2015.

Spyrou, Andrew G. *From T-2 to Supertanker: Development of the Oil Tanker, 1940–2000*. Bloomington, IN: iUniverse, 2011.

Stanik, Joseph. *El Dorado Canyon: Reagan's Undeclared War with Qaddafi*. Annapolis, MD: Naval Institute Press, 2017.

Stewart, Ben. *Don't Trust, Don't Fear, Don't Beg: The Extraordinary Story of the Arctic 30*. New York: New Press, 2013.

Suárez, Thomas. *Early Mapping of the Pacific: The Epic Story of Seafarers, Adventurers and Cartographers Who Mapped the Earth's Greatest Ocean*. North Clarendon, VT: Tuttle, 2004.

Subrahmanyan, Sanjay. *The Career and Legend of Vasco da Gama*. Cambridge: Cambridge University Press, 1997.

Tanaka, Yoshifumi. *The International Law of the Sea*. Cambridge: Cambridge University Press, 2019.

Taylor, Miles, ed. *The Victorian Empire and Britain's Maritime World, 1837–1901: The Sea and Global History*. New York: Palgrave Macmillan, 2013.

Thomson, Charles Wyville et al. *Report on the Scientific Results of the Voyage of H.M.S. Challenger During the Years 1872–76: Under the Command of Captain George S. Nares and the Late Captain Frank Tourle Thomson. Deep-sea deposits.* London: H. M. Stationery Office, 1891.

Thomson, Janice. *Mercenaries, Pirates, and Sovereigns: State-Building and Extraterritorial Violence in Early Modern Europe.* Princeton, NJ: Princeton University Press, 1994.

Thucydides, *History of the Peloponnesian Wars.* Baltimore, MD: Penguin Books, 1972.

United Nations. *Papers Presented at the International Technical Conference on the Conservation of the Living Resources of the Sea.* New York: United Nations, 1956.

United Nations. *United Nations Conference on the Law of the Sea, Official Records.* Washington, DC: United Nations, 1958.

United Nations. *Third United Nations Conference on the Law of the Sea, Official Records.* New York: United Nations, 1975.

United Nations Conference on Trade and Development. *Review of Maritime Transport 2017.*

US Department of Defense. *Maritime Claims Reference Manual.* Washington, DC: US Department of Defense, 2014.

US Department of the Navy. *Sweeping the North Sea Mine Barrage.* Washington, DC: US Department of the Navy, 1919.

US Department of State. *Foreign Relations of the United States.* Washington, DC: US Department of State, various volumes.

Urbina, Ian. *The Outlaw Ocean: Journeys Across the Last Untamed Frontier.* New York: Knopf Doubleday, 2019.

Van Bynkershoek, Cornelius et al. *De Dominio Maris Dissertatio,* edited by James Brown Scot. New York: Oxford University Press, 1923.

Vitug, Marites. *Rock Solid: How the Philippines Won Its Maritime Case Against China.* Manila: Ateneo de Manila University Press, 2018.

Wadsworth, James E. *Global Piracy: A Documentary History of Seaborne Banditry.* New York: Bloomsbury, 2019.

Walters, Francis Paul. *A History of the League of Nations.* New York: Oxford University Press, 1986.

Webster, Jane and Nicholas J. Cooper (eds.), *Roman Imperialism: Post-Colonial Perspectives.* Leicester: University of Leicester, 1996.

Went, A. E. J. *Seventy Years Agrowing: A History of the International Council for the Exploration of the Sea, 1902–1972.* Copenhagen: International Council for the Exploration of the Sea, 1972.

Wharton, Francis. *The Revolutionary Diplomatic Correspondence of the United States,* vol. 2. Washington, DC: Government Printing Office, 1889.

World Bank, Food and Agriculture Organization, Kieran Kelleher, Rolf Willmann, and Ragnar Arnason. *The Sunken Billions: The Economic Justification for Fisheries Reform.* Washington, DC: World Bank, 2009.

Wright, Charles, and Charles Ernest Fayle. *A History of Lloyd's from the Founding of Lloyd's Coffee House to the Present Day.* London: Macmillan, 1928.

Zelko, Frank. *Make It a Green Peace! The Rise of a Countercultural Environmentalism.* Oxford: Oxford University Press, 2013.

Index

For the benefit of digital users, indexed terms that span two pages (e.g., 52–53) may, on occasion, appear on only one of those pages.

The letter *f* following a page locator denotes a figure.